The Old Farmer's Almanac

Calculated on a new and improved plan for the year of our Lord

1998

Being 2nd after LEAP YEAR and (until July 4)
222nd year of American Independence

FITTED FOR BOSTON AND THE NEW ENGLAND STATES, WITH SPECIAL
CORRECTIONS AND CALCULATIONS TO ANSWER FOR ALL THE UNITED STATES.

Containing, besides the large number of Astronomical Calculations
and the Farmer's Calendar for every month in the year, a variety of

NEW, USEFUL, AND ENTERTAINING MATTER.

ESTABLISHED IN 1792

by Robert B. Thomas

*Work as if you were to live a hundred years,
Pray as if you were to die tomorrow.*

– BENJAMIN FRANKLIN
Poor Richard's Almanac, 1757

COVER T.M. REGISTERED
IN U.S. PATENT OFFICE

ISSN 0078-4516

LIBRARY OF CONGRESS
CARD NO. 56-29681

Address all editorial correspondence to

THE OLD FARMER'S ALMANAC, DUBLIN, NH 03444

CONTENTS

The Old Farmer's Almanac • 1998

(contents continued on page 4)

CONTENTS
(continued)

page 190

241
Special Bookstore Supplement
A Compendium of Useful and Unusual Reference Matter

Charts, Tables, and Departments

34
....
☞ How to Use This Almanac

P To ATRONS

Something about the hole, the weather,

and two granite stones . . .

L ast year on this page, we told you about our survey, which revealed that the typical Almanac reader (all nine million of you) spends 5.5 hours each week in the garden, purchases five or more books a year, is more likely than not to own a computer, and so on. Then we mentioned our greatest disappointment of the survey: Only 19 percent of you use the hole we punch in the upper right-hand corner of each copy of the Almanac (with the exception of the hardbound version and the condensed gift edition). Since the hole cost us $43,187 last year, we speculated about whether to continue it.

Well . . . you 19 percent have convinced us. We will keep the hole. Many thanks to the hundreds of you hole-users who wrote to us. We wish we had space to include more of your letters, but anyway, here's a representative four:

■ A. B., Circleville, Ohio: "My husband gets very upset if whoever last used the Almanac doesn't hang it back on the nail where the next person can find it. So, please, keep punching the hole."

■ B. D. T., Tahlequah, Oklahoma: "Yes, I *do* care about the hole. Can't you see me going through the new holeless Almanac two or three pages at a time, with my little handheld punch? Heaven forbid!"

■ T. D., Huntington, West Virginia: "If you punch a hole in every *other* copy, half your hole-users might feel shortchanged but would understand if you explained to them that the savings (maybe $20,000?)

would go to establishing '*The Old Farmer's Almanac* Hole Scholarship Program.' Just a thought."

■ C. W. M., Oklahoma City: "I like my hole, and if you plug it up, I will not renew my classified advertisement. Let's see . . . you'd save $43,187 by not punching the hole, but then you'd lose my $352.75 ad. I realize I don't have much leverage but . . . please?"

Well, that's the hole story. Now let's turn to another popular subject of our mail, the weather. Particularly during this past spring, readers from around the country have been writing to ask how our winter forecasts turned out in regions other than their own. So here's a short summary (slanted only *slightly* in our favor).

First of all, we should say that the weather pattern in the winter of 1996-97 developed a bit later than usual, with the main storm track about 300 miles west of where we expected it would be. That's why the winter was somewhat milder than we predicted in much of the East and colder than we predicted in the northern Great Plains. Still, our predictions were better than other long-range predictions and *much* better than chance or "predicting" by weather averages.

In temperature, we were correct in the direction of departure from normal (or average) in 9 of our 16 regions across the country, and we were close to "right on" in 12 of the 16 regions. Looking at all 16 regions for the five "winter" months (November 1996 to March 1997), we were on the mark in 49 of 80 monthly temperature forecasts and in 48 of 80 precipitation forecasts — that is, about 60 percent for both. We also correctly predicted that the winter would be much milder than the previous winter in the East and warmer than normal in the Southwest.

Truly extreme weather phenomena usually defy all forecasts, but we nonetheless nailed the big April 1 snowstorm in the Northeast ("A big snowstorm may serve as nature's April Fool's joke") and also the record snow for the Great Lakes in November ("Windy, cold, heavy lake snows").

(continued on page 8)

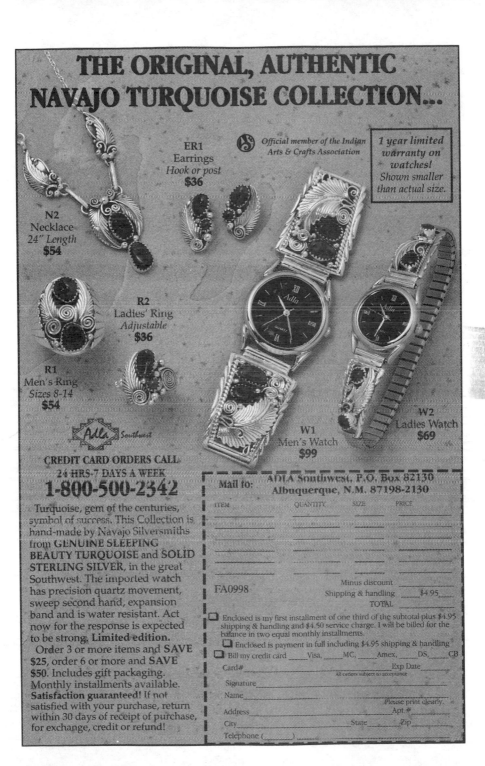

Although we did not predict the magnitude of several other extreme weather conditions, our forecasts at least pointed in the right direction. For example, we said "warm" for the record warm temperatures in the East in February, "heavy rain" before and during the flooding in the Pacific Northwest, and "rain and snow" for the locally heavy rains that flooded Louisville, Kentucky. Our forecast for the Fargo, North Dakota, area and the northern Great Plains called for much colder weather than normal in March and April, with above-normal precipitation. But to say our forecast accurately predicted the tragic and record flooding would not be appropriate nor altogether correct. Our hearts go out to all our readers — and everyone — in that devastated area.

So there you have our weather predictions, our hole situation, and — oh, yes, there's one more thing: We wish to thank John T. O'Malley of Sterling, Massachusetts, for instigating and overseeing (completely as a labor of love) the restoration of the gravestone of our founder, Robert B. Thomas (1766-1846), who is buried in the Legge Cemetery at the intersection of Route 140 and Dana Hill Road in Sterling. The professional stonework was expertly done by A. Rogonini of nearby Clinton, who, at the same time, restored the stone of Robert B.'s wife, Hannah Beaman Thomas (1774-1855). After years of neglect and vandalism, both gravestones are now properly mounted, cleaned, restored — and handsome!

Now, as usual, we will close with the following words of Robert B. Thomas himself, used since 1819 to end this page.

J. D. H. (June 1997)

However, it is by our works and not our words that we would be judged. These, we hope, will sustain us in the humble though proud station we have so long held in the name of,

Your obedient servant,

Robt. B. Thomas.

THE 1998 EDITION OF
THE OLD FARMER'S ALMANAC
Established in 1792 and published every year thereafter

ROBERT B. THOMAS *(1766-1846)*
FOUNDER

EDITOR *(12th since 1792)*: Judson D. Hale Sr.
MANAGING EDITOR: Susan Peery
EXECUTIVE EDITOR: Tim Clark
ART DIRECTOR: Margo Letourneau
COPY EDITOR: Ellen Bingham
ASSISTANT MANAGING EDITOR: Mare-Anne Jarvela
SENIOR ASSOCIATE EDITOR: Debra Sanderson
SENIOR CONSULTING EDITOR: Mary Sheldon
RESEARCH EDITORS: Maude Salinger, Randy Miller
ASTRONOMER: Dr. George Greenstein
SOLAR PROGNOSTICATOR: Dr. Richard Head
WEATHER PROGNOSTICATOR: Michael A. Steinberg
WEATHER GRAPHICS AND CONSULTATION: Accu-Weather, Inc.
ARCHIVIST: Lorna Trowbridge
CONTRIBUTING EDITORS: Jamie Kageleiry; Bob Berman, *Astronomy;* Castle Freeman Jr., *Farmer's Calendar*
PRODUCTION DIRECTOR: Susan Gross
PAGE PRODUCTION MANAGER: David Ziarnowski
SENIOR PRODUCTION ARTISTS: Lucille Rines, Rachel Kipka
PRODUCTION ASSISTANT: Brian Jenkins

GROUP PUBLISHER: John Pierce
PUBLISHER *(23rd since 1792)*: Sherin Wight
ADMINISTRATIVE ASSISTANT: Sarah Duffy
ADVERTISING PRODUCTION / CLASSIFIED: Donna Stone
MAIL ORDER MARKETING MANAGER: Deborah M. Walsh
DIRECT SALES MANAGER: Cindy Schlosser
SPECIAL MARKETS DIRECTOR: Ronda Knowlton

ADVERTISING MARKETING REPRESENTATIVES
Mail Order Advertising
NORTHEAST & WEST: Robert Bernbach, 914-769-0051
MIDWEST: Tom Rickert, 612-835-0506
SOUTH: Sheala Browning, 770-446-9900

General Advertising
MIDWEST: Media Marketers, 312-236-4830
WEST: Fatima Mulholland, 206-842-2959
EAST: Peter Uhry, 203-637-5478

NEWSSTAND CIRCULATION: P.S.C.S.
DISTRIBUTION: Curtis Circulation Company

EDITORIAL, ADVERTISING, AND PUBLISHING OFFICES
P.O. Box 520, Dublin, NH 03444
Phone: 603-563-8111 • Fax: 603-563-8252
Internet Address: www.almanac.com

YANKEE PUBLISHING INC., MAIN ST., DUBLIN, NH 03444
Joseph B. Meagher, *President;* Judson D. Hale Sr., *Senior Vice President;* Brian Piani, *Vice President and Chief Financial Officer;* Jody Bugbee, John Pierce, Joe Timko, and Sherin Wight, *Vice Presidents.*

The Old Farmer's Almanac will not return any unsolicited manuscripts that do not include a stamped and addressed return envelope.

The Old Farmer's Almanac publications are available at special discounts for bulk purchases for sales promotions or premiums. Contact Special Markets, 603-563-8111.

CONSUMER
TASTES & TRENDS
FOR 1998

by Jamie Kageleiry and Christine Schultz

Good News

How High the Moon?

■ The most powerful telescopes once allowed astronomers to see features on the Moon that were the size of football fields but nothing smaller. Now, thanks to a new telescope, aptly named "The Very Large Telescope," astronomers can make out **Neil Armstrong's footprints**. The VLT, actually collections of telescopes on the world's mountaintops, has improved acuity equivalent to that of a legally blind person suddenly attaining 20/20 vision.

The Good (but Not Cheap) Old Days

■ Some household necessities actually **have gotten relatively cheaper** over the years: An automatic clothes washer that runs $380 today would have cost $1,770 in 1947 (in 1997 dollars); a $300 television would have been $3,280; a refrigerator, close to $1,500. Home prices, however, have jumped since the 1950s — a median of $131,500 now versus $49,330 in 1950, in today's dollars.

Live Longer

■ The Metropolitan Life Insurance Company reports that **life expectancy for American men has hit an all-time high.** Once a man has survived to age 65, his average life expectancy is 80.5 years — the increase being attributed to lower mortality from cardiovascular disease.

The Way the Ball Is Bouncing

■ The evolution of women's sports is accelerating. **The National Basketball Association** launched a women's league last summer, the second pro women's league in a year, and a **professional women's soccer league** will make its debut this year. High school sports saw the introduction of the first girl's wrestling team.

Bad News

Sticks and Stones . . .

■ In one of those good news/bad news things, Boston school officials, mirroring a national trend, report that **fighting by boys in school yards** is down. Picking up the slack, unfortunately, are girls, who are resorting less to name-calling and more to punch-throwing.

Annual Weigh-in

■ **Americans, once again, are getting heftier.** For the first time, more than half of the U.S. population weighs more than it should. Standards are based on "body mass index": body weight (in kilograms) divided by height (in meters) squared. This means that a woman who is 5 feet

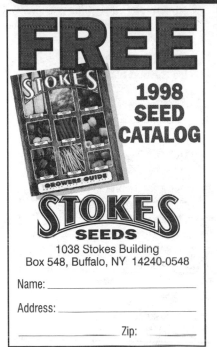

4 inches tall shouldn't weigh more than 145 pounds (a BMI of 25).

Dream On

■ Though the country's chief executive officers report that they **dream of spending more time with their families** in the upcoming year, only seven percent said they would be able to.

Eating In and Eating Out

■ Take-out food orders have **more than doubled** in the last ten years. Only 55 percent of dinners eaten at home include even one homemade dish.

■ Only nine percent of adults are willing to wait more than five minutes for a **waiter to ask for their beverage order**; 20 percent can bear only one minute.

■ Bagel sales in the United States have **increased 500 percent** in the last three years.

■ Watch for an increase in fine restaurants serving doughnuts — indicative of **the relaxed approach** people are taking to dining. The doughnuts reflect a trend back to old-fashioned things, with a twist (would that be a cruller?). One New York restaurateur says doughnuts let grown-ups be children again — an appealing thought for aging baby boomers.

Other food trends include:

■ Health-food backlash.

■ Haute junk food such as **cotton candy** (used as a predessert at one San Francisco restaurant) and **Jell-O** (in a special-edition champagne flavor!). Another old favorite showing up on elegant menus is Boston cream pie.

■ Soup restaurants popping up everywhere. In supermarkets, watch for **Campbell's soup in glass jars** to celebrate the company's centennial.

■ More cooks are purposely making **extra portions** to create leftovers — a practice that's up 30 percent in the last ten years.

Popular cuisines in restaurants:

■ **Malaysian**, which blends Indian, Chinese, and Malay cooking.

■ **Iberian**, both Portuguese and regional Spanish (Catalonian, Andalusian).

■ **Mediterranean Rim**, such as Moroccan, Tunisian, Greek, and Israeli.

Also, **watch for dishes using tea as an ingredient** (such as tea-soaked salmon). And "50s-style" dining has returned, with caviar, escargot, calf's liver, anchovies, and a martini with lunch.

What's New on the Job Scene in 1998

Take the Paycheck and Run

■ The "cashing out" trend will increase across the country, according to trend-forecaster Faith Popcorn, as thousands of Americans leave corporations to **begin their own enterprises.** The numbers support the theory: One in six workers say he or she thinks about quitting work at least weekly. The top three reasons are

stress (32 percent), poor pay/benefits (19 percent), and dissatisfaction with duties (11 percent).

The Office Christmas Party Makes a Comeback

■ The office bash is back. Almost 97 percent of companies in the United States **held a holiday celebration** in 1996, and the trend is likely to continue after having made a comeback

from a low of 16 percent in 1990, when companies were fraught with layoffs and not in the mood for a party.

Son of Nepotism

■ It's not who you know, it's who you're kin to. Nepotism used to be a **dirty word in corporate America,** but it's making a positive revival as companies look for social incentives to create a strong core of loyalty and skill among employees. In the words of *Fast Company* magazine's editor, "The talent pool, it turns out, runs in the gene pool."

Here's to Your Health

High-Altitude Training

■ **Jet-setters who want to hit the ground running when they arrive at their next high-altitude destination can sign up for the world's first "hypoxic" workout room, which simulates a 9,000-foot altitude. The first one was installed in a trendy Manhattan health club in 1997; others in Los Angeles, Chicago, and San Francisco are in the works.**

The New Jurassic Gym

■ **In an effort to keep in step with what *The New York Times* calls the "cultural-intellectual workout movement," museums are offering power-walk tours and exercise facilities. New York's Museum of Natural History has converted itself into an early-morning "Jurassic Gym," where Upper West Siders can squat, lunge, and power-walk their way past the dioramas, pausing for a plié beside the plesiosaur. In a similar vein, Moscow's Palace of Young Pioneers is now being used as the world's biggest recreational complex.**

The Ultimate Health Fad

■ **Culture-watcher Faith Popcorn calls it the "being alive" trend. Followers of this trend show great interest in alternative medicines, including homeopathy, herbs, and acupuncture.**

What's Good For You in 1998

Fans

■ We mean someone to yell, "You can do it!" while you exercise. Researchers found that weight lifters were able to lift up to eight percent more when they got **verbal encouragement** from someone.

Marriage

■ Although the benefits of marriage to health — mental, physical, financial — have been touted for years, there's a new finding: Marriage among young adults causes a one-third **decrease in drug and alcohol use.** Couples who only lived together showed no such drop.

Pass the Vino

■ Grapes and red wine have been known to help **prevent heart disease.** Now, researchers at the University of Illinois think an element in the wine, called *resveratrol*, may be a potent cancer inhibitor. (continued)

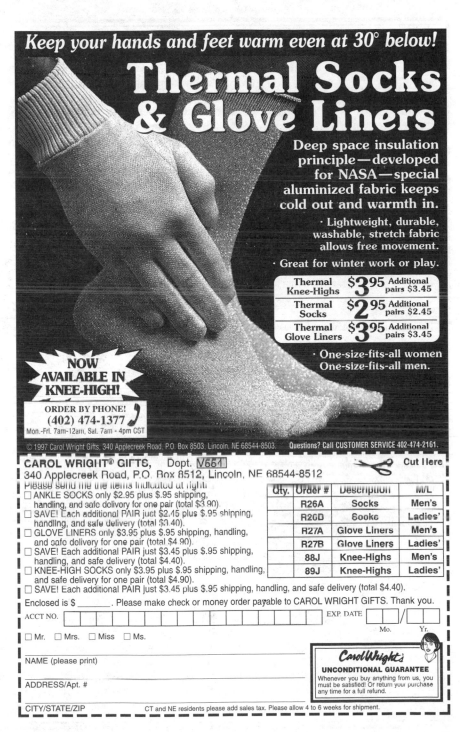

Smoking (?)

■ Now that we have your attention . . . smoking cigarettes, of course, is NOT good for you, but nicotine, researchers have found, may potentially be a **treatment for several major health problems,** including Alzheimer's, Parkinson's, and inflammatory bowel diseases. Don't go out and buy a carton of cigarettes when you're stocking up on wine; your best bet will be to wait until nicotine is available in nontobacco forms, so you don't get lung cancer while preventing Parkinson's.

What's Bad For You in 1998

Mondays

■ Last year, we reported that more people had car accidents on Mondays than any other day. Now the news is out that **heart problems and strokes** peak on Monday mornings. If you are at risk, researchers suggest not scheduling the toughest parts of your week on Monday.

A Career in Advertising

■ It's a wonder the Man in the Grey Flannel Suit ever lived long enough to see a book written about him. In 1996, more people **died on the job** in advertising than did people in electrical-repair shops or in petroleum refineries.

Dialing and Driving

■ Researchers have found that the risk of a car crash quadruples during the five minutes after a driver places a call on a cellular phone — about the same hazard as driving at the legal limit of alcohol consumption. **Having a phone in the car,** they found, *did* come in handy *after* the crash, though.

Juice

■ At least, too much juice. . . . Aside from causing chronic diarrhea and abdominal pain, too much fruit juice (more than eight ounces a day) can put children **at risk for obesity and shortness.** We understand the obesity part: Juice has lots of calories. But short stature? Apparently, kids who drink more than a cup of juice a day get a lot of calories, but not enough of the nutrients that promote skeletal growth.

In Case You Were Wondering

A Bad Hair Day Is Worse than Death

■ According to a recent poll, 63 percent of Americans said they could not live without an automobile; 22 percent said they couldn't live without a TV, and almost 8 percent said life would be over for them without a blow-dryer (that was more than those who said they couldn't face life without a personal computer).

Elevator Eccentricities

■ Over 60 percent of people surveyed reported that they "quickly check out the other passengers" on an elevator, while 27 percent said they prefer to stare at their keys or some other object. Six percent said they try to whistle or hum.

Pet News

What to Spend Your Pet Budget On

■ Les Poochs is not a joke but a **serious dog perfume** sold near people perfume at Bloomingdale's. Millions of bottles of dog perfume, often smelling much like the human stuff — Opium with a hint of Chanel No. 5 — have been snapped up. (continued)

GIANT CLIMBING STRAWBERRIES

59¢ Per Plant

In Just 60 Days You Will Enjoy a Bumper Crop

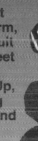

It's Non-Stop Picking for Months On End

Harvest Large, Firm, Juicy Fruit with Sweet Taste! Spirals Up, Adding Beauty and Color

Imagine eating fresh, succulent, juicy strawberries from fast growing vines. Unique climbing vine is a strawberry festival. These perennial plants zoom to heights of 5 feet. Enjoy fresh strawberries throughout the year—summer, fall, and spring. You will harvest handfuls of mouth-watering strawberries in just 60 days.

Produces Runners, Blooms & Fruit—All at the Same Time

Home-grown fruit is not only fresher and tastier, but it is better for you. Known by many as the hardiest of all everbearing varieties. Requires little care. Comes with easy-to-follow instructions. Shipped at proper planting time. We ship plants, not seeds.

FRESH SUCCULENT STRAWBERRIES

Cats and ferrets may enjoy Cologne of the Wild — which calls itself "a provocative spray cologne that brings out the beast in lovable pets."

(Not) Seeing Spots

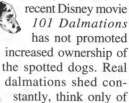

■ **Contrary to widespread predictions,** the recent Disney movie *101 Dalmations* has not promoted increased ownership of the spotted dogs. Real dalmations shed constantly, think only of themselves, and like to eat a steady diet of bread and butter (and your best shoes), according to a dalmation breeder.

The Differences Between Men and Women in 1998

■ **The average woman speaks 25,000 words per day more than the average man does.**

■ **If you're a woman, age 30 to 50, you usually get to pick which film to go to, according to an executive at 20th Century Fox. Teenage girls, however, follow their male dates to the movies.**

■ **Women laugh more than men, unless they're listening to other women, when they tend to be silent.**

Hot Collectibles

■ **Warmth in the well-worn:** In what *USA Today* calls a "cold age of computer printouts and hard drives," well-heeled collectors are finding **warmth in vintage**

Indian blankets. A Chief's blanket, circa 1820, recently sold for more than half a million dollars. Less wealthy collectors will be searching for other antique Native American items.

■ **Old blue jeans:** Levis, in particular, but any antique denim has high value, particularly old, hand-cut pants made from heavy denim. Last spring, the Levi Strauss **company paid $25,000 for a pair of its jeans** found by a vintage clothing dealer in Soho (N.Y.); with a single back pocket and a leather patch on the waistband, the old Levis were made sometime between 1886 and 1902.

■ **Anything that reminds baby boomers of Grandmother's house:** 1950s furniture and toys, anything western, and vintage desk lamps. Also continuing to do well are **old comics**: An original 1938 Action Comics book featuring the first appearance of Superman just sold for $63,000.

Home Sweet Home

■ **The big house:** In the last 20 years, the size of the average new home grew 21 percent, to almost 2,100 square feet; the number of new homes installing **central air-conditioning** leaped from 46 percent to 80 percent. Since 1990, the number of king- and queen-size mattresses sold has risen from 30 percent to 36 percent (something needs to fill all that extra space in the house!).

■ **Television's last stand:** Watch for TV stands to show up on junk heaps as **hang-on-the-wall TVs** come into popularity. Granted, the current price ($14,000-$25,000) will have to drop considerably

before the effect is felt, but according to *The New York Times,* "The arrival of big, flat screens could change everything from the design of living rooms to the configuration of office cubicles."

■ The pantry is back. Ranging in size from a walk-in room lined with deep shelves to a narrow floor-to-ceiling unit, **pantries are what most Americans want** in a house, second only to a linen closet.

■ One new thing to keep in the pantry: a **home coffee-roaster**, soon to be a popular Christmas gift.

■ Green is still the color to decorate with or drive in, reflecting, says a New York color consultant, a **"greening of America."** The popularity of green will peak this year — look for shades of brown and also lighter, brighter colors for decorating; and in cars, colors that change depending on light.

■ The newest trend in garages is hiding them. It is considered unfashionable now to have your **garage doors gaping at the street.** Designers are tucking garages away behind houses, around corners, or bent at an angle from the house.

States of the Union

■ In an age when regionalism is supposedly fading out, state legislatures are busy passing bills marking out all manner of local icons. Texas may become the first to designate an official state molecule — the buckyball. It doesn't stop there. Other official state symbols:

Dance: Shag (South Carolina)
Dessert: Boston cream pie (Massachusetts)
Dog: Boston terrier (where else?)
Fossil: Sea scorpion (New York)
Neckwear: Bolo tie (Arizona)
Peace symbol: Mourning dove (Wisconsin)
Reptile: Red-spotted newt (New Hampshire)
Song: "Oklahoma!" (don't ask)
Sport: Jousting (Maryland)

Agricultural News

Old MacDonald Had a Seaweed-Eating Sheep
■ In Britain, the Rare Breeds Survival Trust is trying to save historic breeds of farm animals from extinction by persuading more people to eat them. The Trust hopes to create a commercial market for exotic animals and thus increase financial incentives for more farmers to raise such rarities as lop-eared Saddleback pigs, North Ronaldsay seaweed-eating sheep of the Orkney Islands, and Manx Loghtan four-horned rams.

Demographica

Seeing Double
■ The average growth rate of the population of the world has slowed since the 1960s but remains high enough so that before another century passes, **the number of people on Earth will have doubled.** Rising births have been exacerbated by the increasing rate of twins and triplets born to Americans. The number of twins alone has risen 30 percent since 1980. The reason for more multiple births: greater use of fertility treatments, and more women over 30 giving birth.

Mom and Pop at the Movies
■ On the other end of the population boom is the increase of older people. A more **mature movie-viewing audience** is encouraging filmmakers to move toward more-sophisticated films. (continued)

State of Romance in 1998

Sweet Words for High-Tech Times

■ A sure sign of the times can be found on Necco candy hearts. In the past, **love messages on the pastel candies** have included such expected endearments as "Kiss Me" and "Be Mine." Now they include the following modern sass: "E-Mail Me," "Page Me," "Awesome," and "I Don't Think So."

Love at First Sight — Read All About It!

■ The latest trend in personal ads puts a new twist on the old tracking game. Personal ads have been converted to "I Saw U" ads. The admirer states where and when the admiree was spotted, **and leaves a number on the newspaper's 900 system.** Being seen has become a status symbol among the Seattle set, and the trend is spreading.

High Tech

Shake, Rattle, and Hold

■ Scientists at Xerox's research center in Palo Alto, California, are hammering out the technology to make highway overpasses and skyscrapers self-adjusting, so that they will no longer crumble at the impact of an earthquake tremor. Minute motors, valves, nozzles, and sensors will respond to changes in heat, light, sound, and motion to get the buildings dancing in sync with Earth's motion.

ET, Phone Home

■ The search for life in the cosmos will heat up in the coming century, as NASA sends more and more "low-cost" spacecraft out to explore the solar system as part of its Origins program. The first two missions to look for life beyond Earth include a trip to Jupiter's moon Europa in 2001 and one to Mars in 2005.

Weirdness

■ Worldwide weirdness was up 2.4 percent overall in 1996, based on the number of bizarre occurrences reported to the *Fortean Times* of London. Up: Reported incidents or sightings of "ineptitude and stupidity," "out-of-place animals," "falls from the sky," and "manimals." Unchanged: "Paranormal experiences," "fires and spontaneous human combustion," and just all-around "bad luck." Down: "Genius and discovery," "crop circles," and "miracles." Weird.

– courtesy Strange Days #2, The Year in Weirdness, by the editors of Fortean Times *Cader Books). Copyright 1997* Fortean Times *and Cader Company, Inc.*

Fashion

■ **Colors:** For women this fall and winter, **black** (does it ever go out of style?), **beige, and shades of brown** (especially nice, rich cocoa) will be popular, as well as oranges and reds.

■ **Styles:** Over all is a theme of softness and lightness — sleekly feminine without too many frills. Dresses are short and wispy. **Micro-minis have returned** (about 16 inches from waist to hem!), but luckily, pants will be popular. Watch for straight-legged pants. Suits will be softened by sheer, sexy blouses and sweater or bolero jackets in different colors. Stylish **shoes** have straps and stiletto heels (which look great with slim pants but don't make podiatrists happy). But chunky heels will be popular as well. **Hairstyles** will also take a turn for the feminine: Look for more Veronica Lake look-alikes.

■ **For men,** casual wear will feature V-necked sweaters with T-shirts peeking

Labels!

Lakefront Realty Co.
10 Bridgewater Dr.
Boca Raton FL 33486
407-555-1849

★ Peel n' Stick roll no dispenser needed
★ Up to 4 lines, 28 spaces per line
★ Choose Block, Italic, or with Initial Monogram

Gold #101
White #102
Clear #103
Rainbow #104

Best Price!
500 for ~~$6.05~~
$4.95
250 for $3.65

Your Child's Name Becomes a Poem

The Beauty of Poetry... The Art of Calligraphy

Folk poet, artist Debra Brim uses the letters of a child's first name to compose an original, inspirational poem.

Frame not included

Reproduced on 8 x 10 parchment weight paper, ideal for framing.

SAVE $3
Child's name poem
~~$6.95~~
$3.95

out, rolled cuffs on trousers, and wider, looser pants. **Suits will take a turn for the conservative.** Look for more suits with vests, and jackets with side vents (not very flattering for heavier guys).

■ **Eyeglasses** have become so trendy that "everyone" (even those stuck at 20/20) is stocking up on several pairs, often designed by people such as Calvin Klein.

The Mood

■ If anything characterizes the nation's mood these days, it may just be comfort. We are **comfortable with our lives** and **comfortable with the perceived stability of our economy.**  This comfort has had a moderating influence on a number of cultural trends. We saw this start last year: backlash against the penny-pinchers and the fat-watchers and the teetotalers. Now the good life is being celebrated again, not with the abandon of the 1980s but more **in the vein of the sensible 1950s.**

■ Status symbols tend to have an "anti-status" glow to them. "I'm going home to see my kids," is considered an admirable, enviable statement for an ambitious corporate executive at the end of the day. **No longer is the workaholic the saint of the workplace** — those successfully balancing family and work are envied.

■ Having free time is one of the most priceless status symbols one can flaunt. **Popular vacations are vigorous learning treks,** such as African safaris or long, grueling bike trips. (As baby boomers grow older, which is the driving demographic behind most of our cultural trends, being fit enough to drive trucks through mud and climb mountains is a status symbol.)

■ All of this is balanced (and balance is a good key word for 1998) by sensibility: **people believing that they must rely on themselves** for such things as retirement income. If given an extra $40,000, most homeowners say they would put it in a mutual fund or savings account.

■ Watch for emphasis on children. In the 1946 to 1964 baby boom, families often had four to six kids; the new boom will see **more families having two children.** Last year, more men and women (about 90 percent) defined success as "being a good husband and father (or wife and mother)" rather than "being a success at work." Education will be in the spotlight, as well as child-rearing issues (such as how to teach manners and impart moral values).

■ Technology, which is embraced by most Americans, does in fact **make most people's lives easier.** And it may be what is allowing a sudden new trend: the move back to rural places. Last year, 1.6 million more Americans moved to rural places than from them. Look for an upsurge in porch swings for quiet summer nights.

So Long, Farewell, Adios

Beyond Rewind
■ Music cassettes are being heaped atop the boxes of vinyl albums at yard sales. CDs now outsell cassettes four to one.

The Remote (Control) Wilderness
■ The remote wilderness will soon become the remote-control wilderness as more urban adventurers carry cellular phones and global-positioning units on their snowmobiles or aircraft when they venture deep into the nation's mountains and forests. Satellite technology will soon make it possible for computers and fax machines to be brought in as well, so people can track stocks while stalking tracks.

NORTH AMERICAN FAIRS and EXPOS

On October 1, 1810, Elkanah Watson, a farmer in the Berkshire Mountains of western Massachusetts, sponsored the first county fair — basically a cattle show — in Pittsfield, Massachusetts. From this fairly humble beginning have evolved the sprawling, earthy, proud events that celebrate all forms of agriculture in the United States and Canada. We list here the top 25 for 1998 as ranked by attendance, from the gigantic State Fair of Texas to the Calgary Stampede and New England's own Big E. There's a fair to remember for everyone!

Information is given in the following order:
- Fair name
- City
- Size/name of fairgrounds
- 1996 attendance
- 1998 dates
- Information number

....

1. State Fair of Texas
- Dallas
- 277-acre Fair Park
- 3,558,749
- Sept. 25-Oct. 18
- 214-565-9931

2. Houston Livestock Show & Rodeo
- Houston, Texas
- 30-acre Astrodomain Complex
- 1,830,265
- Feb. 20-March 8
- 713-791-9000

3. New Mexico State Fair
- Albuquerque
- 236-acre New Mexico State Fairgrounds
- 1,749,275
- Sept. 4-20
- 505-265-1791

4. Canadian National Exhibition
- Toronto, Ontario
- 220-acre Exhibition Place
- 1,706,323
- Aug. 21-Sept. 7
- 416-393-6000

5. Minnesota State Fair
- St. Paul
- 310-acre State Fairgrounds
- 1,673,976
- Aug. 27-Sept. 7
- 612-642-2200

(continued on page 30)

6. State Fair of Oklahoma
- Oklahoma City
- 435-acre State Fair Park
- 1,621,593
- Sept. 18-Oct. 4
- 405-948-6700

7. Western Washington Fair (The Puyallup Fair)
- Puyallup
- 160-acre Puyallup Fairgrounds
- 1,364,625
- Sept. 11-27
- 253-841-5045

8. Los Angeles County Fair
- Pomona, California
- 498-acre Fairplex
- 1,269,573
- Sept. 17-Oct. 4
- 909-623-3111

9. Tulsa State Fair
- Tulsa, Oklahoma
- 240-acre Expo Square
- 1,107,110
- Oct. 1-11
- 918-744-1113

10. Calgary Stampede
- Calgary, Alberta
- 137-acre Stampede Park
- 1,100,007
- July 3-12
- 800-661-1260

Great Ideas and Great Fun All Year Long!

11. The Big E
- West Springfield, Massachusetts
- 175-acre Eastern States Exposition fairgrounds
- 1,078,120
- Sept. 18-Oct. 4
- 413-737-2443

12. Colorado State Fair
- Pueblo
- 80-acre Colorado State Fairgrounds
- 1,063,067
- Aug. 22-Sept. 7
- 719-561-8484

13. Pacific National Exhibition
- Vancouver, British Columbia
- 114-acre Hastings Park
- 1,048,122
- Aug. 22-Sept. 7
- 604-253-2311

14. Del Mar Fair (Southern California Exposition)
- Del Mar
- 400-acre Del Mar Fairgrounds
- 1,018,658
- Mid-June through first week of July
- 619-793-5555

15. Erie County Fair & Expo
- Hamburg, New York
- 275-acre Hamburg Fairground
- 1,004,940
- Aug. 6-16
- 716-649-3900

16. Wisconsin State Fair
- Milwaukee
- 200-acre Wisconsin State Fair Park
- 922,267
- Aug. 6-16
- 414-266-7000

17. Iowa State Fair
- Des Moines
- 400-acre Iowa State Fairgrounds
- 918,600
- Aug. 13-23
- 515-262-3111

18. Arizona State Fair
- Phoenix
- 98-acre Arizona State Fair Park
- 900,613
- late Oct. to early Nov. (18 days)
- 602-252-6771

19. Ohio State Fair
- Columbus
- 360-acre Ohio Expo Center
- 900,318
- Aug. 7-23
- 614-644-FAIR (3247)

20. New York State Fair
- Syracuse
- 375-acre Empire Expo Center
- 848,857
- Aug. 27-Sept. 7
- 315-487-7711

21. San Antonio Stock Show & Rodeo
- San Antonio, Texas
- 170-acre Freeman Coliseum
- 829,945
- Feb. 7-22
- 210-225-5851

22. California State Fair
- Sacramento
- 350-acre Cal Expo Fairgrounds
- 818,071
- Aug. 21-Sept. 7
- 916-263-3000

23. Dade County Fair & Exposition
- Miami, Florida
- 80-acre Fair Expo Center
- 812,422
- March 19-April 5
- 305-223-7060

24. Evergreen State Fair
- Monroe, Washington
- 350-acre Evergreen State Fairgrounds
- 797,570
- Aug. 27-Sept. 7
- 360-794-7832

25. Illinois State Fair
- Springfield
- 366-acre Illinois State Fairgrounds
- 790,028
- Aug. 14-23
- 217-782-6661

□□

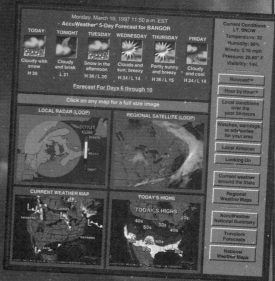

HOW TO USE THIS ALMANAC
Anywhere in the U.S.A.

Annually, for the interest and pleasure of our readers, *The Old Farmer's Almanac* provides a variety of astronomical data calculated for the upcoming year. It covers a wide range of phenomena — the rising and setting times of the Sun and the Moon; the declination of the Sun; the astronomical age and placement of the Moon and its monthly phases; selected times for observing the visible planets; solar and lunar eclipses; the dates and times of meteor showers; the transit times of the bright stars; and a monthly summary of astronomical highlights.

THE LEFT-HAND CALENDAR PAGES
(Pages 60-86)

Much of the data is contained in the Left-Hand Calendar Pages (pages 60-86). For the enlightenment of our readers, part of a sample page is reproduced below, with an explanatory text summarizing the individual entries.

☞ **Please note** that all the times given in this edition of the Almanac are calculated for **Boston, Massachusetts.** Key Letters accompany much of the data and are provided so that readers can correct the Boston times to those of their own localities. Examples given below clarify this procedure. (Times throughout the Almanac are given in Eastern Standard Time [EST], except from 2:00 A.M., April 5, until 2:00 A.M., October 25, when Eastern Daylight Time [EDT] is given.)

SAMPLE LEFT-HAND CALENDAR PAGE
(from November 1997 — page 60)

1 —

1997   NOVEMBER, THE ELEVENTH MONTH

An extraordinary gathering of planets appears at nightfall. While their most dense concentration will occur early next month, now we can observe every planet in the solar system at once! Pluto requires a powerful telescope and good star chart, while Neptune and Uranus demand a telescope or binoculars. The rest stand brightly after sunset, stretched leftward along the solar system's plane (the zodiac) from southwest to southeast. At nightfall, Venus is brightest and lowest, Jupiter far to its left, while less brilliant Saturn rises in the southeast. On the 3rd, the Moon, Mars, and Venus form a striking triangle in the southwest 45 minutes after sunset.

2 —

☽	First Quarter	7th day	16th hour	43rd minute
○	Full Moon	14th day	9th hour	12th minute
☾	Last Quarter	21st day	18th hour	58th minute
●	New Moon	29th day	21st hour	14th minute

Times are given in Eastern Standard Time.

For an explanation of this page, see "How to Use This Almanac," page 34; for values of Key Letters, see Time Correction Tables, page 214.

3 —

Day of Year	Day of Month	Day of Week	☉ Rises h. m.	Key	☉ Sets h. m.	Key	Length of Days h. m.	Sun Fast m.	Declination of Sun	Full Sea Boston A.M. / P.M.	☽ Rises h. m.	Key	☽ Sets h. m.	Key	☽ Place	☽ Age
305	1	Sa.	6 18	D	4 37	B	10 19	32	14s.35	11½ / —	7 14	E	5 46	B	LIB	1
306	2	E	6 19	D	4 36	B	10 17	32	14 54	12 / 12¼	8 13	E	6 27	B	LIB	2
307	3	M.	6 20	D	4 35	B	10 15	32	15 13	12¾ / 12¾	9 11	E	7 13	B	OPH	3
308	4	Tu.	6 21	D	4 34	B	10 13	32	15 31	1¼ / 1½	10 06	E	8 04	B	SAG	4
309	5	W.	6 23	D	4 32	B	10 09	32	15 49	2¼ / 2¼	10 58	E	9 02	B	SAG	5
310	6	Th.	6 24	D	4 31	B	10 07	32	16 07	3 / 3¼	11 45	E	10 04	B	SAG	6
311	7	Fr.	6 25	D	4 30	B	10 05	32	16 25	3¾ / 4	12 29	E	11 10	C	CAP	7

4 —

5 6 7   8   9   10

13

12

11

1. The text heading the calendar page is a summary of the sky sightings for the month. These astronomical highlights appear on each month's calendar page.

2. The dates and times of the Moon's phases for the month. (For more details, see Glossary, page 42.)

3. The days of the year, month, and week are listed on each calendar page. The traditional ecclesiastical calendar designation for Sunday — the Dominical Letter — E for 1997, D for 1998 — is used by the Almanac. (For further explanation, see Glossary, page 42.)

4. Sunrise and sunset times (EST or EDT) for Boston for each day of the month.

5. Key Letter columns. The letters in these two columns are designed to correct to other localities the sunrise/sunset times given for Boston. Note that each sunrise/sunset time has a Key Letter. The values (that is, the number of minutes) assigned to these Key Letters are given in the **Time Correction Tables**, page 214. Simply find your city, or the city nearest you, in the tables, and locate the value in the appropriate Key Letter column. Add or subtract those minutes to the sunrise or sunset time given for Boston. (Because of the complexities of calculation for different locations, times may not be precise to the minute.)

Example:

To find the time of sunrise in Atlanta, Georgia, on November 1, 1997:

Sunrise, Boston, with Key Letter D (p. 34)	6:18 A.M., EST
Value of Key Letter D for Atlanta (p. 214)	+40 minutes
Sunrise, Atlanta	6:58 A.M., EST

Use the same procedure to determine the time of sunset.

6. Length of Days. This column denotes how long the Sun will be above the horizon in Boston for each day of the month. To determine the length of any given day in your locality, follow the procedure outlined in #5 above to determine the sunrise and sunset times for your city. Then add 12 hours to the time of sunset and subtract the time of sunrise, and you will have the length of day.

Example:

Sunset, Miami, Florida, Nov. 1	5:34
Add 12 hours	+ 12:00
	17:34
Subtract sunrise, Miami, Nov. 1	– 6:32
Length of day, Miami, Nov. 1 (11 hr., 02 min.)	11:02

– Beth Krommes

7. The Sun Fast column is designed to change sundial time into clock time in Boston. A sundial reads natural, or Sun, time, which is neither Standard nor Daylight time except by coincidence. Simply subtract the minutes given in the Sun Fast column to get Boston clock time, and use Key Letter C in the Time Correction Tables (page 214) to correct the time for your city.

Example:

To change sundial time into clock time in Boston, Massachusetts, or Denver, Colorado, on November 1, 1997:

Sundial reading, Nov. 1 (Boston or Denver)	12:00 noon
Subtract Sun Fast (p. 34)	– 32 minutes
Clock time, Boston	11:28 A.M., EST
Use Key C for Denver (p. 215)	+ 15 minutes
Clock time, Denver	11:43 A.M., MST

8. This column denotes the declination (angular distance from the celestial equator) of the Sun in degrees and minutes, at noon, EST or EDT.

9. The times of daily high tides in Boston, for morning and evening, are recorded in this column. ("3" under "Full Sea Boston, A.M." on November 6 means that the high tide that morning will be at 3:00 — with the height in feet of the high tides shown for some of the dates on the Right-Hand Calendar Pages. Where a dash is shown under Full Sea, it indicates that time of high water occurs on or after midnight and so is recorded on the next date.) Tide corrections for some localities can be found in the **Tide Correction Tables** on page 210.

10. Moonrise and moonset times (EST or EDT) for Boston for each day of the month. (Dashes indicate that moonrise or moonset occurs on or after midnight and so is recorded on the next date.)

11. Key Letter columns. These columns designate the letters to be used to correct to other localities the moonrise/moonset times for Boston. As explained in #5, the same procedure for calculating sunrise/sunset is used *except* that an additional correction factor based on longitude (see table below) should be used. For the longitude of your city, consult the Time Correction Tables, page 214.

Longitude of city	Correction minutes
58°- 76°	0
77°- 89°	+1
90°-102°	+2
103°-115°	+3
116°-127°	+4
128°-141°	+5
142°-155°	+6

Example:

To determine the time of moonrise in Akron, Ohio, on November 1, 1997:

Moonrise, Boston, with Key Letter E (p. 34)	7:14 A.M., EST	
Value of Key Letter E for Akron (p. 214)	+ 37 minutes	
Correction for Akron longitude 81° 31'	+ 1 minute	
Moonrise, Akron	7:52 A.M., EST	

Use the same procedure to determine the time of moonset.

12. The Moon's Place denoted in this column is its *astronomical* place, i.e., its *actual* placement, in the heavens. (This should not be confused with the Moon's *astrological* place in the zodiac, as explained on page 170.) **All calculations in this Almanac, except for the astrological information on pages 166-170, are based on astronomy, not astrology.**

In addition to the 12 constellations of the astronomical zodiac, five other abbreviations may appear in this column: Auriga (AUR), a northern constellation between Perseus and Gemini; Cetus (CET), which lies south of the zodiac, just south of Pisces and Aries; Ophiuchus (OPH), a constellation primarily north of the zodiac but with a small corner between Scorpius and Sagittarius; Orion (ORI), a constellation whose northern limit first reaches the zodiac between Taurus and Gemini; and Sextans (SEX), which lies south of the zodiac except for a corner that just touches it near Leo.

13. The last column lists the Moon's age, which is the number of days since the previous new Moon. (The average length of the lunar month is 29.53 days.)

Further astronomical data can be found on page 48, which lists the eclipses for the upcoming year, the principal meteor showers, and the dates of the full Moon over a five-year period.

The Visible Planets (pages 46-47) lists selected times for observing Venus, Mars, Jupiter, Saturn, and Mercury for 1998; page 50 carries the transit times of the bright stars for 1998. Both feature Key Letters, designed to convert the Boston times given to those of other localities (see #5 and #11 above).

The Twilight Zone on page 212 is a chart that enables you to calculate the length of twilight and the times of dawn and dark in your area.

THE RIGHT-HAND CALENDAR PAGES

(Pages 61-87)

These pages are a combination of astronomical data; specific dates in mainly the Anglican church calendar, inclusion of which has always been traditional in American and English almanacs (though we also include some other religious dates); tide heights at Boston (the Left-Hand Calendar Pages include the daily times of high tides; the corrections for your locality are on page 210); quotations; anniversary dates; appropriate seasonal activities; and a rhyming version of the weather forecasts for New England. (Detailed forecasts for the entire country are presented on pages 120-149.)

The following list classifies some of the entries from the Right-Hand Calendar Pages, with a sample (the first part of November 1997) of a calendar page explained. Also, following the Almanac's tradition, the Chronological Cycles and Eras for 1998 are listed.

– Beth Krommes

MOVABLE FEASTS AND FASTS FOR 1998

Septuagesima Sunday	Feb. 8
Shrove Tuesday	Feb. 24
Ash Wednesday	Feb. 25
Palm Sunday	Apr. 5
Good Friday	Apr. 10
Easter Day	Apr. 12
Rogation Sunday	May 17
Ascension Day	May 21
Whitsunday-Pentecost	May 31
Trinity Sunday	June 7
Corpus Christi	June 11
1st Sunday in Advent	Nov. 29

THE SEASONS OF 1997-1998

Fall 1997	Sept. 22, 7:56 P.M., EDT
Winter 1997	Dec. 21, 3:07 P.M., EST
Spring 1998	Mar. 20, 2:55 P.M., EST
Summer 1998	June 21, 10:03 A.M., EDT
Fall 1998	Sept. 23, 1:37 A.M., EDT
Winter 1998	Dec. 21, 8:56 P.M., EST

CHRONOLOGICAL CYCLES FOR 1998

Golden Number (Lunar Cycle)	4
Epact	2
Solar Cycle	19
Dominical Letter	D
Roman Indiction	6
Year of Julian Period	6711

Era	Year	Begins
Byzantine	7507	Sept. 14
Jewish (A.M.)*	5759	Sept. 20
Roman (A.U.C.)	2751	Jan. 14
Nabonassar	2747	Apr. 24
Japanese	2658	Jan. 1
Grecian (Seleucidae)	2310	Sept. 14
		(or Oct. 14)
Indian (Saka)	1920	Mar. 22
Diocletian	1715	Sept. 11
Islamic (Hegira)*	1419	Apr. 27
Chinese (Lunar)	4696	Jan. 28
(Tiger)		

Year begins at sunset

DETERMINATION OF EARTHQUAKES

☞ Note the dates, on right-hand pages 61-87, when the Moon (☾) "rides high" or "runs low." The date of the high begins the most likely five-day period of earthquakes in the Northern Hemisphere; the date of the low indicates a similar five-day period in the Southern Hemisphere. You will also find on these pages a notation for Moon on the Equator (☾ on Eq.) twice each month. These times indicate a two-day earthquake period in both hemispheres.

NAMES AND CHARACTERS OF THE PRINCIPAL PLANETS AND ASPECTS

☞ Every now and again on the Right-Hand Calendar Pages, you will see symbols conjoined in groups to tell you what is happening in the heavens. For example, ♂♂☾ opposite November 4, 1997 (see below), means

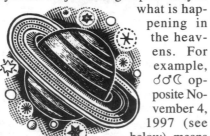

that on that date, Mars ♂ and the Moon ☾ are in conjunction ♂ or apparently near each other.

– Beth Krommes

Here are the symbols used . . .

☉	Sun	♅	Uranus
○ ● ☾	Moon	♆	Neptune
☿	Mercury	♇	Pluto
♀	Venus	♂	Conjunction, or in
⊕	Earth		the same degree
♂	Mars	☊	Ascending Node
♃	Jupiter	☋	Descending Node
♄	Saturn	☍	Opposition, or
			180 degrees

EARTH AT APHELION AND PERIHELION 1998

☞ Earth will be at perihelion on January 4, 1998, when it will be 91,400,005 miles from the Sun. Earth will be at aphelion on July 3, 1998, when it will be 94,512,258 miles from the Sun.

SAMPLE RIGHT-HAND CALENDAR PAGE

(from November 1997 — page 61)

Day of the month.   Day of the week.   For detailed regional forecasts, see pages 120-149.

The Dominical Letter for 1997 was E because the first Sunday of the year fell on the fifth day of January. The Letter for 1998 is D.

Conjunction — closest approach — of Neptune and the Moon.

St. Leo the Great was elected Bishop of Rome in 440. By interceding with Attila, he prevented the city's massacre by invading Huns. (Certain religious feasts and civil holidays appear in this typeface.)

The Moon is at perigee, the point in its orbit closest to Earth.

Morning tide at Boston, shown to be at 10:15 A.M. on the left-hand page, will be 12.1 feet. The 11 P.M. tide will be 11.0 feet.

26th Sunday after Pentecost. (Sundays and special holy days generally appear in this typeface.)

D. M.	D. W.	Dates, Feasts, Fasts, Aspects, Tide Heights	Weather ↓
1	Sa.	All Saints • Famous "Dark Day" in New England, 1716 • Tides {10.4 / —	Cool
2	E	24th ⬤. af. ℟. • James K. Polk born, 1795 • {9.6 / 10.5 •	and
3	M.	All Souls • Never try to wear a hat that has more character than you do. • {9.5 / 10.4	wet,
4	Tu.	♂♂☾ • ♂♀☾ • Election Day • {9.4 / 10.4 •	the
5	W.	☾ runs low • First U.S. cross-country airplane flight, 1911 • Tides {9.3 / 10.3 •	Sun
6	Th.	♀ Gr. Elong. (47° E.) • ♂♆☾ • Tides {9.2 / 10.1 •	with-
7	Fr.	♂♅☾ • ♂♃☾ • Joni Mitchell born, 1943 •	holds
8	Sa.	Take care that old age does not wrinkle your spirit even more than your face. • {9.4 / 10.0 •	its
9	E	25th ⬤. af. ℟. • ☾ at ☋	blessing,
10	M.	St. Leo the Great • Richard Burton born, 1925 • Tides {10.3 / 10.4 •	and
11	Tu.	St. Martin • Veterans Day • ☾ on Eq. • Occn. ♄ by ☾ •	we
12	W.	☾ at perig. • If All Saints brings out winter, St. Martin brings out Indian Summer. •	we
13	Th.	Great Leonid meteor display, midnight to dawn, 1833 • Tides {11.8 / 11.0 •	all
14	Fr.	Full Beaver ○ • Mamie Eisenhower born, 1896 • Tides {12.1 / 11.0 •	get
15	Sa.	Keep a green tree in your heart and perhaps the singing bird will come. • {12.1 / 10.8 •	colds.
16	E	26th ⬤. af. ℟. • W. C. Handy born, 1873 • {— / 11.9 •	Awake
17	M.	St. Hugh of Lincoln • ☾ rides high • Suez Canal opened, 1869 •	to
18	Tu.	St. Hilda • CBS sold its record division to Sony, 1987 • {10.1 / 11.0 •	flakes.

For a more complete explanation of terms used throughout the Almanac, see Glossary, page 42.

Totally Gross Secrets About Losing Weight

By Sharon Louise Brodie

Did you ever notice that when you're fat, people actually stare at you while you eat. It's as if they want to tap you on the shoulder and say, "If you wouldn't eat that stuff, you wouldn't be so fat!"

Hello. My name is Sharon Brodie. You don't know me from Adam. But I'm a real person. I live near Sandy Springs, Georgia. And, up until two years ago, I was the fat lady that everyone was staring at.

I was too tired to go out with my friends at night. I was even embarrassed to go out on weekends by myself. I waddled when I walked. I sweat when I ate. I wore anything loose that would hang straight down and wouldn't cling. I couldn't even cross my legs. I wasn't just "overweight." I was fat. I was 5'4" and weighed 202 pounds.

I went to my doctor for help. But I wasn't optimistic. During the past seven years I had tried 16 *different* diets. One by one. And I failed at all of them.

My doctor listened carefully then recommended an entirely different program. This wasn't a "diet." It was a special weight-loss program researched by a team of bariatric physicians — specialists who treat the severely obese. The program itself was developed by James Cooper, M.D. of Atlanta, Georgia.

I started the program on May 17th. Within the first four days, I only lost three pounds. So I was disappointed. But during the three weeks that followed, my weight began to drop. Regularly. Week after week. Within the next 196 days, I went from 202 pounds to 129 pounds. To me it was a miracle. This was the first time in my life I'd ever lost weight and not felt like I was starving to death.

The real reason the program worked was simple: I was *always eating!*

I could eat *six times every day.* So I never felt deprived. Never hungry. I could snack in the morning. I could snack before dinner. I could even snack at night while I was watching TV.

How can you eat so much and still lose weight?

The secret is not in the amount of food you eat. It's in the prescribed combination of foods you eat in each 24-hour period. Nutritionally dense portions of special fiber, unrefined carbohydrates, and certain proteins which create a metabolic process which continues all day long ... a complete 24-hour calorie-burning cycle. Food is metabolized over a much longer period — not just in unhealthy "spurts" like many diets. That's why it lets you shed pounds without hunger ... without nervousness ... without feeling deprived.

And it's all good wholesome food. Nothing strange. And *wonderful variety.* You'll enjoy delicious meats, chicken, fish, vegetables, potatoes, pasta, sauces — plus your favorite snacks. Lots of snacks.

This special program must be the best-kept secret in America. Because for years it was only available to doctors. No one else. In fact, The Clinic-30 Program has been used by a wide variety of doctors and family physicians throughout the U.S. and Canada.

So it's *doctor-tested!*

And now it's available to the public.

There are other benefits too ...

- There are no amphetamines. No drugs. No pills. No powders.
- There's nothing artificial. No chalky-tasting drinks to mix.
- Everything you'll need is at your local supermarket. Good healthy food.
- You don't count calories. Just follow the program. It's very easy to follow.
- It's low in sodium. You don't hold water.
- You can eat the foods you enjoy. Great variety. Great taste.

But here's the best part ...

Once you lose the weight, you can keep it off. Because you're *not starving yourself.* You're not hungry all the time.

Let's face it. We all have "eating lifestyles." Our eating habits usually include three meals a day plus two or three snacks. We all love snacks. Especially at night.

But most "diets" force us to change all that.

And that's *precisely* why they fail!

The Clinic-30 Program is different. It lets you continue your *normal eating lifestyle.* You can eat six times a day. You can snack when you wish. So when you lose the weight, you can keep it off. Because no one's forcing you to change.

One person commented, "... there's so much food on the program, I can hardly eat it all!"

Here are a few of the other people who participated in The Clinic-30 Program ...

Kitty R. lost 56 pounds and went from a size 18 to a size 10 dress.

"The Clinic-30 Program works! I'm an example. What I like best is that I can eat six times a day and lose weight! I recommended it to a couple of friends and they started losing weight, too!"

Anne G., High Point, NC loves wearing a size 10!

"I lost 25 lbs. in two months. I talk about it so much that others in my workplace have bought their own programs. I was even able to keep it off during the holidays. I am so proud of myself!"

Obviously, everyone's results will vary because each of us is different. But consider this:

We've received *literally stacks* of *unsolicited* letters from people all over America telling us how much weight they lost. One couple even wrote to say "... Between the two of us we've lost 150 pounds!"

Before I began the Clinic-30 Program, a lot of people offered me advice about losing weight. Some of them were really weird.

1. I read in a tabloid that an overweight woman in England literally *wired* her mouth shut! That didn't last.

2. A friend suggested that I stick pins in my ears. It was supposed to control my appetite.

3. My cousin tried to get me to spend the night in a cemetery. She said I'd lose 5 pounds. No thanks.

The Clinic-30 Program worked for me when *nothing else* would. Nothing. No fad diet. No pills. No weird stuff.

It's doctor researched. And doctor tested.

We'll be happy to send you the program to examine for 35 days. Show it to your doctor. Try it. There's no *obligation.* In fact, your check won't be cashed for 31 days. You may even post-date it 31 days in advance, if you wish.

Choose a day and start the program. If you don't begin losing weight within five days — and continue losing weight — we'll promptly return your original uncashed check. No delays. No excuses.

Or keep it longer. Try it for six months. Even then, if you're not completely satisfied, we'll send you a refund. Promptly. And without question. This is the fairest way we know to prove to you how well this program works.

To order, just send your name, address and postdated check for $12.95 (plus $3.00 shipping/handling) to The Clinic-30 Program, c/o Green Tree Press, Inc., Dept. 182, 3603 West 12th Street, Erie, PA 16505.

Holidays and Observances, 1998

(*) Recommended as holidays with pay for all employees
(**) State observances only

Jan. 1 (*) New Year's Day
Jan. 19 (*) Martin Luther King Jr.'s Birthday *(observed)*; (**) Robert E. Lee's Birthday *(Ark., Fla., Ga., La., S.C., Tenn., Tex.)*
Feb. 2 Groundhog Day
Feb. 12 Abraham Lincoln's Birthday
Feb. 14 Valentine's Day
Feb. 16 (*) Presidents Day
Feb. 22 George Washington's Birthday
Feb. 24 (**) Mardi Gras *(Ala., La.)*
Mar. 2 (**) Texas Independence Day
Mar. 15 (**) Andrew Jackson Day *(Tenn.)*
Mar. 17 (**) St. Patrick's Day; Evacuation Day *(Boston and Suffolk Co., Mass.)*
Apr. 2 (**) Pascua Florida Day
Apr. 13 (**) Thomas Jefferson's Birthday *(Ala., Okla.)*
Apr. 20 (**) Patriots Day *(Maine, Mass.)*
Apr. 24 National Arbor Day
May 1 May Day
May 8 (**) Truman Day *(Mo.)*
May 10 Mother's Day
May 16 Armed Forces Day
May 18 Victoria Day *(Canada)*
May 25 (*) Memorial Day *(observed)*
June 5 World Environment Day
June 11 (**) King Kamehameha I Day *(Hawaii)*
June 14 Flag Day
June 17 (**) Bunker Hill Day *(Boston and Suffolk Co., Mass.)*
June 20 (**) West Virginia Day
June 21 Father's Day
July 1 Canada Day
July 4 (*) Independence Day
July 24 (**) Pioneer Day *(Utah)*
Aug. 3 (**) Colorado Day
Aug. 10 (**) Victory Day *(R.I.)*
Aug. 16 (**) Bennington Battle Day *(Vt.)*
Aug. 26 Women's Equality Day
Sept. 7 (*) Labor Day
Sept. 9 (**) Admission Day *(Calif.)*
Sept. 12 (**) Defenders Day *(Md.)*
Oct. 9 Leif Eriksson Day
Oct. 12 (*) Columbus Day *(observed)*; Thanksgiving Day *(Canada)*; (**) Native Americans Day *(S. Dak.)*
Oct. 18 (**) Alaska Day
Oct. 31 Halloween; (**) Nevada Day
Nov. 3 Election Day
Nov. 4 (**) Will Rogers Day *(Okla.)*
Nov. 11 (*) Veterans Day; (**) Admission Day *(Wash.)*
Nov. 19 (**) Discovery Day *(Puerto Rico)*
Nov. 26 (*) Thanksgiving Day
Dec. 10 (**) Wyoming Day
Dec. 25 (*) Christmas Day
Dec. 26 Boxing Day *(Canada)*

RELIGIOUS OBSERVANCES

Epiphany	Jan. 6
Ash Wednesday	Feb. 25
Palm Sunday	Apr. 5
Good Friday	Apr. 10
First day of Passover	Apr. 11
Easter Day	Apr. 12
Orthodox Easter	Apr. 19
Islamic New Year	Apr. 28
Whitsunday-Pentecost	May 31
Rosh Hashanah	Sept. 21
Yom Kippur	Sept. 30
First day of Chanukah	Dec. 14
First day of Ramadan	Dec. 20
Christmas Day	Dec. 25

How the Almanac Weather Forecasts Are Made

Our weather forecasts are determined by the use of a secret formula devised by the founder of this Almanac in 1792, enhanced by the most modern scientific calculations based on solar activity. We believe nothing in the universe occurs haphazardly; there is a cause-and-effect pattern to all phenomena, including weather. It follows, therefore, that we believe the weather is predictable. It is obvious, however, that neither we nor anyone else has as yet gained sufficient insight into the mysteries of the universe to predict weather with anything resembling total accuracy.

GLOSSARY

Aph. – Aphelion: The point in a planet's orbit that is farthest from the Sun.

Apo. – Apogee: The point in the Moon's orbit that is farthest from Earth.

Celestial Equator: The circle on the celestial sphere that is halfway between the celestial poles. It can be thought of as the plane of Earth's equator projected out onto the sphere.

Celestial Sphere: An imaginary sphere projected into space, with an observer on Earth as its center. It represents the entire sky. All celestial bodies other than Earth are imagined as being on its inside surface; it is used for describing their positions and motions.

Conj. – Conjunction: The apparent closest approach to each other of two celestial bodies. **Inf. – Inferior:** A conjunction in which the planet is between the Sun and Earth. **Sup. – Superior:** A conjunction in which the Sun is between the planet and Earth.

Declination: The angular distance of a celestial body measured perpendicularly north or south of the celestial equator — analogous to latitude on Earth. The Almanac gives the Sun's declination at noon EST or EDT.

Dominical Letter: The letter used to denote the Sundays in the ecclesiastical calendar in a particular year; determined by the date on which the first Sunday of that year falls. If Jan. 1 is a Sunday, the letter is A; if Jan. 2 is a Sunday, the letter is B; and so on to G. In a leap year, the letter applies through February and then takes the preceding letter.

Eclipse, Lunar: The Moon, at full phase, enters the shadow of Earth. **Total:** The Moon passes completely into the umbra (central dark part) of Earth's shadow. **Partial:** Only part of the Moon passes through the umbra. **Penumbral:** The Moon passes through only the penumbra (an area of partial darkness that surrounds the umbra).

Eclipse, Solar: The Moon passes between Earth and the Sun, and all three bodies are aligned in the same plane. **Annular:** The Moon appears silhouetted against the Sun, with a ring of sunlight showing around it.

Epact: A number from 1 to 30 that indicates the Moon's age at the instant Jan. 1 begins at the meridian of Greenwich, England; used for the ecclesiastical calendar.

Eq. – Equator: A great circle of Earth that is equidistant from the two poles.

Equinox, Autumnal: The Sun appears to cross the celestial equator from north to south. **Vernal:** The Sun appears to cross the celestial equator from south to north.

Era, Chronological: A system of reckoning time by numbering the years from an important occurrence or a particular point in time.

Evening Star: A planet that is above the western horizon at sunset and less than 180 degrees east of the Sun in right ascension.

Golden Number: A number in the 19-year cycle of the Moon, so called because of its importance in determining Easter. (The Moon repeats its phases approximately every 19 solar years.) To find the Golden Number of any year, add 1 to that year, and divide the result by 19. The remainder is the Golden Number. When there is no remainder, the Golden Number is 19.

Gr. El. – Greatest Elongation: The greatest apparent angular distance of a planet from the Sun as seen from Earth.

Julian Period: A period of 7,980 years, beginning at 4713 B.C. and providing a chronological basis for the study of ancient history. Its system of astronomical dating, devised by 16th-century scholar Joseph Scaliger and named in honor of his father, Julius, allows the difference between two dates to be calculated more easily than with conventional civil calendars. To find the Julian year, add 4,713 to any year.

Moon Age: The number of days since the previous new Moon.

Moon on Equator: The Moon is on the celestial equator.

Moon Phases: Four particular states in the Moon's appearance, based on its position at each quarter of its complete cycle around Earth. **First Quarter:** The right half of the Moon is illuminated. **Full:** The Sun and the Moon are in opposition; the entire disk of the Moon is illuminated as viewed from Earth. **Last Quarter:** The left half of the Moon is illuminated. **New:** The Sun and the Moon are in conjunction; the entire disk of the Moon is darkened as viewed from Earth.

Moon Place, Astronomical: The actual position of the Moon within the constellations on the celestial sphere. **Astrological:** The position of the Moon within the astrological zodiac

(continued on page 44)

Best Fishing Days, 1998

(and other fishing lore from the files of
*The Old Farmer's Almanac***)**

Probably the best fishing time is when the ocean tides are restless before their turn and in the first hour of ebbing. All fish in all waters — salt or fresh — feed most heavily at that time.

Best temperatures for fish species vary widely, of course, and are chiefly important if you are going to have your own fishpond. Best temperatures for brook trout are 45° to 65° F. Brown trout and rainbows are more tolerant of higher temperatures. Smallmouth black bass do best in cool water. Horned pout take what they find.

Most of us go fishing when we can get time off, not because it is the best time. But there are best times:

■ One hour before and one hour after high tide, and one hour before and one hour after low tide. (The times of high tides are given on pages 60-86 and corrected for your locality on pages 210-211. Inland, the times for high tides would correspond with the times the Moon is due south. Low tides are halfway between high tides.)

■ "The morning rise" — after sunup for a spell — and "the evening rise" — just before sundown and the hour or so after.

■ Still water or a ripple is better than a wind at both times.

■ When there is a hatch of flies — caddis flies or mayflies, commonly. (The fisherman will have to match the hatching flies with *his* fly — or go fishless.)

■ When the breeze is from a westerly quarter rather than north or east.

■ When the barometer is steady or on the rise. (But, of course, even in a three-day driving northeaster, the fish aren't going to give up feeding. Their hunger clock keeps right on working, and the smart fisherman will find something to eat.)

■ When the Moon is between new and full.

Moon Between New & Full, 1998

Jan. 1-12	Apr. 26-May 11	Sept. 20-Oct. 5
Jan. 28-Feb. 11	May 25-June 10	Oct. 20-Nov. 4
Feb. 26-Mar. 12	June 23-July 9	Nov. 18-Dec. 3
Mar. 27-Apr. 11	July 23-Aug. 7	Dec. 18-31
	Aug. 21-Sept. 6	

GLOSSARY *(continued)*

according to calculations made over 2,000 years ago. Because of precession of the equinoxes and other factors, this is not the Moon's actual position in the sky.

Moon Rides High or Runs Low: The Moon is highest above or farthest below the celestial equator.

Moonrise & Moonset: The Moon's rising above and descending below the horizon.

Morning Star: A planet that is above the eastern horizon at sunrise and less than 180 degrees west of the Sun in right ascension.

Node: Either of the two points on opposite sides of the celestial sphere where the Moon's orbit intersects the ecliptic.

Occn. – Occultation: The eclipse of a star or planet by the Moon or another planet.

Opposition: The Moon or a planet appears on the opposite side of the sky from the Sun (elongation 180 degrees).

Perig. – Perigee: The point in the Moon's orbit that is closest to Earth.

Perih. – Perihelion: The point in a planet's orbit that is closest to the Sun.

R.A. – Right Ascension: The coordinate on the celestial sphere for measuring the east/west positions of celestial bodies; analogous to longitude on Earth.

Roman Indiction: A number in a 15-year cycle, established Jan. 1, A.D. 313, as a fiscal term. Add 3 to any given year in the Christian era and divide by 15; the remainder is the Roman Indiction. When there is no remainder, the Roman Indiction is 15.

Solar Cycle: A period of 28 years, at the end of which the days of the month return to the same days of the week.

Solstice, Summer: The Sun is at its maximum (23.5°) north of the celestial equator. **Winter:** The Sun is at its maximum (23.5°) south of the celestial equator.

Stat. – Stationary: Halted apparent movement of a planet against the background of the stars just before it comes to opposition.

Sun Fast/Slow: The adjustment needed to reconcile sundial time to standard clock time. This adjustment factor is given in the Left-Hand Calendar Pages.

Sunrise & Sunset: The visible rising and setting of the Sun's upper limb across the unobstructed horizon of an observer whose eyes are 15 feet above ground level.

Twilight: The period of time between full darkness and sunrise or between sunset and full darkness.

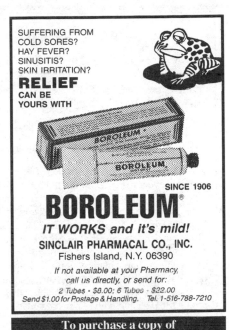

THE VISIBLE PLANETS, 1998

The times (EST/EDT) of the visible rising or setting of the planets Venus, Mars, Jupiter, and Saturn on the 1st, 11th, and 21st of each month are given below. The approximate times of their visible rising or setting on other days can be found with sufficient accuracy by interpolation. For an explanation of Key Letters (used in adjusting the times given here for Boston to the times in your town), see page 35 and pages 214-218. Key Letters appear as capital letters beside the times. (For definitions of morning and evening stars, see pages 42-44.)

VENUS is not prominent this year. The planet stretches away from the Sun in the spring, just when its orbit makes its skinniest, lowest angle to the horizon. After plunging into evening twilight in early January, Venus emerges as a dazzling but low morning star from February through May. The rest of the year finds it lurking within the Sun's glare. Venus is in conjunction with Mercury on January 26, August 25, and September 10; with Jupiter on April 22; with Saturn on May 28; and with Mars on August 4.

MARS has its close encounters with Earth at 25- or 26-month intervals, meaning that the red planet grows big and bright biannually. This is one of its "off" years, when it glides behind the Sun. However, Mars starts brightening during the final three months of 1998, while beginning to rise around midnight. Wait until then to point a telescope its way. Mars is in conjunction with Jupiter on January 20, with Mercury on March 11 and March 30, and with Venus on August 4.

Boldface — P.M.		Lightface — A.M.			Boldface — P.M.		Lightface — A.M.	
Jan. 1	set **6:16** A	July 1	rise 3:12 A		Jan. 1	set **6:48** A	July 1	rise 4:13 A
Jan. 11	" **5:23** B	July 11	" 3:15 A		Jan. 11	" **6:50** B	July 11	" 4:03 A
Jan. 21	rise 6:10 D	July 21	" 3:24 A		Jan. 21	" **6:52** B	July 21	" 3:54 A
Feb. 1	" 5:09 D	Aug. 1	" 3:40 A		Feb. 1	" **6:54** B	Aug. 1	" 3:45 A
Feb. 11....	" 4:32 D	Aug. 11	" 3:59 A		Feb. 11....	" **6:55** B	Aug. 11	" 3:38 A
Feb. 21....	" 4:11 D	Aug. 21	" 4:21 A		Feb. 21....	" **6:56** B	Aug. 21	" 3:32 A
Mar. 1	" 4:00 D	Sept. 1.....	" 4:48 B		Mar. 1	" **6:57** C	Sept. 1.....	" 3:25 A
Mar. 11 ...	" 3:51 D	Sept. 11...	" 5:12 B		Mar. 11 ...	" **6:57** C	Sept. 11...	" 3:18 A
Mar. 21 ...	" 3:44 D	Sept. 21...	" 5:37 B		Mar. 21 ...	" **6:57** C	Sept. 21...	" 3:11 B
Apr. 1......	" 3:35 D	Oct. 1	" 6:01 C		Apr. 1......	" **6:57** D	Oct. 1	" 3:04 B
Apr. 11....	" 4:26 D	Oct. 11	" 6:26 C		Apr. 11....	" **7:57** D	Oct. 11	" 2:57 B
Apr. 21....	" 4:16 C	Oct. 21	" 6:51 D		Apr. 21....	" **7:56** D	Oct. 21	" 2:49 B
May 1	" 4:05 C	Nov. 1.....	set **4:42** B		May 1	" **7:55** D	Nov. 1.....	" 1:39 B
May 11 ...	" 3:53 C	Nov. 11...	" **4:36** A		May 11 ...	" **7:54** D	Nov. 11...	" 1:30 B
May 21 ...	" 3:41 B	Nov. 21...	" **4:35** A		May 21 ...	rise 5:11 A	Nov. 21...	" 1:20 C
June 1	" 3:29 B	Dec. 1	" **4:40** A		June 1	" 4:53 A	Dec. 1	" 1:09 C
June 11 ...	" 3:20 B	Dec. 11 ...	" **4:50** A		June 11 ...	" 4:38 A	Dec. 11 ...	" 12:58 C
June 21 ...	rise 3:14 A	Dec. 21 ...	" **5:07** A		June 21 ...	rise 4:25 A	Dec. 21 ...	" 12:45 C
		Dec. 31 ...	set 5:29 A				Dec. 31 ...	rise 12:32 C

JUPITER has a wonderful year. The giant planet is briefly seen sinking into the western evening twilight during the first weeks of January. Then it spends March through September in the morning sky, rising higher and growing brighter. By summer, it rises at midnight, reaching opposition on September 15 — its brightest appearance in a decade. That month it's visible all night as the sky's brightest "star," and it remains prominent through December. Jupiter is in conjunction with Mars on January 20 and with Venus on April 22.

SATURN comes closer to us than it has since 1989, while it also climbs higher. The result is a very bright "star" that spends its first two months of 1998 low in the west before emerging in the morning sky in May. Gradually rising higher and earlier through the summer, it reaches greatest brilliancy when at opposition on October 23 and out all night. Though prominent through year's end, Saturn's prime time is definitely the autumn. Saturn is in conjunction with Mercury on May 12 and with Venus on May 28.

IVPITER

SATVRN9

Boldface — P.M.   Lightface — A.M.

Jan. 1	set	**7:46**	B	July 1 ...... rise	12:02 C
Jan. 11	"	**7:18**	B	July 11 .... **rise**	**11:24** C
Jan. 21	"	**6:50**	B	July 21 .... "	**10:45** C
Feb. 1......	"	**6:20**	B	Aug. 1..... "	**10:01** C
Feb. 11	"	**5:53**	B	Aug. 11... "	**9:20** C
Feb. 21	"	**5:26**	B	Aug. 21... "	**8:39** C
Mar. 1	rise	6:14	D	Sept. 1..... "	**7:53** C
Mar. 11 ...	"	5:41	D	Sept. 11... "	**7:11** C
Mar. 21 ...	"	5:07	D	Sept. 21... set	6:05 B
Apr. 1......	"	4:30	D	Oct. 1 ...... "	5:14 B
Apr. 11....	"	4:56	C	Oct. 11 .... "	4:29 B
Apr. 21....	"	4:21	C	Oct. 21 .... "	3:46 B
May 1	"	3:46	C	Nov. 1..... "	1:59 B
May 11 ...	"	3:11	C	Nov. 11... "	1:19 B
May 21 ...	"	2:36	C	Nov. 21... "	12:40 B
June 1	"	1:57	C	Dec. 1...... "	12:04 B
June 11 ...	"	1:20	C	Dec. 11 ... **set**	**11:28** B
June 21 ...	rise	12:40	C	Dec. 21 ... "	**10:55** B
				Dec. 31 ... **set**	**10:22** B

Boldface — P.M.   Lightface — A.M.

Jan. 1	set	12:10	C	July 1 ...... rise	1:30 B
Jan. 11	set	**11:29**	C	July 11 .... "	12:53 B
Jan. 21	"	**10:53**	C	July 21 .... "	12:15 B
Feb. 1......	"	**10:14**	C	Aug. 1..... **rise**	11:33 B
Feb. 11	"	**9:39**	C	Aug. 11... "	10:54 B
Feb. 21	"	**9:05**	C	Aug. 21... "	10:15 B
Mar. 1	"	**8:38**	C	Sept. 1..... "	9:32 B
Mar. 11 ...	"	**8:04**	C	Sept. 11... "	8:51 B
Mar. 21 ...	"	**7:31**	C	Sept. 21... "	8:11 B
Apr. 1......	"	**6:55**	D	Oct. 1 ...... "	7:26 B
Apr. 11....	"	**7:22**	D	Oct. 11 .... "	6:45 B
Apr. 21....	rise	5:30	B	Oct. 21 .... "	6:04 B
May 1	"	5:14	B	Nov. 1..... set	5:31 D
May 11 ...	"	4:38	B	Nov. 11... "	4:48 D
May 21 ...	"	4:01	B	Nov. 21... "	4:05 D
June 1	"	3:21	B	Dec. 1...... "	3:23 D
June 11 ...	"	2:44	B	Dec. 11 ... "	2:41 D
June 21 ...	rise	2:07	B	Dec. 21 ... "	2:01 D
				Dec. 31 ... set	1:21 D

MERCURY has a fairly good year, ducking in and out of the Sun's glare on its brisk carousel ride. Its best showing as an evening star, low in the western twilight, is from March 15 to 24, with a less favorable apparition the first 11 days of July. As a morning star low in eastern twilight, the charbroiled world is clearly visible the first two weeks of the year and then not again until the last days of August through mid-September and again in mid-December.

DO NOT CONFUSE 1) Mercury with Mars in early March and with Saturn in mid-May; on both occasions, Mercury is the brighter object. 2) Venus with Jupiter in the eastern predawn sky in April and May. Venus is always brighter than Jupiter. 3) Mars and Leo's bright star, Regulus, in late September and the first half of October. Mars is orange and Regulus is blue. 4) Mars and Virgo's main star, Spica, in late December. Mars is orange and Spica is blue.

ECLIPSES FOR 1998

There will be five eclipses in 1998, two of the Sun and three of the Moon, all listed below. One of the solar eclipses will not be visible in the United States or Canada. (Solar eclipses are visible in certain areas; lunar eclipses are technically visible from the entire night side of Earth, but this year's are penumbral, which means that the dimming of the Moon's illumination is so slight as to be scarcely noticeable.)

1. Total eclipse of the Sun, February 26. (For details, see feature on page 52.)

2. Penumbral eclipse of the Moon, March 12-13. The beginning phase will be visible in North America except Alaska and northwestern Canada; the end will be visible in North America. The Moon enters penumbra on March 12 at 9:14 P.M., EST (6:14 P.M., PST). The Moon leaves penumbra March 13 at 1:26 A.M., EST (March 12, 10:26 P.M., PST).

3. Penumbral eclipse of the Moon, August 7. The beginning phase will be visible in eastern North America. The end will be visible in North America except northern and western Canada and Alaska. The Moon enters penumbra at 9:32 P.M., EDT (6:32 P.M., PDT). The Moon leaves penumbra at 11:18 P.M., EDT (8:18 P.M., PDT).

4. Annular eclipse of the Sun, August 21. This eclipse will not be visible in the United States or Canada.

5. Penumbral eclipse of the Moon, September 6. The beginning phase will be visible in North America except the extreme east. The end will be visible in western North America. The Moon enters penumbra at 5:14 A.M., EDT (2:14 A.M., PDT). The Moon leaves penumbra at 9:06 A.M., EDT (6:06 A.M., PDT).

Full Moon Days

	1998	1999	2000	2001	2002
Jan.	12	1/31	20	9	28
Feb.	11	—	19	8	27
Mar.	12	2/31	19	9	28
Apr.	11	30	18	7	26
May	11	30	18	7	26
June	10	28	16	5	24
July	9	28	16	5	24
Aug.	7	26	15	4	22
Sept.	6	25	13	2	21
Oct.	5	24	13	2	21
Nov.	4	23	11	1/30	19
Dec.	3	22	11	30	19

Principal Meteor Showers

Shower	Best Hour (EST/EDT)	Radiant Direction*	Date of Maximum**	Approx. Peak Rate (/hr.)	Associated Comet
Quadrantid	5 A.M.	N.	Jan. 4	40-150	—
Lyrid	5 A.M.	S.	Apr. 21	10-15	1861 I
Eta Aquarid	5 A.M.	S.E.	May 4	10-40	Halley
Delta Aquarid	3 A.M.	S.	July 30	10-35	—
Perseid	5 A.M.	N.	Aug. 11-13	50-100	1862 III
Draconid	10 P.M.	N.W.	Oct. 9	10	Giacobini-Zinner
Orionid	5 A.M.	S.	Oct. 20	10-70	Halley
Taurid	midnight	S.	Nov. 9	5-15	Encke
Leonid	5 A.M.	S.	Nov. 16	5-20	1866 I
Andromedid	10 P.M.	S.	Nov. 25-27	10	Biela
Geminid	2 A.M.	S.	Dec. 13	50-80	—
Ursid	5 A.M.	N.	Dec. 22	10-15	—

* Direction from which the meteors appear to come.
** Date of actual maximum occurrence may vary by one or two days in either direction.

BRIGHT STARS, 1998

The upper table shows the time (EST or EDT) when each star transits the meridian of Boston (i.e., lies directly above the horizon's south point there) and its altitude above that point at transit on the dates shown. The time of transit on any other date differs from that on the nearest date listed by approximately four minutes for each day. For a location outside Boston, the local time of the star's transit is found by correcting the time at Boston by the value of Key Letter "C" for that location. (See footnote.)

| Star | Constellation | Magni- tude | Time of Transit (EST/EDT) Boldface — P.M. Lightface — A.M. | | | | | | Alt. |
			Jan. 1	Mar. 1	May 1	July 1	Sept. 1	Nov. 1	
Altair	Aquila	0.8	**12:50**	8:58	5:58	1:58	**9:50**	**4:50**	56.3
Deneb	Cygnus	1.3	**1:40**	9:48	6:49	2:49	**10:41**	**5:41**	92.8
Fomalhaut	Psc. Austr.	1.2	**3:55**	**12:03**	9:03	5:03	12:56	**7:56**	17.8
Algol	Perseus	2.2	**8:06**	**4:14**	**1:14**	9:14	5:10	12:10	88.5
Aldebaran	Taurus	0.9	**9:33**	**5:41**	**2:41**	10:41	6:38	1:38	64.1
Rigel	Orion	0.1	**10:11**	**6:19**	**3:20**	11:20	7:16	2:16	39.4
Capella	Auriga	0.1	**10:13**	**6:21**	**3:21**	11:21	7:18	2:18	93.6
Bellatrix	Orion	1.6	**10:22**	**6:30**	**3:30**	11:30	7:27	2:27	54.0
Betelgeuse	Orion	var. 0.4	**10:52**	**7:00**	**4:00**	**12:00**	7:57	2:57	55.0
Sirius	Can. Maj.	−1.4	**11:42**	**7:50**	**4:50**	**12:50**	8:46	3:46	31.0
Procyon	Can. Min.	0.4	12:40	**8:44**	**5:44**	**1:44**	9:40	4:40	52.9
Pollux	Gemini	1.2	12:45	**8:50**	**5:50**	**1:50**	9:46	4:46	75.7
Regulus	Leo	1.4	3:09	**11:13**	**8:13**	**4:13**	**12:09**	7:09	59.7
Spica	Virgo	var. 1.0	6:25	2:33	**11:29**	**7:29**	**3:25**	10:26	36.6
Arcturus	Bootes	−0.1	7:16	3:24	12:20	**8:20**	**4:16**	11:16	66.9
Antares	Scorpius	var. 0.9	9:28	5:36	2:37	**10:33**	**6:29**	**1:29**	21.3
Vega	Lyra	0.0	11:36	7:44	4:44	12:40	**8:37**	**3:37**	86.4

RISINGS AND SETTINGS

The times of the star's rising and setting at Boston on any date are found by applying the interval shown to the time of the star's transit on that date. Subtract the interval for the star's rising; add it for its setting. The times for a location outside Boston are found by correcting the times found for Boston by the values of the Key Letters shown. (See footnote.) The directions in which the star rises and sets, shown for Boston, are generally useful throughout the United States. Deneb, Algol, Capella, and Vega are circumpolar stars — this means that they do not appear to rise or set but stay above the horizon.

Star	Interval hr. m.	Rising Key	Dir.	Setting Key	Dir.
Altair	6:36	B	EbN	E	WbN
Fomalhaut	3:59	E	SE	D	SW
Aldebaran	7:06	B	ENE	D	WNW
Rigel	5:33	D	EbS	B	WbS
Bellatrix	6:27	B	EbN	D	WbN
Betelgeuse	6:31	B	EbN	D	WbN
Sirius	5:00	D	ESE	B	WSW
Procyon	6:23	B	EbN	D	WbN
Pollux	8:01	A	NE	E	NW
Regulus	6:49	B	EbN	D	WbN
Spica	5:23	D	EbS	B	WbS
Arcturus	7:19	A	ENE	E	WNW
Antares	4:17	E	SEbE	A	SWbW

NOTE: The values of Key Letters are given in the Time Correction Tables (pages 214-218).

Sand, cat-hairs, dust and dust-mites...
Nothing gets by the 8-lb. ORECK XL!

The favorite vacuum of thousands of hotels
and more than 1 million professional and private users.
Now you can use this powerful vacuum to clean your
home better than ever before.

**Exclusive Filter System assures hypo-
allergenic cleaning with Germastat®**
Ideal for those who suffer from dust-related or
allergic discomforts. There's virtually no after dust.
Its special top-fill action carries the litter up
through the handle and deposits it on the inside
top of the bag. Yesterday's dirt can't seep out.
And the metal-tube top-fill performance works
without hoses to crack, leak or break.

**The lightest full-size vacuum
available.** It weighs just 8 pounds. So stairs
are a snap. It's super-powerful, with amazing
cleaning power: the fast, double helical brushes
revolve at an incredible 6,500 times a minute.

ORECK's Helping Hand® handle is
orthopedically designed on the principles
of ergonomics. To put it simply: no need to
squeeze your hand or bend your wrist.
A godsend for people with hand or wrist
problems.

Exclusive New Microsweep® gets
bare floors super clean, without any hoses,
attachments or adjustments.

A full 10-year Guarantee against breakage
or burnout of the housing PLUS a full 3-year
Warranty on the extended life motor. We'll let you
try the ORECK XL in your home for 15 days.
If you don't love it, you don't keep it.

FREE with purchase

Super Compact Canister

The 4-lb. dynamo
you've seen on TV.
The motor's so
powerful it lifts a
16-lb. bowling ball!
Hand-holdable and
comfortable. Cleans
under refrigerators...
car seats... books...
ceilings... even typewriter, computer and piano keys. With 8
accessories. Yours FREE when you purchase an ORECK
XL upright. Offer limited, so act now.

**FOR FREE INFORMATION,
CALL NOW TOLL-FREE**
1-800-286-8900
**and ask for Ext. 21001.
No salesperson will visit.**

ORECK CORPORATION
100 Plantation Road, New Orleans, LA 70123

A1-NC

The GREAT ECLIPSE of 1998

It has a lot going for it: In our neighborhood, it's the last total solar eclipse of the millennium. To see it at its best, you'll have to travel to the Caribbean in February. Hey, it's tough work, but someone's got to do it . . . author BOB BERMAN, for instance.

No spectacle in nature can match a total solar eclipse. And both elements — total and solar — are essential to the full experience. Partial solar eclipses are interesting, but not mind-blowing; lunar eclipses are nice, but not overwhelming. On **February 26,** an eclipse of the Sun will be visible in its partial phase from sections of the United States and Canada. Specifically, everyone east and south of a diagonal line from the Canadian Maritimes to Minneapolis to Los Angeles can view this event.

An even bigger thrill, however, awaits those willing to make the ultimate sacrifice and travel to the Caribbean, where the spectacle will be at its maximum, and where hundreds of research teams will converge. The lure is great: For our part of the world, this is the last *total* solar eclipse for the next two decades. And it is totality that you want, when the Moon and the Sun — both the same apparent size in our sky, in the greatest coincidence of nature — perfectly align so that the Sun is completely blocked for a time.

There's one problem in viewing a total solar eclipse. Because the Moon's shadow tapers to a slender 100-mile-wide line by the time it reaches Earth, just a narrow slash of geography falls inside the enchanted zone of darkness. Across a much larger area (in this case, much of the United States and part

---

Protect Your Eyes!

DO NOT ATTEMPT TO OBSERVE THE PARTIAL PHASE OF THIS ECLIPSE WITH THE NAKED EYE.

■ The easiest way to keep your eyes from turning into carbon during the partial phase of a solar eclipse (in this case, for all observers in the United States and Canada and for Caribbean observers during the partial phase) is to pick up an inexpensive pair of shade number 14 welder's goggles at any welding supply store. (No, you won't find them at the mall.)

of Canada), the event is a partial eclipse, where you need eye protection to safely see it at all, and where the amazing apparitions of totality never materialize.

For any given location on Earth, a total eclipse happens just once every 360 years, on average. (If it's cloudy, you have to hang around for another 360 years.) Usually, however, some small segment of North America manages to sit within the path of totality every decade or so. Unfortunately, a bizarre total-eclipse drought has afflicted us. The last time the Moon's shadow touched the U.S. or Canadian mainland was in February 1979, when a few northwestern states hosted that rare umbral swath. And the next time for the United States won't be until August 2017, and for Canada, 2024.

Only once a decade or so do all factors conspire for a really favorable eclipse, and that's what's in store on February 26. First there's the relatively long duration of totality: four minutes and eight seconds at the point of maximum eclipse. (Doesn't sound like much? Consider that the longest eclipse of the century was under seven minutes and that people have chartered flights to witness totalities as brief as one second!) Then there's the location: the Caribbean in February. That has a better ring to it than Siberia in March, where last year's event occurred. Next, factor in climatological prospects: Experts say the odds of clear weather for this one range between 80 and 85 percent.

So cruise ships are enjoying heavy bookings, as nature buffs and scientific expeditions plan for the millennium's final — and convenient — total solar eclipse.

Bob Berman, author of *Secrets of the Night Sky* (Morrow, 1995), was eclipse astronomer during four total-solar-eclipse expeditions.

A Sight "Beyond Words"
(but we'll try anyway)

■ The eclipse shadow crosses northwestern Venezuela before passing over Curaçao, Aruba, and the Leeward Islands of Montserrat, Antigua, and Guadeloupe. In those places, you can first expect an hour-long partial phase, where you need eye protection. For viewers in the Caribbean, the Sun during the partial phase becomes an odd, thin crescent.

A minute or two before totality, all light-colored surfaces, such as beaches, suddenly exhibit shadow bands. These dramatic, shimmering dark lines, which look a bit like the wiggles at the bottom of a swimming pool, appear everywhere. This weird curiosity cannot be photographed. (Try it! Your pictures will show the scene without them.) Only recently explained, shadow bands are the edges of atmospheric temperature cells, or air pockets, projected onto the ground by the dazzling remnant of the Sun.

Then comes totality. The delicate tendrils of the Sun's corona, or atmosphere, leap into the surrounding sky in a manner wholly different from the image in photos, which over- or underexpose various sections of the phenomenon. But beyond the lovely sight of the fully eclipsed Sun lies a sensation that is almost universally described as "beyond words." Animals act up; in fact, a total eclipse makes an estimated 50 percent of all observers shout and babble. A profound presence overwhelms all onlookers as the Sun, the Moon, and your spot on Earth form a perfectly straight line in space.

Maybe that's why it's so addictive. Eclipses are conventions for some people, who have often assumed extra jobs or second mortgages, whatever it took, to confront the Moon's shadow once again. But if you cannot travel, you can at least enjoy the partial eclipse from home. Observed from the United States and Canada, where the eclipse reaches its maximum at around noon in the Southwest and Texas, around 1:00 P.M. along the East Coast, and around 3:00 P.M. in eastern Canada, the Sun will appear less than 50 percent obscured by the Moon.

□ □

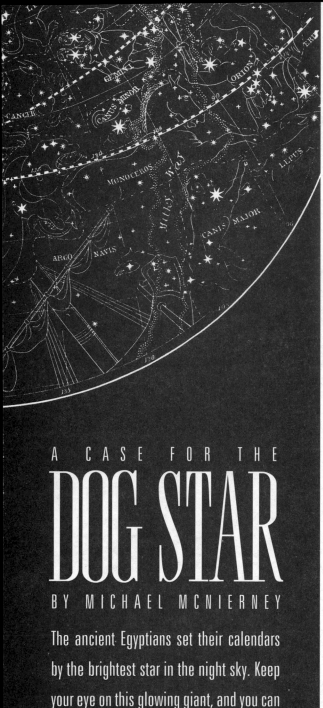

A CASE FOR THE
DOG STAR

BY MICHAEL MCNIERNEY

The ancient Egyptians set their calendars by the brightest star in the night sky. Keep your eye on this glowing giant, and you can do the same.

One winter night not long ago, I glanced out my window at about two in the morning. The snow glowed in the platinum light of the Moon, and in the barren branches of cottonwoods to the south, a single white light shone so brightly that it startled me.

It was Sirius, the Dog Star, lead star of the winter constellation Canis Major, the Greater Dog. Sirius is far and away the brightest star in the night sky. In fact, at magnitude -1.46, it is nearly ten times as bright as the average first-magnitude star. It can actually be seen in broad daylight with a small telescope, if you know where to look.

From prehistory until urban civilization began to blast the night sky with artificial illumination, people looked to this magnificent celestial light as a beacon telling the change in seasons and predicting the future. The origin of the name Sirius is unknown, but ancient writers explained it as relating to a word for blazing, burning, or parching. This association is at least as old as Homer, whose *Iliad* mentions "Orion's Dog" as a star in the summer dawn and also as a star in the evening sky at harvesttime. In both cases, it "brings down killing fevers on wretched men."

In ancient Egypt, the appearance of Sirius above the eastern horizon just before dawn occurred around the time of the summer solstice. This event, called the heliacal rising of the

☆ ☆ ☆ ☆ ☆ ☆ ☆ ☆ ☆ ☆ ☆ ☆ ☆ ☆

star, was an occasion of great joy. The return each year of Sirius to its place near the morning Sun meant that the Nile was about to flood, bringing water and rich soil to the desert along its banks. The Egyptians began their year with the heliacal rising of Sirius and calibrated their calendar according to it.

To inhabitants of the Mediterranean shore farther north, however, the same summer rising of Sirius portended disease and death. Both the Greeks and the Romans noted that the star's appearance seemed to bring on the worst heat of summer, a time when people felt lethargic and feverish, and crops withered. Since Sirius was the dominant star in the constellation of the Dog, it was called the Dog Star, and the time after its solstice rising was known as the Dog Days, a term we still use for the 40 or so days in the hottest part of the summer.

Ancient medicine sought to explain disease and health as various combinations of heat and cold, dryness and moisture. If the Dog Star was thought to cause fevers in people, then naturally, it must affect dogs, too. Under its influence, dogs could become so hot and dry that they developed rabies — *lyssa* in Greek, which means "wolfishness."

The Greeks made the connection between madness, rabies, and wolves, and associated Sirius with the "excessive dryness" that caused men to act like or even change into wolves. To describe the insane, uncontrollable rage of men in battle (*berserk* in Old Norse), the Greeks used the word for rabies. When Achilles mangled the corpse of his fallen enemy for days after the battle, Homer says he was seized by *lyssa*.

For us today, all of the mythical mysteries and dire associations of Sirius are gone. It is simply a star a little less than twice the size of our Sun. Though 23 times as bright as the Sun, it is a fairly ordinary star by astronomical standards. Its prominence in our sky and our history is due to the accident of distance: It is only 8.7 light years away, the fifth-closest star known.

To regain a little of the fear and awe once felt at the sight of Sirius, try this: During fall and winter, keep an eye on the star. Gaze at that burning arc light in the sky a few times a month and notice how its position changes in relation to the hour and the horizon. As it rises earlier each night, the Dog Star leads us into the season of our own special days of celebration. On Thanksgiving, it rises shortly before 9:30 P.M., EST. By Christmas Eve, it appears in the east around 7:30 P.M. About midnight on New Year's Eve, it is as high in the southern sky as it ever climbs, a symbol of the inexorable revolution of the years. ☐ ☐

About midnight on New Year's Eve, it is as high in the southern sky as it ever climbs.

Canis Major — illustration by Sara Mintz Zwicker

WHERE THE SUN RISES AND SETS

By using the table below and a compass, you can determine accurately where on the horizon the Sun will rise or set on a given day. The top half of the table is for those days of the year, between the vernal and autumnal equinoxes, when the Sun rises north of east and sets north of west. March 21 through June 21 are listed in the left column, June 21 through September 22 appear in the right column. Similarly arranged, the bottom half of the table shows the other half of the year, when the Sun rises south of

east and sets south of west. Here's how it works. Say you live in Gary, Indiana, and need to know where the Sun will rise or set on October 10. Use the Time Correction Tables (pages 214-218) to determine the latitude of your city or the listed city nearest to you. Gary is at 41° latitude. Find the 40° latitude column and you see that on October 10 the Sun rises 8° south of east and sets 8° south of west. Of course, you can determine figures for other latitudes and days not actually shown in the table by using extrapolation.

Latitude Date	0°	10°	20°	30°	40°	50°	60°	Latitude Date
Mar. 21	0°	0°	0°	0°	0°	0°	0°	Sept. 22
Mar. 31	4° N	4° N	4° N	4° N	5° N	6° N	8° N	Sept. 14
Apr. 10	8° N	8° N	8° N	9° N	10° N	12° N	15° N	Sept. 4
Apr. 20	11° N	12° N	12° N	13° N	15° N	18° N	23° N	Aug. 24
May 1	15° N	16° N	16° N	17° N	20° N	23° N	31° N	Aug. 14
May 10	17°N	18° N	19° N	20° N	23° N	28° N	37° N	Aug. 4
May 20	20° N	21° N	21° N	23° N	26° N	32° N	43° N	July 25
June 1	22° N	22° N	23° N	26° N	29° N	36° N	48° N	July 13
June 10	23° N	24° N	24° N	27° N	31° N	37° N	51° N	July 4
June 21	23½° N	25° N	25° N	27° N	31° N	38° N	53° N	June 21
Sept. 22	0°	0°	0°	0°	0°	0°	0°	Mar. 21
Oct. 1	3° S	3° S	3° S	3° S	4° S	5° S	6° S	Mar. 14
Oct. 10	6° S	7° S	7° S	7° S	8° S	10° S	13° S	Mar. 5
Oct. 20	10° S	11° S	11° S	12° S	13° S	16° S	20° S	Feb. 23
Nov. 1	15° S	15° S	15° S	16° S	18° S	22° S	29° S	Feb. 12
Nov. 10	17° S	18° S	18° S	20° S	22° S	27° S	36° S	Feb. 2
Nov. 20	20° S	21° S	21° S	23° S	26° S	31° S	42° S	Jan. 23
Dec. 1	22° S	23° S	23° S	25° S	29° S	35° S	48° S	Jan. 13
Dec. 10	23° S	24° S	24° S	27° S	30° S	37° S	51° S	Jan. 4
Dec. 21	23½° S	25° S	25° S	27° S	31° S	38° S	53° S	Dec. 21

Special Offer to Our Readers

An extraordinary gathering of planets appears at nightfall. While their most dense concentration will occur early next month, now we can observe every planet in the solar system at once! Pluto requires a powerful telescope and good star chart, while Neptune and Uranus demand a telescope or binoculars. The rest stand brightly after sunset, stretched leftward along the solar system's plane (the zodiac) from southwest to southeast. At nightfall, Venus is brightest and lowest, Jupiter far to its left, while less brilliant Saturn rises in the southeast. On the 3rd, the Moon, Mars, and Venus form a striking triangle in the southwest 45 minutes after sunset.

☽	First Quarter	7th day	16th hour	43rd minute
○	Full Moon	14th day	9th hour	12th minute
☾	Last Quarter	21st day	18th hour	58th minute
●	New Moon	29th day	21st hour	14th minute

Times are given in Eastern Standard Time.

For an explanation of this page, see "How to Use This Almanac," page 34; for values of Key Letters, see Time Correction Tables, page 214.

Day of Year	Day of Month	Day of Week	☉ Rises h. m.	Key	☉ Sets h. m.	Key	Length of Days h. m.	Sun Fast m.	Declination of Sun ° '	Full Sea Boston A.M.	Full Sea Boston P.M.	☽ Rises h. m.	Key	☽ Sets h. m.	Key	☽ Place	☽ Age
305	1	Sa.	6 18	D	4 37	B	10 19	32	14 s.35	11½	—	7 ᴹ 14	E	5 ᴾᴹ 46	B	LIB	1
306	2	**E**	6 19	D	4 36	B	10 17	32	14 54	12	12¼	8 13	E	6 27	B	LIB	2
307	3	M.	6 20	D	4 35	B	10 15	32	15 13	12¾	12¾	9 11	E	7 13	B	OPH	3
308	4	Tu.	6 21	D	4 34	B	10 13	32	15 31	1¼	1½	10 06	E	8 04	B	SAG	4
309	5	W.	6 23	D	4 32	B	10 09	32	15 49	2¼	2¼	10 58	E	9 02	B	SAG	5
310	6	Th.	6 24	D	4 31	B	10 07	32	16 07	3	3¼	11 ᴬᴹ 45	E	10 04	B	SAG	6
311	7	Fr.	6 25	D	4 30	B	10 05	32	16 25	3¾	4	12 ᴾᴹ 29	E	11 ᴹ 10	C	CAP	7
312	8	Sa.	6 26	D	4 29	A	10 03	32	16 43	4¾	5	1 09	D	— —	—	CAP	8
313	9	**E**	6 28	D	4 28	A	10 00	32	17 00	5¾	6¼	1 46	D	12 ᴬᴹ 18	C	AQU	9
314	10	M.	6 29	D	4 27	A	9 58	32	17 17	6¾	7¼	2 22	D	1 29	D	AQU	10
315	11	Tu.	6 30	D	4 26	A	9 56	32	17 33	7¾	8¼	2 57	D	2 40	D	PSC	11
316	12	W.	6 31	D	4 25	A	9 54	31	17 50	8¾	9¼	3 34	C	3 53	D	PSC	12
317	13	Th.	6 33	D	4 24	A	9 51	31	18 05	9½	10	4 13	B	5 05	E	CET	13
318	14	Fr.	6 34	D	4 23	A	9 49	31	18 21	10¼	11	4 56	B	6 17	E	ARI	14
319	15	Sa.	6 35	D	4 22	A	9 47	31	18 36	11¼	11¾	5 43	B	7 25	E	TAU	15
320	16	**E**	6 36	D	4 21	A	9 45	31	18 51	—	12	6 33	B	8 29	E	TAU	16
321	17	M.	6 38	D	4 20	A	9 42	31	19 06	12½	12¾	7 28	B	9 27	E	ORI	17
322	18	Tu.	6 39	D	4 20	A	9 41	31	19 20	1½	1½	8 25	B	10 17	E	GEM	18
323	19	W.	6 40	D	4 19	A	9 39	30	19 34	2¼	2½	9 23	B	11 01	E	GEM	19
324	20	Th.	6 41	D	4 18	A	9 37	30	19 48	3¼	3¼	10 21	B	11 ᴬᴹ 40	D	CAN	20
325	21	Fr.	6 42	D	4 17	A	9 35	30	20 01	4	4¼	11 ᴾᴹ 18	B	12 ᴾᴹ 14	D	LEO	21
326	22	Sa.	6 44	D	4 17	A	9 33	30	20 14	5	5¼	— —	—	12 44	D	LEO	22
327	23	**E**	6 45	D	4 16	A	9 31	29	20 26	6	6¼	12 ᴬᴹ 15	D	1 13	D	LEO	23
328	24	M.	6 46	D	4 16	A	9 30	29	20 38	6¾	7¼	1 12	D	1 41	D	VIR	24
329	25	Tu.	6 47	D	4 15	A	9 28	29	20 50	7½	8	2 09	D	2 09	C	VIR	25
330	26	W.	6 48	D	4 15	A	9 27	28	21 01	8¼	8¾	3 06	D	2 38	C	VIR	26
331	27	Th.	6 49	E	4 14	A	9 25	28	21 12	9	9½	4 05	E	3 10	B	VIR	27
332	28	Fr.	6 51	E	4 14	A	9 23	28	21 23	9¾	10¼	5 04	E	3 44	B	LIB	28
333	29	Sa.	6 52	E	4 13	A	9 21	27	21 34	10½	11	6 04	E	4 23	B	LIB	0
334	30	**E**	6 53	E	4 13	A	9 20	27	21 s.43	11	11½	7 ᴬᴹ 04	E	5 ᴾᴹ 08	B	OPH	1

NOVEMBER hath 30 days. 1997

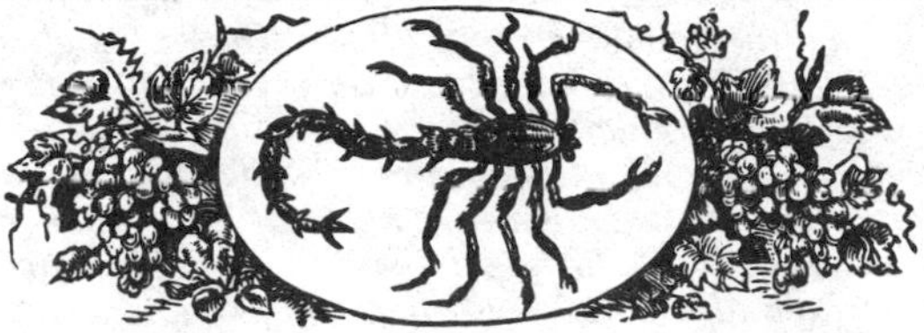

No shade, no shine, no butterflies,
no bees
No fruit, no flowers, no leaves,
no birds — No-vember!
– Thomas Hood

D. M.	D. W.	Dates, Feasts, Fasts, Aspects, Tide Heights	Weather ↓
1	Sa.	**All Saints** • Famous "Dark Day" in New England, 1716 • Tides {10.4 — •	*Cool*
2	**E**	**24th S. af. P.** • James K. Polk born, 1795 • {9.6 10.5 •	*and*
3	M.	**All Souls** • *Never try to wear a hat that has more character than you do.* • {9.5 10.4	*wet,*
4	Tu.	☌♂☾ • ☌♀☾ • Election Day • {9.4 10.4 •	*the*
5	W.	☾ runs low • First U.S. cross-country airplane flight, 1911 • Tides {9.3 10.3 •	*Sun*
6	Th.	♀ Gr. Elong. (47° E.) • ☌♆☾ • Tides {9.2 10.1 •	*with-*
7	Fr.	☌♅☾ • ☌♃☾ • Joni Mitchell born, 1943 •	*holds*
8	Sa.	*Take care that old age does not wrinkle your spirit even more than your face.* • {9.4 10.0 •	*its*
9	**E**	**25th S. af. P.** • ☾ at ☋ •	*blessing,*
10	M.	**St. Leo the Great** • Richard Burton born, 1925 • Tides {10.3 10.4 •	*and*
11	Tu.	**St. Martin** • **Veterans Day** • ☾ on Eq. • Occn. ♄ by ☾ •	
12	W.	☾ at perig. • *If All Saints brings out winter, St. Martin brings out Indian Summer.* •	*we*
13	Th.	Great Leonid meteor display, midnight to dawn, 1833 • Tides {11.8 11.0 •	*all*
14	Fr.	**Full Beaver** ○ • Mamie Eisenhower born, 1896 • Tides {12.1 11.0 •	*get*
15	Sa.	*Keep a green tree in your heart and perhaps the singing bird will come.* • {12.1 10.8 •	*colds.*
16	**E**	**26th S. af. P.** • W. C. Handy born, 1873 • {— 11.9 •	*Awake*
17	M.	**St. Hugh of Lincoln** • ☾ rides high • Suez Canal opened, 1869 •	*to*
18	Tu.	**St. Hilda** • CBS sold its record division to Sony, 1987 • {10.1 11.0 •	*flakes.*
19	W.	Ford Motor Co. discontinued the Edsel, 1959 • Roy Campanella born, 1921 •	*In*
20	Th.	Alistair Cooke born, 1908 • Robert F. Kennedy born, 1925 • {9.3 9.8 •	*the*
21	Fr.	Mayflower Compact signed, 1620 • Stan Musial born, 1920 • {9.0 9.4 •	*woods*
22	Sa.	U.S. ended 22-year ban on travel to mainland China, 1972 • Billie Jean King born, 1943 •	*the*
23	**E**	**27th S. af. P.** • ☾ at ☊ • ☾ at apo. •	*deer's*
24	M.	☾ on Eq. • *If you add to the truth, you subtract from it.* • Tides {9.1 8.9 •	*a*
25	Tu.	Pope John XXIII born, 1881 • Joe DiMaggio born, 1914 • {9.3 8.9 •	*wraith,*
26	W.	Charles M. Schulz born, 1922 • Sojourner Truth died, 1883 • Tides {9.6 9.1 •	*as*
27	Th.	**Thanksgiving** • ♇ in ☌ with ☉ • Tides {9.9 9.2 •	*we*
28	Fr.	☿ Gr. Elong. (22° E.) • Cocoanut Grove nightclub fire, 1942 • {10.2 9.4	*ponder*
29	Sa.	New ● • C. S. Lewis born, 1898 • Tides {10.5 9.5 •	*Pilgrim*
30	**E**	**1st S. in Advent** • Winston Churchill born, 1874 •	*faith.*

You've got to be very careful if you don't know where you are going, because you might not get there. – Yogi Berra

Farmer's Calendar

The attack of the Asian ladybugs is no myth: You can read about it in *The New York Times.* The invader is *Harmonia axyridis*, a quarter-inch beetle, orange and covered with black speckles. In the northeastern states for the past few years, *H. axyridis* has begun turning up in people's houses around this time. It's looking for a warm place to hibernate. That is what everybody in this part of the country needs, and most householders wouldn't begrudge the ladybug its winter shelter — except that the little things arrive in large numbers. Now, *H. axyridis* is harmless. In fact, as a predator of insect pests, it's highly beneficial. Still, as the *Times* report observed, "If a woman wakes up in the morning and finds 20,000 ladybugs on her kitchen ceiling, she doesn't care that they eat aphids."

The Asian ladybug has traveled up here from the south, where it was introduced to control aphids and other harmful insects. It does that admirably, but it also swarms in alarming numbers and inconvenient places. The story of *H. axyridis*, therefore, would seem to be a classic of unintended consequences, another case in which importing exotic creatures for a good reason comes to a bad end. But wait a minute. Not all foreign transplants go wrong. I myself, I reflect, am no native of New England. I was imported from farther west. But I feel I have settled in pretty well, and if I don't exhibit conspicuously beneficial behavior (I don't eat aphids, for example), neither do I do much serious harm. Nor does *H. axyridis*, and it may be that is all that should be asked of either of us, especially as both the beetle and I are certainly here to stay.

1997 DECEMBER, THE TWELFTH MONTH

The year ends on a spectacular note as all the planets bunch into one side of the heavens, simultaneously visible. Mercury scrapes the low southwest horizon a half hour after sunset. Higher and leftward stands the closely spaced duo of dim Mars and dazzling Venus (awesome at magnitude -5). Then come naked-eye-invisible Uranus and Neptune; even further leftward brilliant Jupiter hovers some 30 degrees above the southern horizon. Saturn is the solitary bright "star" in the southeast. This is the century's final simultaneous display of all planets and a holiday feast for all who look heavenward. Winter begins on the 21st at 3:07 P.M., EST.

☽	First Quarter	7th day	1st hour	9th minute
○	Full Moon	13th day	21st hour	37th minute
☾	Last Quarter	21st day	16th hour	43rd minute
●	New Moon	29th day	11th hour	56th minute

Times are given in Eastern Standard Time.

For an explanation of this page, see "How to Use This Almanac," page 34; for values of Key Letters, see Time Correction Tables, page 214.

Day of Year	Day of Month	Day of Week	☉ Rises h. m.	Key	☉ Sets h. m.	Key	Length of Days h. m.	Sun Fast m.	Declination of Sun ° '	Full Sea Boston A.M.	Full Sea Boston P.M.	☽ Rises h. m.	Key	☽ Sets h. m.	Key	☽ Place	☽ Age
335	1	M.	6 54	E	4 13	A	9 19	27	21s.52	11¾	—	8 A.M. 01	E	5 P.M. 59	B	OPH	2
336	2	Tu.	6 55	E	4 12	A	9 17	26	22 01	12¼	12½	8 55	E	6 55	B	SAG	3
337	3	W.	6 56	E	4 12	A	9 16	26	22 10	1	1¼	9 45	E	7 57	B	SAG	4
338	4	Th.	6 57	E	4 12	A	9 15	26	22 17	1¾	2	10 30	E	9 02	C	CAP	5
339	5	Fr.	6 58	E	4 12	A	9 14	25	22 25	2¾	2¾	11 11	D	10 09	C	AQU	6
340	6	Sa.	6 59	E	4 12	A	9 13	25	22 32	3½	3¾	11 A.M. 48	D	11 P.M. 18	C	AQU	7
341	7	**E**	7 00	E	4 12	A	9 12	24	22 39	4½	4¾	12 P.M. 24	D	— —	–	AQU	8
342	8	M.	7 01	E	4 11	A	9 10	24	22 46	5½	5¾	12 58	D	12 A.M. 27	D	PSC	9
343	9	Tu.	7 02	E	4 11	A	9 09	23	22 52	6½	7	1 32	C	1 37	D	PSC	10
344	10	W.	7 03	E	4 12	A	9 09	23	22 57	7½	8	2 09	C	2 47	E	PSC	11
345	11	Th.	7 03	E	4 12	A	9 09	23	23 02	8¼	9	2 48	B	3 57	E	ARI	12
346	12	Fr.	7 04	E	4 12	A	9 08	22	23 06	9¼	9¾	3 32	B	5 05	E	TAU	13
347	13	Sa.	7 05	E	4 12	A	9 07	22	23 10	10	10¾	4 20	B	6 11	E	TAU	14
348	14	**E**	7 06	E	4 12	A	9 06	21	23 14	10¾	11½	5 13	B	7 12	E	TAU	15
349	15	M.	7 06	E	4 12	A	9 06	21	23 17	11¾	—	6 09	B	8 06	E	GEM	16
350	16	Tu.	7 07	E	4 13	A	9 06	20	23 20	12¼	12½	7 07	B	8 54	E	GEM	17
351	17	W.	7 08	E	4 13	A	9 05	20	23 22	1	1¼	8 06	B	9 36	E	CAN	18
352	18	Th.	7 08	E	4 13	A	9 05	19	23 23	1¾	2	9 05	C	10 13	E	CAN	19
353	19	Fr.	7 09	E	4 14	A	9 05	19	23 24	2¾	2¾	10 03	C	10 45	D	LEO	20
354	20	Sa.	7 10	E	4 14	A	9 04	18	23 25	3½	3¾	11 00	D	11 15	D	LEO	21
355	21	**E**	7 10	E	4 14	A	9 04	18	23 25	4¼	4½	11 P.M. 57	D	11 A.M. 43	D	LEO	22
356	22	M.	7 11	E	4 15	A	9 04	17	23 25	5	5½	— —	–	12 P.M. 11	C	VIR	23
357	23	Tu.	7 11	E	4 15	A	9 04	17	23 25	6	6¼	12 A.M. 54	D	12 39	C	VIR	24
358	24	W.	7 12	E	4 16	A	9 04	16	23 24	6¾	7¼	1 52	D	1 09	C	VIR	25
359	25	Th.	7 12	E	4 17	A	9 05	16	23 22	7½	8¼	2 50	E	1 42	B	LIB	26
360	26	Fr.	7 12	E	4 18	A	9 06	15	23 20	8½	9	3 50	E	2 18	B	LIB	27
361	27	Sa.	7 12	E	4 18	A	9 06	15	23 17	9¼	9¾	4 50	E	3 00	B	SCO	28
362	28	**E**	7 13	E	4 19	A	9 06	14	23 14	9¾	10½	5 49	E	3 49	B	OPH	29
363	29	M.	7 13	E	4 20	A	9 07	14	23 11	10½	11¼	6 46	E	4 44	B	SAG	0
364	30	Tu.	7 13	E	4 21	A	9 08	13	23 07	11¼	—	7 40	E	5 45	B	SAG	1
365	31	W.	7 13	E	4 21	A	9 08	13	23s.03	12	12	8 A.M. 28	E	6 P.M. 51	B	SAG	2

DECEMBER hath 31 days. 1997

All glory be to God on high,
And to the earth be peace;
Good-will henceforth from heaven to men
Begin, and never cease! – *Nahum Tate*

D. M.	D. W.	Dates, Feasts, Fasts, Aspects, Tide Heights	*Weather* ↓
1	M.	☌ ☿ ☾ • Boys Town founded near Omaha, Neb., 1917 • {10.8 / —	*'Tis the*
2	Tu.	☾ runs low • Ford unveiled the Model A, 1927 • Tides {9.6 / 10.8 •	*season*
3	W.	☌ ♂ ☾ • ☌ ♀ ☾ • ☌ ♆ ☾ • {9.6 / 10.8 •	*for*
4	Th.	☌ ♅ ☾ • Last American hostage released, Lebanon, 1991 • {9.7 / 10.7 •	*rain*
5	Fr.	☌ ♃ ☾ • Walt Disney born, 1901 • Tides {9.7 / 10.5 •	*that's*
6	Sa.	St. Nicholas • Explosion destroyed Halifax, Nova Scotia, 1917 •	*freezin'.*
7	E	**2nd S. in Advent** • ☾ at ☋ • ☿ stat. • ☌ ♀ ♆	
8	M.	☾ on Eq. • James Thurber born, 1894 • Tides {10.2 / 9.9 •	*Hang*
9	Tu.	☌ ♄ ☾ • ☾ at perig. • 61° F, Boston 1 A.M., 1980 •	*mistletoe*
10	W.	*Opportunity is missed by most people because it is dressed in overalls and looks like work.* •	*as*
11	Th.	♀ Greatest Brilliancy • Snow, Phoenix, Arizona, 1985 • Tides {11.2 / 10.1 •	*you*
12	Fr.	Francis Chichester completed solo voyage, England to Australia, 1966 •	*whistle "O*
13	Sa.	St. Lucy • Full Cold ○ • {11.7 / 10.3 •	*Tannenbaum."*
14	E	**3rd S. in Advent** • Halcyon Days • {11.6 / 10.2 •	*Build a*
15	M.	☾ rides high • ☌ ♂ ♆ • Tides {11.5 / — •	*snowman;*
16	Tu.	*Always put off till tomorrow what you shouldn't do at all.* • Tides {10.0 / 11.2 •	*watch*
17	W.	☿ in inf. ☌ • ♄ stat. • Ember Day • Tides {9.8 / 10.7 •	*him*
18	Th.	Ty Cobb born, 1886 • Antonio Stradivari died, 1737 • {9.6 / 10.3 •	*melt down*
19	Fr.	Ember Day • National Hockey League began first pro season, 1917 •	*as the*
20	Sa.	☾ at ☊ • Ember Day • Branch Rickey born, 1881 • {9.1 / 9.3 •	*rain*
21	E	**4th S. in Advent** • Winter Solstice • ☾ at apo. •	*begins*
22	M.	St. Thomas • ☾ on Eq. • ☌ ♀ ♂ • Tides {9.0 / 8.6 •	*to*
23	Tu.	Boogie-woogie music first performed at Carnegie Hall, 1938 • {9.0 / 8.5 •	*pelt down.*
24	W.	First day of Chanukah • Beware the Pogonip. • {9.2 / 8.5 •	*Gather*
25	Th.	**Christmas Day** • ♀ stat. • {9.4 / 8.6 •	*friends*
26	Fr.	St. Stephen • ☌ ♂ ♅ • Boxing Day (Canada) • {9.8 / 8.8 •	*and*
27	Sa.	St. John • ☿ stat. • ☌ ☿ ☾ • {10.1 / 9.0 •	*celebrate:*
28	E	**1st S. af. C.** • Woodrow Wilson born, 1856 •	*peace*
29	M.	Holy Innocents • ☾ runs low • New ● • {10.8 / 9.6 •	*and*
30	Tu.	*Begin the new year square with every man.* (Robert B. Thomas) • Tides {11.1 / — •	*joy*
31	W.	☌ ♆ ☾ • ☌ ♀ ☾ • ☌ ♅ ☾ • {9.9 / 11.2 •	*in '98!*

Farmer's Calendar

It is a question for the ages whether people who live in cities envy country people as much as they say they do — or whether if they don't, they should. Peace is what they want, or so they say. But how peaceful do they think it is up here? And anyway, how much peace can a person stand?

Well, these are not questions we can settle in this space today, but let us admit one realm in which rural life seems plainly to have an advantage: the realm of the weather. Weather of all kinds, but especially winter weather, visits the city more harshly than it does less settled districts. Consider a moderately heavy snowstorm: In Vermont it's a struggle. In Boston it's a calamity. In part that's because of the inevitable obstacle put in the way of transportation by snow as it falls. But surely the worst of a snowstorm in the city comes from other reasons, reasons related to the rhythm or tempo of a storm in town compared to one in the country.

Up here, to oversimplify only a little, when a storm is over, it's over. When the snow stops falling, the ordeal is finished, and we can get on to other things. In the city when the snow stops falling, the ordeal has only begun. You have to plow out, clear off, and shovel, but you can't because there's no place to put the snow. You can't put it in the street, because the street must be clear for cars. You can't put it beside the street, because the sidewalk must be clear for people. In New York they solve the problem by piling the snow up at the street *corners* and climbing over it with ropes. You can see how a day or so of that leads to envy of those located some place — anyplace — else.

1998 JANUARY, THE FIRST MONTH

New Year's Day finds bright Jupiter and the crescent Moon meeting low in the southwest soon after sunset. Early risers can observe Mercury, at its best from the 2nd to the 16th, in the east just before dawn. Quadrantid meteors, normally the year's third- or fourth-best shower, occur under dark, moonless conditions on January 3. Earth skims closest to the Sun (perihelion) on the 4th, at a distance of 91,400,005 miles, making southern hemisphere summers warmer than they would be otherwise. Venus reaches inferior conjunction on the 16th, when it passes between Earth and the Sun and is closest to us though lost in the solar glare.

☽	First Quarter	5th day	9th hour	18th minute
○	Full Moon	12th day	12th hour	24th minute
☾	Last Quarter	20th day	14th hour	40th minute
●	New Moon	28th day	1st hour	1st minute

Times are given in Eastern Standard Time.

For an explanation of this page, see "How to Use This Almanac," page 34; for values of Key Letters, see Time Correction Tables, page 214.

Day of Year	Day of Month	Day of Week	☼ Rises h. m.	Key	☼ Sets h. m.	Key	Length of Days h. m.	Sun Fast m.	Declination of Sun ° ′	Full Sea Boston A.M.	Full Sea Boston P.M.	☽ Rises h. m.	Key	☽ Sets h. m.	Key	☽ Place	☽ Age
1	1	Th.	7 14	E	4 22	A	9 08	12	22s.58	12¾	12¾	9 A.M. 11	E	7 P.M. 59	C	AQU	3
2	2	Fr.	7 14	E	4 23	A	9 09	12	22 53	1½	1¾	9 51	D	9 09	D	CAP	4
3	3	Sa.	7 14	E	4 24	A	9 10	11	22 47	2¼	2½	10 27	D	10 19	D	AQU	5
4	4	D	7 14	E	4 25	A	9 11	11	22 41	3¼	3½	11 02	C	11 P.M. 28	D	PSC	6
5	5	M.	7 14	E	4 26	A	9 12	10	22 34	4¼	4½	11 A.M. 36	C	— —	–	CET	7
6	6	Tu.	7 13	E	4 27	A	9 14	10	22 27	5	5½	12 P.M. 11	C	12 A.M. 38	D	PSC	8
7	7	W.	7 13	E	4 28	A	9 15	10	22 20	6	6¾	12 48	B	1 46	E	CET	9
8	8	Th.	7 13	E	4 29	A	9 16	9	22 11	7	7¾	1 28	B	2 53	E	TAU	10
9	9	Fr.	7 13	E	4 30	A	9 17	9	22 03	8	8¾	2 13	B	3 58	E	TAU	11
10	10	Sa.	7 13	E	4 31	A	9 18	8	21 54	9	9¾	3 02	B	5 00	E	TAU	12
11	11	D	7 12	E	4 32	A	9 20	8	21 45	9¾	10½	3 56	B	5 56	E	ORI	13
12	12	M.	7 12	E	4 33	A	9 21	8	21 35	10¾	11¼	4 53	B	6 47	E	GEM	14
13	13	Tu.	7 12	E	4 34	A	9 22	7	21 25	11½	—	5 52	B	7 31	E	CAN	15
14	14	W.	7 12	E	4 36	A	9 24	7	21 14	12	12	6 51	C	8 10	E	CAN	16
15	15	Th.	7 11	E	4 37	A	9 26	6	21 04	12¾	12¾	7 50	C	8 45	D	LEO	17
16	16	Fr.	7 10	E	4 38	A	9 28	6	20 52	1½	1½	8 48	D	9 16	D	LEO	18
17	17	Sa.	7 10	E	4 39	A	9 29	6	20 40	2	2¼	9 45	D	9 45	D	LEO	19
18	18	D	7 09	E	4 40	A	9 31	5	20 28	2¾	3	10 42	D	10 13	D	VIR	20
19	19	M.	7 09	E	4 42	A	9 33	5	20 16	3½	3¾	11 P.M. 39	D	10 41	C	VIR	21
20	20	Tu.	7 08	E	4 43	A	9 35	5	20 03	4¼	4¾	— —	–	11 09	C	VIR	22
21	21	W.	7 07	E	4 44	A	9 37	4	19 50	5¼	5¾	12 A.M. 36	E	11 A.M. 40	B	VIR	23
22	22	Th.	7 07	E	4 45	A	9 38	4	19 36	6	6½	1 35	E	12 P.M. 14	B	LIB	24
23	23	Fr.	7 06	D	4 47	A	9 41	4	19 22	7	7½	2 34	E	12 53	B	LIB	25
24	24	Sa.	7 05	D	4 48	A	9 43	4	19 08	7¾	8¼	3 33	E	1 37	B	OPH	26
25	25	D	7 04	D	4 49	A	9 45	3	18 53	8½	9¼	4 31	E	2 29	B	SAG	27
26	26	M.	7 04	D	4 50	A	9 46	3	18 38	9½	10	5 26	E	3 27	B	SAG	28
27	27	Tu.	7 03	D	4 52	A	9 49	3	18 22	10¼	10¾	6 18	E	4 32	B	SAG	29
28	28	W.	7 02	D	4 53	A	9 51	3	18 06	11	11½	7 05	E	5 41	C	CAP	0
29	29	Th.	7 01	D	4 54	A	9 53	3	17 50	11¾	—	7 47	E	6 52	C	CAP	1
30	30	Fr.	7 00	D	4 56	A	9 56	2	17 34	12¼	12½	8 26	D	8 05	D	AQU	2
31	31	Sa.	6 59	D	4 57	A	9 58	2	17s.17	1	1½	9 A.M. 03	D	9 P.M. 17	D	AQU	3

JANUARY hath 31 days. 1998

O Winter, ruler of the inverted year,
Thy scattered hair with sleet like ashes filled,
Thy breath congealed upon thy lips, thy cheeks
Fringed with a beard made white with other snows . . .
I love thee. – *William Cowper*

D. M.	D. W.	Dates, Feasts, Fasts, Aspects, Tide Heights	*Weather* ↓
1	Th.	New Year's Day • **Circumcision** • ☌ ♃ ☾ •	*Rain*
2	Fr.	State highway speeds limited to 55 mph, 1974 • Georgia became 4th state, 1788 • {10.2 / 11.2	*and*
3	Sa.	☾ at perig. • ☾ at ☋ • Alaska became 49th state, 1959 • {10.3 / 10.9	*snow*
4	D	**2nd S. af. Ch.** • ⊕ at perihelion • ☾ on Eq.	*com-*
5	M.	St. Elizabeth Seton • ☌ ♄ ☾ • Twelfth Night • {10.4 / 10.1 •	*pete*
6	Tu.	**Epiphany** • ☿ Gr. Elong. (23° W.) • Carl Sandburg born, 1878 •	*for*
7	W.	St. Distaff's Day • Japanese Emperor Hirohito died, 1989 • {10.5 / 9.5	*airtime;*
8	Th.	*He who makes no mistakes, makes nothing.* • Tides {10.6 / 9.4 •	*flurries*
9	Fr.	☌ ♀ ♆ • 40 inches of snow cover, Newton, N.J., 1996 •	*alternate*
10	Sa.	Thomas Paine published *Common Sense,* 1776 • Ethan Allen born, 1738 • {10.9 / 9.6 •	*with*
11	D	**1st S. af. Ep.** • ☾ rides high • {11.0 / 9.6 •	*fair time.*
12	M.	Full Wolf ○ • Plough Monday • Jack London born, 1876 • {11.0 / 9.7	*Sun*
13	Tu.	St. Hilary • First public radio broadcast, 1910 • Horatio Alger born, 1834 •	*peeks*
14	W.	Snowflakes seen in San Diego, Calif., 1882 • Propitious day for birth of women. • {9.7 / 10.7	*and*
15	Th.	The Greenbay Packers defeated the Kansas City Chiefs in Super Bowl I, 1967 •	*frozen*
16	Fr.	♅ in inf. ☌ • ☾ at ☊ • A. J. Foyt Jr. born, 1935 •	*cheeks.*
17	Sa.	Benjamin Franklin born, 1706 • *The used key is always bright.* • Tides {9.4 / 9.7 •	*A*
18	D	**2nd S. af. Ep.** • ☾ at apo. • ☾ on Eq. • {9.2 / 9.3	*thaw*
19	M.	Martin Luther King Jr.'s Birthday • ☌ ♆ ⊙ • {9.1 / 8.9	*is*
20	Tu.	St. Fabian • ☌ ♂ ♃ • "Buzz" Aldrin born, 1930 •	*hinting,*
21	W.	St. Agnes • First Kiwanis Club chartered, 1915 • {9.0 / 8.3 •	*then cold*
22	Th.	St. Vincent • *St. Vincent opens the seed.* • {9.0 / 8.2 •	*unstinting.*
23	Fr.	Lowest temperature ever recorded, -80° F, Prospect Creek Camp, Alaska, 1971 •	*Skater*
24	Sa.	*Deliver your words not by number but by weight.* • Eskimo Pie ice cream bar patented, 1922	*grins,*
25	D	**3rd S. af. Ep.** • Al Capone died, 1947 • Tides {10.0 / 8.9 •	*skier*
26	M.	Conversion of Paul • ☌ ☿ ♀ • ☌ ♀ ☾ • ☾ runs low •	
27	Tu.	Leontyne Price debuted at the Met, 1961 • Tides {11.0 / 9.9 •	*thrives*
28	W.	St. Thomas Aquinas • New ● • ☌ ♅ ⊙ •	*in*
29	Th.	☌ ♃ ☾ • ☌ ♂ ☾ • Tides {11.6 / — •	*scenes from*
30	Fr.	☾ at perig. • ☾ at ☋ • Mahatma Gandhi assassinated, 1948 •	*Currier*
31	Sa.	☾ on Eq. • First Social Security check issued, 1940 • Tides {10.9 / 11.5 •	*& Ives.*

Farmer's Calendar

What is a tool? Well, it's an object or instrument that helps in doing some task. The task comes first: You find you need to dig a hole; therefore, you get a spade. So at least the business ought to go; so it often does go — but not always. For there are tools, like spades, that assist in the completing of a task, and then there are tools that *create* the task they assist in. These might be called "second-order tools." You must be able to spot second-order tools at a safe distance, so to speak, because it's usually a good idea to avoid them. There are two identifying signs: Second-order tools either cost a lot of money or, if cheap, are funny looking.

I am contemplating one of the cheap ones as I write. I was given it for Christmas several years ago by people who, I thought, had no reason to wish me ill. It consists of a sectional metal tube 15 feet long, at the end of which is fixed a 2-foot crosspiece that looks like an oversize boot-scraper. You use the thing to clear your roof of snow. You stand on the ground and reach well up onto the roof with the long pole, and pull the accumulated snow down so it doesn't build up and cause leaks.

It looks easy. It isn't. Maneuvering a 15-foot rod above your head at arm's length is tough. Maneuvering it in any wind at all is tougher. But the worst of it is you have a new care. For years, my roof went uncleared of snow. Did it leak? Sure, sometimes. But life was good anyway, mainly. Now when the snow begins to fall, I become gloomy. I am heavy where I was light, because I have taken on the weight of a dangerous helper.

1998 FEBRUARY, THE SECOND MONTH

Venus climbs rapidly into the eastern sky in morning twilight this month and becomes positively dazzling, reaching its highest and most prominent position on the 23rd. This same morning, it stands next to the crescent Moon and offers its own crescent for those using steadily braced binoculars or small telescopes. The new Moon on the 26th passes directly in front of the Sun for observers in the Caribbean, presenting the final total solar eclipse near the United States until the second decade of the 21st century. A partial eclipse occurs for some U.S. and Canadian observers (see the feature on page 52). The sky's brightest tableau now dominates the south at nightfall. Orion and his friends offer no fewer than eight first-magnitude stars, the year's greatest concentration of stellar brilliance.

☽	First Quarter	3rd day	17th hour	53rd minute
○	Full Moon	11th day	5th hour	23rd minute
☾	Last Quarter	19th day	10th hour	27th minute
●	New Moon	26th day	12th hour	26th minute

Times are given in Eastern Standard Time.

For an explanation of this page, see "How to Use This Almanac," page 34; for values of Key Letters, see Time Correction Tables, page 214.

Day of Year	Day of Month	Day of Week	☉ Rises h. m.	Key	☉ Sets h. m.	Key	Length of Days h. m.	Sun Fast m.	Declination of Sun ° '	Full Sea Boston A.M.	Full Sea Boston P.M.	☽ Rises h. m.	Key	☽ Sets h. m.	Key	☽ Place	☽ Age
32	1	**D**	6 58	D	4 58	A	10 00	2	17s.00	2	2¼	9ᴀᴍ38	C	10ᴘᴍ28	D	CET	4
33	2	M.	6 57	D	4 59	A	10 02	2	16 43	2¾	3¼	10 13	C	11ᴘᴍ38	D	PSC	5
34	3	Tu.	6 56	D	5 01	A	10 05	2	16 25	3¾	4¼	10 50	C	—	—	CET	6
35	4	W.	6 55	D	5 02	A	10 07	2	16 08	4¾	5¼	11ᴀᴍ29	B	12ᴀᴍ45	E	ARI	7
36	5	Th.	6 54	D	5 03	A	10 09	2	15 50	5¾	6¼	12ᴘᴍ12	B	1 51	E	TAU	8
37	6	Fr.	6 52	D	5 05	A	10 13	2	15 31	6¾	7½	12 59	B	2 53	E	TAU	9
38	7	Sa.	6 51	D	5 06	A	10 15	1	15 12	7¾	8½	1 50	B	3 50	E	ORI	10
39	8	**D**	6 50	D	5 07	B	10 17	1	14 53	8¾	9½	2 45	B	4 41	E	GEM	11
40	9	M.	6 49	D	5 09	B	10 20	1	14 34	9¾	10¼	3 42	B	5 27	E	GEM	12
41	10	Tu.	6 48	D	5 10	B	10 22	1	14 15	10½	11	4 40	C	6 08	E	CAN	13
42	11	W.	6 46	D	5 11	B	10 25	1	13 55	11¼	11¾	5 39	C	6 44	D	LEO	14
43	12	Th.	6 45	D	5 13	B	10 28	1	13 35	11¾	—	6 37	C	7 17	D	LEO	15
44	13	Fr.	6 44	D	5 14	B	10 30	1	13 15	12¼	12½	7 35	D	7 47	D	LEO	16
45	14	Sa.	6 42	D	5 15	B	10 33	1	12 55	1	1	8 32	D	8 15	D	VIR	17
46	15	**D**	6 41	D	5 16	B	10 35	1	12 34	1½	1¾	9 29	D	8 43	C	VIR	18
47	16	M.	6 39	D	5 18	B	10 39	1	12 14	2¼	2½	10 26	D	9 11	C	VIR	19
48	17	Tu.	6 38	D	5 19	B	10 41	2	11 53	2¾	3¼	11ᴘᴍ23	D	9 41	B	VIR	20
49	18	W.	6 37	D	5 20	B	10 43	2	11 32	3½	4	—	—	10 13	B	LIB	21
50	19	Th.	6 35	D	5 21	B	10 46	2	11 10	4½	5	12ᴀᴍ20	E	10 48	B	LIB	22
51	20	Fr.	6 34	D	5 23	B	10 49	2	10 49	5¼	5¾	1 18	E	11ᴀᴍ29	B	OPH	23
52	21	Sa.	6 32	D	5 24	B	10 52	2	10 27	6¼	6¾	2 15	E	12ᴘᴍ15	B	OPH	24
53	22	**D**	6 31	D	5 25	B	10 54	2	10 05	7	7¾	3 11	E	1 09	B	SAG	25
54	23	M.	6 29	D	5 27	B	10 58	2	9 43	8	8¾	4 03	E	2 09	B	SAG	26
55	24	Tu.	6 28	D	5 28	B	11 00	2	9 21	9	9½	4 52	E	3 16	C	CAP	27
56	25	W.	6 26	D	5 29	B	11 03	2	8 58	9¾	10¼	5 37	E	4 27	C	AQU	28
57	26	Th.	6 25	D	5 30	B	11 05	3	8 36	10½	11¼	6 19	D	5 40	D	AQU	0
58	27	Fr.	6 23	D	5 31	B	11 08	3	8 13	11½	—	6 57	D	6 55	D	AQU	1
59	28	Sa.	6 21	D	5 33	B	11 12	3	7s.51	12	12¼	7ᴀᴍ34	D	8ᴘᴍ09	D	PSC	2

FEBRUARY hath 28 days. 1998

The sleet streams;
The snow flies;
The fawn dreams
With wide brown eyes.
– William Rose Benét

D. M.	D. W.	Dates, Feasts, Fasts, Aspects, Tide Heights	Weather ↓
1	**D**	**4th S. af. Ep.** • ☌ ♄ ☾ • {11.0 / 11.1 •	*Blinking*
2	M.	**Candlemas** • Groundhog Day • ☌ ☿ ♆ •	*ground-*
3	Tu.	On this day in 1982: 86° F, Fort Myers, Fla.; -40° F, International Falls, Minn. • {10.8 / 10.0	*hogs*
4	W.	*He that complies against his will is of his own opinion still.* • Tides {10.5 / 9.0 •	*don*
5	Th.	**St. Agatha** • ♀ stat. • Hank Aaron born, 1934 •	*sunglasses;*
6	Fr.	Massachusetts became sixth state, 1788 • Ronald Reagan born, 1911 •	*moving*
7	Sa.	☾ rides high • Charles Dickens born, 1812 • Tides {10.2 / 9.0 •	*slow as*
8	**D**	**Septuagesima** • ☌ ☿ ♅ • Tides {10.3 / 9.2 •	*cold*
9	M.	Inaugural flight, Boeing 727, 1963 • Inaugural flight, Boeing 747, 1969 •	*molasses.*
10	Tu.	*A man of words and not of deeds is like a garden full of weeds.* • Tides {10.5 / 9.5 •	*Milder*
11	W.	**Full Snow** ○ • Vatican City independence, 1929 • Thomas Edison born, 1847 •	*now*
12	Th.	☾ at ☊ • Abraham Lincoln born, 1809 • Tides {10.4 / — •	*and rain*
13	Fr.	Chuck Yeager born, 1923 • *There is luck in odd numbers.* • {9.6 / 10.3 •	*spreads,*
14	Sa.	**St. Valentine** • **Sts. Cyril & Methodius** • ☾ on Eq. • {9.6 / 10.0 •	*then*
15	**D**	**Sexagesima** • ☾ at apo. • Tides {9.6 / 9.7 •	*pull your*
16	M.	**Presidents Day** • DuPont Corp. patented nylon, 1937 •	*blankets*
17	Tu.	First gas street lights, Baltimore, Md., 1817 • Winter's back breaks. • {9.3 / 8.9 •	*over*
18	W.	Sonja Henie won her sixth women's world figure-skating title, 1932 • {9.2 / 8.5 •	*heads.*
19	Th.	♀ Greatest Brilliancy • Stan Kenton born, 1912 • Tides {9.1 / 8.3 •	*Rain's*
20	Fr.	Metropolitan Museum of Art in New York City opened, 1872 • Phil Esposito born, 1942 •	*still*
21	Sa.	*We soon believe what we desire.* • First telephone directory, New Haven, Conn., 1878 •	*fallin' —*
22	**D**	**Quinquagesima** • ☿ in sup. ☌ • ☾ runs low • {9.5 / 8.6	
23	M.	☌ ♃ ☉ • ☌ ♀ ☾ • John Quincy Adams died, 1821 •	*trade*
24	Tu.	**St. Matthias** • **Shrove Tuesday** • ☌ ♆ ☾ • ☌ ♅ ☾ •	
25	W.	**Ash Wednesday** • Enrico Caruso born, 1873 • {11.1 / 10.3 •	*those*
26	Th.	**New** ● • Eclipse ☉ • ☾ at ☋ • {11.6 / 10.9 •	*parkas*
27	Fr.	☾ at perig. • ☌ ♂ ☾ • John Steinbeck born, 1902 • {11.9 / — •	*for*
28	Sa.	☾ on Eq. • B&O Railroad incorporated, 1827 • {11.4 / 11.9 •	*tarpaulins.*

Laughter is the Sun that drives winter from the human face.
– Victor Hugo

Farmer's Calendar

February 2, as some readers may have forgotten, is the 116th anniversary of the birth of the Irish novelist James Joyce. It is also, as every reader certainly remembers, Groundhog Day — a coincidence Joyce himself knew of and liked to celebrate.

Groundhog Day, the event, has about it some of the character of a jolly pagan nature festival, but it also thrives as a thoroughly up-to-date, managed episode for the press and broadcasters, and (no surprise) it has a commercial side, adding its not-inconsiderable quantity to the economy of Jefferson County, Pennsylvania. Groundhog Day also furnishes a classic study in the peculiar logic of folk weather lore. Recall the formula: On this day in Punxsutawney, Pa., a woodchuck, or groundhog, leaves the burrow in which it has passed the winter in hibernation. If the groundhog, upon emerging, should see its shadow, six more weeks of winter weather are ahead. If it should not see its shadow, winter is over and spring is near.

Observe two points. First, the rodent itself is quite irrelevant to the predictive force of the affair, for its seeing its shadow or not comes to this: The Sun is shining — or it isn't. Then, suppose the day is gray and the creature casts no shadow: Winter is over — or it isn't. The chances that the groundhog's annual prediction will be accurate are exactly 50 percent. The same is true of most traditional folk forecasts. They are, essentially, a coin toss, and their quaint apparatus of groundhogs, caterpillars, and the like have no more to do with the reality they ostensibly predict than has, well, the author of *Finnegans Wake*.

1998 MARCH, THE THIRD MONTH

The Moon hovers near Saturn on the 1st. Mercury offers its best apparition of the year in fading evening twilight in the western sky from the 15th to the 24th. The small, airless ball floats near Saturn on the 19th. The crescent Moon and Venus perform an eye-catching conjunction in the eastern sky just before dawn on the 24th. The vernal equinox occurs at 2:55 P.M., EST, on the 20th, when days and nights are supposedly equal. Actually, our atmosphere bends the Sun's image upward at both sunrise and sunset, causing day to be at least seven minutes longer than night on this date for most of the United States.

☽	First Quarter	5th day	3rd hour	41st minute
○	Full Moon	12th day	23rd hour	34th minute
☾	Last Quarter	21st day	2nd hour	38th minute
●	New Moon	27th day	22nd hour	14th minute

Times are given in Eastern Standard Time.

For an explanation of this page, see "How to Use This Almanac," page 34; for values of Key Letters, see Time Correction Tables, page 214.

Day of Year	Day of Month	Day of Week	☉ Rises h. m.	Key	☉ Sets h. m.	Key	Length of Days h. m.	Sun Fast m.	Declination of Sun ° '	Full Sea Boston A.M.	Full Sea Boston P.M.	☽ Rises h. m.	Key	☽ Sets h. m.	Key	☽ Place	☽ Age
60	1	**D**	6 20	D	5 34	B	11 14	3	7 s.28	12¾	1	8 A.M. 11	C	9 P.M. 22	E	PSC	3
61	2	M.	6 18	D	5 35	B	11 17	3	7 05	1½	2	8 49	C	10 34	E	PSC	4
62	3	Tu.	6 17	D	5 36	B	11 19	4	6 42	2½	3	9 28	B	11 P.M. 42	E	ARI	5
63	4	W.	6 15	D	5 38	B	11 23	4	6 19	3¼	4	10 11	B	— —	–	TAU	6
64	5	Th.	6 13	D	5 39	B	11 26	4	5 56	4¼	5	10 57	B	12 A.M. 46	E	TAU	7
65	6	Fr.	6 12	D	5 40	B	11 28	4	5 33	5¼	6	11 A.M. 47	B	1 45	E	TAU	8
66	7	Sa.	6 10	D	5 41	B	11 31	4	5 09	6½	7¼	12 P.M. 40	B	2 39	E	GEM	9
67	8	**D**	6 08	D	5 42	B	11 34	5	4 46	7½	8¼	1 36	B	3 26	E	GEM	10
68	9	M.	6 07	D	5 44	B	11 37	5	4 23	8½	9¼	2 34	B	4 08	E	CAN	11
69	10	Tu.	6 05	D	5 45	B	11 40	5	3 59	9½	10	3 32	C	4 45	E	CAN	12
70	11	W.	6 03	D	5 46	B	11 43	5	3 36	10¼	10½	4 30	C	5 18	D	LEO	13
71	12	Th.	6 02	C	5 47	B	11 45	6	3 12	10¾	11¼	5 27	D	5 49	D	LEO	14
72	13	Fr.	6 00	C	5 48	B	11 48	6	2 48	11½	11¾	6 24	D	6 18	C	LEO	15
73	14	Sa.	5 58	C	5 49	B	11 51	6	2 25	—	12	7 21	D	6 45	C	VIR	16
74	15	**D**	5 56	C	5 51	B	11 55	6	2 01	12½	12¾	8 18	D	7 13	C	VIR	17
75	16	M.	5 55	C	5 52	B	11 57	7	1 38	1	1¼	9 15	E	7 42	C	VIR	18
76	17	Tu.	5 53	C	5 53	B	12 00	7	1 14	1½	2	10 12	E	8 13	B	LIB	19
77	18	W.	5 51	C	5 54	B	12 03	7	0 50	2¼	2¾	11 P.M. 09	E	8 47	B	LIB	20
78	19	Th.	5 50	C	5 55	B	12 05	8	0 26	3	3½	— —	–	9 25	B	SCO	21
79	20	Fr.	5 48	C	5 56	C	12 08	8	0s. 03	3¾	4¼	12 A.M. 05	E	10 08	B	OPH	22
80	21	Sa.	5 46	C	5 57	C	12 11	8	0n.21	4½	5¼	1 00	E	10 57	B	SAG	23
81	22	**D**	5 44	C	5 59	C	12 15	9	0 44	5½	6¼	1 52	E	11 A.M. 53	B	SAG	24
82	23	M.	5 43	C	6 00	C	12 17	9	1 07	6½	7¼	2 41	E	12 P.M. 54	B	SAG	25
83	24	Tu.	5 41	C	6 01	C	12 20	9	1 31	7½	8¼	3 27	E	2 01	C	CAP	26
84	25	W.	5 39	C	6 02	C	12 23	9	1 55	8½	9	4 09	E	3 12	C	CAP	27
85	26	Th.	5 37	C	6 03	C	12 26	10	2 18	9¼	9¾	4 49	D	4 26	D	AQU	28
86	27	Fr.	5 36	C	6 04	C	12 28	10	2 42	10¼	10¾	5 26	D	5 41	D	AQU	0
87	28	Sa.	5 34	C	6 05	C	12 31	10	3 05	11	11½	6 03	C	6 57	D	CET	1
88	29	**D**	5 32	C	6 07	C	12 35	11	3 29	—	12	6 41	C	8 11	E	PSC	2
89	30	M.	5 30	C	6 08	C	12 38	11	3 52	12¼	12¾	7 21	B	9 24	E	CET	3
90	31	Tu.	5 29	C	6 09	C	12 40	11	4n.15	1¼	1¾	8 A.M. 04	B	10 P.M. 33	E	TAU	4

MARCH hath 31 days. 1998

We like March, his shoes are purple
He is new and high;
Makes he mud for dog and peddler,
Makes he forest dry.
– Emily Dickinson

D. M.	D. W.	Dates, Feasts, Fasts, Aspects, Tide Heights	Weather ↓
1	D	1st S. in Lent • ☌ ♄ ☾ • Glenn Miller born, 1904 •	*Don't*
2	M.	St. David • St. Chad • **Pure Monday** • Sam Houston born, 1793 •	*put*
3	Tu.	Florida became 27th state, 1845 • 17° F, Hague, Fla., 1980 • Tides {11.4 10.6 •	*away*
4	W.	Ember Day • Knute Rockne born, 1888 • Charles Goren born, 1901 • {11.0 9.9 •	*that*
5	Th.	*If every man would sweep before his own door, the city would soon be clean.* • {10.6 9.3	*shovel,*
6	Fr.	Ember Day • Louisa May Alcott died, 1888 • Tides {10.2 8.9 •	*Susie —*
7	Sa.	St. Perpetua • ☾ rides high • ☌ ♀ ♆ • Ember Day •	*one*
8	D	2nd S. in Lent • **Sunday of Orthodoxy** •	*more*
9	M.	Napoleon Bonaparte married Josephine de Beauharnais, 1796 • Tides {9.8 9.1 •	*storm*
10	Tu.	*Saddle your dreams afore you ride 'em.* • Clare Boothe Luce born, 1903 • {9.9 9.3 •	*and*
11	W.	☾ at ☊ • ☌ ☿ ♂ • Lawrence Welk born, 1903 • {10.1 9.5 •	*it's*
12	Th.	St. Gregory • ♇ stat. • **Full Sap** ○ • Eclipse ☾ • {10.1 9.7 •	*a*
13	Fr.	Percival Lowell born, 1855 • Susan B. Anthony died, 1906 • {10.1 9.8 •	*doozy!*
14	Sa.	☾ on Eq. • ☾ at apo. • Halley's Comet returned, 1986 • {— 10.1 •	*Drifts*
15	D	3rd S. in Lent • Beware the Ides of March. • {9.9 9.9	*shrinking*
16	M.	The Federal Trade Commission began operating, 1915 • Tides {9.9 9.7 •	*we're*
17	Tu.	St. Patrick • Franklin D. and Eleanor Roosevelt were wed, 1905 • {9.8 9.4	*thinking*
18	W.	Speed limit raised from 55 to 65 mph on rural highways, 1987 • Tides {9.7 9.0 •	*Dark*
19	Th.	St. Joseph • ☌ ♀ ♅ • ☿ Gr. Elong. (19° E.) • {9.5 8.7 •	*clouds*
20	Fr.	**Vernal Equinox** • Isaac Newton died, 1727 • B. F. Skinner born, 1904 •	*gather*
21	Sa.	☾ runs low • Alcatraz prison closed, 1963 • Julio Gallo born, 1910 • Tides {9.3 8.4	*in*
22	D	4th S. in Lent • Corn starch patented, 1841 • Tides {9.4 8.5 •	*skies*
23	M.	☌ ♆ ☾ • Handel's *Messiah* first performed, 1743 • {9.6 8.9 •	*above:*
24	Tu.	☌ ♅ ☾ • ☌ ♀ ☾ • Harry Houdini born, 1874 • {10.0 9.5 •	*This*
25	W.	Annunciation • Lord Baltimore and colonists landed at Maryland, 1634 • {10.6 10.2 •	*is*
26	Th.	☾ at ☋ • Occn. of ♃ by ☾ • Tides {11.1 10.9 •	*weather*
27	Fr.	**New** ● • ☾ on Eq. • ☿ stat. • ♀ Gr. Elong. (47° W.) •	*only*
28	Sa.	☾ at perig. • The New York Titans became the New York Jets, 1963 • {11.8 12.0 •	*a*
29	D	5th S. in Lent • Oscar Mayer born, 1859 • {— 11.8 •	*mudder*
30	M.	☌ ☿ ♂ • **F**EAR: **F**alse **E**xpectation **A**ppearing **R**eal • {12.2 11.6 •	*could*
31	Tu.	Whitcomb Judson patented the first zipper, 1896 • Al Gore born, 1948 • {12.1 11.1 •	*love!*

Farmer's Calendar

If March comes in like a lion, we say, it will go out like a lamb; if it comes in like a lamb, it will go out like a lion. There are many, however, who are glad to see March go out under whatever sign it wishes. I am one of these. March can go out like a lion, it can go out like a lamb, it can go out like the Queen of Abyssinia for all I care. Just so it goes.

No doubt there is ingratitude here. We ought to be glad for whatever time is given us, whatever seasons. But March does somehow always *take too long*. It wears out its welcome considerably before it ends. Partly it's a matter of foul weather. In many years, where I live, March brings the heaviest snows of the winter, and its storms are apt to finish in ice and frozen rain, the wretchedest weather we have. Then, it's a month that seems to have less than its share of sun, I think. A week in March is too often like a tunnel of foggy, gloomy, gray days. As much as from its weather, though, March feels prolonged because it's a time of waiting. After all, it's this month, opening in snow and ice and finishing in mud and robins, that goes across from winter to spring. March is the bridge, and it's a long one, a Golden Gate in the year.

Yes, March is a weary haul. But what can we do? The calendar is not something we can fix. If there is a solution to the tedium of this protracted month, it will not be, so to speak, mechanical. Rather, we must bring our very idea of the problem onto a different level and see the subject fresh. We must be bold. We must free our minds. Never an easy thing to do, but possible, if we take thought . . .

APRIL, THE FOURTH MONTH

A half hour before sunrise on the 23rd, the three brightest nighttime objects rendezvous low in the eastern sky in the growing twilight. This is the year's most spectacular gathering. The slender crescent Moon, Venus, and Jupiter form an imposing triangle, with Venus and Jupiter especially close. For observers with an unobstructed eastern view, it is well worth setting the alarm clock. Because these "morning stars" appear in the springtime this year, they will sit much closer to the horizon than when they appear in the autumn, as will be the case next year. Daylight Saving Time begins at 2:00 A.M. on the 5th.

☽	First Quarter	3rd day	15th hour	18th minute
○	Full Moon	11th day	18th hour	23rd minute
☾	Last Quarter	19th day	15th hour	53rd minute
●	New Moon	26th day	7th hour	41st minute

After 2:00 A.M. on April 5, Eastern Daylight Time (EDT) is given.

For an explanation of this page, see "How to Use This Almanac," page 34; for values of Key Letters, see Time Correction Tables, page 214.

Day of Year	Day of Month	Day of Week	☉ Rises h. m.	Key	☉ Sets h. m.	Key	Length of Days h. m.	Sun Fast m.	Declination of Sun ° '	Full Sea Boston A.M.	Full Sea Boston P.M.	☽ Rises h. m.	Key	☽ Sets h. m.	Key	☽ Place	☽ Age
91	1	W.	5 27	B	6 10	C	12 43	12	4N.39	2	2¾	8 A.M. 50	B	11 P.M. 37	E	TAU	5
92	2	Th.	5 25	B	6 11	C	12 46	12	5 02	3	3½	9 41	B	— —	–	TAU	6
93	3	Fr.	5 24	B	6 12	C	12 48	12	5 25	4	4¾	10 34	B	12 A.M. 34	E	GEM	7
94	4	Sa.	5 22	B	6 13	C	12 51	12	5 48	5	5¾	11 A.M. 30	B	1 24	E	GEM	8
95	5	**D**	6 20	B	7 14	D	12 54	13	6 11	7	7¾	1 P.M. 28	B	3 08	E	CAN	9
96	6	M.	6 18	B	7 16	D	12 58	13	6 33	8	8¾	2 26	C	3 47	E	CAN	10
97	7	Tu.	6 17	B	7 17	D	13 00	13	6 56	9	9¾	3 24	C	4 21	D	LEO	11
98	8	W.	6 15	B	7 18	D	13 03	14	7 18	10	10½	4 21	D	4 52	D	LEO	12
99	9	Th.	6 13	B	7 19	D	13 06	14	7 40	10¾	11	5 18	D	5 21	D	LEO	13
100	10	Fr.	6 12	B	7 20	D	13 08	14	8 03	11½	11¾	6 15	D	5 49	D	VIR	14
101	11	Sa.	6 10	B	7 21	D	13 11	14	8 25	—	12	7 12	D	6 17	C	VIR	15
102	12	**D**	6 08	B	7 22	D	13 14	15	8 47	12¼	12¾	8 09	E	6 45	C	VIR	16
103	13	M.	6 07	B	7 23	D	13 16	15	9 08	1	1¼	9 07	E	7 15	B	LIB	17
104	14	Tu.	6 05	B	7 25	D	13 20	15	9 30	1½	2	10 04	E	7 48	B	LIB	18
105	15	W.	6 04	B	7 26	D	13 22	15	9 51	2	2½	11 00	E	8 24	B	SCO	19
106	16	Th.	6 02	B	7 27	D	13 25	16	10 13	2¾	3¼	11 P.M. 55	E	9 05	B	OPH	20
107	17	Fr.	6 00	B	7 28	D	13 28	16	10 34	3½	4	— —	–	9 52	B	SAG	21
108	18	Sa.	5 59	B	7 29	D	13 30	16	10 55	4¼	4¾	12 A.M. 47	E	10 44	B	SAG	22
109	19	**D**	5 57	B	7 30	D	13 33	16	11 16	5	5¾	1 36	E	11 A.M. 42	B	SAG	23
110	20	M.	5 56	B	7 31	D	13 35	17	11 36	6	6¾	2 22	E	12 P.M. 44	C	CAP	24
111	21	Tu.	5 54	B	7 32	D	13 38	17	11 57	7	7¾	3 04	E	1 51	C	AQU	25
112	22	W.	5 53	B	7 34	D	13 41	17	12 17	8	8¾	3 43	D	3 02	C	AQU	26
113	23	Th.	5 51	B	7 35	D	13 44	17	12 37	9	9½	4 20	D	4 14	D	AQU	27
114	24	Fr.	5 50	B	7 36	D	13 46	17	12 57	10	10½	4 56	D	5 28	D	PSC	28
115	25	Sa.	5 48	B	7 37	D	13 49	18	13 17	11	11¼	5 33	C	6 43	E	PSC	29
116	26	**D**	5 47	B	7 38	D	13 51	18	13 36	11¾	—	6 11	C	7 58	E	CET	0
117	27	M.	5 45	B	7 39	D	13 54	18	13 55	12	12¾	6 53	B	9 11	E	ARI	1
118	28	Tu.	5 44	B	7 40	D	13 56	18	14 14	1	1½	7 38	B	10 20	E	TAU	2
119	29	W.	5 42	B	7 41	D	13 59	18	14 33	1¾	2½	8 28	B	11 P.M. 22	E	TAU	3
120	30	Th.	5 41	B	7 43	D	14 02	18	14N.51	2¾	3¼	9 A.M. 22	B	— —	–	ORI	4

Loveliest of trees, the cherry now
Is hung with bloom along the bough,
And stands about the woodland ride
Wearing white for Eastertide.
     – A. E. Housman

Farmer's Calendar

There is a law of the garden that has little to do with the care of crops and much to do with the mind (so-called) of the gardener, as it crosses blissfully over from enthusiasm to obsession. The law says: *If you grew it, you will eat it.*

Some years ago, our winter began with a Thanksgiving snow that, essentially, never went away. The next April, when I went into the garden to plant my peas, I found under the remnants of snow and ice the prostrate but still more or less green tops of a few of last year's carrots. I pulled one and examined it. She looked to be a shade on the tough side. Took a bite. That carrot was the root equivalent of a Louisville Slugger that had been passed slowly over a cup of carrot juice. I ate it anyway, though, all of it, as I have also eaten forgotten radishes that looked and tasted like cherry bombs, and beans that seemed to come from the bottom of my grandmother's handbag. Why? Duty, Stern Daughter of the Voice of God. These plants are my responsibility, I feel. I started them and I will, by golly, finish them.

This isn't gardening; it's a darker and more compulsive activity, an empty ceremony of obligation. At least in my case it has its limits, related to the physical condition of the aged harvest. I'll eat my own produce, however old, as long as it is merely tough. Some crops, though, like those of the squash tribe, go over the hill into a semiliquid state. Those I won't touch. So the law, perhaps, needs refining, as follows: If you grew it, *and you can bring yourself to pick it up,* you will eat it.

D.M.	D.W.	Dates, Feasts, Fasts, Aspects, Tide Heights	Weather ↓
1	W.	**All Fools** *If it thunders on All Fools Day, It brings good crops of corn and hay.* ●	*Foolish*
2	Th.	First U.S. mint established, Philadelphia, Pa., 1792 ● Tides { 11.2 / 9.9	*pleasure*
3	Fr.	☾ rides high ● The Pony Express began mail delivery, 1860 ● *TV Guide* began publication, 1953 ●	*is*
4	Sa.	The Reverend Martin Luther King Jr. assassinated, 1968 ● Tides { 10.0 / 9.0 ●	*ours*
5	**D**	**Palm Sunday** ● **Daylight Saving Time begins, 2:00 A.M.** ● { 9.6 / 8.8 ●	*to*
6	M.	☿ in inf. ☌ ● Lowell Thomas born, 1892 ● Tides { 9.4 / 8.9 ●	*treasure.*
7	Tu.	Walter Winchell born, 1879 ● W. K. Kellogg born, 1860 ● { 9.5 / 9.1 ●	*Arbitrary*
8	W.	☾ at ☍ ● First intercollegiate rodeo, Godshall Ranch, Calif., 1939 ● { 9.6 / 9.4 ●	*and*
9	Th.	S. R. Percy of New York patented dried milk, 1872 ● Tides { 9.7 / 9.7 ●	*capricious;*
10	Fr.	**Good Friday** ● ☾ on Eq. ● ☾ at apo. ●	*first it's*
11	Sa.	**First day of Passover** ● **Full Pink** ○ ● Tides { 9.8 / 9.8 ●	*dank,*
12	**D**	**Easter** *The Sun dances on Easter morn.* ● Herbie Hancock born, 1940 ●	*and*
13	M.	☌ ♄ ☉ ● Harold Washington became Chicago's first black mayor, 1983 ● { 10.1 / 9.7 ●	*then*
14	Tu.	President Abraham Lincoln fatally wounded, 1865 ● George Frederick Handel died, 1759 ●	*then*
15	W.	*If lying paid a tax, it would pay the national debt.* ● Tides { 10.1 / 9.3 ●	*delicious.*
16	Th.	Baseball's longest night game (6 hr., 6 min.) was completed after 24 innings, 1968 ●	*Spring*
17	Fr.	Thornton Wilder born, 1897 ● Benjamin Franklin died, 1790 ● { 9.8 / 8.9 ●	*should*
18	Sa.	☾ runs low ● ☿ stat. ● London Bridge sold to U.S. company, 1968 ● { 9.7 / 8.8 ●	*be*
19	**D**	**1st ☉. af. Easter** ● **Orthodox Easter** ● ☌ ♆ ☾ ●	*here,*
20	M.	☌ ☽ ☾ ● Hot Springs National Park established, 1832 ● Tides { 9.7 / 9.0 ●	*here,*
21	Tu.	**St. Anselm** ● Charlotte Brontë born, 1816 ● Mark Twain died, 1910 ●	*but*
22	W.	☾ at ☍ ● ☌ ♀ ♃ ● First Earth Day celebrated, 1970 ●	*you*
23	Th.	**St. George** ● ☌ ♃ ☾ ● ☌ ♀ ☾ ● { 10.6 / 10.7	*wouldn't*
24	Fr.	☾ on Eq. ● ☌ ☿ ☾ ● Robert B. Thomas born, 1766 ●	*know it;*
25	Sa.	**St. Mark** ● ☾ at perig. ● Anders Celsius died, 1744 ● { 11.3 / 12.0 ●	*April*
26	**D**	**2nd ☉. af. Easter** ● **New** ● ● Tides { 11.5 ●	*is*
27	M.	92° F, New York City, 1915 ● Ulysses S. Grant born, 1822 ● { 12.3 / 11.5 ●	*cruel,*
28	Tu.	Captain Cook landed in Australia, 1770 ● Mutiny on the *Bounty,* 1789 ● Tides { 12.4 / 11.2 ●	*said*
29	W.	**St. Catherine** ● Duke Ellington born, 1889 ● Modern zipper patented, 1913 ●	*the*
30	Th.	☾ rides high ● New York World's Fair opened, 1939 ● Tides { 11.7 / 10.3 ●	*poet.*

There are some people that if they don't know, you can't tell 'em.   – Louis Armstrong

MAY, THE FIFTH MONTH

The crescent Moon performs two bright and striking conjunctions, meeting Jupiter on the 20th and a fading Venus on the 22nd. Venus meets Saturn on the 29th in a particularly close and eye-catching encounter, low in the east in morning twilight. Both will fit in the same low-power telescope field. Saturn's rings show their greatest tilt in six years and will be spectacular from now through the end of the year. This is also the time of year when space satellites are most visible; you can see one crossing the sky every minute or two during the first hour after nightfall.

☽	First Quarter	3rd day	6th hour	4th minute
○	Full Moon	11th day	10th hour	29th minute
☾	Last Quarter	19th day	0 hour	35th minute
●	New Moon	25th day	15th hour	32nd minute

Times are given in Eastern Daylight Time.

For an explanation of this page, see "How to Use This Almanac," page 34; for values of Key Letters, see Time Correction Tables, page 214.

Day of Year	Day of Month	Day of Week	☉ Rises h. m.	Key	☉ Sets h. m.	Key	Length of Days h. m.	Sun Fast m.	Declination of Sun ° '	Full Sea Boston A.M.	Full Sea Boston P.M.	☽ Rises h. m.	Key	☽ Sets h. m.	Key	☽ Place	☽ Age
121	1	Fr.	5 40	B	7 44	D	14 04	18	15N.09	3½	4¼	10 A.M. 20	B	12 A.M. 18	E	GEM	5
122	2	Sa.	5 38	B	7 45	D	14 07	19	15 27	4½	5¼	11 A.M. 18	B	1 06	E	CAN	6
123	3	**D**	5 37	B	7 46	D	14 09	19	15 45	5½	6¼	12 P.M. 18	B	1 47	E	CAN	7
124	4	M.	5 36	A	7 47	D	14 11	19	16 03	6½	7¼	1 16	C	2 23	D	LEO	8
125	5	Tu.	5 34	A	7 48	D	14 14	19	16 20	7½	8¼	2 14	C	2 55	D	LEO	9
126	6	W.	5 33	A	7 49	D	14 16	19	16 37	8½	9	3 12	D	3 25	D	LEO	10
127	7	Th.	5 32	A	7 50	D	14 18	19	16 53	9½	9¾	4 08	D	3 53	C	VIR	11
128	8	Fr.	5 31	A	7 51	D	14 20	19	17 10	10¼	10½	5 05	D	4 20	C	VIR	12
129	9	Sa.	5 30	A	7 52	D	14 22	19	17 26	11	11¼	6 03	D	4 48	C	VIR	13
130	10	**D**	5 28	A	7 54	D	14 26	19	17 41	11½	11¾	7 00	E	5 17	C	VIR	14
131	11	M.	5 27	A	7 55	D	14 28	19	17 57	—	12¼	7 58	E	5 49	B	LIB	15
132	12	Tu.	5 26	A	7 56	D	14 30	19	18 12	12¼	1	8 55	E	6 24	B	LIB	16
133	13	W.	5 25	A	7 57	D	14 32	19	18 26	1	1½	9 52	E	7 04	B	OPH	17
134	14	Th.	5 24	A	7 58	D	14 34	19	18 41	1½	2¼	10 45	E	7 49	B	OPH	18
135	15	Fr.	5 23	A	7 59	E	14 36	19	18 55	2¼	3	11 P.M. 35	E	8 39	B	SAG	19
136	16	Sa.	5 22	A	8 00	E	14 38	19	19 09	3	3¾	— —	–	9 35	B	SAG	20
137	17	**D**	5 21	A	8 01	E	14 40	19	19 23	3¾	4½	12 A.M. 22	E	10 35	B	CAP	21
138	18	M.	5 20	A	8 02	E	14 42	19	19 36	4¾	5¼	1 04	E	11 A.M. 40	B	AQU	22
139	19	Tu.	5 19	A	8 03	E	14 44	19	19 49	5½	6¼	1 42	E	12 P.M. 47	C	AQU	23
140	20	W.	5 18	A	8 04	E	14 46	19	20 02	6½	7¼	2 19	D	1 56	D	AQU	24
141	21	Th.	5 17	A	8 05	E	14 48	19	20 14	7½	8¼	2 53	D	3 07	D	PSC	25
142	22	Fr.	5 17	A	8 06	E	14 49	19	20 26	8¾	9	3 28	C	4 20	D	CET	26
143	23	Sa.	5 16	A	8 07	E	14 51	19	20 37	9½	10	4 04	C	5 33	E	PSC	27
144	24	**D**	5 15	A	8 08	E	14 53	19	20 48	10½	11	4 43	C	6 46	E	ARI	28
145	25	M.	5 14	A	8 09	E	14 55	19	20 59	11½	11¾	5 26	B	7 57	E	TAU	0
146	26	Tu.	5 14	A	8 09	E	14 55	19	21 10	—	12½	6 14	B	9 04	E	TAU	1
147	27	W.	5 13	A	8 10	E	14 57	19	21 20	12½	1¼	7 06	B	10 05	E	TAU	2
148	28	Th.	5 12	A	8 11	E	14 59	18	21 30	1½	2	8 03	B	10 58	E	GEM	3
149	29	Fr.	5 12	A	8 12	E	15 00	18	21 39	2¼	3	9 03	B	11 P.M. 43	E	GEM	4
150	30	Sa.	5 11	A	8 13	E	15 02	18	21 48	3¼	3¾	10 04	B	— —	–	CAN	5
151	31	**D**	5 11	A	8 14	E	15 03	18	21N.57	4	4¾	11 A.M. 05	C	12 A.M. 22	D	LEO	6

MAY hath 31 days. 1998

The glittering leaves of the rhododendrons
Balance and vibrate in the cool air;
While in the sky above them
White clouds chase each other.
– *John Gould Fletcher*

D. M.	D. W.	Dates, Feasts, Fasts, Aspects, Tide Heights	Weather ↓
1	Fr.	Sts. Philip & James • May Day • Mother Jones born, 1830 •	*Moist*
2	Sa.	St. Athanasius • Lou Gehrig played his record-making 2,130th game, 1939 • {10.5 9.4	*at*
3	D	3rd S. af. Easter • Invention of the Cross • {9.9 9.1 •	*foist.*
4	M.	♆ stat. • ☿ Gr. Elong. (27° W.) • Audrey Hepburn born, 1929 •	*Warmer*
5	Tu.	☾ at ☊ • Cy Young pitched baseball's third perfect game, 1904 • {9.2 9.1 •	*days*
6	W.	*Great talkers are like leaky pitchers, everything runs out of them.* • Tides {9.1 9.3 •	*begin*
7	Th.	☾ on Eq. • First President's Inaugural Ball, New York, 1789 • Tides {9.2 9.5 •	*to*
8	Fr.	Julian of Norwich • ☾ at apo. • V-E Day, 1945 • {9.3 9.8 •	*bless*
9	Sa.	St. Gregory of Nazianzus • Portland, Oregon, latest freeze, 1894 • {9.4 10.0 •	*us;*
10	D	4th S. af. Easter • George Vancouver died, 1798 •	*even*
11	M.	Three • Full Flower ○ • Martha Graham born, 1894 • {— 9.5 •	*cold*
12	Tu.	Chilly • ☌ ☿ ♄ • ☌ ♂ ☉ • {10.3 9.5 •	*showers*
13	W.	Saints • Joseph Pulitzer III born, 1913 • *Nature is the art of God.* •	*cannot*
14	Th.	John D. Rockefeller donated $100,000,000 to establish the Rockefeller Foundation, 1913 •	*depress*
15	Fr.	☾ runs low • U.S. Dept. of Agriculture created by Congress, 1862 • Tides {10.3 9.3 •	*us.*
16	Sa.	First U.S. five-cent coin authorized, 1866 • *Life is short and so is money.* •	*Meadows*
17	D	Rogation S. • ☌ ♆ ☾ • ♅ stat. • ☌ ♅ ☾ •	*are*
18	M.	Victoria Day (Canada) • Mount St. Helens erupted, 1980 • {10.0 9.4	*bursting*
19	Tu.	St. Dunstan • ☾ at ☋ • Johns Hopkins born, 1795 • {10.0 9.6	*with*
20	W.	☌ ♃ ☾ • 10 inches snow, Stafford, Vermont, 1892 • {10.0 10.0	*violets*
21	Th.	Ascension • ☾ on Eq. • American Red Cross founded, 1881 • {10.1 10.6 •	*and*
22	Fr.	☌ ♀ ☾ • Sir Arthur Conan Doyle born, 1859 • {10.4 11.1 •	*vetch:*
23	Sa.	☌ ♄ ☾ • ☾ at perig. • *There are spots even on the Sun.* • Tides {10.6 11.6 •	*If*
24	D	1st S. af. Asc. • ☌ ☿ ☾ • Tides {10.8 12.0 •	*daisies*
25	M.	St. Bede • Memorial Day • New ● • Tides {10.9 12.2 •	*were*
26	Tu.	St. Augustine of Canterbury • John Wayne born, 1907 •	*dollars,*
27	W.	The Golden Gate Bridge opened, San Francisco, Calif., 1937 • Tides {12.2 10.7 •	*we'd*
28	Th.	Orthodox Ascension • ☾ rides high • ♇ at ☍ • ☌ ♀ ♄ •	
29	Fr.	Rhode Island became 13th state, 1790 • Wisconsin became 30th state, 1848 • {11.5 10.1	*all*
30	Sa.	*It is easier to find a traveling companion than to get rid of one.* • {11.0 9.8 •	*be*
31	D	Whit S. • Pentecost • Shavuot • {10.4 9.5 •	*rich.*

Farmer's Calendar

May 15. Wasting time in the woodlot, I thought I heard geese overhead. Looked aloft and saw nothing — then I spotted them at last, a small flight of 10 or 12 heading north over the river, very high. They were the first I'd seen that year, and I saw no more all day. For Canada geese and at least some other famous migrators, and for those who watch them pass, spring has a very different action from the fall.

In the fall, the geese move through by thousands, by ten thousands. All day long the sky is full of them. The long lines of geese, distantly honking, move south overhead, one after another, with a regularity worthy of a railroad, recalling the Pin Stripe Limiteds that carry the day's commuters to Penn Station and Grand Central. On a good goose afternoon in October, you can see a flight almost any time you want to look up.

In the spring, the situation is otherwise. Roughly the same numbers of geese return north in the spring as go south in the fall, right? But where are they? In April and May, I'll see a flight or two one day, then no more geese till the next week. There are few or no days when they pass like armies of the air, as in the fall. Why should this be? Do the geese go north by a different route? I don't think so, for you do see some in spring. Hawks, I believe, are known to fly south in flocks but to fly north less conspicuously, singly or in pairs. Do geese do the same? Do they fly more by night in spring? I've read up a little, looking for the answer here, but only a little. I find it's a mystery I'm not eager to put an end to.

Morning conjunctions are getting easier to see as the two largest and most telescopically interesting planets climb higher each dawn and stand nicely visible in the east well before sunrise. Look for a fatter, higher crescent Moon meeting Jupiter on the morning of the 17th and Saturn on the 19th. The summer solstice occurs at 10:03 A.M., EDT, on the 21st. As if to celebrate, the Moon stands near Venus on that day; both float quite low in the morning twilight just ahead of the sunrise. The full Moon of June 10 is the lowest of the year, barely climbing 25 degrees for observers in the northern half of the United States and Canada.

☽	First Quarter	1st day	21st hour	45th minute
○	Full Moon	10th day	0 hour	18th minute
☾	Last Quarter	17th day	6th hour	38th minute
●	New Moon	23rd day	23rd hour	50th minute

Times are given in Eastern Daylight Time.

For an explanation of this page, see "How to Use This Almanac," page 34; for values of Key Letters, see Time Correction Tables, page 214.

Day of Year	Day of Month	Day of Week	☉ Rises h. m.	Key	☉ Sets h. m.	Key	Length of Days h. m.	Sun Fast m.	Declination of Sun ° '	Full Sea Boston A.M.	Full Sea Boston P.M.	☽ Rises h. m.	Key	☽ Sets h. m.	Key	☽ Place	☽ Age
152	1	M.	5 10	A	8 14	E	15 04	18	22N.05	5	5¾	12ᴾ04	C	12ᴹ57	D	LEO	7
153	2	Tu.	5 10	A	8 15	E	15 05	18	22 13	6	6½	1 02	C	1 27	D	LEO	8
154	3	W.	5 09	A	8 16	E	15 07	18	22 20	6¾	7½	2 00	D	1 56	D	VIR	9
155	4	Th.	5 09	A	8 17	E	15 08	17	22 27	7¾	8¼	2 57	D	2 24	C	VIR	10
156	5	Fr.	5 08	A	8 17	E	15 09	17	22 34	8¾	9	3 54	D	2 51	C	VIR	11
157	6	Sa.	5 08	A	8 18	E	15 10	17	22 40	9½	9¾	4 51	E	3 20	C	VIR	12
158	7	D	5 08	A	8 19	E	15 11	17	22 46	10¼	10½	5 49	E	3 50	B	LIB	13
159	8	M.	5 07	A	8 19	E	15 12	17	22 52	11	11¼	6 48	E	4 24	B	LIB	14
160	9	Tu.	5 07	A	8 20	E	15 13	17	22 57	11¾	11¾	7 45	E	5 02	B	OPH	15
161	10	W.	5 07	A	8 20	E	15 13	16	23 01	—	12½	8 41	E	5 45	B	OPH	16
162	11	Th.	5 07	A	8 21	E	15 14	16	23 05	12½	1	9 33	E	6 34	B	SAG	17
163	12	Fr.	5 07	A	8 21	E	15 14	16	23 09	1¼	1¾	10 21	E	7 29	B	SAG	18
164	13	Sa.	5 07	A	8 22	E	15 15	16	23 13	2	2½	11 05	E	8 28	B	SAG	19
165	14	D	5 07	A	8 22	E	15 15	16	23 16	2¾	3¼	11ᴹ45	E	9 32	B	CAP	20
166	15	M.	5 07	A	8 23	E	15 16	15	23 19	3½	4	— —	—	10 38	C	CAP	21
167	16	Tu.	5 07	A	8 23	E	15 16	15	23 21	4¼	5	12ᴬ21	D	11ᴬ46	D	AQU	22
168	17	W.	5 07	A	8 23	E	15 16	15	23 23	5¼	6	12 56	D	12ᴾ55	D	AQU	23
169	18	Th.	5 07	A	8 24	E	15 17	15	23 24	6¼	6¾	1 30	D	2 05	D	CET	24
170	19	Fr.	5 07	A	8 24	E	15 17	14	23 25	7¼	7¾	2 04	C	3 16	E	PSC	25
171	20	Sa.	5 07	A	8 24	E	15 17	14	23 25	8¼	8¾	2 40	B	4 27	E	CET	26
172	21	D	5 07	A	8 25	E	15 18	14	23 25	9¼	9¾	3 19	B	5 37	E	ARI	27
173	22	M.	5 08	A	8 25	E	15 17	14	23 25	10¼	10½	4 03	B	6 45	E	TAU	28
174	23	Tu.	5 08	A	8 25	E	15 17	14	23 25	11¼	11½	4 53	B	7 49	E	TAU	0
175	24	W.	5 08	A	8 25	E	15 17	13	23 24	—	12	5 47	B	8 46	E	ORI	1
176	25	Th.	5 09	A	8 25	E	15 16	13	23 22	12¼	1	6 46	B	9 35	E	GEM	2
177	26	Fr.	5 09	A	8 25	E	15 16	13	23 20	1¼	1¾	7 47	B	10 18	E	CAN	3
178	27	Sa.	5 09	A	8 25	E	15 16	13	23 18	2	2½	8 49	C	10 55	E	CAN	4
179	28	D	5 10	A	8 25	E	15 15	12	23 15	2¾	3½	9 50	C	11 28	D	LEO	5
180	29	M.	5 10	A	8 25	E	15 15	12	23 12	3½	4¼	10 50	C	11ᴹ58	D	LEO	6
181	30	Tu.	5 11	A	8 25	E	15 14	12	23N.09	4½	5	11ᴹ49	D	— —	—	LEO	7

JUNE hath 30 days. 1998

A bird in the boughs sang "June,"
And "June" hummed a bee
In a bacchic glee
As he tumbled over and over
Drunk with the honey-dew. – *Clinton Scollard*

D. M.	D. W.	Dates, Feasts, Fasts, Aspects, Tide Heights	*Weather* ↓
1	M.	Visit. of Mary • ☾ at ☊ • Tides 9.8 / 9.2 •	*Students*
2	Tu.	Grover Cleveland became first U.S. President to get married in the White House, 1886 • 9.4 / 9.1 •	*are*
3	W.	☾ on Eq. • Ember Day • Allen Ginsberg born, 1926 • 9.0 / 9.2 •	*grumbling,*
4	Th.	☾ at apo. • *Nature does nothing in vain.* •	*thunderstorms*
5	Fr.	St. Boniface • Ember Day • Tides 8.8 / 9.5 •	*rumbling.*
6	Sa.	Ember Day • First drive-in movie, Camden, N.J., 1933 • Tides 8.9 / 9.8 •	*Soddenly*
7	D	Trinity • Orthodox Pentecost • Paul Gaugin born, 1848 •	*less*
8	M.	President Teddy Roosevelt offered to mediate in the Russo-Japanese War, 1905 •	*summer.*
9	Tu.	Secretariat became first horse in 25 years to win Triple Crown, 1973 • Tides 9.2 / 10.4 •	*It's*
10	W.	Full Strawberry ○ • ☿ in sup. ☌ • — / 9.3 •	*coming*
11	Th.	St. Barnabas • Corpus Christi • ☾ runs low • 10.5 / 9.4 •	*down*
12	Fr.	*Cleopatra*, the costliest film ever made, premiered in New York City, 1963 •	*hard'n*
13	Sa.	☌ ♆ ☾ • U.S. Supreme Court Miranda decision, 1966 • 10.7 / 9.6 •	*weeds*
14	D	2nd S. af. P. • Orthodox All Saints • ☌ ♅ ☾ •	
15	M.	St. Basil • ☾ at ☋ • Magna Carta sealed, 1215 • Tides 10.6 / 9.8 •	*are*
16	Tu.	*A trusting heart is an easy mark for the cunning scoundrel.* • Tides 10.4 / 10.0 •	*taking*
17	W.	☾ on Eq. • ☌ ♃ ☾ • Amelia Earhart flew across the Atlantic, 1928 •	*over*
18	Th.	First American fly-casting tournament, Utica, N.Y., 1861 • Tides 10.1 / 10.5 •	*the*
19	Fr.	☌ ♄ ☾ • U.S. government established 8-hour work day, 1912 •	*garden.*
20	Sa.	☾ at perig. • Willie Mays graduated from high school, 1950 • 10.0 / 11.2 •	*Time*
21	D	3rd S. af. P. • Summer Solstice • ☌ ♀ ☾ • 10.1 / 11.5	*for*
22	M.	Mary Livingstone (Mrs. Jack Benny) born, 1909 • 10.2 / 11.7 •	*diplomas*
23	Tu.	New ● • Midsummer Eve • Bob Fosse born, 1927 • 10.3 / 11.8 •	*and*
24	W.	Nativ. John the Baptist • ☾ rides high • — / 11.8 •	*barbecue*
25	Th.	☌ ☿ ☾ • Custer's Last Stand, 1876 • 11.7 / 10.3 •	*aromas.*
26	Fr.	Abner Doubleday born, 1819 • "Babe" Didrikson Zaharias born, 1914 •	*June*
27	Sa.	100° F at Fort Yukon, Alaska, 1915 • *A good leak in June sets all in tune.* • 11.2 / 9.9 •	*is*
28	D	4th S. af. P. • ☾ at ☊ • Tides 10.7 / 9.7 •	*rusting*
29	M.	Sts. Peter & Paul • Interstate highway system authorized, 1953 • 10.2 / 9.5 •	*out*
30	Tu.	Charles Blondin crossed Niagara Falls on a tightrope, 1859 • Tides 9.7 / 9.3	*all over.*

Gravitation cannot be held responsible for people falling in love. –Albert Einstein

Farmer's Calendar

At the turn of June, the lilacs bloom and the swallowtail butterflies flock to meet them like high school kids at the arrival of a rock star, in a kind of delirium of welcome that is, surely, a bit excessive. Not that the new lilacs aren't gorgeous. With their delicate colors, their abundance, and their extraordinary scent, they are one of the flowers that make an event in the year all by themselves. Everybody loves the lilacs, everybody is refreshed when they appear. But these butterflies go too far.

The big, yellow tiger swallowtails (*Papilio glaucus*) are the ones I mean. Normally, they are a sane butterfly, efficiently visiting the garden flowers. They're alert and shy and don't let you get too close. When the lilacs bloom and their dusky purple flower heads bend their boughs, the swallowtails go nuts. They dive into the lilac clusters avidly and hang from them, ecstatically feeding, their wings aquiver. Usually a solitary butterfly, they come to the lilacs in gangs, often crowding three and four to the same flower. They wallow in the lilacs, they roll in them like puppies in the grass. Sometimes you can approach one of them as it hovers obliviously on a lilac and stroke its wing, and it scarcely seems to notice.

The other swallowtail in my area is the black swallowtail, as beautiful as the tiger but smaller, rarer, and more consistently self-possessed. The black swallowtail likes the lilacs, too, and visits them in their season. But it doesn't make a spectacle of itself like its cousin. Only the tiger swallowtail is a fool at lilac time. Still, it's good to see an insect have so much fun.

1998   JULY, The Seventh Month

Earth reaches its farthest distance from the Sun (aphelion) this year on the night of July 3, when it will be 94,512,258 miles away. This makes northern hemisphere summers more moderate than they would be otherwise. Mercury puts in a brief, one-week performance in evening twilight from the 4th to the 11th; look for it low in the west. The waning gibbous Moon stands near Jupiter on the 14th and Saturn on the 17th. Both planets now rise around midnight and stand high up at dawn.

☽ First Quarter	1st day	14th hour	43rd minute
○ Full Moon	9th day	12th hour	1st minute
☾ Last Quarter	16th day	11th hour	13th minute
● New Moon	23rd day	9th hour	44th minute
☽ First Quarter	31st day	8th hour	5th minute

Times are given in Eastern Daylight Time.

For an explanation of this page, see "How to Use This Almanac," page 34; for values of Key Letters, see Time Correction Tables, page 214.

Day of Year	Day of Month	Day of Week	☉ Rises h. m.	Key	☉ Sets h. m.	Key	Length of Days h. m.	Sun Fast m.	Declination of Sun ° '	Full Sea Boston A.M.	Full Sea Boston P.M.	☽ Rises h. m.	Key	☽ Sets h. m.	Key	☽ Place	☽ Age
182	1	W.	5 11	A	8 25	E	15 14	12	23N.05	5¼	5¾	12ᴘₘ46	D	12ᴀₘ26	C	VIR	8
183	2	Th.	5 12	A	8 25	E	15 13	12	23 00	6¼	6¾	1 43	D	12 54	C	VIR	9
184	3	Fr.	5 12	A	8 24	E	15 12	12	22 56	7	7½	2 41	D	1 21	C	VIR	10
185	4	Sa.	5 13	A	8 24	E	15 11	11	22 50	8	8¼	3 38	E	1 51	B	LIB	11
186	5	**D**	5 13	A	8 24	E	15 11	11	22 45	8¾	9¼	4 36	E	2 23	B	LIB	12
187	6	M.	5 14	A	8 24	E	15 10	11	22 39	9¾	10	5 34	E	2 59	B	SCO	13
188	7	Tu.	5 14	A	8 23	E	15 09	11	22 33	10½	10¾	6 31	E	3 40	B	OPH	14
189	8	W.	5 15	A	8 23	E	15 08	11	22 26	11¼	11¼	7 26	E	4 26	B	SAG	15
190	9	Th.	5 16	A	8 23	E	15 07	10	22 19	—	12	8 17	E	5 19	B	SAG	16
191	10	Fr.	5 17	A	8 22	E	15 05	10	22 11	12	12¾	9 03	E	6 18	B	SAG	17
192	11	Sa.	5 18	A	8 22	E	15 04	10	22 03	12¾	1½	9 45	E	7 22	B	CAP	18
193	12	**D**	5 18	A	8 21	E	15 03	10	21 55	1½	2¼	10 24	D	8 29	C	CAP	19
194	13	M.	5 19	A	8 20	E	15 01	10	21 46	2¼	3	10 59	D	9 37	D	AQU	20
195	14	Tu.	5 20	A	8 20	E	15 00	10	21 37	3¼	3¾	11ᴘₘ33	D	10 47	D	AQU	21
196	15	W.	5 21	A	8 19	E	14 58	10	21 28	4	4½	— —	–	11ᴀₘ56	D	PSC	22
197	16	Th.	5 21	A	8 19	E	14 58	10	21 18	5	5½	12ᴀₘ07	C	1ᴘₘ06	D	PSC	23
198	17	Fr.	5 22	A	8 18	E	14 56	10	21 08	6	6½	12 42	B	2 16	E	CET	24
199	18	Sa.	5 23	A	8 17	E	14 54	9	20 58	7	7½	1 19	B	3 25	E	ARI	25
200	19	**D**	5 24	A	8 16	E	14 52	9	20 47	8	8½	2 00	B	4 32	E	TAU	26
201	20	M.	5 25	A	8 16	E	14 51	9	20 36	9	9½	2 46	B	5 36	E	TAU	27
202	21	Tu.	5 26	A	8 15	E	14 49	9	20 24	10	10¼	3 37	B	6 35	E	ORI	28
203	22	W.	5 27	A	8 14	E	14 47	9	20 12	11	11¼	4 33	B	7 27	E	GEM	29
204	23	Th.	5 28	A	8 13	E	14 45	9	20 00	11¾	—	5 32	B	8 12	E	GEM	0
205	24	Fr.	5 29	A	8 12	E	14 43	9	19 47	12	12¾	6 34	B	8 52	E	CAN	1
206	25	Sa.	5 30	A	8 11	E	14 41	9	19 35	12¾	1½	7 35	C	9 27	D	LEO	2
207	26	**D**	5 31	A	8 10	D	14 39	9	19 22	1½	2¼	8 36	C	9 58	D	LEO	3
208	27	M.	5 32	A	8 09	D	14 37	9	19 08	2¼	2¾	9 36	C	10 27	D	LEO	4
209	28	Tu.	5 33	A	8 08	D	14 35	9	18 55	3	3½	10 34	D	10 55	D	VIR	5
210	29	W.	5 34	A	8 07	D	14 33	9	18 41	3¾	4¼	11ᴀₘ32	D	11 23	C	VIR	6
211	30	Th.	5 35	A	8 06	D	14 31	9	18 26	4½	5	12ᴘₘ29	D	11ᴘₘ52	B	VIR	7
212	31	Fr.	5 36	A	8 05	D	14 29	9	18N.11	5½	6	1ᴘₘ26	E	— —	–	VIR	8

JULY hath 31 days. 1998

Cool in the very furnace of July
 The water-meadows lie;
The green stalks of their grasses and their flowers
They still refresh at fountains never dry.
– John Drinkwater

D. M.	D. W.	Dates, Feasts, Fasts, Aspects, Tide Heights	*Weather* ↓
1	W.	**Canada Day** • ☾ on Eq. • *Ne'er trust a July sky.* •	*Fireworks*
2	Th.	☾ at apo. • B. J. Lane patented the gas mask, 1850 • Tides {8.9 / 9.2 •	*shows*
3	Fr.	⊕ at aphelion • Dog Days begin. • George M. Cohan born, 1878 •	*are*
4	Sa.	**Independence Day** • Thomas Jefferson and John Adams died, 1826 • {8.5 / 9.4 •	*put*
5	D	**5th S. af. P.** • Phineas T. Barnum born, 1810 • {8.5 / 9.6 •	*to*
6	M.	Louis Pasteur gave first successful anti-rabies shot to a human, 1885 • {8.7 / 9.9 •	*shame*
7	Tu.	Jack Walsh set world weight-lifting record of 4,235 pounds, 1950 • Tides {8.8 / 10.2 •	*by*
8	W.	*Nature, Time, and Patience are the three great physicians.* • {9.1 / 10.5 •	*Nature's*
9	Th.	☾ runs low • **Full Thunder** ○ • 106° F, New York City, 1936 •	*nightly*
10	Fr.	☌♆☾ • Communications satellite *Telstar* launched, 1962 • {10.7 / 9.6 •	*flash*
11	Sa.	☌♅☾ • *Skylab I* returned to Earth after six years in space, 1979 • {11.0 / 9.8 •	*and*
12	D	**6th S. af. P.** • ☾ at ☋ • Tides {11.1 / 10.1 •	*flame.*
13	M.	First U.S. military draft sparks four days of rioting, New York City, 1863 • {11.1 / 10.3 •	*Praise*
14	Tu.	☌♃☾ • Bastille Day • Ingmar Bergman born, 1918 • {10.9 / 10.4 •	*the*
15	W.	**St. Swithin** • ☾ on Eq. • Clement Moore born, 1779 • {10.7 / 10.6 •	*Lord*
16	Th.	☾ at perig. • ☿ Gr. Elong. (27° E.) • Ginger Rogers born, 1911 • {10.4 / 10.6 •	*and*
17	Fr.	☌♄☾ • First U.S. dental school established at Harvard, 1867 • {10.0 / 10.7 •	*pass*
18	Sa.	♃ stat. • Rome burned while Nero fiddled, A.D. 64 • *Mein Kampf* published, 1925 •	*the*
19	D	**7th S. af. P.** • Cornscateous air is everywhere. • {9.6 / 11.0 •	*sun-*
20	M.	*Where everyone goes, the grass never grows.* • Sir Edmund Hillary born, 1919 • {9.6 / 11.1	*tan*
21	Tu.	☌♀☾ • ☌♂☾ • Ernest Hemingway born, 1899 •	*lotion.*
22	W.	**St. Mary Magdalene** • ☾ rides high • Tides {9.8 / 11.3 •	*Brief*
23	Th.	**New** ● • ♆ at ☍ • Haile Selassie born, 1892 • {9.9 / — •	*relief,*
24	Fr.	Hulda Crooks, age 91, climbed Mt. Fuji, 1987 • Bella Abzug born, 1920 • {11.2 / 9.9 •	*then*
25	Sa.	**St. James** • ☾ at ☊ • ☌☿☾ • {11.1 / 9.9 •	*hot as*
26	D	**8th S. af. P.** • U.S. Post Office established, 1775 • {10.8 / 9.9 •	*Hades;*
27	M.	**St. Ann** • Korean War armistice signed, 1953 • Tides {10.5 / 9.7 •	*find a*
28	Tu.	☾ on Eq. • *Whatever July and August do not boil, September cannot fry.* • {10.1 / 9.6 •	*spot*
29	W.	**Sts. Mary & Martha** • New York Yacht Club founded, 1844 •	*that's*
30	Th.	☿ stat. • ☾ at apo. • Jimmy Hoffa disappeared, 1975 • {9.2 / 9.3 •	*shady,*
31	Fr.	Hail fell to 12 inches deep; remained for 30 hours, Scituate, Mass., 1769 • {8.8 / 9.2 •	*ladies.*

Farmer's Calendar

After midsummer, the hawkweed appears in the meadows in drifts of orange polka dots that, for a while, give to plain New England pastures the bright, illuminated look of an Impressionist landscape. Orange hawkweed (*Hieracium aurantiacum*) is the medium here, a dandelion-like member of the daisy family, with a fuzzy, ground-hugging rosette of leaves and a single, red-orange flower that has a curious thickness or freshness of color, as though it had been dipped in paint. It's always a welcome flower to me, but it's a flower that has a dark side, or anyway did have for the first European settlers on the land.

"Devil's paintbrush" they called this plant. They, too, noticed how the odd vividness of its color resembled paint, and they thought they knew who was the painter: the Prince of Darkness. Those old colonists were no nature lovers. On the contrary, the evidence is that, living so much in nature, they were scared to death of it. One sign is the names they gave to common plants, not once or twice but over and over. *Gray's Botany,* a standard catalog of North American plants, lists at least a dozen whose English names allude to the Devil. There's devil's club, devil's walking-stick, even devil's grandmother. Any wild plant that could support the remotest association with some human object, the name-givers ascribed to the Devil. Now, a people as devoted to their Bible as the early northern settlers were don't fool with the name of Satan. Perhaps the devil's thises and devil's thats were a kind of joke, but they were an uneasy joke.

1998 AUGUST, THE EIGHTH MONTH

The Moon washes out all but the brightest meteors when the Perseids reach their maximum on the night of August 11-12. This is the only year of the decade in which a bright Moon spoils both of the premier meteor showers (the other is December's Geminids). Fortunately, the usually subdued Leonids may rise to the occasion and perform much better than usual (see November). Arguably the finest constellation grouping now floats in the southern sky at 10:00 P.M., EDT. Beautiful Scorpius, its heart defined by the red giant star Antares, is followed (on its left) by teapot-shaped Sagittarius, which also marks the direction toward the center of our galaxy.

○	Full Moon	7th day	22nd hour	10th minute
☾	Last Quarter	14th day	15th hour	48th minute
●	New Moon	21st day	22nd hour	3rd minute
☽	First Quarter	30th day	1st hour	6th minute

Times are given in Eastern Daylight Time.

For an explanation of this page, see "How to Use This Almanac," page 34; for values of Key Letters, see Time Correction Tables, page 214.

Day of Year	Day of Month	Day of Week	☉ Rises h. m.	Key	☉ Sets h. m.	Key	Length of Days h. m.	Sun Fast m.	Declination of Sun ° '	Full Sea Boston A.M.	Full Sea Boston P.M.	☽ Rises h. m.	Key	☽ Sets h. m.	Key	☽ Place	☽ Age
213	1	Sa.	5 37	A	8 04	D	14 27	9	17 N.56	6¼	6¾	2 P.M. 24	E	12 A.M. 22	A	LIB	9
214	2	**D**	5 38	A	8 03	D	14 25	9	17 41	7¼	7½	3 21	E	12 56	A	LIB	10
215	3	M.	5 39	A	8 01	D	14 22	9	17 25	8¼	8½	4 18	E	1 34	B	OPH	11
216	4	Tu.	5 40	A	8 00	D	14 20	9	17 09	9	9¼	5 14	E	2 17	B	OPH	12
217	5	W.	5 41	A	7 59	D	14 18	10	16 53	10	10	6 07	E	3 07	B	SAG	13
218	6	Th.	5 42	A	7 58	D	14 16	10	16 36	10¾	10¾	6 56	E	4 04	B	SAG	14
219	7	Fr.	5 43	A	7 56	D	14 13	10	16 19	11½	11¾	7 41	E	5 06	B	CAP	15
220	8	Sa.	5 44	A	7 55	D	14 11	10	16 02	—	12¼	8 21	E	6 13	C	AQU	16
221	9	**D**	5 45	A	7 54	D	14 09	10	15 45	12½	1	8 59	D	7 23	C	AQU	17
222	10	M.	5 46	A	7 52	D	14 06	10	15 28	1¼	1¾	9 35	D	8 34	D	AQU	18
223	11	Tu.	5 47	A	7 51	D	14 04	10	15 10	2	2½	10 09	D	9 45	D	PSC	19
224	12	W.	5 48	A	7 50	D	14 02	10	14 53	2¾	3¼	10 44	C	10 A.M. 57	D	CET	20
225	13	Th.	5 49	A	7 48	D	13 59	11	14 34	3¾	4¼	11 P.M. 21	B	12 P.M. 07	E	PSC	21
226	14	Fr.	5 50	A	7 47	D	13 57	11	14 16	4¾	5¼	— —	–	1 17	E	ARI	22
227	15	Sa.	5 51	B	7 45	D	13 54	11	13 57	5¾	6¼	12 A.M. 00	B	2 24	E	TAU	23
228	16	**D**	5 52	B	7 44	D	13 52	11	13 38	6¾	7¼	12 44	B	3 28	E	TAU	24
229	17	M.	5 53	B	7 42	D	13 49	11	13 19	7¾	8¼	1 32	B	4 28	E	TAU	25
230	18	Tu.	5 54	B	7 41	D	13 47	12	13 00	9	9¼	2 25	B	5 21	E	GEM	26
231	19	W.	5 55	B	7 39	D	13 44	12	12 40	10	10¼	3 23	B	6 08	E	GEM	27
232	20	Th.	5 56	B	7 38	D	13 42	12	12 20	10¾	11	4 23	B	6 50	E	CAN	28
233	21	Fr.	5 58	B	7 36	D	13 38	12	12 00	11½	11¾	5 23	C	7 26	E	LEO	0
234	22	Sa.	5 59	B	7 35	D	13 36	13	11 40	—	12¼	6 24	C	7 59	D	LEO	1
235	23	**D**	6 00	B	7 33	D	13 33	13	11 20	12½	1	7 24	D	8 28	D	LEO	2
236	24	M.	6 01	B	7 32	D	13 31	13	11 00	1¼	1½	8 23	D	8 57	D	VIR	3
237	25	Tu.	6 02	B	7 30	D	13 28	13	10 39	1¾	2¼	9 21	D	9 25	C	VIR	4
238	26	W.	6 03	B	7 28	D	13 25	14	10 18	2½	3	10 19	D	9 53	B	VIR	5
239	27	Th.	6 04	B	7 27	D	13 23	14	9 58	3¼	3½	11 A.M. 16	E	10 22	B	VIR	6
240	28	Fr.	6 05	B	7 25	D	13 20	14	9 36	4	4¼	12 P.M. 13	E	10 54	B	LIB	7
241	29	Sa.	6 06	B	7 23	D	13 17	14	9 15	4¾	5¼	1 09	E	11 P.M. 30	B	LIB	8
242	30	**D**	6 07	B	7 22	D	13 15	15	8 53	5¾	6	2 06	E	— —	–	OPH	9
243	31	M.	6 08	B	7 20	D	13 12	15	8 N.32	6½	7	3 P.M. 01	E	12 A.M. 10	B	OPH	10

AUGUST hath 31 days. 1998

Summer declines and roses have grown rare,
But cottage crofts are gay with hollyhocks,
And in old garden walks you breathe an air
Fragrant of pinks and August-smelling stocks.
– John Todhunter

D. M.	D. W.	Dates, Feasts, Fasts, Aspects, Tide Heights	*Weather* ↓
1	Sa.	Lammas Day • Jerry Garcia born, 1942 • Tides {8.5 9.2 •	*Dreamy,*
2	D	9th S. af. P. • Fifth Avenue opened, New York, 1824 • {8.4 9.3 •	*then*
3	M.	⛢ at ☍ • *August needs the dew as much as men need their bread.* •	*steamy.*
4	Tu.	☌♀♂ • U.S. acquired Virgin Islands, 1916 • {8.5 9.8	*Equatorial–*
5	W.	☾ runs low • "Little Orphan Annie" comic strip debuted in New York *Daily News*, 1924 •	*We*
6	Th.	Transfiguration • ☌♆☾ • Tides {9.2 10.6 •	*fear*
7	Fr.	Name of Jesus • ☌⛢☾ • Full Green Corn ○ • Eclipse ☾	
8	Sa.	St. Dominic • Snow showers over Lake Michigan, 1882 • {— 10.0 •	*"Hot*
9	D	10th S. af. P. • ☾ at ☋ • {11.3 10.5 •	*enough*
10	M.	St. Laurence • ☌♃☾ • Tides {11.5 10.8 •	*for ya?"*
11	Tu.	St. Clare • ☾ on Eq. • ☾ at perig. • Dog Days end. • {11.4 11.0	*will*
12	W.	U.S. formally annexed the Hawaiian Islands, 1898 • Tides {11.2 11.1 •	*be all*
13	Th.	☌♄☾ • ☿ in inf. ☌ • Fidel Castro born, 1927 • {10.8 11.0 •	*we*
14	Fr.	*A near neighbor is better than a far-dwelling kinsman.* • Tides {10.4 10.9 •	*hear.*
15	Sa.	Assumption • Woodstock Music and Arts Fair opened, 1969 •	*Delugin's*
16	D	11th S. af. P. • ♄ stat. • Babe Ruth died, 1948 • {9.5 10.6 •	*of*
17	M.	Cat Nights begin. • Davy Crockett born, 1786 • {9.3 10.6 •	*grandeur.*
18	Tu.	☾ rides high • ♇ stat. • 19th Amendment ratified, 1920 • {9.3 10.6 •	*We're*
19	W.	☌♂☾ • Gail Borden patented condensed milk, 1856 • Tides {9.5 10.7 •	*not*
20	Th.	☌♀☾ • Vitas Jonas Bering discovered Alaska, 1741 •	*teasin'–*
21	Fr.	New ● • Eclipse ☉ • Hawaii became 50th state, 1959 • {9.8 10.8 •	*it's*
22	Sa.	☾ at ☊ • The "Mona Lisa" stolen from the Louvre in Paris, 1911 •	*hurricane*
23	D	12th S. af. P. • ☿ stat. • Tides {10.7 9.9 •	*season.*
24	M.	St. Bartholomew • *At St. Bartholomew there comes cold dew.* • {10.5 9.9 •	*Look*
25	Tu.	☾ on Eq. • ☌☿♀ • U.S. National Park Service created, 1916 •	*back*
26	W.	Krakatoa erupted, 1883 • 19th Amendment went into effect, 1920 • Tides {9.9 9.7	*with*
27	Th.	☾ at apo. • First commercial oil well struck oil, Pennsylvania, 1859 • {9.5 9.6	*damp*
28	Fr.	St. Augustine of Hippo • Roger Tory Peterson born, 1908 •	*eyes*
29	Sa.	Ingrid Bergman born, 1915; died 1982 • Oliver Wendell Holmes born, 1809 • {8.8 9.3 •	*on*
30	D	13th S. af. P. • Ted Williams born, 1918 • {8.5 9.2 •	*summer's*
31	M.	☿ Gr. Elong. (18° W.) • *Great talkers fire too fast to take aim.* • {8.3 9.2 •	*demise.*

Farmer's Calendar

The earliest scientific observers of nature found that wild birds and animals had lives that resembled those of people, not individually but politically, so to speak. Aristotle in his *History of Animals* (c. 330 B.C.) described a complicated system of enmities and alliances subsisting between creatures of various kinds. Most often, according to Aristotle, adversaries in the world of animals and birds are pitted against each other because they compete for food or because one is food for the other. "The eagle and the snake are enemies, for the eagle lives on snakes. . . ." Here the accuracy of the report seems plain enough, but it's remarkable that the author invariably expressed predator-prey relationships not as matters of simple survival but as warfare.

The alliances Aristotle discovered in nature are more interesting and curious than the oppositions. "The crow and the heron are friends, as also are the sedge-bird and the lark. . . ." While conflicts among animals are practical and based on survival, their alliances seem to involve subtler affinities. Friendships in the animal world are traditional, *historic*, we might almost say, like the friendship between England and the United States.

It's all pretty quaint. These observations are the product of a time when science had our eyes but not our mind. Today we are constantly on guard against the Pathetic Fallacy, in which we attribute to animals human thoughts and feelings. Aristotle's natural history took the fallacy a large step further, giving to the birds and animals not only ideas and emotions but also foreign relations.

1998   SEPTEMBER, The Ninth Month

Mercury puts in a good performance as a morning star in the east during the first half of the month. Following their conjunction, brilliant Venus and Mercury are an extremely close and spectacular pair on the 11th and 12th, very low in the bright predawn twilight. But the spotlight this month is on Jupiter, the bright "star" near the full Moon on the 6th. This largest planet reaches opposition (at its closest and brightest) on the 15th — its best apparition since 1987. The autumnal equinox occurs on the 23rd at 1:37 A.M., EDT.

○ Full Moon	6th day	7th hour	21st minute
☾ Last Quarter	12th day	21st hour	58th minute
● New Moon	20th day	13th hour	1st minute
☽ First Quarter	28th day	17th hour	11th minute

Times are given in Eastern Daylight Time.

For an explanation of this page, see "How to Use This Almanac," page 34; for values of Key Letters, see Time Correction Tables, page 214.

Day of Year	Day of Month	Day of Week	☼ Rises h. m.	Key	☼ Sets h. m.	Key	Length of Days h. m.	Sun Fast m.	Declination of Sun ° ′	Full Sea Boston A.M.	Full Sea Boston P.M.	☽ Rises h. m.	Key	☽ Sets h. m.	Key	☽ Place	☽ Age
244	1	Tu.	6 09	B	7 18	D	13 09	15	8 N.10	7½	7¾	3 $_M^P$54	E	12$_M^A$56	B	SAG	11
245	2	W.	6 10	B	7 17	D	13 07	16	7 48	8½	8¾	4 45	E	1 49	B	SAG	12
246	3	Th.	6 11	B	7 15	D	13 04	16	7 26	9¼	9½	5 31	E	2 47	B	SAG	13
247	4	Fr.	6 12	B	7 13	D	13 01	16	7 04	10¼	10½	6 14	E	3 52	B	CAP	14
248	5	Sa.	6 13	B	7 12	D	12 59	17	6 42	11	11¼	6 54	D	5 01	C	CAP	15
249	6	D	6 14	B	7 10	D	12 56	17	6 19	11¾	—	7 31	D	6 13	D	AQU	16
250	7	M.	6 16	B	7 08	D	12 52	17	5 57	12	12½	8 07	D	7 26	D	AQU	17
251	8	Tu.	6 17	B	7 06	D	12 49	18	5 34	12¾	1¼	8 43	C	8 40	D	CET	18
252	9	W.	6 18	B	7 05	C	12 47	18	5 12	1¾	2	9 20	B	9 53	E	PSC	19
253	10	Th.	6 19	B	7 03	C	12 44	18	4 49	2½	3	9 59	B	11$_M^A$05	E	CET	20
254	11	Fr.	6 20	B	7 01	C	12 41	19	4 26	3½	3¾	10 42	B	12$_M^P$16	E	TAU	21
255	12	Sa.	6 21	B	6 59	C	12 38	19	4 03	4½	4¾	11$_M^P$30	B	1 22	E	TAU	22
256	13	D	6 22	B	6 58	C	12 36	19	3 40	5½	5¾	— —	–	2 23	E	TAU	23
257	14	M.	6 23	B	6 56	C	12 33	20	3 17	6½	7	12$_M^A$22	B	3 18	E	GEM	24
258	15	Tu.	6 24	B	6 54	C	12 30	20	2 54	7¾	8	1 17	B	4 07	E	GEM	25
259	16	W.	6 25	B	6 52	C	12 27	21	2 31	8¾	9	2 16	B	4 49	E	CAN	26
260	17	Th.	6 26	B	6 51	C	12 25	21	2 08	9¾	10	3 16	B	5 27	D	CAN	27
261	18	Fr.	6 27	B	6 49	C	12 22	21	1 45	10½	10¾	4 16	C	6 00	D	LEO	28
262	19	Sa.	6 28	B	6 47	C	12 19	22	1 22	11¼	11½	5 16	C	6 30	D	LEO	29
263	20	D	6 29	C	6 45	C	12 16	22	0 58	—	12	6 15	D	6 59	D	LEO	0
264	21	M.	6 30	C	6 43	C	12 13	22	0 35	12¼	12½	7 13	D	7 27	C	VIR	1
265	22	Tu.	6 31	C	6 42	C	12 11	23	0 N.11	12¾	1	8 10	D	7 54	C	VIR	2
266	23	W.	6 32	C	6 40	C	12 08	23	0 S.11	1½	1¾	9 08	D	8 23	B	VIR	3
267	24	Th.	6 34	C	6 38	C	12 04	23	0 34	2	2¼	10 04	E	8 54	B	LIB	4
268	25	Fr.	6 35	C	6 36	C	12 01	24	0 58	2¾	3	11 01	E	9 28	B	LIB	5
269	26	Sa.	6 36	C	6 35	C	11 59	24	1 21	3½	3¾	11$_M^A$57	E	10 06	B	SCO	6
270	27	D	6 37	C	6 33	C	11 56	24	1 44	4¼	4½	12$_M^P$52	E	10 48	B	OPH	7
271	28	M.	6 38	C	6 31	B	11 53	25	2 08	5	5¼	1 45	E	11$_M^P$37	B	SAG	8
272	29	Tu.	6 39	C	6 29	B	11 50	25	2 31	6	6¼	2 35	E	— —	–	SAG	9
273	30	W.	6 40	C	6 28	B	11 48	25	2 S.54	7	7¼	3 $_M^P$22	E	12$_M^A$31	B	SAG	10

SEPTEMBER hath 30 days. 1998

A touch of gold in the Autumn night
I walked abroad,
And saw the ruddy moon lean over a hedge
Like a red-faced farmer.
– *T. E. Hulme*

D. M.	D. W.	Dates, Feasts, Fasts, Aspects, Tide Heights	*Weather* ↓
1	Tu.	☾ runs low • 100° F, Los Angeles, Calif., 1955 • Tides {8.4 9.4 •	*School*
2	W.	V-J Day, 1945 • Great Fire of London began, 1666 • Tides {8.6 9.8 •	*bells*
3	Th.	☌♆☾ • ☌♅☾ • Sarah Orne Jewett born, 1849 • {9.0 10.3	*and*
4	Fr.	Swimmer Mark Spitz became first Olympian to win seven gold medals, 1972 • {5.1 6.2	*cooler*
5	Sa.	☾ at ☋ • First Labor Day parade held, New York City, 1882 • {10.2 11.3 •	*spells.*
6	D	**14th S. af. P.** • **Full Barley** ○ • Eclipse ☾ •	*The*
7	M.	**Labor Day** • ☾ on Eq. • ☌♃☾ • Tides {11.6 11.2 •	*first*
8	Tu.	☾ at perig. • *As the weather on the 8th, so will it be for the next four weeks.* • {11.7 11.6	*red*
9	W.	☌♄☾ • Gordie Howe retired from NHL, 1971 • Tides {11.6 11.7 •	*leaf*
10	Th.	☌☿♀ • Elias Howe patented the lock-stitch sewing machine, 1846 •	*appears*
11	Fr.	7 inches of snow, Helena, Mont., earliest in 80 years, 1949 • Tides {10.8 11.4	*on the*
12	Sa.	*Friday night's dream on the Saturday told, is sure to come true be it never so old.* • {10.3 11.0 •	*hill;*
13	D	**15th S. af. P.** • Highest world temperature, 136° F, Azizia, Libya, 1922 •	*it's*
14	M.	**Holy Cross** • ☾ rides high • President William McKinley died, 1901 •	*chilly*
15	Tu.	♃ at ☍ • *U.S.A. Today* began publication, 1982 • Tides {9.2 10.2 •	*out,*
16	W.	Ember Day • U.S. Episcopal Church approved ordination of women priests, 1976 •	*and*
17	Th.	☌♂☾ • Reggie Jackson hit his 500th home run, 1984 • {9.5 10.3 •	*damper.*
18	Fr.	☾ at ☊ • Ember Day • Cornerstone laid for U.S. Capitol, 1793 •	*Make*
19	Sa.	Ember Day • Melville R. Bissell patented the carpet sweeper, 1876 • Tides {9.9 10.3 •	*a*
20	D	**16th S. af. P.** • **New** ● • Tides {— 10.0 •	*picnic,*
21	M.	**St. Matthew** • **Rosh Hashanah** • ☾ on Eq. • {10.3 10.1 •	*end*
22	Tu.	*Fiddler on the Roof* opened on Broadway, the first of 3,242 performances, 1964 • {10.2 10.1 •	*the*
23	W.	**Autumnal Equinox** • ☾ at apo. • Harvard held first commencement, 1642 •	*month*
24	Th.	*Truth is stranger than fiction; fiction has to make sense.* • Tides {9.7 9.9 •	*not with*
25	Fr.	☿ in sup. ☌ • Sequoia National Park established, 1890 • Tides {9.4 9.7 •	*a*
26	Sa.	Shamu, first killer whale born in captivity to survive, born, 1985 • Tides {9.1 9.5 •	*binge*
27	D	**17th S. af. P.** • New York woman arrested for smoking on Fifth Ave., 1904 •	*but*
28	M.	First night football game played, Mansfield, Pa., 1892 • Tides {8.5 9.2 •	*with*
29	Tu.	**St. Michael** • ☾ runs low • Jerry Lee Lewis born, 1935 • {8.4 9.3 •	*a*
30	W.	**St. Jerome** • **Yom Kippur** • ☌♆☾ •	*hamper.*

The best smell is bread, the best savor salt, the best love that of children.

Farmer's Calendar

This house and its lands were once part of a hill farm that started sometime around 1790 and was worked until about 1925. On the place today are five wells that served the old farm. One is little more than a spring a couple of feet deep that's been scooped out and lined with stones. The others are more ambitious structures. Twelve to 15 feet deep and 4 feet across, they are finished with large stones laid skillfully in the manner of a house foundation, the subterranean version of the stone walls that everywhere cross the property.

I try to imagine how you'd go about building one of these wells. First, you'd have to dig out the hole, plumb, six or seven feet wide and as deep as needed. Two or three could work on the digging, I guess, but once the hole was dug and the work of laying up the stones begun, only one worker could carry on at a time; there is no room for more in the stone-sided cylinder of the well. Putting up the stones, you'd be alone down there. And, of course, the stones would be above. Somebody would have to lower them to you on ropes. You'd want a good man up top. Some of the stones in those wells are the size of a steamer trunk and must weigh several hundred pounds. As the stones rose around you, you'd need some kind of staging inside the well to stand on and work from. You'd dismantle it when you were done.

How long would it take to lay up a well? For an experienced stoneworker, I bet, with good help, not long: a day or two. Would you toss a penny down the finished well for good luck? I would. In fact, I have.

OCTOBER, THE TENTH MONTH

The Moon stands near Jupiter on the 3rd, Saturn on the 7th, and Mars on the 16th. Saturn is now at its brightest since 1989 and its highest since 1979. It reaches an excellent opposition (when it is the closest and the most brilliant of the year) on the 23rd. The current favorable conditions are due to the fact that its rings are less edgewise, its distance to Earth is "just" 771 million miles, and it is occupying a more northerly perch on the zodiac, in the constellation Pisces. Daylight Saving Time ends at 2:00 A.M. on the 25th.

○	Full Moon	5th day	16th hour	12th minute
☾	Last Quarter	12th day	7th hour	11th minute
●	New Moon	20th day	6th hour	9th minute
☽	First Quarter	28th day	6th hour	46th minute

After 2:00 A.M. on October 25, Eastern Standard Time (EST) is given.

For an explanation of this page, see "How to Use This Almanac," page 34; for values of Key Letters, see Time Correction Tables, page 214.

Day of Year	Day of Month	Day of Week	☉ Rises h. m.	Key	☉ Sets h. m.	Key	Length of Days h. m.	Sun Fast m.	Declination of Sun ° '	Full Sea Boston A.M.	P.M.	☽ Rises h. m.	Key	☽ Sets h. m.	Key	☽ Place	☽ Age
274	1	Th.	6 41	C	6 26	B	11 45	26	3 s.17	7¾	8	4ᴘ05ᴍ	E	1ᴀ32ᴍ	B	CAP	11
275	2	Fr.	6 42	C	6 24	B	11 42	26	3 41	8¾	9	4 46	D	2 37	C	CAP	12
276	3	Sa.	6 43	C	6 22	B	11 39	26	4 04	9½	10	5 23	D	3 47	C	AQU	13
277	4	**D**	6 44	C	6 21	B	11 37	27	4 27	10½	10¾	6 00	D	4 59	D	AQU	14
278	5	M.	6 46	C	6 19	B	11 33	27	4 50	11¼	11¾	6 36	D	6 14	D	PSC	15
279	6	Tu.	6 47	C	6 17	B	11 30	27	5 13	—	12	7 13	C	7 29	E	PSC	16
280	7	W.	6 48	C	6 16	B	11 28	28	5 36	12½	12¾	7 53	B	8 44	E	CET	17
281	8	Th.	6 49	C	6 14	B	11 25	28	5 59	1¼	1¾	8 36	B	9 59	E	ARI	18
282	9	Fr.	6 50	C	6 12	B	11 22	28	6 22	2¼	2½	9 23	B	11ᴀ09ᴍ	E	TAU	19
283	10	Sa.	6 51	C	6 11	B	11 20	28	6 45	3¼	3½	10 15	B	12ᴘ15ᴍ	E	TAU	20
284	11	**D**	6 52	C	6 09	B	11 17	29	7 07	4¼	4½	11ᴘ11ᴍ	B	1 14	E	ORI	21
285	12	M.	6 53	C	6 07	B	11 14	29	7 30	5¼	5½	— —	—	2 06	E	GEM	22
286	13	Tu.	6 55	C	6 06	B	11 11	29	7 52	6¼	6½	12ᴀ10ᴍ	B	2 50	E	CAN	23
287	14	W.	6 56	D	6 04	B	11 08	29	8 14	7¼	7¾	1 10	B	3 29	E	CAN	24
288	15	Th.	6 57	D	6 02	B	11 05	30	8 37	8½	8¾	2 10	C	4 03	D	LEO	25
289	16	Fr.	6 58	D	6 01	B	11 03	30	8 59	9¼	9½	3 09	C	4 34	D	LEO	26
290	17	Sa.	6 59	D	5 59	B	11 00	30	9 21	10	10½	4 08	C	5 02	D	LEO	27
291	18	**D**	7 00	D	5 58	B	10 58	30	9 42	10¾	11	5 06	D	5 30	C	VIR	28
292	19	M.	7 02	D	5 56	B	10 54	31	10 04	11½	11¾	6 04	D	5 57	C	VIR	29
293	20	Tu.	7 03	D	5 55	B	10 52	31	10 26	—	12	7 01	D	6 26	C	VIR	0
294	21	W.	7 04	D	5 53	B	10 49	31	10 47	12½	12½	7 58	E	6 56	B	LIB	1
295	22	Th.	7 05	D	5 52	B	10 47	31	11 08	1	1¼	8 55	E	7 28	B	LIB	2
296	23	Fr.	7 06	D	5 50	B	10 44	31	11 29	1¾	1¾	9 51	E	8 04	B	LIB	3
297	24	Sa.	7 08	D	5 49	B	10 41	31	11 50	2¼	2½	10 47	E	8 45	B	OPH	4
298	25	**D**	6 09	D	4 47	B	10 38	31	12 11	2	2¼	10 40	E	8 31	B	OPH	5
299	26	M.	6 10	D	4 46	B	10 36	32	12 32	2¾	3	11ᴀ30ᴍ	E	9 22	B	SAG	6
300	27	Tu.	6 11	D	4 44	B	10 33	32	12 52	3½	3¾	12ᴘ17ᴍ	E	10 19	B	SAG	7
301	28	W.	6 12	D	4 43	B	10 31	32	13 12	4½	4¾	1 01	E	11ᴘ20ᴍ	B	CAP	8
302	29	Th.	6 14	D	4 42	B	10 28	32	13 32	5½	5½	1 41	D	— —	—	CAP	9
303	30	Fr.	6 15	D	4 40	B	10 25	32	13 52	6¼	6½	2 18	D	12ᴀ25ᴍ	C	AQU	10
304	31	Sa.	6 16	D	4 39	B	10 23	32	14 s.11	7¼	7½	2ᴘ54ᴍ	D	1ᴀ34ᴍ	D	AQU	11

OCTOBER hath 31 days. 1998

October's face, benign and mellow,
Turns nuts to brown and leaves to yellow;
But (like the Scorpion, sting in tail)
He ends with frost and scourging hail.
– Jan Struther

D. M.	D. W.	Dates, Feasts, Fasts, Aspects, Tide Heights	*Weather* ↓
1	Th.	**St. Remigius** • ☌ ♅ ☾ • Julie Andrews born, 1935 •	*Gutters*
2	Fr.	☾ at ☋ • "Peanuts" comic strip began, 1950 • Tides {9.4, 10.4 •	*sing*
3	Sa.	First episode of *Captain Kangaroo* aired, 1955 • Tides {10.1, 10.9 •	*lullabies,*
4	D	**18th S. af. P.** • ☌ ♃ ☾ • {10.8, 11.3 •	*drippley—*
5	M.	**St. Francis of Assisi** • **Succoth** • **Full Harvest** ○ • ☾ on Eq. •	
6	Tu.	☾ at perig. • ☌ ♄ ☾ • Jenny Lind born, 1820 •	*drapple.*
7	W.	Football history: Georgia Tech beat Cumberland College 222-0, 1918 • {11.7, 12.2 •	*Nights*
8	Th.	Ozzie and Harriet got married, 1935 • Ozzie and Harriet's radio show debuted, 1944 •	*as crisp*
9	Fr.	*Courage ought to have eyes as well as arms.* • Charles Walgreen born, 1873 • {11.2, 12.0	*as a*
10	Sa.	Snow Hurricane: 12 to 36 inches snow and northerly gales, N.J. to Maine, 1804 •	*McIntosh*
11	D	**19th S. af. P.** • ☾ rides high • ♆ stat. • {10.2, 11.0	*apple.*
12	M.	**Columbus Day** • **Thanksgiving Day (Canada)** • Tides {9.7, 10.4	*Foliage*
13	Tu.	Greenwich, England, adopted as universal time meridian of longitude, 1884 •	*carpets*
14	W.	Dr. Martin Luther King Jr. was awarded the Nobel Peace Prize, 1964 • Tides {9.3, 9.8 •	*the*
15	Th.	☾ at ☊ • *I Love Lucy* premiered on TV, 1951 • {9.4, 9.8 •	*foothills*
16	Fr.	☌ ♂ ☾ • *Some people can stay longer in an hour than others can in a week.* •	*with*
17	Sa.	**St. Ignatius of Antioch** • Earthquake, San Francisco, 1989 •	*color;*
18	D	**20th S. af. P.** • ☾ on Eq. • ♅ stat. • {10.0, 9.9	*rain*
19	M.	**St. Luke** • St. Luke's Little Summer • Amy Carter born, 1967 • {10.1, 9.9	*tears*
20	Tu.	**New** ● • Bella Lugosi born, 1884 • Tides {—, 10.2 •	*the leaves*
21	W.	☾ at apo. • ☌ ☿ ☾ • Whitey Ford born, 1928 • {9.8, 10.2 •	*down*
22	Th.	First volume of the Gutenberg *Bible* sold at auction for a record $5.39 million, 1987 • {9.7, 10.2	*and*
23	Fr.	♄ at ☍ • Swallows leave San Juan Capistrano • Tides {9.5, 10.1 •	*makes*
24	Sa.	*Goodness is easier to recognize than to define.* • Tides {9.3, 9.9 •	*our*
25	D	**21st S. af. P.** • **Daylight Saving Time ends, 2:00 A.M.** •	*minds*
26	M.	**St. Crispin** • ☾ runs low • Erie Canal opened, 1825 • {8.8, 9.5 •	*duller.*
27	Tu.	☌ ♆ ☾ • Teddy Roosevelt born, 1858 • {8.7, 9.4 •	*Halloween's*
28	W.	**Sts. Simon & Jude** • ☌ ♅ ☾ • Tides {8.7, 9.4 •	*haunted*
29	Th.	♀ in sup. ☌ • 0° F, Denver, Colo., 1917 • 90° F, Los Angeles, Calif., 1965 •	*by*
30	Fr.	☾ at ☋ • *Autumn is the hush before winter.* • Tides {9.3, 9.9	*beggars*
31	Sa.	**All Hallows Eve** • ☌ ♃ ☾ • {9.9, 10.3 •	*undaunted.*

Farmer's Calendar

In the antique lore of the zodiac, this month is presided over by the constellation Libra, the balance, a sign associated with commerce, trade, and gain, by allusion to the scales on which the old merchant weighed his coin. Nowhere today is that ancient image more apt than in upcountry New England in October, a season that in these parts becomes a kind of Gold Rush in reverse: Hereabouts, the eager prospectors don't come looking for gold. They bring it with them.

Each weekend in October, they come to enjoy the fairest month of the year and its brilliant, clear days, frosty nights, sweet air, yellow light, autumn leaves, and harvest fields. Unaided, nature in October would bring half the world to the hills, but we want the other half, as well, and so we spread over the country a feast of good things, in hopes the happy visitors will pause, enjoy, and, if they feel inclined, unbelt. Yard sales, bake sales, antiques fairs, foliage festivals, church suppers, firehouse suppers, lodge suppers — ten thousand such events are laid on to celebrate the season and catch an honest penny. It works, too.

The only trouble is, it all ends too soon. October's perfect days and vigorous getting and spending are over long before we want them to be. How sad. But, wait. Here's an idea. Refer to the notes for March. What do we find? We want less March, more October. Let us take a weekend in March and — that's right — *move it* to October. Don't laugh. We'd get another 20 percent on the bottom line now, and next spring — spiritual relief. A silly idea, you say? No, a bold one. Get me the governor.

1998 NOVEMBER, The Eleventh Month

The full Moon on the night of the 3rd-4th is the closest Moon of the year, passing just 216,000 miles from Earth. This will produce a dramatically large range of high and low tides. Any storms at sea at this time will produce coastal flooding. The Moon passes near a brightening but still unspectacular Mars on the 13th. Look for the ultrafast Leonid meteors, which may put on a good show this year on the nights of the 17th and 18th. Moonlight will be absent, offering optimal conditions for this sometimes spectacular shower. The Moon returns to pass Jupiter on the 27th and Saturn on the 30th.

○	Full Moon	4th day	0 hour	18th minute
☾	Last Quarter	10th day	19th hour	28th minute
●	New Moon	18th day	23rd hour	27th minute
☽	First Quarter	26th day	19th hour	23rd minute

Times are given in Eastern Standard Time.

For an explanation of this page, see "How to Use This Almanac," page 34; for values of Key Letters, see Time Correction Tables, page 214.

Day of Year	Day of Month	Day of Week	☉ Rises h. m.	Key	☉ Sets h. m.	Key	Length of Days h. m.	Sun Fast m.	Declination of Sun ° '	Full Sea Boston A.M.	Full Sea Boston P.M.	☽ Rises h. m.	Key	☽ Sets h. m.	Key	☽ Place	☽ Age
305	1	**D**	6 17	D	4 38	B	10 21	32	14 s.31	8	8½	3ᴘₘ29	D	2ᴀₘ46	D	AQU	12
306	2	M.	6 19	D	4 36	B	10 17	32	14 50	9	9½	4 05	C	4 00	D	CET	13
307	3	Tu.	6 20	D	4 35	B	10 15	32	15 08	9¾	10¼	4 43	B	5 15	E	PSC	14
308	4	W.	6 21	D	4 34	B	10 13	32	15 27	10½	11¼	5 24	B	6 31	E	ARI	15
309	5	Th.	6 22	D	4 33	B	10 11	32	15 45	11½	—	6 10	B	7 46	E	TAU	16
310	6	Fr.	6 24	D	4 32	B	10 08	32	16 03	12	12¼	7 02	B	8 57	E	TAU	17
311	7	Sa.	6 25	D	4 30	B	10 05	32	16 21	1	1¼	7 58	B	10 02	E	TAU	18
312	8	**D**	6 26	D	4 29	A	10 03	32	16 39	1¾	2	8 58	B	10 59	E	GEM	19
313	9	M.	6 27	D	4 28	A	10 01	32	16 56	2¾	3	10 00	B	11ᴀₘ48	E	GEM	20
314	10	Tu.	6 29	D	4 27	A	9 58	32	17 13	3¾	4	11ᴘₘ01	C	12ᴘₘ30	E	CAN	21
315	11	W.	6 30	D	4 26	A	9 56	32	17 29	4¾	5¼	— —	–	1 06	D	LEO	22
316	12	Th.	6 31	D	4 25	A	9 54	32	17 46	6	6¼	12ᴀₘ02	C	1 38	D	LEO	23
317	13	Fr.	6 32	D	4 24	A	9 52	31	18 02	7	7¼	1 02	C	2 07	D	LEO	24
318	14	Sa.	6 34	D	4 23	A	9 49	31	18 17	7¾	8	2 00	D	2 34	D	VIR	25
319	15	**D**	6 35	D	4 22	A	9 47	31	18 33	8½	9	2 58	D	3 02	C	VIR	26
320	16	M.	6 36	D	4 21	A	9 45	31	18 47	9¼	9¾	3 55	D	3 29	C	VIR	27
321	17	Tu.	6 37	D	4 21	A	9 44	31	19 02	9¾	10¼	4 52	E	3 58	B	VIR	28
322	18	W.	6 39	D	4 20	A	9 41	31	19 16	10½	11	5 49	E	4 30	B	LIB	0
323	19	Th.	6 40	D	4 19	A	9 39	30	19 30	11	11½	6 46	E	5 04	B	LIB	1
324	20	Fr.	6 41	D	4 18	A	9 37	30	19 44	11¾	—	7 42	E	5 43	B	OPH	2
325	21	Sa.	6 42	D	4 18	A	9 36	30	19 58	12¼	12¼	8 37	E	6 28	B	OPH	3
326	22	**D**	6 43	D	4 17	A	9 34	30	20 11	1	1	9 29	E	7 17	B	SAG	4
327	23	M.	6 45	D	4 16	A	9 31	29	20 23	1½	1¾	10 17	E	8 12	B	SAG	5
328	24	Tu.	6 46	D	4 16	A	9 30	29	20 36	2¼	2½	11 01	E	9 11	B	SAG	6
329	25	W.	6 47	D	4 15	A	9 28	29	20 47	3	3¼	11ᴀₘ41	E	10 13	C	CAP	7
330	26	Th.	6 48	D	4 15	A	9 27	29	20 59	4	4¼	12ᴘₘ18	D	11ᴘₘ19	C	CAP	8
331	27	Fr.	6 49	E	4 14	A	9 25	28	21 10	4¾	5¼	12 52	D	— —	–	AQU	9
332	28	Sa.	6 50	E	4 14	A	9 24	28	21 21	5¾	6¼	1 26	D	12ᴀₘ26	D	AQU	10
333	29	**D**	6 51	E	4 13	A	9 22	28	21 31	6¾	7¼	2 00	C	1 36	D	PSC	11
334	30	M.	6 53	E	4 13	A	9 20	27	21 s.41	7¾	8	2ᴘₘ35	C	2ᴀₘ49	D	PSC	12

NOVEMBER hath 30 days. 1998

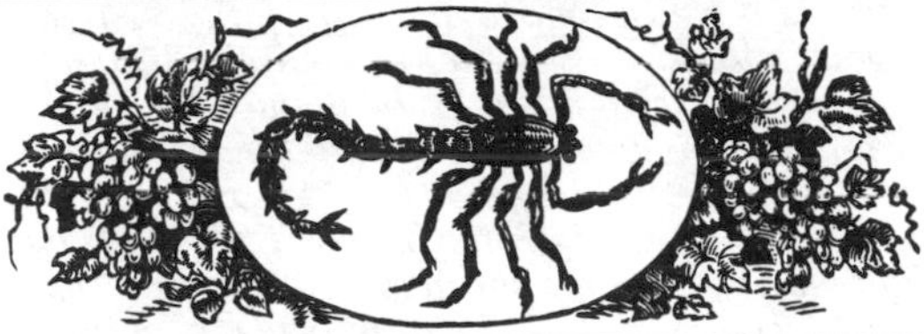

Now is the time for the burning of the leaves.
They go to the fire; the nostril pricks with smoke
Wandering slowly into a weeping mist.
Brittle and blotched, ragged and rotten sheaves!
– Laurence Binyon

D. M.	D. W.	Dates, Feasts, Fasts, Aspects, Tide Heights	Weather ↓
1	D	22nd S. af. P. • All Saints • ☾ on Eq. • {10.6 / 10.8	*In*
2	M.	All Souls • *Flowers in bloom late in autumn indicate a bad winter.* • {11.3 / 11.1	*the*
3	Tu.	☌ ♄ ☾ • ☾ at perig. • Election Day •	*mountains,*
4	W.	Full Beaver ○ • Tomb of King Tut discovered, 1922 • Tides {12.4 / 11.5 •	*the*
5	Th.	Eight teams joined together to form the American Football League, 1959 • {12.5 / — •	*first*
6	Fr.	Adolph Sax born, 1814 • *Music is the poetry of the air.* • Tides {11.3 / 12.4 •	*snow*
7	Sa.	New Jersey became first state to allow girls to play little league baseball, 1973 • {11.0 / 12.1 •	*is*
8	D	23rd S. af. P. • ☾ rides high • {10.6 / 11.5 •	*falling;*
9	M.	First issue of *The Atlantic Monthly* hit the newsstands, 1857 • {10.1 / 10.8 •	*geese*
10	Tu.	St. Leo the Great • The *Edmund Fitzgerald* sank, 1975 • {9.7 / 10.2	*are*
11	W.	St. Martin • Veterans Day • ☾ at ☊ • ☿ Gr. Elong (23° E.) •	
12	Th.	*If All Saints brings out winter, St. Martin brings out Indian summer.* • {9.3 / 9.4 •	*heading*
13	Fr.	☌ ♂ ☾ • ♃ stat. • *You never know your luck.* •	*south.*
14	Sa.	☾ on Eq. • Dow Jones closed above 1,000 mark, first time in 76 years, 1972 •	*We*
15	D	24th S. af. P. • Georgia O'Keefe born, 1887 • {9.7 / 9.4	*pause*
16	M.	6 inches snow, Tucson, Ariz., 1958 • Suez Canal opened, 1869 • {9.9 / 9.4 •	*at*
17	Tu.	St. Hugh of Lincoln • ☾ at apo. • August Mobius born, 1790 •	*our*
18	W.	St. Hilda • New ● • Tides {10.2 / 9.4 •	*feast*
19	Th.	Lincoln delivered his short speech at Gettysburg, Pa., 1863 • Tommy Dorsey born, 1905 •	*to*
20	Fr.	☌ ☿ ☾ • Edwin Powell Hubble born, 1889 • {10.3 / — •	*hear*
21	Sa.	☿ stat. • *As November 21, so the winter.* • Tides {9.3 / 10.2 •	*their*
22	D	25th S. af. P. • ☾ runs low • Tides {9.2 / 10.1 •	*loud*
23	M.	St. Clement • First jukebox installed, San Francisco, Calif., 1889 •	*calling,*
24	Tu.	☌ ♆ ☾ • ☌ ♅ ☾ • Scott Joplin born, 1868 • Tides {9.0 / 9.8 •	*a*
25	W.	*Loyalty to a petrified opinion never yet broke a chain or freed a human soul.* •	*forkful*
26	Th.	Thanksgiving • ☾ at ☋ • Tommy Dorsey died, 1956 • {9.1 / 9.7 •	*of*
27	Fr.	☌ ♃ ☾ • Bat Masterson born, 1853 • Tides {9.3 / 9.7 •	*turkey*
28	Sa.	First skywriting, "Hello USA," written over New York City, 1922 •	*halfway*
29	D	1st S. in Advent • ☾ on Eq. • {10.3 / 10.1 •	*to our*
30	M.	St. Andrew • ☌ ♇ ☉ • ☌ ♄ ☾ • {10.9 / 10.4	*mouth.*

I don't make jokes — I just watch the government and report the facts. –Will Rogers

Farmer's Calendar

A big blow last night: winds up to 40 miles per hour, the report this morning says. All night, the wind galloped and shouted about the house with a racket like world war. Soldiers recall that going into battle you least expect the noise. The sound of battle, they write, is more than the sounds of the particular things that must make it up: guns, cries, machinery, violent motion. Battle has a strange noise of its own, greater than all these.

So it is with a high wind. You can analyze its noise only so far. You can hear the trees being bent, the wind boiling around the corners of the house. You can hear doors banging, windows rattling, the banshee wail of a loose piece of roofing metal. But over all is a wild orchestral roar — the sound of the wind itself.

The worst of it is, you can't sleep. There is something in a strong wind by night that gets under the lid of your brain, just as it does with your window shutters, and makes rest impossible. I can sleep in snow and rain and even in the perpetual emergency that is night in a great city. But let the wind blow hard, and I find I can do nothing but lie there and listen to it. It's not all suffering, though. Windborne sleeplessness, for one thing, is good medicine against self-congratulation. Over and over again, you think of every stupid thing you have ever done, said, believed, and wanted. That's bad. Then you think of every stupid thing you have *not* done, said, and so on. That's far worse. In the end, if you can, you do best to give yourself up to the gale. Tomorrow morning, the world will look like Fifth Avenue after the parade has passed.

1998   DECEMBER, The Twelfth Month

Look for Mercury in the east before dawn from the 11th to the 26th. This innermost planet floats below the crescent Moon on the 16th and above it the next morning. Jupiter, currently the night's most brilliant "star," and bright Saturn well to its left are now both high in the sky at nightfall and well placed throughout the night. The Moon keeps Jupiter company on the 24th and passes Saturn on the 27th. The winter solstice occurs on the 21st, at 8:56 P.M., EST. While members of the mass media correctly announce this as the shortest day, the earliest sunset occurred two weeks earlier, and afternoon daylight is already growing longer.

○	Full Moon	3rd day	10th hour	19th minute
☾	Last Quarter	10th day	12th hour	53rd minute
●	New Moon	18th day	17th hour	42nd minute
☽	First Quarter	26th day	5th hour	46th minute

Times are given in Eastern Standard Time.

For an explanation of this page, see "How to Use This Almanac," page 34; for values of Key Letters, see Time Correction Tables, page 214.

Day of Year	Day of Month	Day of Week	☉ Rises h. m.	Key	☉ Sets h. m.	Key	Length of Days h. m.	Sun Fast m.	Declination of Sun ° '	Full Sea Boston A.M.	Full Sea Boston P.M.	☽ Rises h. m.	Key	☽ Sets h. m.	Key	☽ Place	☽ Age
335	1	Tu.	6 54	E	4 13	A	9 19	27	21s.50	8½	9	3ᴹ13	C	4ᴹ03	E	CET	13
336	2	W.	6 55	E	4 12	A	9 17	26	21 59	9½	10	3 56	B	5 17	E	ARI	14
337	3	Th.	6 56	E	4 12	A	9 16	26	22 08	10¼	11	4 45	B	6 31	E	TAU	15
338	4	Fr.	6 57	E	4 12	A	9 15	26	22 16	11	11¾	5 39	B	7 41	E	TAU	16
339	5	Sa.	6 58	E	4 12	A	9 14	25	22 23	—	12	6 39	B	8 44	E	GEM	17
340	6	D	6 59	E	4 12	A	9 13	25	22 30	12¾	12¾	7 42	B	9 39	E	GEM	18
341	7	M.	7 00	E	4 12	A	9 12	24	22 37	1½	1¾	8 46	C	10 26	E	CAN	19
342	8	Tu.	7 01	E	4 11	A	9 10	24	22 44	2½	2¾	9 50	C	11 05	E	CAN	20
343	9	W.	7 01	E	4 11	A	9 10	24	22 50	3¼	3½	10 51	C	11ᴬ40	D	LEO	21
344	10	Th.	7 02	E	4 12	A	9 10	23	22 56	4¼	4½	11ᴹ51	C	12ᴾ10	D	LEO	22
345	11	Fr.	7 03	E	4 12	A	9 09	23	23 00	5¼	5½	— —	—	12 38	D	VIR	23
346	12	Sa.	7 04	E	4 12	A	9 08	22	23 05	6¼	6½	12ᴬ49	D	1 06	C	VIR	24
347	13	D	7 05	E	4 12	A	9 07	22	23 09	7	7½	1 47	D	1 33	C	VIR	25
348	14	M.	7 06	E	4 12	A	9 06	21	23 13	7¾	8¼	2 44	E	2 01	C	VIR	26
349	15	Tu.	7 06	E	4 12	A	9 06	21	23 16	8½	9	3 41	E	2 31	B	LIB	27
350	16	W.	7 07	E	4 13	A	9 06	20	23 19	9¼	9¾	4 39	E	3 04	B	LIB	28
351	17	Th.	7 08	E	4 13	A	9 05	20	23 21	10	10½	5 36	E	3 42	B	SCO	29
352	18	Fr.	7 08	E	4 13	A	9 05	19	23 23	10¾	11¼	6 31	E	4 25	B	OPH	0
353	19	Sa.	7 09	E	4 14	A	9 05	19	23 24	11¼	11¾	7 25	E	5 13	B	SAG	1
354	20	D	7 09	E	4 14	A	9 05	18	23 25	—	12	8 15	E	6 06	B	SAG	2
355	21	M.	7 10	E	4 15	A	9 05	18	23 25	12½	12½	9 01	E	7 04	B	SAG	3
356	22	Tu.	7 10	E	4 15	A	9 05	17	23 25	1¼	1¼	9 43	E	8 06	B	CAP	4
357	23	W.	7 11	E	4 16	A	9 05	17	23 25	2	2	10 21	D	9 10	C	CAP	5
358	24	Th.	7 11	E	4 16	A	9 05	16	23 24	2¾	2¾	10 56	D	10 17	C	AQU	6
359	25	Fr.	7 12	E	4 17	A	9 05	16	23 23	3½	3¾	11ᴬ29	D	11ᴾ24	C	AQU	7
360	26	Sa.	7 12	E	4 17	A	9 05	15	23 21	4½	4¾	12ᴾ01	D	— —	—	PSC	8
361	27	D	7 12	E	4 18	A	9 06	15	23 18	5¼	5¾	12 34	C	12ᴬ33	D	CET	9
362	28	M.	7 13	E	4 19	A	9 06	14	23 15	6¼	6¾	1 09	C	1 43	E	PSC	10
363	29	Tu.	7 13	E	4 20	A	9 07	14	23 12	7¼	7¾	1 48	B	2 55	E	ARI	11
364	30	W.	7 13	E	4 20	A	9 07	13	23 09	8¼	8¾	2 32	B	4 07	E	TAU	12
365	31	Th.	7 13	E	4 21	A	9 08	13	23s.04	9	9¾	3ᴹ22	B	5ᴹ18	E	TAU	13

Give human nature reverence for the sake
Of One who bore it, making it divine
With the ineffable tenderness of God.
— *John Greenleaf Whittier*

Farmer's Calendar

Five miles down the road is a little, one-horse ski area that caters to locals: beginners, families, school groups. It's not a resort. You can ski, and you can eat a hamburger: no condominiums, no shopping, no fine dining. A nice place. Early in December, before the real winter storms begin, they roll out their snowmaking guns. I like to watch them in action.

On the first clear nights to get sharply cold, the snow guns appear. They look like large, ungainly water birds: storks or pelicans lined up at intervals on the ski trails that climb the hill. The snow guns are, I guess, essentially powerful sprayers, lawn sprinklers on steroids. They spray a fine stream of water 50 to 60 feet into the dry, cold air, where it freezes and falls back to the ground as snow in brilliant, shimmering parabolas. Under the night lights, snowmaking looks like a fireworks show: the glorious Fourth strayed into the wrong season. At my ski area, they run the snow guns all night long, and in the morning, they're ready for business.

It's the damnedest thing, too, when you think about it. Snow, at first, would seem to be a brute fact, the simple, inescapable condition of winter in the North. You love it or you hate it. But no: It's not snow that matters, it's where the snow is. If nature doesn't furnish snow where we want it, we'll figure out a way to put it there, even if doing so means we have to spend millions to make our own. At the same time, 100 feet away, we're spending more millions to *remove* snow from other places, like roads and parking lots. What better image for the mind of man: so smart, so dumb?

D.M.	D.W.	Dates, Feasts, Fasts, Aspects, Tide Heights	Weather ↓
1	Tu.	☿ in inf. ♂ • First "Christmas Club," Carlisle, Pa., 1909 {11.5 / 10.7	Bright
2	W.	☾ perig. • Barney Clark received first artificial heart, 1982 {12.0 / 10.9	and
3	Th.	Full ○ Cold • Oberlin College, first true co-ed college, opened, 1833 {12.3 / 10.9	bitter
4	Fr.	*A Streetcar Named Desire opened in New York City, 1947* {12.4 / 10.9	before
5	Sa.	☾ rides high • Prohibition ended with ratification of the 21st Amendment, 1933	the
6	D	2ⁿᵈ S. in Advent • Dave Brubeck born, 1920 {10.7 / 11.9	cold
7	M.	St. Nicholas • Pearl Harbor attacked, 1941 • Larry Bird born, 1956	eases.
8	Tu.	☾ at ☍ • *The history of the world is but the biography of great men.* {10.0 / 10.7	Snow
9	W.	U.S. Golf Association legalized steel-shaft golf clubs, 1926 {9.7 / 10.0	flurries
10	Th.	70° F, New York City, 1946 • Emily Dickinson born, 1830 {9.4 / 9.5	blow
11	Fr.	☿ stat. • U.S. soldiers camped in Arizona attacked by wild longhorn bulls, 1846	in
12	Sa.	☾ on Eq. • ♂♂☾ • George Grant patented the golf tee, 1899 {9.2 / 8.8	on
13	D	3ʳᵈ S. in Advent • Tides {9.3 / 8.8	boreal
14	M.	St. Lucy • First day of Chanukah • ☾ at apo.	breezes.
15	Tu.	Bill of Rights ratified, 1791 • *They have rights who dare maintain them.* {9.7 / 8.9	The
16	W.	♂☿☾ • Ember Day • Boston Tea Party, 1773 {9.9 / 9.0	Sun
17	Th.	Orville and Wilbur Wright made first successful airplane flights at Kitty Hawk, N.C., 1903 {10.1 / 9.1	is
18	Fr.	New ● • Ember Day • Thirteenth Amendment ratified, 1865 {10.3 / 9.1	so
19	Sa.	☿ Gr. Elong. (22° W.) • Ember Day • Halcyon Days {10.3 / 9.2	weak
20	D	4ᵗʰ S. in Advent • ☾ runs low • Tides {10.4	even
21	M.	St. Thomas • Winter Solstice • ♂♆☾ • {9.2 / 10.4	charity
22	Tu.	♂♁☾ • Beware the Pogonip. • Connie Mack born, 1862	freezes.
23	W.	☾ at ☍ • Federal Reserve System created, 1913 {9.4 / 10.2	But
24	Th.	"Silent Night, Holy Night" composed, 1818 • Tides {9.5 / 10.1	remember
25	Fr.	Christmas Day • ♂♃☾ • Tides {9.6 / 9.9	the
26	Sa.	St. Stephen • ☾ on Eq. • Boxing Day (Canada) {9.8 / 9.7	star,
27	D	1ˢᵗ S. af. Ch. • ♂♄☾ • Tides {10.1 / 9.7	and
28	M.	St. John • Holy Innocents • *Dare to be wise.* • Texas statehood, 1848 {10.5 / 9.7	the
29	Tu.	Gas lighting was installed at the White House, 1848 • Rudyard Kipling born, 1865	stable,
30	W.	♄ stat. • ☾ perig. {11.3 / 10.0	and
31	Th.	*Each day the world is born anew For him who takes it rightly.* —Lowell {11.7 / 10.2	Jesus.

"We're looking for people

by Alvin Tresselt, *Dean of Faculty*

IF YOU WANT TO WRITE and see your work published, I can't think of a better way to do it than writing books and stories for children and teenagers. Ideas flow naturally, right out of your own life. And while it's still a challenge, the odds of getting that first, unforgettable check from a children's publisher are better than they are from any other kind of publisher I know.

Your words will never sound as sweet as they do from the lips of a child reading your books and stories. And the joy of creating books and stories that truly reach young people is an experience you won't find anywhere else.

A surprisingly big market

But, that's not all. The financial rewards go far beyond most people's expectations, because there's a surprisingly big market out there for writers who are trained to tap it. More than $1.5 *billion* worth of children's books are purchased annually, and almost 500 publishers of books and 600 publishers of magazines related to children and teenagers buy freelance writing. That means that *there are thousands of manuscripts being purchased every month of the year!*

Yet two big questions bedevil nearly every would-be writer…"Am I really qualified?" and "How can I get started?"

"Am I really qualified?"

At the Institute of Children's Literature®, this is our definition of a "qualified person": someone with an aptitude for writing who can take constructive criticism, learn from it, and turn it into a professional performance.

To help us spot potential authors, we've developed a reliable test for writing aptitude based upon our 27 years of experience. It's free, and we don't charge for our evalua-

tion. Those who pass are eligible to enroll and receive our promise:

You will complete at least one manuscript for submission to an editor or publisher by the time you finish the course.

You learn by corresponding with your own personal instructor—a nationally published writer or professional editor—in the privacy and comfort of your own home.

One-on-one training with your own instructor

This is the way I work with my students, and my fellow instructors work more or less the same way:

• When you're ready—at your own time and your own pace—you mail your assignment to me.

• I read it and reread it to get everything out of it that you've put into it.

• Then I edit your assignment just the way a publishing house editor would—if he or she had the time.

Writing for Children and Teenagers is recommended for college credits by the Connecticut Board for State Academic Awards and approved by the Connecticut Commissioner of Higher Education.

*The students' statements in this ad were provided voluntarily by them, without remuneration, from 1990 to 1997.

to write children's books"

• I mail it back with a detailed letter explaining my comments. I tell you what your strong points and weaknesses are, and just what you can do to improve.

It's a matter of push and pull. You push and I pull, and between us both, you learn how to write and how to market your writing.

"I hit pay dirt"

This method really works. The proof of the pudding is offered by our students.

"My first two attempts met with rejection, and on the third, I hit pay dirt with *Listen Magazine*," says Marjorie Kashdin, East Northport, NY. "My instructor was invaluable…It's not everyone who has his own 'guardian editor!'"

"I was attracted by the fact that you require an aptitude test," says Nikki Arko, Raton, NM. "Other schools sign you up as long as you have the money to pay, regardless of talent or potential."

"…a little bird…has just been given…freedom"

"The course has helped me more than I can say," writes Jody Drueding, Boston, MA. "It's as if a little bird that was locked up inside of me has just been given the freedom of the garden."

Romy Squeri, Havertown, PA says, "I met two of your students in my critique group and realized that they were the best writers there."

"I'd take the course again in a heartbeat!"

"I'd take the course again in a heartbeat!" says Tonya Tingey, Woodruff, UT. "It made my dream a reality."

"…it is comforting to know that there are still people out there who deliver what they promise," writes Meline Knago, Midland, TX. "The Institute is everything it says it is—and maybe even more."

Of course, not everyone gets published; we simply promise you the best training available.

FREE—Writing Aptitude Test, illustrated brochure, and *How to Manage Your Writing Time*

We offer a free Writing Aptitude Test to people who are interested in writing for children and teenagers, and we don't charge for our professional evaluation of it.

We also offer a free, illustrated brochure describing our course, *Writing for Children and Teenagers,* and the current market for children's literature.

In addition, you'll receive a free copy of *How to Manage Your Writing Time*.

If your test reveals a true aptitude for writing, you'll be eligible to enroll. But that's up to you.

There is no obligation.

Get all three free

Institute of Children's Literature
93 Long Ridge Road
West Redding, CT 06896-0812

Yes, please send me your free Writing Aptitude Test, illustrated brochure, and *How to Manage Your Writing Time*. I understand I'm under no obligation, and no salesperson will visit me.

Please circle one and print name clearly:

Mr.   Mrs.   Ms.   Miss   C3562

Name

Street

City

State   Zip

— — COPYRIGHT © ICL 1997, A DIVISION OF THE INSTITUTE, INC. — —

"By God, I Believe I've

James Marshall (below) *discovered gold while supervising construction of Sutter's mill. It did not take long for headlines such as this one* (background) *from the* California Herald *to spread gold fever across the country.*

There was so much gold in

California's hills in 1848 that

miners could pry chunks of it

from rocks with a jackknife.

It seemed — at first —

that there would be plenty

for everyone.

by Dayton Duncan

John Sutter (right) *had ambitious dreams of creating an agricultural empire on his prospering ranch of 50,000 acres before gold was discovered on his land in 1848.*

Found a Gold Mine"

ASK MOST AMERICANS TO NAME THE EVENTFUL YEAR WHEN THE DISCOVERY OF GOLD in California transformed the nation, and they'll probably say 1849. Even San Francisco's professional football team preserves '49 as the year to remember.

But it was 150 years ago, in 1848, that the gold was first discovered. It all began inauspiciously enough on the morning of January 24, 1848, on the south fork of the American River, a fast-running stream that courses down the western slope of the Sierra Nevada. There a small mill was being built for John Sutter, a Swiss-born entrepreneur trying to establish an agricultural empire of wheat, cattle, and orchards on 50,000 acres centered around what is now Sacramento.

James W. Marshall, a former carpenter from New Jersey who had drifted west four years earlier, was supervising the sawmill's construction. That day, as he inspected a ditch for the mill's tailrace, Marshall noticed something glinting under a few inches of water. He stooped to pick it up. The dull yellow metal consisted mostly of thin flakes, though some of it was in small grains, the largest being about "half the size of a pea."

"Hey, boys," he called out to the others as he placed his tiny treasure in a crease in the crown of his hat. "By God, I believe I've found a gold mine."

If Marshall and his crew were excited by the prospects of the discovery, it did not prevent them from continuing their work on the sawmill. Not until four days later, when it was time to get supplies, did Marshall show his employer what he'd found. The two consulted Sutter's battered encyclopedia to learn how to test the sample's mineral content. It was nearly pure gold. **(c o n t i n u e d)**

91

Above left: Sutter's sawmill, which prospectors later converted into living quarters.

Above right: Sam Brannan, a Mormon elder, was a shrewd businessman who became, briefly, one of California's wealthiest men.

Back at the river, work continued on the mill. The crew members were mostly Mormons, like young Azariah Smith, age 19, who had arrived in California during the Mexican-American war. Although they were desperately trying to earn some hard cash so they could join their families in Utah, the idea of simply abandoning the construction project for full-time prospecting apparently never occurred to them.

"Mr. Marshall grants us the privilege of picking up gold [during] odd spells and Sundays," Azariah noted in his diary in mid-February. "Today I picked up a little more of the root of all evil." For the "privilege," Marshall was charging the workers half of their gold.

By mid-March, the mill was completed. More significantly, word of the gold discovery had started to seep out across central California, despite Sutter's and Marshall's desire for secrecy. Another group of Latter Day Saints, after visiting their brethren at the sawmill and learning of the gold, had discovered an even richer lode farther downstream at Mormon Island. Rumors had reached the seacoast, but most people discounted them.

Sam Brannan was among the few who decided to check out the rumors firsthand. He was the leader of a Mormon colony in California,

Left: Wagon trains of gold seekers made the arduous journey overland to California.

Kill Foot Pain Dead!

Total Relief Guaranteed–Risk-Free.

Don't blame foot pain on your shoes! Most foot pain comes from misalignment of the bones in your feet.

Foot pain begins when your foot's balance and natural elasticity is gone. Corns, calluses, bunions, even hammertoes can develop, as well as toe cramps, fallen arches, burning skin, tender blisters, flaking and chafing. Ankle, leg, knee, hip - even lower back pain, can result from improper foot alignment. And when your feet hurt, you hurt all over.

Now! No More Foot Pain. Guaranteed!

Featherspring® Foot Supports, a remarkable discovery from Europe are unlike anything you have ever tried. First, they are *custom-formed* for your feet and your feet only! Secondly, they help restore and maintain the elastic support you had when you were younger. They actually help realign your feet, while absorbing shock and relieving pain.

© Featherspring, 712 N. 34th Street, Seattle, WA 98103-8881

For over 40 years, Feathersprings have brought blessed relief to more than 3,000,000 foot pain sufferers world wide. No other foot support has ever given so much relief to so many people.

It doesn't matter whether you are a woman or man, whether your feet are size 4 or 14, what width your foot is, how low or high your arches are, how old you are or how long you've had foot pain... we know Feathersprings will work for you.

Guaranteed To Kill Your Foot Pain Dead! We'll Prove It To You Risk Free!

If you are bothered by aches and pains of the feet, legs, or lower back, we state without reservation that Feathersprings will bring you relief or *you risk nothing*.

Send today for FREE Fact Kit.

Cut out and mail in the coupon below TODAY for FREE information, including details of our risk-free money back guarantee.

Custom–Formed Feathersprings end foot pain... once and for all!

publisher of the *California Star*, and co-owner of a store at Sutter's Fort — and, taking full advantage of all three positions once he saw that the rumors were true, he also became the gold rush's first millionaire.

As California's highest-ranking Mormon, Brannan announced that he would collect the church's tithe at Mormon Island and Coloma, the site of Sutter's mill. Azariah Smith, now reporting in his diary that he had amassed nearly $400 in his diggings, was among those who willingly handed over their percentage. The money, however, never made it from Brannan to church headquarters. When an angry Brigham Young wrote to demand the "Lord's money," Brannan reportedly answered that he wouldn't turn it over without a receipt "signed by the Lord." Within three years, the church excommunicated him.

At Mormon Island and Coloma, Brannan opened new stores and stocked them with picks, shovels, and other supplies he knew would be indispensable to prospectors. Then he returned to San Francisco to use his newspaper and his flamboyant personality to make sure his stores had plenty of customers. On May 12, Brannan began walking the streets of the small town of 800 people, waving a quinine bottle filled with gold dust and shouting, "Gold! Gold! Gold from the American River!"

It worked. Within two weeks, even Brannan's competitor, the *Californian*, was reporting that the territory from San Francisco "to the base of the Sierra Nevada resounds to the sordid cry of 'gold! Gold!! GOLD!!!' while the field is left half planted, the house half built, and everything neglected but the manufacture of shovels and pick-axes."

By mid-June, three quarters of the men living in San Francisco had left for the gold fields. At the town's school, the teacher had locked the doors and even taken a few pupils with him to go prospecting.

> "The people are running over the country and picking [gold] out of the earth here and there, just as a thousand hogs, let loose in a forest, would root up ground nuts ..."

Gold samples soon reached Monterey, where the Reverend Walter Colton reported sailors jumping ship, though it meant forfeiting four years' pay, and a whole platoon of soldiers deserting their fort. "The people are running over the country and picking [gold] out of the earth here and there, just as a thousand hogs, let loose in a forest, would root up ground nuts," Colton wrote. "One old woman declared she would never again break an egg or kill a chicken, without first examining yolk and gizzard."

Meanwhile, the fortune seekers were reaping bonanzas. They had no previous mining experience, but it didn't seem to matter. They found gold in eddies and sandbars, wedged in rocks, and lodged in places it had been sitting in for centuries, as if it had

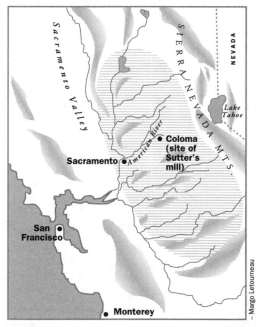

The 400-mile-long area where gold was being mined is indicated by the shaded lines on the map.

– Margo Letourneau

"They *gasped* when I sprayed <u>beer</u> on my lawn. But you should see my golf-course green grass now!"

MILWAUKEE (Special) That's right — I spray beer on my lawn, and use baby shampoo, ammonia, and instant tea to grow mouth watering vegetables and flowers prettier than a florist!

My name is Jerry Baker, and I'm known as America's Master Gardener.® I've got hundreds of amazing lawn and garden secrets and "make-it-yourself" home remedies I'd like to share with you. The best part is *you'll save money since everything you need to make them is found in your home!*

Your Plants Will Love 'Em, Too

Since 1964, I've taught over 19.8 million people how to beautify their yards and gardens using common household products on my national radio show – *On the Garden Line*, on *Good Morning America*, *The Tonight Show*...in *Sports Illustrated, Mature Outlook*...and in my 40 best-selling lawn and gardening books.

Now, you can get an *extraordinary collection* of my all-time favorite tonics for super lawns, trees, shrubs, flowers, vegetables, roses and houseplants in my new *Year 'Round Garden Magic Program*. This jam-packed program reveals over 200 of my amazing secrets like how a little corn syrup and baby shampoo will invigorate your trees.

Plus, you'll learn how...
- Instant tea energizes flowers
- Ashes make bulbs bloom bigger
- Roses love banana peels
- Laundry soap controls crabgrass
- Whiskey – the key to houseplant success
- Tabasco Sauce® stimulates perennials
- Pantyhose produces heftier tomatoes

Cures For Your Toughest Gardening Problems

You'll also learn that...
- Beer bombs lawn thatch
- Coke® really gets your compost a cookin'
- Epsom salts power packs soil
- Mouthwash fights off lawn disease
- Chewin' tobacco sends pests a packin'

Have Fun, Save Money and Enjoy a *Showcase* Yard!

Do my 200+ secrets really work? You bet! Enthusiastic gardeners write: "Our flowers never stood so tall"..."My lawn is magnificent... great program... and very, **very** inexpensive to boot"..."Giant produce in giant quantities." I love hearing how much fun people are having mixing up my homemade formulas, and *how much money they are saving* by using common household products.

Save 67% and Receive 4 <u>FREE</u> Gifts

My *Year 'Round Garden Magic Program* is just $9.95 (a $12.95-value). Plus, I'll send you my step-by-step "Growing Power" cassette tape (a $9.95-value), FREE. *And, if you order within 7 days,* I'll send you 3 extra FREE gifts – a "Garden Secrets" Summary Chart, handy Calendar Reminder Stickers and a handsome carrying case (a $6.95-value). That's a total value of $29.85 for just $9.95, a 67% savings!

TO ORDER: Simply print your name, address and the words "Garden Secrets" on a piece of paper, and mail it with only $9.95 plus $2.95 S&H (total – **$12.90**) to Year Round Garden Magic, 50222 Pontiac Trail, Dept. 1274, Wixom, MI 48393. VISA/ MasterCard send card number, signature, and expiration date.

Want to save even more? Order an extra copy for family and friends for only $20.00 postage paid.

There's <u>no risk</u> - you're protected by my <u>100% money-back guarantee for 90 days.</u> **So order today!**

just been waiting patiently for someone to come along and scoop it up.

Nuggets weighing five to eight ounces (gold was worth $10 an ounce at the time) were pried loose with jackknives. A greenhorn from Los Angeles, using only a spoon to dig, filled a wooden bowl with gold until it was too heavy to lift. A farmer wrote home to Missouri that "my girls can make from $5 to $25 per day washing gold in pans." His own average, he added, "will be about $150 a day."

A man who had once mined gold in Georgia showed up and began using a rocker, a relatively simple cradlelike device that sifts larger quantities of sand, dirt, and rock from a riverbed. Soon others were imitating him, many of them hiring local Indians to do the shoveling. In one week, two men employing a hundred Indians and four white laborers cleared $17,000.

California's residents were amazed at their good fortune, particularly the 2,700 Americans who had emigrated there over the previous decade seeking only fertile land and a healthy climate. "We are in our infancy in wealth," wrote James Frazier Reed, whose own family had barely survived the horrible ordeal of the Donner Party two years earlier to reach California. "The poor man in the course of 60 days is raised into comparative ease, and many become wealthy. Plenty for all, for years to come."

In July, ships reached the Hawaiian Islands with credible accounts of the gold discovery; as hundreds of people embarked for California, the gold report sailed on toward China. In August, two thirds of Ore-

gon's male population began heading south when they learned the news. Around the same time, it was spreading through Mexico and on toward South America. Boats set out from seaports in Peru and Chile.

In the aftermath of the war with Mexico, California's affairs were being administered by Colonel Richard B. Mason, the temporary military governor. (The treaty ceding California, New Mexico, and the Southwest to the United States had actually been signed in far-off Guadalupe Hidalgo nine days after Marshall's discovery, by dignitaries unaware of what he had found.) Mason, in turn, was relying heavily on his young adjutant, 28-year-old Lieutenant William Tecumseh Sherman. With the soldiers deserting and all but one of the officers' servants having disappeared — one of them with Sherman's favorite shotgun — the lieutenant recommended a personal inspection of the gold fields in midsummer.

Mason and Sherman were amazed at what they saw. The gold district now stretched for 400 miles along the western front of the Sierras, and there were already 4,000 miners in the region, half of them Indians. They were pulling out up to $50,000 a day in gold — enough, he predicted, to "pay the cost of the war with Mexico a hundred times over." He was equally surprised by the lack of crime. Men slept in brush shelters or the open air, some of them with thousands of dollars' worth of gold, yet reports of thefts or robberies were nonexistent, which Mason attributed to the fact that "the gold is so abundant that for the present there is room and enough for all."

Lieutenant William Tecumseh Sherman (above) inspected the gold fields for a report to President Polk.

Sherman was struck by the exorbitant prices of supplies. A meal cost $3. Shoes, if a store had any, brought $10. Spades and shovels had skyrocketed from $1 to $10 apiece; at one place, $50 had been offered. Sam Brannan's strategically located stores, Sherman calculated, were clearing $2,000 a day in profits.

The two officers hurried back to Monterey, wrote out a lengthy official report to President James K. Polk, and sent it with a courier who boarded a ship to Washington on August 30. With it, as proof that their words weren't fiction, they sent a tea caddy packed with 230 ounces of gold. Sherman went back to the gold fields, ostensibly to keep an eye on things, although he and some other officers also started their own store at Coloma. Each of the partners, he admitted in his memoirs, quickly made a $1,500 profit off a $500 investment.

Mason and Sherman's report did not reach the

Early miners used any available tool to dig for gold; later, more-sophisticated equipment such as this sluice box (opposite) were put to use.

capital until late November. Polk officially announced the discovery to America — and the world — in a special message to Congress on December 5, nearly 11 months after the discovery. The president put the tea caddy filled with gold on display at the War Department so no one could doubt what had been considered fanciful rumors and wild exaggerations.

"We have seen in our day manias, fevers, and excitements of all sorts," the *New York Express* wrote soon after Polk's message, "but . . . the fact is, this last gold news has unsettled the minds of even the most cautious and careful among us."

As 1848 drew to a close, people from every corner of the globe were busily making plans to converge on California. Some 89,000 arrived the next year, in the first big surge that will forever associate the gold rush with 1849. Even more came in subsequent years. All pursued the easy wealth that the lucky prospectors of 1848 had truthfully reported; but few achieved it.

Azariah Smith (below) left California with a modest sum in 1848, returning to San Francisco half a century later to attend the 50th anniversary celebration of the gold discovery.

Losers and Winners

Even some of those at the center of the 1848 bonanza were ruined in the end. Convinced that **James Marshall** had special "powers of divination," hordes of newcomers dogged his every movement, then threatened to lynch him when he failed to lead them to "color." Another mob chased him into hiding for standing up against the new miners' mistreatment of local Indians. **John Sutter's** domain was overrun by squatters who rustled his cattle, stripped his buildings, and took over his lands. "There is a saying that men will steal everything but a milestone and a millstone," he reflected ruefully. "They stole my millstones." After cheating Sutter out of some prime building lots in burgeoning Sacramento, **Sam Brannan** amassed a fortune in San Francisco real estate but soon lost it all in a series of misguided speculations. All three men — Marshall, Sutter, Brannan — died embittered and impoverished.

After going broke in a banking panic in San Francisco in the 1850s, **William Tecumseh Sherman** headed east in disappointment (not knowing that greater fame awaited him). "My

– California History Room, California State Library, Sacramento, California

opinion is the very nature of the country begets speculation, extravagance, failures, and rascality," he wrote upon his departure. "Everything is chance, everything is gambling, and I shall feel relieved when I am not dependent on the people of California for my repose."

But **Azariah Smith** left California a happy man. And, incredibly, he left it in 1848, while the pickings were still easy and the rest of the world was just starting to pant feverishly to be in his shoes. "I was homesick," he remembered later. "I wanted to see my mother, and I did not care whether there was gold in the locality or not."

He arrived in Utah at the end of September with $500 in gold. After reuniting with his parents, he went to Brigham Young, paid his tithe in person, and donated $1 for each of the Mormon church's 12 apostles plus something extra for the poor. For the next 50 years, except for short trips to attend church conferences in Salt Lake City, he never left his home for more than two nights in a row.

But in 1898, as one of four surviving witnesses of Marshall's great discovery, Azariah agreed to come to San Francisco for the 50th anniversary celebration. "I have never regretted leaving the mines, never wished myself back there," he told the *San Francisco Examiner* of the momentous year of discovery. "If I had stayed there, I would have been under the ground in a short time. By coming away, I have lived to be 69 years of age." He lived to age 83 before dying — contentedly — at home. □□

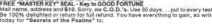

How to Hypnotize a Frog

I have two clear memories of watching someone hypnotize a frog. The first is of my father, ankle-deep in a pond with his pant legs rolled up, hypnotizing a large frog as he slowly crouched down to pick it up. The more recent is of my daughter and her cousin, then six and seven years old, hypnotizing frogs at a summer picnic.

I asked my daughter and her cousin, now both teenagers, if they remember hypnotizing the frogs. They both said that they *do* remember and that it worked. I knew *I* hadn't taught them this skill, so I concluded that the kids must have learned it directly from my father. Wanting to know more, I called him.

"Hi, Dad. How do you hypnotize a frog?" I asked.

"I don't know. How?" he replied. He thought I was telling a joke. He was silent, waiting for the punchline.

"No, Dad," I said. "Really, how *do* you hypnotize a frog?" More silence. I reminded him about the kids hypnotizing frogs at the picnic years ago. Finally, he remembered them doing it but said he hadn't taught them.

At this point, I became more determined. "Well, Dad, I know I remember something about you catching frogs. I'm sure of it. Something about red flannel . . ."

"Oh, I remember that!" At last I was getting somewhere. Dad continued, "You take a piece of red flannel and tie it to the end of a string; then you tie the other end of the string to a stick, like a fishing pole; then you dangle it in front of the frog's face, and the frog will bite the flannel and won't let go."

I searched my memories of childhood, trying to remember my sister and me catching frogs this way, but came up empty. "Does it really work?" I asked him.

In his dry Yankee way, he replied, "Don't know. Never tried it, just heard it."

Well, I now had an unexpected piece of frog folklore but not the one I was looking for. My next hunch was that my deceased father-in-law had been the source of the skill. One of my brothers-in-law thought it was their Aunt Martha in Maine who had taught them to do it one summer. I called my mother-in-law and she cleared up the mystery. It was Aunt Martha's husband who used to take the boys to a stream behind his house to catch frogs by hypnotizing them. She thought he had learned the trick from Maine fishermen, who caught frogs to use for bait.

This is how to hypnotize a frog:

First, put your hand out in front of you, palm outward and fingers together, as if you are signaling someone in front of you to stop. **Second,** start making small circles in the air with that hand.

a Frog (In a pinch, it'll work on certain cats, too.)

by Laraine Howard

– illustrated by Jim Carson

Third, walk slowly toward the frog, bringing your circling hand closer and closer to the frog's face.
Fourth, slowly crouch down as you approach the frog, keeping the circling motion going.

Fifth, pick up the frog with your free hand.

I don't know if I have the knack for hypnotizing frogs, but I once used this technique to catch a feral cat when I was working at our local humane society. The cat was barely more than a kitten and didn't look too wild, but as soon as its carrier was opened, the cat bolted across the quarantine room and attempted to run up the wall. Four of us were trying to catch it when it scrambled up a pile of boxes in the corner, standing on its hind legs and frantically scratching the walls trying to go higher.

I told the others I thought I could catch it. I felt pretty foolish as I walked toward the cat, slowly moving my hand in small circles in the air. I heard a snicker behind me but kept going. The cat remained motionless, watching my hand. When I got close enough, I laid my other hand on the scruff of its neck and lifted it off the pile of boxes.

My one fatal error in judgment was to discontinue the hand circles on the way to the quarantine cage. It was like carrying the Tasmanian Devil. I wondered if there was any way to get the cat into the cage and get my arm out before it became a bloody stump. In cats, I concluded, the hypnotic effect is short-lived.

While trying to track down the origins of frog hypnosis, I asked each person why he or she thought it worked. The answers ranged from the distraction theory to an explanation that a frog's eyes can't rotate in a complete circle and thus can't watch the whole movement of the hand, so the resulting confusion overwhelms its brain.

My own theory is that we look so ridiculous circling our hands in the air that frogs just sit there in amazement, dumbfounded.

P.S. Don't try to catch a prince this way. It doesn't work. □□

FOR *Crying Out Loud*

᛫[OR OTHERWISE]᛫

A woman stands at a sink. We can't see what she's doing, but she's slumped over a bit.
Her hair hides her face. She sniffles. Then her hand comes up and brushes her cheek. A tear?
She's crying. Has her husband been cross to her? Or is she peeling an onion?

BY JAMIE KAGELEIRY

Humans cry. There are unproven anecdotes of crying elephants and tearful golden retrievers, but humans are virtually the only creatures to shed emotional tears. Although Bartlett's *Familiar Quotations* has far fewer entries for *cry* and *crying* than it does for *love*, popular music relies heavily on the word (either using it in lyrics or evoking an emotion that moves you to tears). Until recently, scientific resources were scarce on this most elemental of human functions. There has been research on infant cries but not much about the rest of us. As Dr. William Frey (director of the Ramsey Dry Eye and Tear Research Center in St. Paul, Minnesota) and Jeffrey Kottler (author of *The Language of Tears*) have discovered, crying is no simple thing.

The woman at the sink, for instance. If we could scoop up that brushed tear and analyze it, we might know why she is crying. If her tears are due to a tiff with her husband, they will contain more proteins — complex elemental substances that include essential compounds such as enzymes or hormones — than if her eyes are merely irritated by peeling an onion. Though other scientists aren't sure yet, Frey thinks this difference means that "something unique happens when people cry emotional tears." Frey was able to isolate in emotional tears the hormone prolactin, which is released by the pituitary gland at times of intense emotion or stress and makes its way to the lachrymal (or tear) glands. Too much prolactin in your system can become toxic, so crying is a way of cleansing the body of this during stress, just as irritant tears help cleanse the eye of smoke, onion fumes, or a stray eyelash.

Women average 5.3 cries a month. When men cry, it's often hard to tell — usually their eyes brim, but not many tears escape down their face.

The fact that crying flushes away excess prolactin during stress probably accounts for the fact that 85 percent of women and 73 percent of men say they feel better after crying, and why some studies even indicate that men who do not cry, or who consider crying a sign of weakness, are more apt to suffer stress-related illnesses such as colitis.

Imagine the woman, let's name her Nadia, at the sink again. We've discovered that she's sad. Chances are, she cries emotional tears four times more often than her ogre of a husband. No surprise — women average 5.3 cries a month. When men cry, it's often hard to tell — usually their eyes brim, but not many tears escape down their face.

Before puberty, boys and girls cry about the same amount. Then, by some combination of a "big boys don't cry" culture (at least in this country) and biological differences, women pull way ahead. Men's and women's tear glands are structurally different, but there's something else that may cause women to cry more — that sneaky prolactin again. Not only is the hormone present during emotional times, it's crucial in promoting the secretion of milk. Women need prolactin to nurse their babies, and their bodies contain 60 percent more of it than do men's.

TIME IS A RIVER OF TEARS

So a woman stands crying. Only this time, it's not at a sink. It's beside a fire, and she is early *Homo sapiens*. A neurophysiologist named Paul MacLean thinks that humans first began to cry 1.4 million years ago when they started using fire. He pictures the smoke from the first fire making those standing around it cry irritant tears. Then, as tribespeople habitually gathered around the fires for social activities — cooking, tending the sick, even disposing of loved ones in cremation ceremonies — tearing became a conditioned reflex associated with separation. MacLean suggests that it is the ability to cry tears in response to separation from loved ones that sets us apart from other animals. (Though there is the story of the lost golden retriever. His owners finally tracked him down hundreds of miles away from their home. As they walked up to the shelter to get him, out he came with tears running down his face. But we didn't run into many of these stories.)

Jeffrey Kottler notes that Charles Darwin — who believed that no human behavior is useless but is naturally selected based on its adaptive value in helping an organism survive — could think of no use for tears. But think about babies. And, once more, picture Nadia at the sink. This time, she stops what she is doing and turns her head quickly. Her three-month-old baby is crying. She listens for a second: Is he just trying to get to sleep? Is he hungry? Or sick? Or wet? Studies have found that though fathers can correctly identify their own child's cry out of a group 84 percent of the time, mothers are nearly infallible; and mothers are better than fathers at being able to discern what their baby's cries mean. Nadia can tell by the sharpness of her baby's cry that he is hungry, and she picks him up and soothes him. His cries have stimulated milk production in Nadia, and she feeds him. He won't be able to speak words for another year, but he has gotten his message across and his needs met.

Take a different look at Nadia. She stands in her office at a major law firm where she works as the chief litigator. Her boss has just spoken crossly to her — probably even

more sharply than her husband did that morning. But she stands with her hands on her hips, dry-eyed. As women move into traditional male worlds, the tears aren't as automatic. Nadia cries at home. She would never cry at work. In our culture, where more people of both sexes tend to cry more often than those of other cultures, one's occupation is as good a predictor as any for this tendency: Nurses cry, doctors don't (as often); therapists cry, engineers don't. And, as with Nadia, it all depends on where you are when you feel like crying.

"LAUGH, AND THE WORLD LAUGHS WITH YOU; WEEP, AND YOU WEEP ALONE. . . ."

Well, that all depends on your culture. If you're English, you might cry only in private. If a tear slips out in public, chances are those with you will look away in embarrassment or discomfort. An Italian, though, is more likely to cry in public, whether happy or sad.

If you are one of the Bosavi people in New Guinea, it gets more complicated. If visitors from another village come, for instance, they are expected to perform a night of singing and dancing for their hosts. Suddenly, a local villager will grab a torch and burn one of the visiting Bosavins on the shoulder. The victim will not cry or even show he is in pain. The villagers, though, will scream, cry, and carry on all night. The longer and harder the crying, the more successful the ritual is deemed to be. This ceremony, writes Kottler, is one "of grief, of violence, of tribute and reciprocity. . . . The object of this exercise is to elicit strong emotional reactions in the participants, to make them cry." Anthropologists observing the Bosavi think the songs are presented not as taunts but in the same spirit of sympathy with which the guests themselves weep at the end of the ceremony for their hosts who have suffered. The entire ritual is a way of contriving tragedy so that everyone may cry in the end.

Just as some women are learning to withhold tears in certain situations, men in America are coming around to the idea that crying can serve a purpose.

This may sound bizarre, but when you think about it, it's not a lot different from what we do when we purposely play a song that makes us cry, or go to an opera or film that will make us weep. "Both within the culture of the Bosavi," says Kottler, "and in our own community, we have institutionalized 'tear ceremonies' that help us to reflect on our feelings about our own existence through the lives of others" — allowing us to experience our emotions safely, without rocking the boat too much.

The ability to turn on tears, or even to withhold tears as Nadia did at work, functions as communication. Think about the late Senator Edmund Muskie. In 1972, Muskie, then seeking his party's presidential nomination,

WHEN IT'S YOUR JOB TO CRY

*H*ow do they cry so easily in the movies? When the Tin Man cried in *The Wizard of Oz* (making Dorothy and the Scarecrow fear he would rust), chances are he had a secret device supplying water. But in a scene such as the opener in *Truly, Madly, Deeply,* where actress Juliet Stevenson sobs to her therapist about how much she misses her recently deceased lover, the actor must invoke the tears on the spot.

One veteran of the stage (which doesn't allow the luxury of multiple "takes") tells us the best way to cry is to try not to. "You sort of empty yourself out and listen hard to the words you're saying and avoid any conscious effort to tear up. In fact, it sometimes works better to try to stifle any sad feelings, because then they come on hard. If it works, it works. If it doesn't, it's still good acting because it stays simple. One of the worst things you can do as an actor is get so emotional that the audience can't understand what you're saying." Others say that conjuring up tragic thoughts does the trick.

Deborah Kerr in *An Affair to Remember.*

purportedly wept at a rally in Manchester, New Hampshire, while denouncing a newspaper publisher for printing a derogatory letter about his wife. His "weakness" did in his campaign. Yet the 1996 campaign season was, according to the *Wall Street Journal*, "the weepiest on record." Bill Clinton and Bob Dole were both comfortable blubbering in public. It had become, in the words of one reporter, "increasingly cool to cry."

So perhaps the next time we see someone sobbing at the sink, it may be Nadia's husband or her son crying over *Field of Dreams*. Or maybe it's just onions.

TEARJERKER HALL OF FAME
{ Our nominations for the weepiest movies, books, and music }

An Affair to Remember

Baby Jessica, the movie about the little girl who was taken from her adoptive home to live with her birth parents — watching it on the news was just as bad

Bambi, the Disney movie

Beaches, at the end when Barbara Hershey dies

The Bridges of Madison County, by Robert James Waller (book or movie)

Camille, with Greta Garbo

Casablanca

The Champ, the scene where the dad is dying

A Christmas Story, Truman Capote's short story

ET, at the end when he has to "go home"

Ghost, when Patrick Swayze dies

Heidi, the Shirley Temple version, when the grandfather calls for her

Homeward Bound, the pets arriving home

I Have a Dream, the speech by Martin Luther King Jr.

Lassie Come Home

The Little Fir Tree, a story by Hans Christian Andersen — you see the truth and the sadness in it more and more as you get older

The Little Match Girl, another Andersen story

Little Women, by Louisa May Alcott (book or movie), when sister Beth dies

The Lost Dog, by Edwin Way Teale (a true story, suitable for any age)

Love Story

My Girl

Old Yeller

The Prince of Tides, about half of all the scenes

The Red Shoes, original version

St. Matthew Passion, by J. S. Bach, the chorales at the end

Schindler's List

Sense and Sensibility, at the end when the heroine breaks into great sobs and tears . . . of happiness!

Shadowlands

Sophie's Choice, by William Styron (book or movie), especially the scene where she has to choose which of her children to give up

The Sound of Music, Maria's wedding

The Star-Spangled Banner, played at the Olympics

Tears in Heaven, sung by Eric Clapton

Terms of Endearment

The Way We Were

Where the Red Fern Grows, by Wilson Rawls (book or movie)

First minted 85 years ago, the nickel with a Plains Indian on one side and a buffalo on the other captured the romance of the American West. Numismatists are still arguing about

The Face on the

The 1913 Indian Head Nickel.

– photo courtesy the Museum of the American Numismatic Association

FOR MANY AMERICANS, THE INDIAN Head, or Buffalo, nickel is the most familiar obsolete coin in existence. The design is unforgettable. On one side is the head of a warrior, his hair braided and decorated with three feathers, his expression proud. The reverse of the coin portrays an adult male bison (the proper term for buffalo) atop a grassy mound. Released on March 4, 1913, and minted until 1938, the nickel

helped transform our coinage from the purely practical to the uniquely American.

The nickel was designed by James Earle Fraser, a sculptor raised on the northern prairies of the Midwest. As a boy in the 1880s, Fraser traveled through the West with his family (his father was a mechanical engineer and railroad builder) and spent ten years on a ranch in South Dakota. The boy began to draw his surroundings at an early age, and shortly afterward began to create small sculptures from stone quarried near his home. The romance of the West and the sad plight of the Native American and the buffalo impressed young Fraser. While still in his teens, he completed his first major work, "The End of the Trail," a statuette depicting a lean Indian hunter astride his exhausted horse, their heads bowed in despair and fatigue. The emotional intensity Fraser portrayed won him international recognition and led him to study under the preeminent

"The End of the Trail," James Earle Fraser's first major work, won him international recognition.

– National Cowboy Hall of Fame and Western Heritage Center, Oklahoma City

sculptor of the day, Augustus Saint-Gaudens, in Paris and in Cornish, New Hampshire.

Saint-Gaudens had been commissioned by President Theodore Roosevelt to design coins for the United States as beautiful as those of the ancient Greeks. His first design

by Victoria Doudera

the identity of the Indian model. (But they've identified the buffalo!)

Indian Head Nickel

Top: Sculptor Augustus Saint-Gaudens in 1905. *Above:* Detail of the $20 "double eagle" gold coin designed by Saint-Gaudens — considered to be the most beautiful ever struck in the United States.

was for the 1907 "double eagle," a $20 gold piece — featuring the standing Liberty on the obverse (front) carrying a torch in one hand and an olive branch in the other, and an American eagle in flight on the reverse — considered by many to be the most beautiful coin ever struck in the United States. Although Saint-Gaudens died just as his coins were being prepared for circulation, his work inspired other artists.

Fraser was 35 when word reached him that the Treasury Department was considering a replacement for the Liberty Head nickel of 1883. His preliminary sketches for the director of the mint proposed a "purely American" coin in honor of Native Americans and the nearly extinct bison. Fraser's enthusiasm, artistic reputation, and persistence won him the job, and on January 13, 1912, the sculptor was given the go-ahead to refine the sketches.

Fraser's final designs were at the mint, ready to be cast, when manufacturers of vending machines objected bitterly to the raised design. After months of delay, the Secretary of the Treasury gave final approval to the new coin. On February 17, 1913, Indian Head nickels were struck in Philadelphia, Denver, and San Francisco, and released for circulation on March 4.

The new nickels were barely minted when folks began trying to guess the identity of the Native American portrayed. Sculptor Fraser stated that the profile on his coin was representative of many Indians, but no one was content with that answer. After the Treasury Department had received hundreds of letters asking the model's

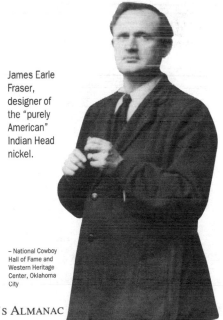

James Earle Fraser, designer of the "purely American" Indian Head nickel.

– National Cowboy Hall of Fame and Western Heritage Center, Oklahoma City

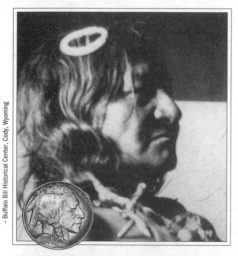

identity, Fraser admitted that the profile was a composite of three Indians known to him. When asked for specific identities, he named Two Moons, a Northern Cheyenne, and Iron Tail, a Sioux, but said he could not remember the third.

Two Moons was a leader in the War for the Black Hills of 1876-77 and was present at General Custer's defeat at Little Bighorn. His eyewitness account of that battle was told to the writer Hamlin Garland, whose article "General Custer's Last Fight as Seen by Two Moons" was published in 1898. One of Two Moons' descendants, Morgan J. Wheeler of New York, says there was never any debate in his family as to whether his famous ancestor posed for the nickel. "He did sit for Fraser and most people have heard that he is the man on the nickel," says Wheeler, whose birth name is Justin Two Moons. "But it's not him, or at least not totally. That's definitely not his nose. In my family, we've always believed that the portrayal on the nickel was a composite."

Iron Tail was a war chief who also served as an aide to Sitting Bull at Little Bighorn. He later joined William "Buffalo Bill" Cody's Wild West Show and toured with the extravaganza through Europe in 1889. Photographs of Iron Tail, especially in profile, look remarkably like Fraser's Indian. According to Fraser's wife, Laura Gardin Fraser, Iron Tail was her husband's favorite subject.

But who was the third man?

"Fraser was rather unclear as to his identity," says Robert Van Ryzin, editor of *Coins* magazine, "and over the years there have been quite a few pretenders." Van Ryzin re-

---

Top: Two Moons, a northern Cheyenne, modeled for Fraser. *Center:* Isaac John, also known as Chief John Big Tree, was an actor who claimed to have posed for the nickel. *Left:* Big Tree, a Kiowa, also known as Adoeette, was likely Fraser's third model.

counts that Two Guns White Calf, a Blackfoot, claimed in the late 1920s to be the mystery man, but Fraser publicly denied it. From the 1930s on, many enterprising men tried to make their fortunes by claiming at country fairs, sideshows, and the like that they had posed for the nickel.

One such man was Chief John Big Tree, a Seneca, who also claimed to have posed for Fraser's "The End of the Trail." Interestingly, both the Bureau of Indian Affairs and *Who's Who in Native Americans* name him as the third model. But according to Van Ryzin, there are a few holes in Chief John Big Tree's story.

"His real name was Isaac 'Johnny' John and he was a Hollywood actor," says Van Ryzin. "He starred in several of John Ford's silent films, including *Drums Along the Mohawk* and *The Iron Horse.* Chief John Big Tree began claiming in the 1950s and 60s that he was chosen to pose 'because of his classic facial features,' but he's never mentioned in Fraser's

– Buffalo Bill Historical Center, Cody, Wyoming

Iron Tail *(right)*, a Sioux, was Fraser's favorite subject and may have been the main model for the Indian profile.

What About the Buffalo?

■ The creature Fraser immortalized was named Black Diamond, a Great Plains bison who never roamed the West but who was born and raised in New York City's Bronx Park Zoo. Reputed to be the largest bison ever held in captivity, Black Diamond weighed almost a ton. He proved to be a temperamental star who exasperated the sculptor by refusing to stay in profile. Despite his celebrity status, Black Diamond met with a sad end. Shortly after modeling for Fraser, he was deemed too old for the zoo and was sold to a poultry and game dealer. In 1915, two years after the coin bearing his likeness was released, the animal was slaughtered. His hide became a blanket, his meat was sold as "Black Diamond Steaks," and his shaggy head was mounted. This same head appeared at a coin convention some 70 years later.

correspondence. He was only 30 at the time the nickel was designed, while both Iron Tail and Two Moons were in their sixties.

"I've read Fraser's letters and my research points to another Big Tree, a member of the Kiowa, who was also known as Adoeette," says Van Ryzin. He notes that Laura Gardin Fraser confirmed that Adoeette modeled for Fraser prior to 1912. "He certainly was much more famous in his day than John Big Tree," writes Van Ryzin in his book *Twisted Tails*. But until Adoeette is positively identified, confusion over the identity of Fraser's third model will persist.

The Indian Head nickel was replaced in 1938 by the coin we use today, featuring President Jefferson and his home, Monticello. Old issues were still in circulation in 1951 when James Earle Fraser received one of the most distinguished awards given to artists in the United States, the gold medal of the National Institute of Arts and Letters and the American Academy of Arts and Letters. Fraser died two years later at the age of 77. □□

Collecting Indian Head Nickels

■ The coin with two nicknames — Buffalo and Indian Head — was a favorite with nearly everyone from the start, although it was quickly apparent that Fraser's design required a slight change. The problem lay in the grassy mound beneath the buffalo's feet. Its thickness prevented the coin from stacking properly, and it exposed the words *FIVE CENTS* to heavy wear. It also could not enter the coin slot of streetcar and bus fare boxes, requiring most fare boxes around the country to be changed.

Chief engraver Charles Barber modified the dies, lowering the mound beneath the buffalo and adding a thin line above the *FIVE CENTS*. The modified nickel was again minted at all three mints and released into circulation in 1913. Thanks to this second minting, six varieties of the Indian Head nickels exist for that year: Type 1 coins (with the higher mound) and Type 2s (with Barber's modifications) hail from each mint.

A die mishap caused this 1937 minting of a "three-legged buffalo" nickel, now worth as much as $2,400.

According to Bob Slaymin, owner of Downeast Coins and Collectibles in Bangor, Maine, there are plenty of common date (1934-1938) Indian Head nickels out there in decent condition, worth about 50¢ to $1 each. Visit your local coin or hobby shop, or call the American Numismatic Association at 719-632-2646 for a list of dealers near you.

Besides the rare earlier dates, watch for the "three-legged buffalo," a 1937 coin minted in Denver in which Black Diamond, due to a die mishap, has only three legs. In mint condition, a 1937-D three-legged can fetch up to $2,400 or more, while those in good condition are worth about $80. Probably the most valuable type of Indian Head nickel is known as a 1916 doubled die. A minting error stamped the year twice on these coins, and experts estimate good examples are worth from $800 to $2,500.

If you search your attic and that rare specimen doesn't appear, take heart. As Slaymin says, "The hard-to-come-by dates are scarce, unless some kid spends his father's coin collection." He chuckles, and adds, "Which *does* happen."

60 LBS OF TOMATOES FROM ONE TREE PLANT

Constantly Harvesting all season. Treat it like any fruit tree!

Imagine! Now you can have large, red, juicy tomatoes up to 60 pounds each year. So why settle for a few short weeks of tomatoes every year? Not to mention the back breaking time it takes to plant them. Our perennial tomato harvesting tree yields garden fresh succulent tomatoes so abundant they seem to grow as quickly as you pick them. There's plenty of these delicious, plump tomatoes to go around for family and friends. So simply step back and watch your tree quickly zoom to the full height desired and supply you with yummy fresh garden tomatoes.

This incredible horticultural concept from New Zealand is not to be confused with an ordinary vine or a tomato plant. It is really a tomato tree that bears bushel after bushel of mouth watering flavor - up to 7 months outdoors and all year round indoors. No special care is needed. Grows to a full 8 ft. high or you can simply trim this exotic beautiful tree to any size.

Orders Shipped At Proper Planting Time

ONE LARGE TOMATO FOR LESS THAN 1¢ each

JUICY AND DELICIOUS!

AS SEEN ON TV

Can be grown indoors or on outdoor patios
- No Staking • No Pruning
- No Caging • No Trimming

You save on your grocery bill while enjoying these delectable tomatoes. They're simply fabulous in your salads, sandwiches, and spaghetti sauce. Even eating these yummy tomatoes by themselves is a real treat. There's nothing like the taste of fresh home grown tomatoes. All plants are guaranteed to arrive in perfect condition. We ship mature plants, not seeds. Shipped in time to plant for this season.

PREDICTING THE WEATHER FOR THE 21st CENTURY

Feeling chilly? Solar scientists who
study farming records in medieval England and
geological residue on the shores of
Hudson Bay think we may be in for a spell of cold, wet weather.

BY CLIFFORD NIELSEN

emember 20 years ago when the weather buzzword was "global cooling"? The Brazilian coffee crop and the grain yield in the Soviet Union had both just been devastated by unusual cold. Glaciers showed an alarming advance throughout the Northern Hemisphere, and for the first time in 80 years, sea ice had become a problem for shipping in both the North Atlantic and the Arctic Oceans. Scientists warned that Earth was headed into a devastating ice age, with particulate matter in the atmosphere (from industrial burning and even the contrails of jet aircraft) acting to screen out sunlight, thus causing the cooling.

But by 1978, the weather was warming up. Since then, the weather buzzword has been "greenhouse warming." Scientists who in the 1970s had predicted massive world crop failures due to frost began to warn of similar crop failures from drought and parching caused by man-made greenhouse gases, primarily carbon dioxide. Given this dramatic seesaw in popular scientific opinion, one might well ask: Is there any means of gauging climate in the near future, the next century, or even the next half century?

The answer is that there may well be. The evidence comes from geological residue on the east coast of Hudson Bay that portrays the dynamic nature of our climate since the Ice Age.

That huge burden of ice, which originated more than 100,000 years ago and grew to more than a mile thick, compressed Earth's crust in a wide area surrounding what is now Hudson Bay. About 12,000

years. That record, in turn, may give us a distant mirror that can reflect future climate.

What is most striking about the Hudson Bay record is a repeated pattern of sea-level  rise for 350 to 360 years, followed by a period of falling levels for an identical time span. The best scientific explanation is that sea levels fall when increased cold locks water in glaciers and ice caps; sea levels rise when warming releases the water. The entire cycle from a cold trough, known as a *climatic pessimum*, to a warm peak, called a *climatic optimum*, and back to cold requires 700 to 720 years. If the record of sea-level change during a complete cycle is as accurate as it seems to be, it is possible to look back from our own time to what may well have been a similar period of climate 700 years ago in the late 13th century.

The decade of the 1280s seems to have been a prosperous and optimistic period in Europe. In southern England, small  vineyards had flourished for much of the century. The quality of wine produced was high enough to worry French vintners, who attempted to have English vineyards closed down as part of a treaty settlement.

Here's how scientists use the past to mirror the future.

years ago, when the glaciers had completely melted, the land began rising at a predictable rate in what is known as *isostatic rebound*. The continued rising has made it possible to read the record of sea-level fluctuations on the east shore of the bay for the last 10,000

The fact that the English vineyards prospered indicates that temperatures were something like 1.1° to 1.6° F (0.7° to 1.0° C) warmer than during our own warmest period of the 20th century, a period that has been defined as a climatic optimum. **(continued)**

Throughout the decade beginning in 1310, crops failed in many parts of Europe because the fields were too swampy to support growth.

The relatively good growing conditions during the 13th century were not limited to vineyards. Tillage and general agriculture were practiced at much higher altitudes and latitudes than is possible today. In the British Isles, records exist of farming at altitudes 500 to 600 feet higher than is now practicable. In Scandinavia, grain was cultivated and boreal forests grew 200 miles farther north than has been possible since.

The prosperity of the 1280s did not last long, unfortunately. The best evidence indicates that the vineyards had completely quit producing by 1300 or a bit later. Oncoming colder conditions also made farming impossible in the northern reaches of Scandinavia and the highlands of the British Isles. Continued cooling in the next decade led to one of the greatest weather disasters in Europe. The cold, in itself, was not as intense as it became in the late 1600s and early 1700s (a period now seen as the depth of what is known as the Little Ice Age), but the cooling caused a phenomenon equally as devastating: torrential rainfall.

Throughout the decade beginning in 1310, crops failed in many parts of Europe because the fields were too swampy to support growth. The most disastrous year was 1315, when virtually the entire grain harvest failed in Europe. Great numbers of sheep and cattle also died in *murrains*, or epidemics of disease, that swept the sodden landscapes. So dire was the famine that

instances of cannibalism were recorded. It was a disaster thought by many historians to have been the cause of the century of chaos that is best remembered for the Hundred Years' War between England and France.

– Culver Pictures

In Asia, significant flooding of China's central river valleys was common from about 1300 on. The greatest flood, in 1332, led to the death of over seven million people. Almost every year after 1327 saw famine caused by flooding and poor harvests in much of China. And in 1344,

– Culver Pictures

the dikes on the Yellow River were breached, flooding vast areas and causing the dislocation of a previously isolated rodent, which carried fleas that, in turn, were host to the bubonic plague. Within a quarter century, the Black Death was decimating Europe, deepening the misery.

One explanation for that historical quick shift in climate is that the period was marked by a decline in solar activity. Unfortunately, no one in Europe was counting sunspots that early. But during the warm period from 1050 to 1250, the Chinese had recorded what could be called a riot of sunspots. After 1300, accounts of sunspots are rare in Chinese chronicles.

Solar scientists now believe that solar activity became unusually quiet during the early 1300s. They have named that period

Major Climate Changes, A.D. 1040 to 2020

PERIOD	CLIMATE CHARACTERISTICS	TEMPERATURES (C)
Little Climatic Optimum **1040 to 1300**	Wine grapes cultivated in England by 1200; spruce trees and grain cultivated in Norway 200 miles north of present limits. Drought common on U.S. Great Plains. Vikings colonized Greenland. The analog period, based on the Little Ice Age Cycle of 720 years, is 1760 to 2020.	1025 1075 1125 1175
Wolf and Spörer Sunspot Minima **1300 to 1480**	Torrential storms in northern Europe during the 1310s. Grain crops failed in much of Europe. Devastating floods in China during the 1330s. Vikings had to take more southerly route to Greenland because of sea ice. After 1430, the Baltic, in the area of the Danish islands, and the Lagoon of Venice froze nine times. Alpine glaciers advanced. Analog period, 2020 to 2200.	1225 1275 1325 1375
16th Century Warming and Maunder Minimum **1480 to 1760**	Gradual warming until about 1540 followed by severe weather much like that of the 1300s. Regional crop failures in England. Beginning of the "Freneau Period" of general glacial advance in the Northern Hemisphere. Coldest temperatures in northern Europe were from 1680 to 1710. Last European settlers of Greenland succumbed to the plague. Ice fairs were common on the frozen Thames. Analog period, 2200 to 2480.	1425 1475 1525 1575 1625
Modern Optimum **1760 to 2020**	Noticeable warming by the 1780s followed by general cooling from 1800 to 1820. "Year Without a Summer" recorded in 1816. Gradual retreat of glaciers in Northern Hemisphere after 1820. Grain cultivated at relatively northern latitudes in North America. Drought common in U.S. Great Plains (1930s, 1950s, 1970s). Analog period, 2480 to 2740.	1675 1725 1775 1825 1875 1925 1975

Scale: 6°C   8°C   10°C

Temperatures on the graph are average yearly temperatures for England. Winter temperatures tended to be warmer than average during the optimum temperature periods and colder during the "pessimums." The Fahrenheit range on the graph is from 42.8° (6° C) to 50° (10° C). Temperature information is based on H. H. Lamb's book, *Climate, History and the Modern World* (Methuen, New York: 1982).

climate change such as that experienced in 1310 could spell global disaster rivaling the scenarios predicted about global warming.

is: What are the implications for mankind in the 21st century? One viewpoint is that we can adapt to it, as did the 17th-century colonials in North America, who flourished during the coldest period of the Little Ice Age.

the Wolf Sunspot Minimum. It was the first of three periods of quiet solar activity, followed by the Spörer (latter part of the 1400s) and Maunder (late 1600s) Sunspot Minima, all of which are now associated with the colder periods of the Little Ice Age.

Much of this analysis is conjectural. The greatest argument *against* a solar influence on climate is that the change between an active Sun (the period when sunspots appear) and a quiet Sun is minuscule, only one to three watts per square meter at the top of the atmosphere. Opponents argue that no physical mechanism has been discovered to explain such a solar-climate relationship.

The historical record, however, remains. Sea-level fluctuations along Hudson Bay averaging 710 years have been recorded 14 times, accounting for a span of nearly 10,000 years. By the mid-1600s, sunspots (the few that happened) were finally being counted in Europe. Looking back to that period, a correlation exists between low solar activity and falling sea levels caused by cooling. The record since has allowed us to witness exactly half of a Little Ice Age Cycle, a 360-year period during which climate has, with ups and downs, grown progressively warmer while the Sun has become intermittently more active, peaking in intensity in the 1950s. Sea levels in Hudson Bay have risen proportionally.

Assuming that the Sun and climate follow the anticipated cooling pattern predicted by the Hudson Bay record, the obvious question

Because too much rain is deadly to grain crops, development of other crops may well be an answer. During the Little Ice Age in Europe, for example, people made potatoes a staple crop when heavy rains made the grain crop vulnerable.

On the other hand, a climate change such as that experienced in 1310 could spell global disaster rivaling the scenarios predicted about global warming. Should the atmosphere cool by as little as 1° F (-17° C), an onslaught of precipitation similar to that

of the 1300s might well be expected. Such continued heavy precipitation is easy to understand in meteorological terms. After a period of great warmth, the oceans, which are highly efficient heat sinks, remain warm, while the atmosphere cools. The combination of cold air and warm water is the perfect recipe for deluge after deluge.

Given the record, it might almost be hoped that greenhouse warming *would* occur to help mitigate any coming cool period. A repeat of the 50 or so years of the Wolf Sunspot Minimum may bring about a recurrence, in the coming century, of some of the coldest weather of the past millennium, when ice fairs were held on the frozen Thames, livestock froze in the fields, and hens' eggs were worth their weight in silver.

This article is excerpted from the author's forthcoming book, The Sun, Changing Climate, and the Coming Ice. □□

GENERAL WEATHER FORECAST

1997-1998

(For details, see the regional forecasts beginning on page 122.)

The year ahead may be the warmest on record overall, with a mild winter in much of the country and a substantial risk of drought in the summer across the nation's breadbasket.

NOVEMBER THROUGH MARCH will start relatively chilly from the eastern seaboard into the Ohio Valley and Great Lakes regions, with November and December near normal, except from Maryland to Florida, where it will be well below normal. However, most of this region will be unusually mild during January and February. March will be a bit cooler than normal from New England westward to Wisconsin, with mild temperatures in the Southeast. The western regions will start relatively mild, but cold temperatures will be the rule from January through March from the Dakotas southward to Kansas and westward to the Pacific Northwest. Temperatures from Texas to southern California will stay close to normal. Precipitation will be above normal from New England and New York through Michigan, Illinois, Iowa, Kansas, and North Texas, and also from northern California to western Washington. Elsewhere, it will be below normal. Snowfall will be above normal in much of New England, the Rocky Mountain states, and interior Washington; from the North Carolina and Tennessee mountains northward to southwest Pennsylvania; and from the Great Lakes into the northern Great Plains. It will be below normal in most of New York and Pennsylvania, the mid-Atlantic states, the Ohio and Tennessee Valleys, Oklahoma, and North Texas.

APRIL THROUGH JUNE will be cool in the mid-Atlantic states, Florida, the Pacific states, and the Desert Southwest. The Rocky Mountain states will remain chilly. Coastal New England and New York will be near normal, and the northern and central Great Plains will be warm in April and May. Elsewhere, it will be warmer than normal. Precipitation will be below normal in most of the country. Exceptions include the northern Rockies, southern and central California, Oregon, the Deep South, Tennessee, and western Kentucky and Indiana.

JULY AND AUGUST will be hotter than normal from New England and New York across to the northern and central Great Plains. The mid-Atlantic states and Southeast will be a bit above normal, with Florida, the Deep South, Texas, and southern California near normal. The Rocky Mountain states, Desert Southwest, and West Coast will be cooler than normal. Rainfall will be above normal from New England southward to the mid-Atlantic states, and in the Desert Southwest and the northern tier from Minnesota to Washington. There is a possibility of a hurricane or two in August in the Northeast. Rainfall will be below normal, with a drought likely, from Texas and Oklahoma north through Kansas, Nebraska, and South Dakota, and east through much of the Ohio Valley and Great Lakes regions.

SEPTEMBER AND OCTOBER will be warmer than normal. Rainfall will be above normal from New England southward to Florida, in the Pacific Northwest, and in portions of Texas, Missouri, and Illinois. Elsewhere, below-normal rainfall is expected, with the drought continuing in the Midwest, the Dakotas, Oklahoma, and portions of Texas, Wisconsin, and the Ohio Valley.

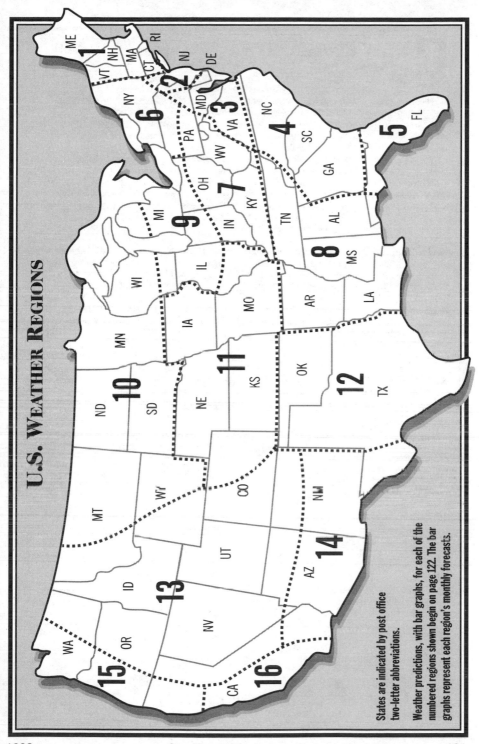

U.S. Weather Regions

States are indicated by post office two-letter abbreviations.

Weather predictions, with bar graphs, for each of the numbered regions shown begin on page 122. The bar graphs represent each region's monthly forecasts.

SUMMARY: Cold periods in November may lead some to believe a severe winter is on the way, but January and February will feature above-normal temperatures. Despite a turn to below-normal cold in March, temperatures from November through March will average higher than normal. Precipitation and snowfall will also be somewhat higher than normal, with the best chances for heavy snowfall in mid-December, toward Christmas, and in early and late March. The coldest period during the winter will occur in late January and early February.

April will be cooler and drier than normal. May will be close to normal, but a heat wave beginning near Memorial Day will make the month as a whole warmer than normal, a prelude to a very hot summer.

Temperatures from June through August will average 3 degrees above normal, with the best chance for record heat in mid-June, early and late July, and mid- and late August. August will be a record month, with heat waves punctuated by severe thunderstorms, alternating with brief chilly spells. Watch for a hurricane late in the month. September will bring comfortable temperatures and more-tranquil weather. October will have above-normal rainfall, with some pleasant spells between the rainy periods.

NOV. 1997: Temp. 47° (2° above avg.; avg. southeast); precip. 3" (1" below avg. northwest; 2" above southeast). 1-5 Showers, cool. 6-9 Rainy. 10-19 Sunny days. 20-25 Rainy, mild. 26-30 Rain southeast, flurries northwest.

DEC. 1997: Temp. 32° (avg.); precip. 3.5" (0.5" above avg.). 1-3 Heavy rain. 4-9 Flurries, cold. 10-14 Snow, then rain. 15-17 Seasonable. 18-22 Heavy rain coast, snow inland. 23-26 White Christmas. 27-31 Sunny, cold nights.

JAN. 1998: Temp. 32° (3° above avg.); precip. 3" (avg.). 1-6 Rain and snow. 7-11 Periods of snow. 12-17 Partly sunny, chilly. 18-24 Milder, then cold. 25-31 Seasonable, flurries.

FEB. 1998: Temp. 30° (1° above avg.); precip. 3.5" (0.5" above avg.). 1-4 Sunshine, cold. 5-8 Snow, then very cold. 9-12 Milder, rain, snow interior. 13-18 Warm, rain to snow, then very cold. 19-22 Rain and snow. 23-28 Milder, few showers.

MAR. 1998: Temp. 37° (2° below avg.); precip. 4.5" (1" above avg.). 1-5 Cooler, then rain. 6-10 Mild, then heavy snow. 11-14 Milder. 15-18 Warm, then cooler; showers. 19-20 Rainy. 21-24 Cool, then mild. 25-31 Rain, wet snow inland.

APR. 1998: Temp. 48° (0.5° below avg.); precip. 2.5" (1" below avg.). 1-6 Sunny, warmer. 7-10 Rainy, raw, then milder. 11-15 Chilly rain, then warm. 16-19 Cool, then warm. 20-26 Cool, showers. 27-30 Mild, then a cold rain.

MAY 1998: Temp. 58° (1.5° above avg.); precip.

2.5" (1" below avg.; avg. west). 1-3 Rainy, raw. 4-8 Sunny, warmer. 9-14 Showers, cooler. 15-21 Mild, showers. 22-28 Hot, dry. 29-31 Showers, then cooler.

JUNE 1998: Temp. 68° (2° above avg. west; 1° below east); precip. 4.5" (1" above avg.). 1-7 Warm with thunderstorms, then cooler. 8-13 Cool, showers. 14-17 Warm, then damp and cool. 18-23 Hot. 24-30 Rain.

JULY 1998: Temp. 77° (4° above avg.); precip. 2" (2" below avg.; 1" above east). 1-4 Hazy, hot, humid. 5-8 Hot, thunderstorms. 9-11 Thunderstorms, then cooler. 12-17 Hot, then thunderstorms, cooler. 18-22 Hazy, hot, humid. 23-24 Brief relief. 25-27 Record heat. 28-31 Thunderstorms, warm.

AUG. 1998: Temp. 76° (4° above avg.); precip. 6.5" (3" above avg.; 8" above east). 1-3 Cool. 4-9 Heat wave, then thunderstorms. 10-14 Showers, cool nights. 15-18 Heavy rain. 19-20 Hot. 21-24 Possible hurricane. 25-29 Hot, then thunderstorms, cooler. 30-31 Showers, seasonable.

SEPT. 1998: Temp. 64° (0.5° above avg.); precip. 2.5" (0.5" below avg.). 1-9 Cool, then warmer with showers. 10-14 Cool. 15-19 Cool, showers. 20-23 Sunny, hot. 24-27 Thunderstorms, cooler. 28-30 Rain, then chilly nights.

OCT. 1998: Temp. 57° (2° above avg.); precip. 4.5" (1" above avg.). 1-5 Milder, rainy periods. 6-9 Mild days, crisp nights. 10-12 Rainy, warm. 13-17 Sunny. 18-21 Heavy rain. 22-27 Showers, mild, then cooler. 28-31 Sprinkles.

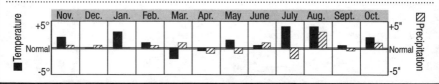

50 Legendary Songs Of The Old West

From out of the Golden West we bring you a giant memory-stirring treasury of unforgettable cowboy favorites. Here are America's beloved singing cowboys with all the romantic western songs that helped build the legends of the Old West.

Settle back and close your eyes – hear the jingle of spurs and the gentle clippity-clop of horses on the range as the famous cowboys of yesteryear bring you 50 classic hits. Legends like Gene Autry, Tex Ritter, Rex Allen and the Sons of the Pioneers will serenade you with their plaintive harmonies and the easy rhythms of the trail. Imagine having all the great western stars of radio and the movies right in your own home. It's a goldmine of musical memories. Don't miss out! Be sure to order now.

I'M BACK IN THE SADDLE AGAIN
Gene Autry

TUMBLING TUMBLEWEEDS
Sons Of The Pioneers

CATTLE CALL
Eddy Arnold

BURY ME NOT ON THE LONE PRAIRIE
Tex Ritter

NEW SAN ANTONIO ROSE
Bob Wills

THE LAST ROUNDUP
Rex Allen

COOL WATER
Sons Of The Pioneers

RIDERS IN THE SKY
Vaughn Monroe

HIGH NOON
Tex Ritter

SOMEDAY YOU'LL WANT ME TO WANT YOU
Elton Britt

HOME ON THE RANGE
Gene Autry

THE SHIFTING, WHISPERING SANDS
Jim Reeves

WHOOPIE TI YI YO (GET ALONG LITTLE DOGGIE)
Sons Of The Pioneers

EL RANCHO GRANDE
Gene Autry

NOBODY'S DARLIN' BUT MINE
Jimmie Davis

MEXICALI ROSE
Jim Reeves

THE STREETS OF LAREDO
Marty Robbins

DON'T FENCE ME IN
Bing Crosby

GOODNIGHT IRENE
Ernest Tubb & Red Foley

I WANT TO BE A COWBOY'S SWEETHEART
Patsy Montana

I'M AN OLD COWHAND
Patsy Montana

EMPTY SADDLES
Sons Of The Pioneers

DOWN IN THE VALLEY
Slim Whitman

WHEN IT'S SPRINGTIME IN THE ROCKIES
Montana Slim

SOUTH OF THE BORDER
Patsy Cline

I'M THINKING TONIGHT OF MY BLUE EYES
The Carter Family

ALONG THE NAVAJO TRAIL
Sons Of The Pioneers

SIOUX CITY SUE
Bing Crosby

BEAUTIFUL, BEAUTIFUL BROWN EYES
Jimmy Wakely

RED RIVER VALLEY
Slim Whitman

MULE TRAIN
Frankie Laine

DEEP IN THE HEART OF TEXAS
Bob Wills

MY LITTLE CHEROKEE MAIDEN
Bob Wills

JEALOUS HEART
Tex Ritter

TAKE ME BACK TO MY BOOTS AND SADDLE
Jimmy Wakely

HAVE I TOLD YOU LATELY THAT I LOVE YOU
Gene Autry

PISTOL PACKIN' MAMA
Al Dexter

YOU ARE MY SUNSHINE
Jimmie Davis

WAGON WHEELS
Sons Of The Pioneers

HAPPY TRAILS
Roy Rogers & Dale Evans

AND MORE!

GREATER NEW YORK-NEW JERSEY
F O R E C A S T

SUMMARY: The period from November through March will be relatively mild, with above-normal rainfall but a good chance for less snow than normal. The best time for snowstorms will be early and late in the winter season, with little snow during the heart of winter. Temperatures will average about a degree above normal but 2 to 4 degrees above normal during January and February. November will be a damp month, with precipitation close to normal from December through March.

April will be somewhat drier than normal. Temperatures will be near or a bit above normal during April and May.

The summer season will start out cool in June, but July and August will be much hotter than normal, with overall temperatures 3 to 4 degrees above average. Especially hot weather will occur just after Independence Day, the latter part of July, and mid- and late August. Rainfall during July and the first part of August will be well below normal, but heavy thunderstorms and tropical storms or hurricanes may bring flooding during the latter half of August. September and October will continue warmer than normal, with below-normal rainfall in September and heavy rain in October.

NOV. 1997: Temp. 47° (0.5° below avg.); precip. 5.5" (2" above avg.). 1-5 Showers, cooler. 6-9 Rainy, raw. 10-18 Sunny days, chilly nights. 19-25 Rainy, mild. 26-30 Cooler, showers.

DEC. 1997: Temp. 35.5° (1° below avg.); precip. 3.5" (avg.). 1-5 Rain, then colder. 6-12 Cold, few flurries. 13-17 Rain, then seasonable. 18-22 Rainy, windy. 23-26 Cold, flurries. 27-31 Becoming milder.

JAN. 1998: Temp. 35° (4° above avg.); precip. 3.5" (0.5" above avg.). 1-3 Rainy, quite mild. 4-7 Cloudy, rather mild. 8-11 Showers, flurries north and west. 12-16 Sunshine, seasonable. 17-19 Rain and snow. 20-25 Cold, dry. 26-31 Showers, then colder with flurries.

FEB. 1998: Temp. 35° (2° above avg.); precip. 3" (avg.). 1-4 Sunny, cold. 5-7 Snow, very cold. 8-11 Milder, rain. 12-14 Very mild. 15-17 Rain to snow, colder. 18-21 Showers, snow west. 22-28 Mild, then rain.

MAR. 1998: Temp. 42.5° (1° above avg.); precip. 3.5" (0.5" above avg.). 1-5 Rainy, mild. 6-11 Rainy, turning colder, snow inland. 12-15 Becoming warm. 16-20 Showers, mild. 21-24 Seasonable. 25-27 Rain. 28-31 Mild, then cool.

APR. 1998: Temp. 51° (avg.); precip. 2.5" (1" below avg.). 1-6 Sunny, turning warmer. 7-10 Showers. 11-15 Cool, then warm. 16-19 Showers. 20-27 Mild, mainly dry. 28-30 Rainy, raw.

MAY 1998: Temp. 63° (1° above avg.); precip. 2.5" (1" below avg.). 1-4 Rainy episodes. 5-9 Sunshine, becoming hot. 10-15 Sunshine, rather cool. 16-26 Warm, mainly dry. 27-31 Showers.

JUNE 1998: Temp. 70° (1° below avg.); precip. 2.5" (1" below avg.). 1-7 Thunderstorms, then cooler. 8-16 Showers, cool. 17-22 Sunshine, very warm. 23-27 Hazy, humid, scattered thunderstorms. 28-30 Damp, cool.

JULY 1998: Temp. 80.5° (4° above avg.); precip. 2" (2" below avg.). 1-5 Hot, scattered thunderstorms. 6-9 Stifling heat and humidity. 10-20 Thunderstorms, then less hot. 21-27 Oppressive. 28-31 Some sun, a bit cooler.

AUG. 1998: Temp. 78° (3° above avg.); precip. 9" (5" above avg.). 1-4 Cloudy, comfortable. 5-10 Heat wave. 11-13 Thunderstorms, then cooler. 14-18 Possible hurricane. 19-21 Hot, humid. 22-23 Possible hurricane. 24-26 Oppressive heat. 27-31 Mainly dry, seasonable.

SEPT. 1998: Temp. 70° (2° above avg.); precip. 2" (1" below avg.). 1-3 Sunny. 4-10 Warm, few showers. 11-18 Mainly dry, seasonable. 19-24 Hot, afternoon thunderstorms. 25-26 Cooler. 27-30 Rain, cool.

OCT. 1998: Temp. 60° (2° above avg.); precip. 5" (2" above avg.). 1-4 Milder, some rain. 5-9 Sunny, pleasant. 10-12 Rainy, mild. 13-17 Warm with sunshine. 18-21 Heavy rain. 23-31 Seasonable, few showers.

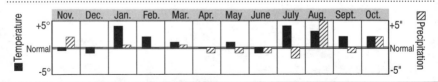

The Most Important Money/Power/Romantic-Love Discovery Since The Industrial Revolution © 1997

Receive Free — The valuable, 8000-word Neo-Tech Information Package

No one can spot the Neo-Tech man. The constant invisible advantages obtained by Neo-Tech appear completely natural, yet are unbeatable. Neo-Tech puts one in the ultimate catbird seat.

An entire new field of knowledge has been discovered by Dr. Frank R. Wallace, a former Senior Research Chemist for E.I. du Pont de Nemours & Co. For over a decade, Dr. Wallace researched Psychuous Advantages to uncover a powerful array of new knowledge called Neo-Tech. That new knowledge allows any person to prosper monetarily, personally, romantically, and financially anywhere in the world, even during personal or financial hard times, inflation, boom times, recession, depression, war.

Neo-Tech is a new, scientific method for capturing major financial and personal advantages everywhere. Neo-Tech is a new knowledge that has nothing to do with positive thinking, religion, or anything mystical. Once a person is exposed to Neo-Tech, he can quietly profit from anyone — anywhere, anytime. He can prosper almost anywhere on earth and succeed under almost any economic or political condition. Combined with Psychuous Advantages, Neo-Tech applies to all money and power gathering techniques — to all situations involving the transfer of money, power, or love.

Neo-Tech has its roots in the constant financial pressures and incentives to develop the easiest, most profitable methods of gaining advantages. Over the decades, all successful salesmen, businessmen, politicians, writers, lawyers, entrepreneurs, investors, speculators, gamers and Casanovas have secretly searched for shortcuts that require little skill yet contain the invisible effectiveness of the most advanced techniques. Dr. Wallace identified those shortcuts and honed them into practical formats called Neo-Tech. Those never-before-known formats transfer money, power, and prestige from the uninformed to the informed. Those informed can automatically take control of most situations involving money and power.

Who is The Neo-Tech Man? He is a man of quiet power — a man who cannot lose. He can extract money at will. He can control anyone unknowledgeable about Neo-Tech — man or woman.

The Neo-Tech man has the power to render others helpless, even wipe them out, but he wisely chooses to use just enough of his power to give himself unbeatable casino-like advantages in all his endeavors for maximum long-range profits. His Neo-Tech maneuvers are so subtle that they can be executed with casual confidence. His hidden techniques let him win consistently and comfortably — year after year, decade after decade. Eventually, Neo-Tech men and women will quietly rule everywhere.

The Neo-Tech man can easily and safely beat any opponent. He can quickly impoverish anyone he chooses. He can immediately and consistently acquire large amounts of money. He has the power to make more money in a week than most people without Neo-Tech make in a full year. He commands profits and respect. He controls business deals and emotional situations to acquire money and power...and to command love. He can regain lost love. He can subjugate a business or personal adversary. He wins any lover at will. He can predict stock prices — even gold and silver prices. He quietly rules all.

Within a week, an ordinary person can become a professional Neo-Tech practitioner. As people gain this knowledge, they will immediately begin using its techniques because they are irresistibly easy and overwhelmingly potent. Within days after gaining this knowledge, a person can safely bankrupt opponents — or slowly profit from them, week after week. He can benefit from business and investment endeavors — from dealing with the boss to the biggest oil deal. He can also benefit from any relationship — from gaining the respect of peers to inducing love from a partner or regaining lost love from an ex-partner. He will gain easy money and power in business, investments, the professions, politics, and personal life.

Indeed, with Neo-Tech, a person not only captures unbeatable advantages over others, but commands shortcuts to profits, power, and romance. The ordinary person can quickly become a Clark Kent — a quiet superman — taking command of all. He can financially and emotionally control whomever he deals with. He becomes the man-on-the-hill, now. He is armed with an unbeatable weapon. All will yield to the new-breed Neo-Tech man, the no-limit man....All except the Neo-Tech man will die unfulfilled...without ever knowing wealth, power, and romantic love.

SUMMARY: The period from November through March will be warmer than normal despite a cold November and December. Precipitation will be near or slightly below average, with less-than-normal snowfall expected. Heavy snow will fall in the mountains in mid-December, but coastal snow will not occur until late winter, if at all. Although Christmas will be cold, and there will be a white one in the mountains, the new year will start unusually mild, with temperatures in January as a whole well above normal.

Relatively mild weather will continue in April, with May slightly cooler and drier than normal. The first hot weather of the season will occur in early May, with warm temperatures to close the month.

The period from June through August will be 1 to 2 degrees warmer than normal, with above-normal rainfall. Hot, humid periods will alternate with cooler weather in June. July and August will be mostly hot, with record heat possible in early and late July, mid-August, and again in late August. Rainfall will be near normal from June through early August, but a tropical storm may bring flooding rain in mid-August. September will be a relatively tranquil month. After a damp beginning, dry and quite mild weather will be the rule. October will start with heavy rain, but the remainder of the month will be pleasant, with temperatures above normal.

NOV. 1997: Temp. 47° (2° below avg.); precip. 3" (avg.). 1-9 Cool, rainy episodes. 10-19 Mainly dry, continued cool. 20-25 Damp, mild. 26-30 Chilly, showers.

DEC. 1997: Temp. 36.5° (3° below avg.); precip. 2.5" (0.5" below avg.). 1-3 Rain, then colder. 4-9 Sprinkles and flurries. 10-13 Rain, snow west. 14-16 Dry, cold. 17-20 Rain, snow west. 21-26 Rain, then very cold. 27-31 Sunny and seasonable.

JAN. 1998: Temp. 38.5° (4° above avg.); precip. 2" (0.5" below avg.). 1-5 Mild, rain north. 6-10 Mainly dry, mild. 11-14 Seasonable. 15-17 Rain to snow. 18-22 Sunshine, chilly. 23-26 Periods of rain and snow. 27-31 Sunny, quite seasonable.

FEB. 1998: Temp. 38.5° (1° above avg.); precip. 2.5" (avg.). 1-4 Sunny, cold. 5-9 Rain, then very cold. 10-15 Rainy, milder. 16-25 Sunny, cold, then milder. 26-28 Warm, rain, then colder.

MAR. 1998: Temp. 49° (2° above avg.); precip. 3.5" (0.5" above avg.). 1-10 Rainy, mild. 11-18 Colder, then milder. 19-24 Rather cool, showers. 25-28 Thunder, warm. 29-31 Colder.

APR. 1998: Temp. 57° (2° above avg.); precip. 3.5" (avg.). 1-7 Sunny, turning warmer. 8-14 Showers, cooler, then warmer. 15-19 Rainy. 20-24 Warm, mainly dry. 25-30 Warm and damp.

MAY 1998: Temp. 65.5° (1° below avg.); precip. 2" (2" below avg.). 1-6 Cloudy, cool. 7-9 Sunny, hot. 10-13 Seasonable. 14-18 Periods of rain. 19-25 Some sun, turning very warm. 26-31 Warm, hazy sun.

JUNE 1998: Temp. 73.5° (2° below avg.); precip. 3.5" (avg.). 1-7 Thunderstorms, then cooler. 8-11 Hot, then thunderstorms. 12-18 Showers, cool. 19-22 Sunshine, warm. 23-24 Rainy, raw. 25-30 Hot, humid, thunderstorms.

JULY 1998: Temp. 82° (2° above avg.); precip. 4" (1" below avg. north; 2" above south). 1-3 Seasonable. 4-10 Hot, hot, and humid. 11-16 Thunderstorms. 17-19 Warm. 20-26 Oppressive. 27-31 Humid, with thunderstorms.

AUG. 1998: Temp. 80.5° (2° above avg.); precip. 8" (4" above avg.). 1-4 A bit cooler. 5-11 Heat wave. 12-13 Cooler. 14-22 Flooding rain, possible hurricane. 23-25 Hot, humid. 26-31 Thunderstorms, then cooler.

SEPT. 1998: Temp. 72° (1° above avg.); precip. 2.5" (1" below avg.). 1-7 Damp, turning cooler. 8-14 Sunny, pleasant. 15-21 Cool, then warmer. 22-28 Showers, cooler. 29-30 Crisp.

OCT. 1998: Temp. 65° (1° above avg.); precip. 4" (1" above avg.; avg. south). 1-5 Some rain, heavy south. 6-8 Sunny. 9-12 Showers, warm. 13-16 Sunny, warm. 17-24 Rain, then cooler. 25-31 Mainly dry.

Baltimore
Washington
Richmond
Roanoke

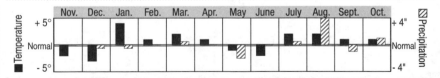

SCIATICA RELIEF!

If you have ever suffered Sciatica symptoms such as pain in the buttocks and lower back, or pain and numbness in your legs and feet, you should get a copy of a new book called *The Sciatica Relief Handbook*. The book shows you how to prevent Sciatica flare-ups, and how to stop pain if you now have a Sciatica problem.

The book contains the latest up-to-date information on Sciatica—what causes painful symptoms, how to best treat them, and how to protect yourself from Sciatica problems. The book gives you specific facts on the latest natural, alternative and medical treatments that can bring prompt and lasting relief—without the use of dangerous drugs or surgery. You'll learn all about these remedies and learn how and why they work to bring dramatic relief.

You'll discover what to immediately do if Sciatica symptoms start and what to avoid at all costs to prevent possible serious problems. You'll even discover a simple treatment that has helped thousands get relief, yet is little known to most people—even doctors.

The book explains all about the Sciatic nerve, the various ways it may become inflamed and cause pain, how to find out what specifically causes distress (you may be surprised), what to do and what not to do—and why over 165 million people experience Sciatica and lower back pain.

Many people are putting up with Sciatica pain—or have had Sciatica pain in the past and are at risk of a recurrence—because they do not know about new prevention and relief measures that are now available.

Get all the facts. The book is available for only $14.95 *(plus $3 postage and handling)*. To order, simply send your name and address with payment to United Research Publishers, 103 North Highway 101, Dept. FAK-1, Encinitas, CA 92024. Your book will be rushed to you. You may return the book within 90 days for a refund if not completely satisfied. ∎

Irritable Colon?

If you suffer problems such as constipation, bloating, diarrhea, gas, stomach cramps, heartburn, pain and discomfort associated with the colon or Irritable Bowel Syndrome (IBS), you should know about a new book, *The Irritable Bowel Syndrome & Gastrointestinal Solutions Handbook*.

The book contains the latest up-to-date information on the digestive system—what can go wrong, how it can best be treated, and how to protect yourself from IBS and stomach problems. The book gives you specific facts on the latest natural and alternative remedies that can bring prompt and lasting relief without the use of dangerous drugs. You'll learn all about these new remedies and find out how and why they work.

You'll discover what you can do to avoid IBS, digestive and stomach problems, what foods actually promote healing, and what to avoid at all costs. The book even explains a simple treatment that has helped thousands rid themselves of IBS and stomach distress, yet is little-known to most people—even doctors.

The book also explains how the gastrointestinal system works, how food is digested, how specific foods affect digestion, why certain foods and activities cause problems, why over 20 million people suffer IBS and gastrointestinal problems—and how people are now able to overcome their problems.

Many Americans are putting up with troublesome IBS, stomach and digestive problems because they are unaware of new natural treatments and the welcome relief that is now available.

Get all the facts. Order today. The book is available for only $14.95 *(plus $3 postage and handling)*. To order, send your name and address with payment to United Research Publishers, 103 North Highway 101, Dept. FAS-4, Encinitas, CA 92024. You may return the book within 90 days for a refund if not satisfied. ∎

PIEDMONT & SOUTHEAST COAST

F O R E C A S T

SUMMARY: Despite a below-normal start, the period from November through March will turn out relatively mild, with temperatures averaging 2 degrees above normal. Precipitation and snowfall will both be below normal. The best chance for snow is relatively early, as storms in late November or early December can bring heavy snow to the interior. January and February will be milder than usual, with record high temperatures most likely to occur in mid- and late February.

Relatively mild weather will continue in April and May, with temperatures 2 degrees above normal. April will be wetter than normal, but May will be relatively dry.

Precipitation will continue below normal from June through August, with temperatures near or above normal. June will be cooler than average, despite hot spells in the second week and again late in the month. July and August will be hotter than usual, with below-normal rainfall in most of the region. New record-high temperatures will be set July 19-22 and August 22-27. A hurricane may hit coastal North Carolina in mid- to late August, but is more likely to make landfall farther north.

September and October will be warmer than normal, with heavy rain in the south, especially in September. The hottest temperatures will occur in early September, with hot spells later in the month.

NOV. 1997: Temp. 50° (2° below avg.); precip. 3" (avg.). 1-9 Cool, rainy episodes. 10-17 Sunny days, chilly nights. 18-24 Rainy, mild. 25-30 Rain, then cold.

DEC. 1997: Temp. 40.5° (1° below avg.); precip. 3" (0.5" below avg.). 1-8 Rain, then seasonable. 9-12 Rain, mountain snow, then cold. 13-16 Dry, chilly. 17-25 Rain, then cold. 26-31 Sunny.

JAN. 1998: Temp. 43° (4° above avg.); precip. 3.5" (0.5" below avg.). 1-5 Showers, mild. 6-10 Sunny, warm. 11-15 Mild south, rain north. 16-18 Sunny, chilly. 19-28 Rainy episodes, mountain snow. 29-31 Seasonable.

FEB. 1998: Temp. 45° (3° above avg.); precip. 2" (1" below avg.). 1-4 Sunny, colder. 5-8 Showers, mild, then colder. 9-11 Heavy rain. 12-14 Sunny, warm. 15-17 Rain, then cold. 18-26 Quite mild, mainly dry. 27-28 Rain.

MAR. 1998: Temp. 54° (2° above avg.); precip. 3" (1" below avg.). 1-10 Warm, few showers. 11-14 Colder, then milder. 15-17 Warm, then showers. 18-26 Damp north, warm south. 27-31 Turning colder.

APR. 1998: Temp. 62° (2° above avg.); precip. 5.5" (2" above avg.). 1-5 Sunny, turning warmer. 6-11 Showers. 12-14 Pleasant. 15-18 Heavy rain. 19-27 Sunny, warm. 28-30 Showers.

MAY 1998: Temp. 69° (2° above avg.); precip. 2.5" (1" below avg.). 1-7 Sunny, warm. 8-15 Sunny, hot. 16-21 Thunderstorms, cooler. 22-24 Dry. 25-29 Rainy. 30-31 Hot.

JUNE 1998: Temp. 74° (2° below avg.); precip. 2.5" (1" below avg.). 1-5 Cooler. 6-10 Sunny, hot. 11-15 Showers, cooler. 16-20 Hot south, comfortable north. 21-30 Hot, humid, thunderstorms.

JULY 1998: Temp. 81° (1° above avg.); precip. 4.5" (1" above avg. north; 1" below south). 1-3 Pleasant. 4-8 Oppressive. 9-14 Hot, afternoon thunderstorms. 15-18 Hazy, thunderstorms. 19-22 Very hot. 23-25 Thunderstorms, then cooler. 26-31 Seasonably hot.

AUG. 1998: Temp. 78° (2° above avg.); precip. 2.5" (1" below avg.). 1-5 Seasonable, few thunderstorms. 6-11 Hazy, hot, humid. 12-21 Warm, mostly dry. 22-27 Very hot. 28-31 Cooler.

SEPT. 1998: Temp. 74° (2° above avg.); precip. 3.5" (1" below avg. north; 1" above south). 1-3 Sunny, hot. 4-9 Showers, cooler. 10-16 Hot, humid. 17-21 Rain south. 22-27 Sunny, hot. 28-30 Showers.

OCT. 1998: Temp. 67° (1° above avg.); precip. 5.5" (2" above avg.). 1-6 Hot south, rain north. 7-10 Warm north, showers south. 11-17 Warm, mainly dry. 18-22 Cooler, few showers. 23-31 Warm days, cool nights.

Raleigh

Columbia

Atlanta   Savannah

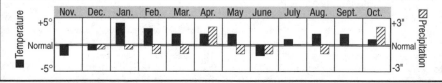

FLORIDA

F O R E C A S T

SUMMARY: Temperatures in the period from November through March will average near normal, with below-normal rainfall. The period will start with relatively cool temperatures, averaging about 3 degrees below normal in November and December. The coldest temperatures, with the best chance for a freeze into central Florida, will occur in mid-December, after the passage of a strong cold front. January, February, and March will be milder than normal, with below-normal rainfall, especially in February.

April and May will bring near- to below-normal temperatures, except in the north, where temperatures will average 2 degrees above normal. Precipitation will be near normal, although continued dry weather in the south will be a prelude to an unusually dry summer.

While temperatures from June through August will be near normal, precipitation will be relatively light, with substantially less thunderstorm activity than usual. The best chances for more widespread thunderstorms are in the latter half of June, in the beginning and at the end of July, and in the middle and latter portions of August. The hottest period for Florida as a whole will occur in the second week of August.

September and October will be warmer than normal, especially in the north. Relatively dry weather will continue in the south, but rainfall in central and northern parts of the state will be above normal.

NOV. 1997: Temp. 65° (3° below avg.); precip. 3" (avg.; 2" above south). 1-3 Showers, warm. 4-13 Mainly sunny, rather cool. 14-19 Rain. 20-23 Sunshine, warm. 24-30 Rather cool, few showers.

DEC. 1997: Temp. 59° (3° below avg.); precip. 3" (1" below avg.). 1-4 Warm. 5-9 Cool, dry. 10-13 Showers, then freeze north. 14-18 Mild, then showers. 19-21 Cool. 22-26 Showers, then chilly. 27-31 Sunny, warmer.

JAN. 1998: Temp. 62° (2° above avg.); precip. 2.5" (1" below avg.). 1-13 Sunny, mild. 14-18 Showers, then cooler. 19-23 Frequent showers. 24-26 Pleasant. 27-31 Rain, then colder.

FEB. 1998: Temp. 63° (2° above avg.; avg. south); precip. 1" (2" below south). 1-5 Sunshine, chilly. 6-10 Warmer, few showers. 11-16 Thunderstorms, then cooler. 17-20 Turning warmer. 21-28 Pleasant north, showers south.

MAR. 1998: Temp. 69° (2° above avg.); precip. 2.5" (1" below avg.). 1-10 Sunshine, turning warmer. 11-14 Showers, cooler. 15-25 Sunny, warm. 26-31 Rain, then chilly.

APR. 1998: Temp. 71° (1° below avg.; 2° above north); precip. 5.5" (avg.). 1-10 Rain, then warmer. 11-20 Seasonable, showers. 21-30 Sunshine, hot.

MAY 1998: Temp. 76° (1° below avg.; 2° above north); precip. 5" (avg. north; 2" below south). 1-8 Sunny, warm. 9-17 Hot north, thunder south. 18-27 Frequent showers. 28-31 Sunny, hot.

JUNE 1998: Temp. 80° (1° below avg.); precip. 4" (2" below avg.). 1-5 Warm, few showers. 6-13 Sunshine, very warm. 14-17 Thunderstorms, heavy south. 18-23 Sunshine, daily thunderstorms. 24-30 Thunderstorms, hot north.

JULY 1998: Temp. 83° (1° below avg.); precip. 4" (1" below avg.). 1-7 Frequent showers. 8-12 Hot north, showers south. 13-19 Seasonable. 20-25 Hot north, showers south. 26-31 Heavy thunderstorms.

AUG. 1998: Temp. 83° (1° above avg.); precip. 3.5" (3" below avg.). 1-6 Seasonable, few thunderstorms. 7-15 Hot, mainly dry. 16-19 Frequent showers. 20-24 Hottest north. 25-31 Hot, thunderstorms.

SEPT. 1998: Temp. 82° (1° above avg.); precip. 6" (avg.; 2" above central). 1-3 Mainly dry. 4-14 Frequent thunderstorms. 15-22 Most rain north. 23-28 Showers south, hot north. 29-30 Thunderstorms.

OCT. 1998: Temp. 75° (avg.; 2° above north); precip. 4" (2" above avg. north; 1" below south). 1-10 Warm, frequent showers. 11-15 Thunderstorms, cooler north. 16-20 Sunny, cool nights. 21-22 Rainy. 23-31 Mild, mainly dry.

Jacksonville

Tampa *Orlando*

Miami

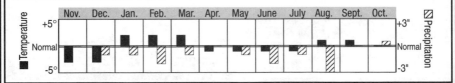

SUMMARY: Temperatures and precipitation will be higher than normal from November through March, but snowfall will be below normal in most of the region. Heavy lake-effect snows will occur in early and late December, with additional snows in mid- to late January. The best chances for more-widespread snowstorms are in mid-December, in early and mid-February, and toward the middle of March. The coldest temperatures will occur in early February, after a relatively mild January.

April and May will be a bit warmer than normal, although Memorial Day weekend will be on the cool side. Precipitation will be normal or slightly below.

After a near normal June, exceptionally hot temperatures will occur in July and August. Heat waves are most likely in the first weeks of both months, when record highs may be set. Rainfall will be well below normal, with July not only very hot but also very dry. The best chance for substantial rain in July is during the latter half of the month, but many spots will have little precipitation until mid-August, when the remnants of a tropical storm may bring heavy rain, especially to the east.

Temperatures in September and October will continue to be warmer than normal. Precipitation in September will be below normal despite rainy periods at the start, the middle, and the end of the month. Heavy rain in mid-October will make the month as a whole wetter than normal.

NOV. 1997: Temp. 41° (1° above avg.); precip. 3.5" (avg.). 1-5 Cooler, showers. 6-8 Heavy rain. 9-20 Mainly dry, seasonable. 21-25 Rainy, quite mild. 26-30 Colder, showers and flurries.

DEC. 1997: Temp. 26.5° (avg.); precip. 3.5" (0.5" above avg.). 1-3 Rainy. 4-11 Cold, lake snows. 12-15 Rain and snow. 16-17 Some sun. 18-22 Snow, rain south. 23-26 Cold, flurries, lake snows. 27-31 Milder.

JAN. 1998: Temp. 24.5° (4° above avg.); precip. 3.5" (1" above avg.). 1-3 Rain, then colder. 4-10 Turning milder, rain, snow north. 11-21 Seasonably cold, flurries, lake snows. 22-24 Cold. 25-31 Seasonable, lake snows.

FEB. 1998: Temp. 24.5° (1° above avg.); precip. 2.5" (0.5" above avg.). 1-7 Snow, then very cold. 8-14 Milder, mainly dry. 15-21 Cold, snowy episodes. 22-24 Mild. 25-28 Rain to snow.

MAR. 1998: Temp. 34° (avg.; 1° below east); precip. 4" (1" above avg.). 1-6 Mild, some rain. 7-10 Snow, cold. 11-16 Milder. 17-22 Colder, flurries. 23-31 Chilly, rain and snow.

APR. 1998: Temp. 47° (1° above avg.); precip. 2" (avg.). 1-6 Turning milder. 7-12 Rain, colder. 13-21 Warmer, rain. 22-30 Mild, then cooler, showers.

MAY 1998: Temp. 59.5° (2° above avg.); precip. 3" (1" below avg.). 1-9 Becoming warmer, few showers. 10-13 Showers, then cooler. 14-20 Warmer, sunshine. 21-25 Warm days, chilly nights. 26-31 Showers, warm.

JUNE 1998: Temp. 67° (avg.); precip. 3" (1" below avg.). 1-5 Cooler, showers. 6-10 Becoming hot. 11-18 Cool, showers. 19-23 Sunny, hot. 24-30 Warm, showers east.

JULY 1998: Temp. 76° (4° above avg.); precip. 1.5" (2" below avg.). 1-8 Sunny, hot, and humid. 9-11 Thunderstorms, then cooler. 12-14 Quite hot. 15-17 Cooler. 18-22 Hot, thunderstorms. 23-26 Hot days, cool nights. 27-31 Thunderstorms, warm.

AUG. 1998: Temp. 74° (4° above avg.); precip. 5" (1" above avg.; 3" above southeast). 1-7 Heat wave. 8-14 Thunderstorms, then cooler. 15-18 Heavy rain east. 19-26 Rather hot, thunderstorms east. 27-31 Cooler, few showers.

SEPT. 1998: Temp. 62° (1° above avg.); precip. 3" (0.5" below avg.). 1-3 Rain. 4-13 Sunshine, pleasant. 14-18 Rain, some heavy. 19-23 Sunny, hot. 24-26 Cooler. 27-30 Rain, then colder.

OCT. 1998: Temp. 52° (2° above avg.); precip. 4.5" (2" above avg.). 1-8 Mild days, crisp nights. 9-12 Rainy, warm. 13-16 Sunny, warm. 17-21 Cooler, heavy rain. 22-31 Showers, seasonable.

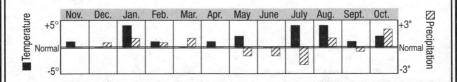

SUMMARY: The period from November through March will be milder and drier than normal, with snowfall below normal, except possibly in the mountains. The season will start on the cold side, with temperatures in November and December some 2 degrees below normal. Snow in mid-December will last long enough for a white Christmas, but a milder regime will start in the west in December and then spread across the whole region, with January temperatures about 5 degrees above normal. February will also be milder than normal, although snow in midmonth will be heavy.

April and May will continue relatively mild, with temperatures about 2 degrees above normal and rainfall below normal.

June will be on the cool side, and July and August will be hotter than normal. Heat waves are most likely in early and mid-July and in early and mid- to late August. Rainfall will be near normal, with the heaviest rain in the west in June and in the east in August. The remains of a tropical storm could bring some heavy rain to the east in mid- to late August.

September and October will be about 2 degrees warmer than normal despite chilly periods. Particularly hot temperatures will occur in September. Rainfall will be near normal but below normal in the west.

NOV. 1997: Temp. 44° (2° below avg.); precip. 2" (1" below avg.). 1-3 Showers, cooler. 4-9 Cold, showers and flurries. 10-21 Sunshine; mild, cold nights. 22-24 Rainy, mild. 25-30 Colder, showers, mountain snow.

DEC. 1997: Temp. 32° (2° below avg.; 1° above west); precip. 2" (1" below avg.). 1-3 Mild, showers. 4-11 Cold, flurries. 12-14 Rain and snow. 15-17 Seasonable. 18-22 Rain and snow. 23-26 Cold, snow showers. 27-31 Milder, then rain.

JAN. 1998: Temp. 34° (5° above avg.); precip. 3" (0.5" above avg.). 1-3 Rain, then colder. 4-10 Milder and rainy. 11-15 Seasonable, mainly dry. 16-19 Cold, snow showers. 20-24 Milder, then cold with flurries. 25-31 Milder, then cold with snowy episodes.

FEB. 1998: Temp. 35° (2° above avg.); precip. 3.5" (0.5" above avg.). 1-3 Very cold. 4-8 Snow, then very cold. 9-14 Turning milder. 15-17 Snow, colder. 18-24 Snow, then milder. 25-28 Rain, then colder.

MAR. 1998: Temp. 44° (avg.); precip. 4" (avg.). 1-8 Mild, rainy. 9-12 Much colder. 13-18 Warm, few showers. 19-22 Showers, then colder with flurries. 23-24 Mild. 25-28 Rain, then colder. 29-31 Cold, flurries.

APR. 1998: Temp. 56° (2° above avg.); precip. 3" (avg. west; 1" below east). 1-6 Sunny, turning warmer. 7-13 Quick changes. 14-18 Showers,

warm. 19-22 Sunny, warm. 23-27 Warm, rainy periods. 28-30 Cooler.

MAY 1998: Temp. 66° (2° above avg.); precip. 3.5" (1" below avg.). 1-8 Becoming warmer, more humid. 9-17 Showers, cooler. 18-22 Sunny, pleasant. 23-31 Showers, warm.

JUNE 1998: Temp. 69° (3° below avg.; 2" above west). 1-4 Cooler, showers. 5-9 Sunny, warmer. 10-18 Rainy, cool. 19-25 Sunshine, hot. 26-30 Cooler, few showers.

JULY 1998: Temp. 78° (2° above avg.); precip. 3"(1" below avg.). 1-9 Hot, humid, mainly dry. 10-12 Thunderstorms, cooler. 13-21 Hot, humid, mainly dry. 22-31 Progressively hotter, few thunderstorms east.

AUG. 1998: Temp. 79° (4° above avg.); precip. 4" (2" above avg. east; 1" below west). 1-8 Heat wave. 9-18 Warm, thunderstorms east. 19-26 Heat wave west, few thunderstorms east. 27-31 Sunny, very warm.

SEPT. 1998: Temp. 70° (2° above avg.); precip. 2" (1" below avg.). 1-3 Hot, then thunderstorms. 4-13 Sunny, warm days, cool nights. 14-16 Thunderstorms, then cooler. 17-23 Sunny, hot. 24-30 Showers, then cooler.

OCT. 1998: Temp. 58° (2° above avg.); precip. 3" (0.5" above avg.; 1" below west). 1-7 Rain, then cool. 8-11 Rainy, warm. 12-15 Sunny, warm. 16-23 Showers, turning cooler. 24-31 Warm days, crisp nights.

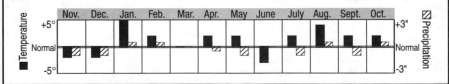

New Poetry Contest
$48,000.00 in Prizes

The National Library of Poetry to award 250 total prizes to amateur poets in coming months

The National Library of Poetry publishes the work of amateur poets in colorful hardbound anthologies like **The Coming of Dawn,** *pictured above. Each volume features poetry by a diverse mix of poets from all over the world.*

Owings Mills, Maryland – The National Library of Poetry has just announced that $48,000.00 in prizes will be awarded over the next 12 months in the brand new North American Open Amateur Poetry Contest. The contest is open to everyone and entry is free.

"We're especially looking for poems from new or unpublished poets," indicated Howard Ely, spokesperson for The National Library of Poetry. "We have a ten year history of awarding large prizes to talented poets who have never before won any type of writing competition."

How To Enter

Anyone may enter the competition simply by sending in *ONLY ONE* original poem, any subject, any style, to:

The National Library of Poetry
Suite 6482
1 Poetry Plaza
Owings Mills, MD 21117-6282

Or enter online at **www.poetry.com**

The poem should be no more than 20 lines, and the poet's name and address must appear on the top of the page. "All poets who enter will receive a response concerning their artistry, usually within seven weeks," indicated Mr. Ely.

Possible Publication

Many submitted poems will also be considered for inclusion in one of The National Library of Poetry's forthcoming hardbound anthologies. Previous anthologies published by the organization have included *On the Threshold of a Dream*, *Days of Future's Past*, *Of Diamonds and Rust*, and *Moments More to Go*, among others.

"Our anthologies routinely sell out because they are truly enjoyable reading, and they are also a sought-after sourcebook for poetic talent," added Mr. Ely.

SUMMARY: November through March will be warmer than normal despite a cold start. Temperatures through mid-December will be 2 to 3 degrees below normal, and 2 to 3 degrees above normal for the rest of the period. The coldest spells will be in early and mid-December and in mid-January. Rainfall will be well below normal, with the rainiest periods most likely in the first half of December, early and mid-January, early and late February, and mid- to late March. The best chances for snow or ice are in early December, in mid- to late January, and in late February.

April and May will be 2 to 3 degrees warmer than normal, with a wet April followed by near-normal rainfall in May. Some of the hottest temperatures of the year will occur during the first half of May.

Temperatures in June through August will be a bit cooler than normal. Hottest temperatures will occur in mid-July. Rainfall will be slightly above normal. The most widespread thunderstorm activity will be in mid- to late July. Tropical storms will be less likely, with more activity in the Atlantic than in the Gulf.

September and October will be relatively warm and dry, with temperatures averaging about 2 degrees above normal and precipitation about half of normal. The greatest chances for significant rainfall are at the start and end of September and in mid-October.

NOV. 1997: Temp. 50.5° (2° below avg.); precip. 3" (2" below avg.). 1-3 Showers, cool. 4-6 Sunny, chilly. 7-18 Rain, then sunny and warmer. 19-25 Rainy periods. 26-30 Sunny, cool.

DEC. 1997: Temp. 41.5° (2° below avg.); precip. 4" (1" below avg.). 1-7 Rain, then colder. 8-16 Rainy, cool north. 17-20 Cold, then milder. 21-31 Showers, then warm.

JAN. 1998: Temp. 43° (3° above avg.); precip. 2.5" (1" below avg.). 1-4 Heavy rain, then colder. 5-10 Cloudy, mild. 11-17 Rainy, then cold. 18-23 Rain, snow north. 24-31 Mainly seasonable.

FEB. 1998: Temp. 46° (2° above avg.); precip. 4" (avg.). 1-5 Cold, then milder. 6-10 Rain, some heavy. 11-13 Mild. 14-17 Showers, then colder. 18-23 Some sun, milder. 24-26 Heavy rain, snow north. 27-28 Mild.

MAR. 1998: Temp. 54° (1° above avg.); precip. 5" (1" above avg. north; 2" below south). 1-9 Some sun, warm. 10-13 Rain, then colder. 14-20 Rain north, warm south. 21-25 Heavy rain. 26-31 Showers, then quite cold.

APR. 1998: Temp. 64° (1° above avg.); precip. 7.5" (2" above avg.). 1-3 Sunny, chilly. 4-10 Warmer, rain. 11-17 Heavy rain. 18-23 Sunny, warm. 24-27 Warm, rain north. 28-30 Seasonable.

MAY 1998: Temp. 77° (3° above avg.); precip. 5" (avg.). 1-14 Mainly dry, hot. 15-18 Humid, showers. 19-23 Warm, thunderstorms south. 24-31 Some sun, afternoon thunderstorms.

JUNE 1998: Temp. 76° (3° below avg.); precip. 3.5" (avg.) 1-3 Cool. 4-8 Sunny, hot. 9-18 Showers, rather cool. 19-23 Sunny, hot. 24-30 Hot, few thunderstorms.

JULY 1998: Temp. 82° (1° below avg.); precip. 5.5" (2" above avg.). 1-11 Hazy, humid, few thunderstorms. 12-15 Hot, with sunshine. 16-22 Frequent thunderstorms. 23-31 Seasonable heat and thunderstorms.

AUG. 1998: Temp. 82° (1° above avg.); precip. 2.5" (1" below avg.). 1-6 Hot north, thunder south. 7-10 Seasonably hot. 11-15 Unsettled. 16-21 Warm, mainly dry. 22-31 Hot, mainly dry.

SEPT. 1998: Temp. 76° (2° above avg.); precip. 1.5" (2" below avg.). 1-3 Few showers. 4-9 Sunny, seasonable. 10-14 Sunny, hot. 15-18 Cooler. 19-26 Sunny, hot. 27-30 Hot south, rain north.

OCT. 1998: Temp. 65° (2° above avg.); precip. 2" (1" below avg.). 1-3 Hot, humid. 4-7 Cooler north. 8-11 Thunderstorms, then cooler. 12-15 Sunny, warmer. 16-22 Showers, then cool. 23-27 Sunny, warm. 28-31 Seasonable.

Nashville

Little Rock

Montgomery

Mobile

Shreveport

New Orleans

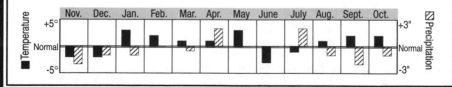

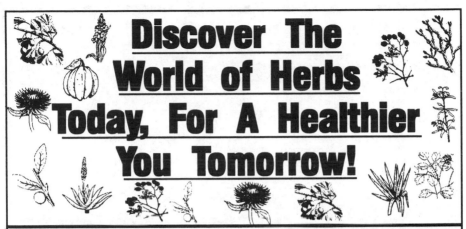

9 CHICAGO & SOUTHERN GREAT LAKES

F O R E C A S T

SUMMARY: November through March will be 1 to 2 degrees warmer than normal, mainly because of a warmer-than-normal January. December and February will both be colder than January, with coldest temperatures expected in early and mid-February. Precipitation overall will be close to normal, although twice the norm in January. The best chances for heavy snow are in mid-December and just after the new year.

April and May will be warmer and drier than normal, a trend that will carry through most of the summer. Temperatures will be quite hot in early May.

Rainfall from June through August will be well below normal, with well-above-normal temperatures. June will actually be cooler than normal, with rainfall only a bit below normal. July and August will bring several heat waves, with infrequent cooling thunderstorms. Especially oppressive heat will occur in the first half and final week of July, and in the first week and through much of the latter half of August. The best chances for much-needed widespread rain are in late July and in mid- and late August.

Warmer, drier-than-normal weather will continue in September and October, despite heavy thunderstorms, followed by a cool-down in early September. Other periods likely to experience significant rain are mid-September and mid- and late October.

NOV. 1997: Temp. 42.5° (1° above avg.); precip. 2" (1" below avg.). 1-8 Turning colder, showers to flurries. 9-21 Sunshine, rather mild. 22-25 Rain, then colder. 26-30 Windy, showers.

DEC. 1997: Temp. 28° (avg.); precip. 2" (1" below avg.). 1-9 Colder, snow showers. 10-11 Sunny, cold. 12-14 Rain and snow. 15-23 Cold, flurries. 24-31 Cold, then milder with rain.

JAN. 1998: Temp. 28° (5° above avg.); precip. 3.5" (2" above avg.). 1-3 Heavy snow. 4-9 Milder with heavy rain. 10-15 Sunny, mild. 16-18 Flurries. 19-24 Mainly dry, seasonable. 25-31 Periods of snow, then cold.

FEB. 1998: Temp. 28° (1° above avg.; 1° below west); precip. 2.5" (0.5" above avg.). 1-3 Cold, flurries. 4-13 Light snow, then milder. 14-17 Rain to snow, then cold. 18-23 Milder. 24-28 Rain.

MAR. 1998: Temp. 37° (1° below avg.); precip. 3" (avg.; 1" above east). 1-4 Rainy episodes. 5-7 Warm west, rain east. 8-11 Colder, flurries. 12-17 Much warmer. 18-23 Rain, then cold. 24-31 Rain changing to snow.

APR. 1998: Temp. 53° (3° above avg.); precip. 2" (1" below avg.). 1-6 Sunny, turning warmer. 7-11 Rain, then cooler. 12-14 Sunny, warmer. 15-18 Showers. 19-24 Sun, then rain. 25-30 Warm, then rain, cooler.

MAY 1998: Temp. 62° (2° above avg.); precip. 2.5" (1" below avg.). 1-7 Sunny, becoming hot. 8-17 Cooler, few showers. 18-25 Sunny, warmer. 26-31 Thunderstorms, warm.

JUNE 1998: Temp. 69° (2° below avg.); precip. 3" (1" below avg.). 1-6 Cool, mainly dry. 7-17 Warm, then cool, frequent showers. 18-24 Sunny, hot. 25-30 Some sun, cooler.

JULY 1998: Temp. 79° (4° above avg.); precip. 2" (2" below avg.). 1-8 Hot, mainly dry, thunderstorms north. 9-13 Hot, thunderstorms west. 14-17 Sunny, warm. 18-22 Warm, thunderstorms. 23-26 Sunny, hot. 27-31 Thunderstorms, oppressively hot.

AUG. 1998: Temp. 79.5° (6° above avg.); precip. 1.5" (2" below avg.). 1-8 Heat wave. 9-17 Thunderstorms, then seasonable. 18-25 Another heat wave. 26-31 Thunderstorms, then cooler east.

SEPT. 1998: Temp. 69° (3° above avg.); precip. 2.5" (1" below avg.). 1-10 Heavy thunderstorms, then sunny, cooler. 11-18 Quick changes. 19-23 Sunny, hot. 24-30 Showers, cooler.

OCT. 1998: Temp. 54° (3° above avg.); precip. 3.5" (1" below avg.). 1-7 Showers, then sunny. 8-11 Rain. 12-15 Sunny, warm. 16-22 Showers, turning cooler. 23-26 Mild. 27-31 Rain, then warm.

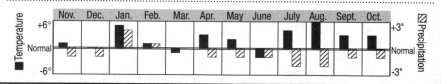

NORTHERN GREAT PLAINS-GREAT LAKES
F O R E C A S T

SUMMARY: Another tough winter is likely, especially in the western part of the region. Although November will be quite mild, temperatures from November through March will average 2 degrees below normal in the west and only 1 degree above normal in the east. February will be especially harsh, with strong winds and temperatures well below normal. The coldest weather is most likely from the latter half of January through February. Precipitation will be slightly below normal, with snowfall near to slightly above normal. The best chances for heavy snow are in early December, mid-February, and the second week of March.

The change from March to April will be dramatic, with both April and May expected to be quite a bit milder than normal. Precipitation during these months will be below normal.

Temperatures in June will be relatively cool, but July and August will be far hotter than normal. Rainfall, especially in the south, will be less than normal, with drought a possibility. The hottest temperatures will occur in early and late July, and the first week and second half of August. The best chances for widespread rain are in mid-June, late July, and mid-August.

Warm and dry weather is expected to continue in September and October, with temperatures about 4 degrees above normal and precipitation half to two thirds of normal.

NOV. 1997: Temp. 38° (5° above avg.); precip. 1" (1" below avg.). 1-6 Colder, showers and flurries. 7-17 Sunny, mild days. 18-27 Clouds, still mild. 28-30 Colder, flurries.

DEC. 1997: Temp. 20° (1° above avg.); precip. 1" (avg.; 1" below east). 1-6 Periods of snow. 7-12 Mainly dry. 13-20 Snow showers. 21-27 Milder, sprinkles and flurries. 28-31 Colder.

JAN. 1998: Temp. 11° (2° below avg.; 3° above east); precip. 1" (avg.). 1-10 Rather mild, some sun. 11-19 Colder, snow showers. 20-23 Sunny, quite cold. 24-31 Cold, occasional flurries.

FEB. 1998: Temp. 12° (6° below avg.; 2° below east); precip. 1.5" (0.5" above avg.). 1-5 Very cold. 6-13 Snowy episodes. 14-18 Frigid. 19-24 Milder, then snow. 25-28 Cold, flurries.

MAR. 1998: Temp. 28° (3° below avg.); precip. 1" (1" below avg.). 1-7 Somewhat milder. 8-12 Snow, then cold. 13-18 Milder, showers. 19-25 Cold, occasional snow. 26-31 Milder, then very cold.

APR. 1998: Temp. 50° (4° above avg.); precip. 1" (1.5" below avg.). 1-6 Much warmer. 7-10 Showers, cooler. 11-20 Sunny, warm. 21-24 Showers. 25-30 Sun, then showers.

MAY 1998: Temp. 63° (5° above avg.); precip. 2" (1" below avg.). 1-6 Sunny, hot. 7-13 Showers, then cooler. 14-23 Sunny, very warm. 24-31 Hot and humid, then showers, cooler.

JUNE 1998: Temp. 66° (2° below avg.); precip. 3" (1" below avg.). 1-4 Sunshine, mild. 5-15 Warm, then cool with thunderstorms. 16-20 Sunny, warm. 21-26 Showers, then cooler.

JULY 1998: Temp. 76° (3° above avg.); precip. 3.5" (avg.; 1" above north). 1-8 Hot, few thunderstorms. 9-11 Sunny, hot. 12-16 Thunderstorms east, hot west. 17-21 Cooler. 22-26 Sunny, hot. 27-31 Quick changes.

AUG. 1998: Temp. 76° (6° above avg.); precip. 3" (1" below avg.; avg. north). 1-7 Heat wave. 8-13 Cooler, few thunderstorms. 14-19 Sunny, warm. 20-24 Heat wave. 25-31 Hot, scattered thunderstorms.

SEPT. 1998: Temp. 64.5° (4° above avg.); precip. 1.5" (1" below avg.). 1-7 Warm, sunny. 8-15 Turning cooler, mainly dry. 16-21 Showers, then hot. 22-26 Cooler, few showers. 27-30 Frequent showers east.

OCT. 1998: Temp. 53° (4° above avg.); precip. 1" (1" below avg.). 1-4 Sunshine. 5-9 Showers, warm. 10-12 Sunny, cool. 13-15 Sunny, quite warm. 16-22 Showers, then cooler. 23-31 Up and down temperatures.

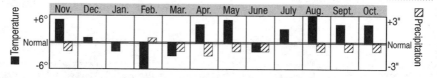

SUMMARY: Temperatures from November through March will vary quite a bit through the region. Western and central areas will be well above normal in November but well below normal thereafter, with temperatures about 2 degrees below average overall. The east will be near normal in November and December but warmer than normal thereafter. Precipitation and snowfall will be near normal, although the central area will have more than usual. Heavy snow is most likely in mid- and late January and late February in the west, and in late November and mid- to late February in the east.

April and May will be milder than usual, with below-normal rainfall, especially in the southwest. Temperatures will be about 3 degrees above normal during each month.

Although June will be cooler than normal, July and especially August will be quite hot. Rainfall will be below normal all three months in most of the region. The possibility of a drought is rather high, with a significant chance of low corn and soybean yields. Hottest periods will be in mid- and late July, and in the first week of and mid- to late August. The greatest chances for significant rains are in late July and mid-August.

Temperatures in September and October will be about 4 degrees above average. Although rainfall will remain below normal, soaking rains will occur in late September and early October.

NOV. 1997: Temp. 43° (5° above avg.; avg. east); precip. 1.5" (1" below avg.). 1-8 Cooler, showers east. 9-20 Sunny, warm. 21-24 Turning cooler, showers. 25-30 Mild west, chilly east.

DEC. 1997: Temp. 23° (1° below avg.); precip. 1.5" (0.5" above avg.; 1" below east). 1-4 Chilly, showers and flurries. 5-11 Dry. 12-16 Mild southwest, flurries northeast. 17-20 Mild. 21-25 Rain and snow, cooler. 26-31 Milder.

JAN. 1998: Temp. 17° (4° below avg. west; 4° above east); precip. 2" (1" above avg.). 1-6 Rain east, then mild. 7-10 Rain, snow west. 11-15 Mild east, cold west. 16-21 Flurries, then milder. 22-28 Snow west, flurries east. 29-31 Very cold.

FEB. 1998: Temp. 19° (5° below avg. northwest; 1° above southeast); precip. 2" (0.5" above avg.; 2" above central). 1-4 Flurries, then milder. 5-11 Snow and rain, then colder. 12-16 Mild, then cold. 17-21 Cloudy and mild east, cold northwest. 22-26 Rain to snow, colder. 27-28 Flurries.

MAR. 1998: Temp. 34° (avg. east; 3° below west); precip. 1" (1" below avg.). 1-4 Rain east, flurries west. 5-7 Milder, then thunderstorms. 8-10 Sunny, cold. 11-15 Sunny, warm. 16-23 Colder, showers. 24-26 Rain to snow. 27-31 Turning cold.

APR. 1998: Temp. 53° (3° above avg.); precip. 2" (1" below avg.). 1-6 Sunny, warmer. 7-11 Thunderstorms, cooler. 12-18 Warm, thunderstorms.

19-22 Hot. 23-30 Thunderstorms east.

MAY 1998: Temp. 65° (3° above avg.); precip. 2" (2" below avg.; avg. central). 1-10 Warm, thunderstorms. 11-17 Cooler, showers. 18-21 Sunny, warm. 22-25 Cooler. 26-31 Thunderstorms.

JUNE 1998: Temp. 69° (3° below avg.); precip. 3" (1" below avg.; 2" below central). 1-6 Warmer, thunderstorms. 7-16 Cooler, showers. 17-24 Thunderstorms west, warm east. 25-30 Thunderstorms.

JULY 1998: Temp. 79° (3° above avg.); precip. 3.5" (avg.; 2" below south). 1-7 Some sun, turning hot. 8-10 Cooler, thunderstorms. 11-17 Hot, thunderstorms. 18-22 Warm, mainly dry. 23-27 Hot, few thunderstorms. 28-31 Heat wave.

AUG. 1998: Temp. 82° (6° above avg.); precip. 2" (2" below avg.). 1-8 Heat wave. 9-14 Thunderstorms, cooler. 15-20 Warm. 21-24 Heat wave. 25-26 Thunderstorms. 27-31 Oppressive.

SEPT. 1998: Temp. 69° (4° above avg.); precip. 2.5" (1" below avg.). 1-2 Hot, then thunderstorms. 3-7 Sunny, warm. 8-12 Very hot. 13-17 Thunderstorms, then cooler. 18-21 Hot. 22-30 Cooler.

OCT. 1998: Temp. 58° (4° above avg.); precip. 2" (1" below avg.; 2" above southeast). 1-7 Rain south and east. 8-11 Showers, warm. 12-14 Sunny, warm. 15-18 Warm. 19-26 Warm, showers east. 27-31 Dry, mild.

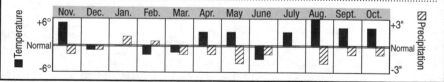

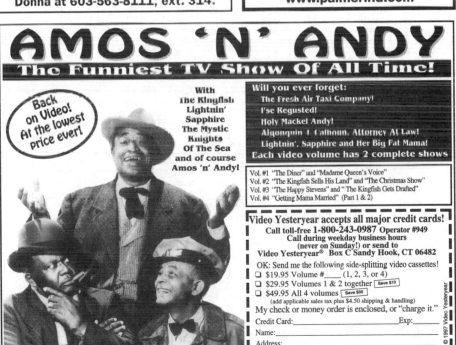

SUMMARY: Although temperatures from November through March will be about 1 degree warmer than normal in the northwest and 2 degrees warmer in the southeast, there will be a few cold periods. Cold air will even reach all the way down to the Rio Grande Valley in mid-December or early January. Precipitation will be near normal, with a drier-than-usual November and March, but with wetter weather in between. The best chances for snow and ice across the northern and perhaps the central regions are in the first half of January and again in early February.

April and May will be warmer and drier than normal. April will be particularly dry, especially in the south and east, while Gulf moisture will bring more frequent showers and thunderstorms in May.

Though June will start showery and cool, hotter temperatures will prevail, with scattered thunderstorms. The first half of July will be hotter and drier than usual, but a possible tropical storm will bring heavy rain to the Valley by midmonth. The remainder of July will be hot and humid. August will be typically hot, with less thunderstorm activity than usual. The combination of summer heat and below-normal rainfall will result in a significant drought by the end of August.

The first half of September will be rather hot despite some thunderstorms, but the latter half of the month will be distinctly cooler. October will feature a couple of much-needed rainy periods.

NOV. 1997: Temp. 57° (avg.; 2° above northwest); precip. 1.5" (1" below avg.). 1-3 Rain south and east. 4-6 Sunny, chilly. 7-9 Turning warmer, some rain. 10-12 Sunny, warm. 13-17 Sunny, rain south. 18-21 Showers. 22-30 Sunny, warm.

DEC. 1997: Temp. 49° (2° above avg.); precip. 2.5" (1" above avg.; avg. east). 1-6 Dry. 7-12 Sunny, cool. 13-16 Rain. 17-22 Sunny, cool. 23-27 Rain. 28-31 Rain east.

JAN. 1998: Temp. 45° (avg. west; 2° above east); precip. 3" (1" above avg.). 1-5 Snow north and west, cooler. 6-10 Warm south, ice to rain north. 11-15 Milder. 16-20 Rain east. 21-25 Warm south, rain northeast. 26-31 Mainly dry, seasonable.

FEB. 1998: Temp. 49° (2° below avg. northwest; 2° above southeast); precip. 2.5" (avg.; 1" above northwest). 1-5 Sunny, warmer. 6-9 Warm southeast, snow northwest. 10-13 Sunny, warmer. 14-17 Showers, then colder. 18-21 Sunny, warmer. 22-28 Showers, then sunny and colder.

MAR. 1998: Temp. 60° (3° above avg.); precip. 2" (1" below avg.). 1-8 Showers, then sunny, warmer. 9-12 Rain, then cooler. 13-20 Sunny, turning warm. 21-25 Hot south, rainy north. 26-31 Sunny, chilly.

APR. 1998: Temp. 68° (1° above avg.); precip. 2" (2" below avg.). 1-3 Sunny, warm. 4-10 Warm, rain north. 11-17 Drizzle south, rain north. 18-23 Sunny, hot. 24-30 Hot, cooler northwest.

MAY 1998: Temp. 77° (3° above avg.); precip. 4" (1" below avg.). 1-9 Mainly dry, warm. 10-15 Cooler west, thunderstorms, hot southeast. 16-20 Sunny, hot. 21-24 Thunderstorms. 25-31 Hot.

JUNE 1998: Temp. 80° (2° below avg.); precip. 2.5" (1" below avg.). 1-6 Showers, then cooler. 7-12 Thunderstorms, then hot. 13-17 Hot south, showers north. 18-21 Seasonable. 22-30 Hot, thunderstorms.

JULY 1998: Temp. 86° (avg.); precip. 2.5" (avg.; 1" below northeast). 1-11 Sunny, hot. 12-14 Possible Gulf hurricane. 15-23 Thunderstorms. 24-31 Hot, few thunderstorms.

AUG. 1998: Temp. 86° (1° above avg.); precip. 1" (2" below avg.). 1-6 Sunny and hot. 7-10 Thunderstorms. 11-15 Sunshine, hot. 16-22 Thunderstorms south. 23-26 Thunderstorms. 27-31 Sunny, hot.

SEPT. 1998: Temp. 82° (2° above avg.; avg. south); precip. 3.5" (avg.; 2" below south). 1-3 Unsettled. 4-12 Sunny, hot, Gulf thunderstorms. 13-19 Cooler, few showers. 20-23 Sunny, hot. 24-30 Thunderstorms, then cooler.

OCT. 1998: Temp. 70.5° (2° above avg.); precip. 3" (1" above avg. west; 1" below east). 1-4 Warm, dry. 5-9 Hot, rain west. 10-13 Cooler, thunderstorms east. 14-20 Sunny, warmer. 21-27 Cooler, then hot. 28-31 Sunny, cooler.

Amarillo ◉

Oklahoma City ◉

Dallas ◉

Houston ◉

San Antonio ◉

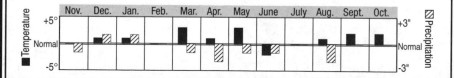

	Nov.	Dec.	Jan.	Feb.	Mar.	Apr.	May	June	July	Aug.	Sept.	Oct.

SUMMARY: The winter season looks like it will be a nasty one, even by Rocky Mountain standards. November will be relatively mild with above-normal temperatures and below-normal precipitation. However, the period from November through March will be about 4 degrees colder than normal, with above-normal snowfall. A mid-December snowstorm will bring a white Christmas to most of the region. Other widespread snowstorms will occur early in the new year, in the beginning and end of February, and in early March.

Colder-than-normal temperatures will occur in April and May. Heavy snow will fall in the mountains and across the north in mid-April and early May, but there will also be some warmth, especially in mid- and late May.

The period from June through August will be about 2 degrees cooler than normal, with near-normal rainfall. Look for heavy rain in central regions in early June, and in the south in midmonth. Rainfall in July and August will be more showery than widespread. The most concentrated thunderstorm activity will be in late July, but a few thunderstorms will pop up on most days. Hottest temperatures are most likely in late June, mid-July, and the first part of August.

The first part of September will be especially hot and dry, but wet and cooler weather will follow. After heavy mountain snow ends in September, October will be relatively tranquil.

NOV. 1997: Temp. 43° (2° above avg.); precip. 0.5" (0.5" below avg.). 1-5 Sunny, cool. 6-7 Few showers. 8-12 Sunny, warm. 13-22 Rain, mountain snow. 23-27 Sunny, mild. 28-30 Showers, flurries.

DEC. 1997: Temp. 28° (3° below avg.); precip. 1" (0.5" below avg.). 1-8 Colder, snow showers. 9-12 Milder. 13-17 Snowstorm. 18-20 Flurries. 21-25 Sunny, cold. 26-31 Milder, then snow showers, very cold.

JAN. 1998: Temp. 24° (3° below avg.; 8° below central); precip. 1.5" (avg.). 1-9 Snow, occasionally heavy. 10-18 Frigid, mainly dry. 19-25 Cold, occasional snow. 26-28 Cold north, milder south. 29-31 Sunny, cold.

FEB. 1998: Temp. 26° (8° below avg.); precip. 1" (0.5" below avg.). 1-3 Sunny, cold. 4-7 Heavy snow. 8-10 Frigid. 11-13 Milder. 14-19 Sunny, bitter, then milder. 20-23 Snowy. 24-28 Snow showers, cold.

MAR. 1998: Temp. 37° (5° below avg.); precip. 1.5" (1" below avg.). 1-6 Blizzard. 7-10 Sunny, cold. 11-17 Milder, showers, mountain snow. 18-25 Sunny, cold. 26-31 Milder, mountain flurries.

APR. 1998: Temp. 46° (4° below avg.); precip. 1.5" (1" below avg.; 1" above north). 1-6 Milder. 7-12 Cold, then milder. 13-18 Cooler, rain and snow north. 19-22 Mild. 23-30 Rain and snow north.

MAY 1998: Temp. 65° (4° below avg.); precip. 2" (0.5" below avg.; 1" above north). 1-6 Cool,

showers, mountain snow. 7-10 Sunny, warmer. 11-14 Showers, cooler. 15-17 Sunny, warm. 18-22 Sunny south, rain and snow north. 23-27 Dry, warm. 28-31 Showers, cooler.

JUNE 1998: Temp. 67° (2° below avg.); precip. 2" (1" above avg.; 0.5" below north). 1-7 Showers, rain central. 8-14 Sunny, cold nights. 15-20 Mainly dry north, rain south. 21-27 Sunny, hot. 28-30 Cooler, showers.

JULY 1998: Temp. 74° (4° below avg.); precip. 0.8" (avg.). 1-15 Cool, thunderstorms north. 16-18 Sunny, hot. 19-24 Hot north, thunderstorms south. 25-28 Thunderstorms. 29-31 Sunny, cool.

AUG. 1998: Temp. 76° (avg.); precip. 1" (avg.). 1-7 Sunny and hot north, thunderstorms south. 8-15 Dry and hot, thunderstorms south. 16-22 Hot, thunderstorms south and central. 23-27 Sunny, thunderstorms south. 28-31 Showers, cooler.

SEPT. 1998: Temp. 72° (1° above avg.); precip. 1.5" (avg.; 1" below east). 1-11 Sunny, hot. 12-15 Thunderstorms, then cooler. 16-21 Warm, then heavy rain, cooler. 22-26 Sunshine, seasonable. 27-30 Showers, mountain snow.

OCT. 1998: Temp. 54° (2° above avg.); precip. 1" (0.5" below avg.). 1-6 Sunny, warm. 7-9 Few showers. 10-13 Sunny, warm. 14-16 Rain north. 17-22 Sunshine, warm. 23-31 Cooler, showers.

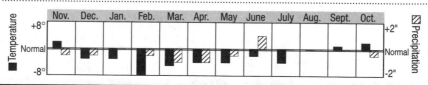

SUMMARY: The period from November through March will be a bit warmer than normal with below-normal rainfall. Although the Rockies will be much colder than normal, the frigid air will have a difficult time pushing farther south. Cold incursions will occur in late December, mid-January, and early and late February. Other cool periods will come in early November and early March. Most places will have little rain during the period, with the best chances for significant rainfall in mid-November, the first half of December, mid-January, early and late February, and early and late March.

April and May will continue drier than normal, with the best chances for rain in late April or the middle or end of May. Temperatures will be a bit below normal, despite a hot spell in mid-April and a few hot periods in May.

Temperatures in June, July, and August will be a bit below normal, but that's still hot. The hottest temperatures will occur in the second week of July. The period from June through August will bring greater-than-normal rainfall, with locally heavy downpours most likely in late July and through August.

Despite clouds and scattered thunderstorms, the first half of September will continue to be hot, perhaps the hottest time of the year. The second half of September will cool down to normal or a bit below. Then October will be much cooler, though still warmer than normal.

NOV. 1997: Temp. 64° (2° above avg.); precip. 0.3" (0.5" below avg.). 1-5 Cool, then warmer. 6-12 Sunny, cool. 13-16 Sunny, warm. 17-22 Some clouds, seasonable. 23-30 Sunny, warm.

DEC. 1997: Temp. 55° (1° above avg.); precip. 0.5" (0.5" below avg.). 1-3 Sunny, warm. 4-14 Warm, showers. 15-21 Sunny, seasonable. 22-28 Sunny, warm. 29-31 Turning colder.

JAN. 1998: Temp. 53° (avg.); precip. 0.2" (avg.). 1-5 Turning milder. 6-12 Rain, heavy west. 13-16 Cool, mainly dry. 17-23 Frequent rain. 24-31 Sunny, turning warmer.

FEB. 1998: Temp. 58° (avg.); precip. 0.2" (0.5" below avg.). 1-3 Sunny, warm. 4-11 Showers, then colder. 12-20 Sunny, turning warmer. 21-26 Showers, then colder. 27-28 Sunny, milder.

MAR. 1998: Temp. 62° (1° above avg.); precip. 0.5" (0.5" below avg.). 1-2 Showers. 3-5 Sunny, cool. 6-13 Sunny, warmer. 14-20 Sunny, seasonable. 21-25 Cooler, showers. 26-28 Sunny, warmer. 29-31 Cooler, showers east.

APR. 1998: Temp. 69° (1° below avg.); precip. 0.2" (0.2" below avg.). 1-5 Sunny, cool east, warm west. 6-10 Seasonable. 11-16 Sunny, cool. 17-21 Sunny, hot. 22-26 Showery. 27-30 Sunny, warm.

MAY 1998: Temp. 76° (3° below avg.; 1° below east); precip. 0.1" (0.2" below avg.). 1-4 Sunny, warm. 5-7 Cool, showers. 8-11 Sunny, hot.

12-15 Clouds, a shower. 16-18 Sunny, hot. 19-28 Sunshine, cool, then hotter. 29-31 Few showers.

JUNE 1998: Temp. 86° (2° below avg.); precip. 0.5" (0.5" above avg.). 1-2 Hot. 3-6 Showers, then cooler. 7-13 Sunny, hot. 14-18 Scattered thunderstorms. 19-22 Sunny, hot. 23-30 Very hot, thunderstorms east.

JULY 1998: Temp. 92° (2° below avg.); precip. 2.8" (2" above avg.). 1-10 Sunny, seasonably hot. 11-14 Sunny, quite hot. 15-22 Hot, thunderstorms, some heavy. 23-31 Cooler, heavy thunderstorms.

AUG. 1998: Temp. 91° (1° below avg.); precip. 2" (1" above avg.). 1-7 Cooler, few thunderstorms. 8-17 Rather hot, local downpours. 18-24 Cooler, clouds, thunderstorms. 25-31 Hot, scattered thunderstorms.

SEPT. 1998: Temp. 86° (1° above avg.); precip. 0.5" (0.5" below avg.). 1-3 Scattered thunderstorms. 4-14 Sunny, very hot. 15-18 Quite hot, thunderstorms east. 19-22 Few thunderstorms. 23-30 Sunny west, thunderstorms east.

OCT. 1998: Temp. 77.5° (3° above avg.); precip. 0.7" (0.3" below avg.). 1-5 Sunny, hot. 6-8 Thunderstorms, some heavy. 9-16 Sunny, very warm. 17-24 Sunny, hot west, cooler east. 25-28 Sunny, warm. 29-31 Sunny, cooler.

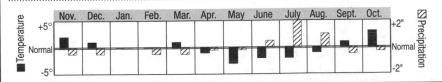

SUMMARY: November through March will probably not be as cold as in the previous year but will again be wetter than normal. November through January will be warmer than normal near the coast, with below-normal temperatures inland, resulting in above-normal rainfall and heavy snow inland. The stormiest periods will occur in mid- and late November, mid- and late December, and early and mid-January, with the best chance for coastal snow in mid-January. February and March will be colder than normal but with below-normal rainfall and storminess. Most precipitation in February will fall across the north. In March, precipitation will be more evenly distributed, and snow early in the month will cover much of the area.

April will be damp and cool, with heavy rain to start the month. Heavy rain will occur in the northern and central areas in midmonth but in the south later on. May will be on the cool side, with below-normal rainfall.

The period from June through August will be nice overall, with cooler-than-normal temperatures and generally below-normal rainfall. The rainiest weather will be across the north and in the mountains.

September will be a bit warmer than normal, with dry weather most days. Rainfall will average near normal, despite heavy rain midmonth. October will be stormy, with frequent heavy rain.

NOV.1997: Temp. 48° (4° above avg. north; 1° above south); precip. 6" (avg. south; 2" above north). 1-5 Sunny, warm. 6-8 Rain north. 9-13 Mild, heavy rain. 14-19 Stormy. 20-23 Mild south, rain north. 24-27 Mainly dry. 28-30 Rain.

DEC. 1997: Temp. 40.5° (2° above avg. coast; 1° below inland); precip. 7" (1" above avg.). 1-2 Rain. 3-4 Some sun. 5-6 Rain south. 7-13 Heavy rain, snow inland. 14-17 Dry, then rain. 18-23 Mainly dry. 24-31 Heavy rain, mountain snow.

JAN. 1998: Temp. 39° (avg. coast; 3° below inland); precip. 6" (avg. north; 2" above south). 1-6 Rain, mountain snow. 7-9 Rain, snow north. 10-11 Dry. 12-14 Sprinkles north, heavy rain south. 15-18 Sprinkles. 19-23 Stormy. 24-28 Light rain north. 29-31 Some sun.

FEB. 1998: Temp. 41° (2° below avg. coast; 5° below inland); precip. 3" (1" below avg.). 1-2 Dry. 3-5 Rain, mountain snow. 6-12 Rain north, showers south. 13-18 Showers north, mild south. 19-21 Showers, mountain snow. 22-25 Sunny, cold. 26-28 Milder south, light rain and snow north.

MAR.1998: Temp. 43° (5° below avg.; 1° below south); precip. 2" (1" below avg.). 1-7 Cold, heavy rain, snow north. 8-12 Sunshine, cold, then milder. 13-18 Colder, rain, mountain snow. 19-24 Mainly dry, chilly. 25-31 Rain, snow inland.

APR. 1998: Temp. 49° (2° below avg.); precip. 4" (1" above avg.; 3" above central). 1-6 Chilly, rain. 7-11 Some sun, warmer. 12-16 Mild south, rain central. 17-22 Rain and mountain snow north, showers south. 23-30 Sprinkles north, rain south and central.

MAY 1998: Temp. 55° (2° below avg.); precip. 1.5" (0.5" below avg.). 1-8 Cool, rain south, sprinkles north. 9-16 Rain north, warm elsewhere. 17-21 Cooler, rain central. 22-27 Mainly dry, hot southeast. 28-31 Showers.

JUNE 1998: Temp. 61° (2° below avg.); precip. 1" (0.5" below avg.). 1-7 Rain north, dry elsewhere. 8-13 Sunny, becoming hot. 14-22 Sunshine, cooler. 23-30 Cool, showers.

JULY 1998: Temp. 64° (4° below avg.); precip. 1" (avg. south; 1" above north). 1-5 Showers, cool. 6-10 Cool, showers north. 11-18 Showers, then warmer. 19-26 Showers, then seasonable. 27-31 Cooler, rain north and central.

AUG. 1998: Temp. 67.5° (1° below avg.); precip. 0.5" (0.5" below avg.). 1-5 Cool, rain north. 6-10 Sunny, warm. 11-22 Sunshine, seasonable. 23-31 Sunny, warm, mountain thunderstorms.

SEPT. 1998: Temp. 64° (1° above avg.); precip. 1.5" (0.5" below avg.; 0.5" above south). 1-4 Cool, sprinkles north. 5-10 Sunny, hot. 11-16 Showers, then cooler. 17-21 Rain. 22-30 Sunshine, cool.

OCT. 1998: Temp. 56.5° (2° above avg.); precip. 3.5" (avg. south; 3" above north). 1-2 Rain. 3-6 Sunshine. 7-11 Rain. 12-16 Stormy. 17-22 Sunny. 23-27 Showers, then cooler. 28-31 Rain.

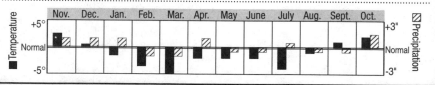

SUMMARY: The period from November through March will be milder than normal with near-normal precipitation. A storm expected in the middle of November will bring heavy thunderstorms to much of the region and snow to the mountains. December will bring some rainy periods, especially in the north. The heaviest rain and mountain snow will occur during the month's second week. January will be the most unsettled month of the season, with a storm at the beginning and two more in midmonth. Although February and March will each start with a storm, the weather overall will be more tranquil, with warm periods in late February and in mid- and late March.

April and May will be cooler and wetter than normal, with a great deal of cloudiness. The heaviest rain will be in late April and early May.

Temperatures from June through August will be cooler than normal, although there will be little, if any, rain. The hottest periods in The Valley will occur in the second week of June, in mid-July, and in early and mid-August. The hottest weather in coastal sections will wait until September, when a Santa Ana wind will bring record highs to Los Angeles. October will start on the warm side, but cooler temperatures will prevail by month's end.

NOV. 1997: Temp. 57° (2° above avg.); precip. 2.5" (avg.). 1-7 Sunshine, warm, then cooler. 8-11 Sunny, warm south. 12-19 Stormy, thunderstorms. 20-26 Sunny, cool north, hot south. 27-30 Sprinkles north, cooler south.

DEC. 1997: Temp. 51.5° (2° above avg.); precip. 3" (2" above avg. north; 0.5" below south). 1-4 Sunshine, seasonable. 5-13 Windy, rains, some heavy. 14-19 Sunny, cool, then showers. 20-26 Warm south, cool north, mountain snow. 27-31 Sunshine, mountain snow.

JAN. 1998: Temp. 48° (1° below avg.); precip. 4.5" (1" above avg.). 1-5 Rainy, cool, mountain snow. 6-10 Sun, then showers. 11-12 Chilly. 13-14 Showers. 15-18 Seasonable. 19-23 Heavy rain, mountain snow. 24-31 Sunshine, turning warmer.

FEB. 1998: Temp. 51° (avg.; 2° below inland); precip. 2" (1" below avg.). 1-4 Windy, showers. 5-12 Sunny, cool, then milder. 13-19 Showers north, then sunny and seasonable. 20-24 Showers, then cooler. 25-28 Sunny, pleasant.

MAR. 1998: Temp. 54° (1° above avg.); precip. 1.5" (1" below avg.). 1-4 Windy, heavy rain, mountain snow. 5-11 Sunny, turning warmer. 12-15 Windy, showers. 16-27 Sunny, seasonable. 28-31 Sunny, warm.

APR. 1998: Temp. 54° (avg. south; 3° below north); precip. 2" (0.5" above avg.). 1-3 Cooler, showers north. 4-8 Sprinkles. 9-12 Sunny, warm. 13-16

Showers north, warm south. 17-19 Sunshine, cool. 20-26 Chilly, rain. 27-28 Cool. 29-30 Rain.

MAY 1998: Temp. 56° (2° below avg.); precip. 1" (1" above avg.; avg. north). 1-6 Showers, locally heavy. 7-9 Dry. 10-11 Showers. 12-21 Coastal fog, sunny inland. 22-23 Hot. 24-31 Warm inland, clouds and sprinkles coast.

JUNE 1998: Temp. 60.5° (avg. south; 2° below north); precip. 0" (avg.). 1-5 Cool, sprinkles coast. 6-13 Hot inland, warm, then cooler coast. 14-18 Cool, coastal fog. 19-26 Sunny, warm, sprinkles north. 27-30 Seasonable.

JULY 1998: Temp. 61.5° (3° below avg.; avg. south); precip. 0" (avg.). 1-8 Cool, sprinkles. 9-18 Sunshine, hot inland. 19-25 Sunny, warm, cool northwest. 26-31 Cool.

AUG. 1998: Temp. 61.5° (3° below avg.; 1° above south); precip. 0" (avg.). 1-7 Sunshine, hot inland, cool coast. 8-15 Sprinkles, then warm with some sun. 16-25 Sunshine, hot inland. 26-31 Sunny, warm, sprinkles northwest.

SEPT. 1998: Temp. 65.5° (1° above avg.); precip. 0.1" (0.2" below avg.). 1-3 Sunshine. 4-11 Santa Ana wind. 12-16 Cool coast, hot inland. 17-20 Showers north, warm south. 21-30 Cool coast, sunny and warm inland.

OCT. 1998: Temp. 60° (1° below avg.); precip. 0.5" (0.5" below avg.). 1-6 Warm, some sun. 7-9 Cooler. 10-15 Warm, then showers. 16-21 Sunshine, warm. 22-27 Cooler, few sprinkles. 28-31 Showers.

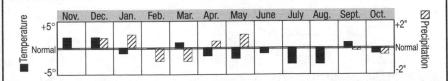

The Truth About
WOOLLY BEARS

In the fall of 1948, Dr. C. H. Curran, curator of insects at the American Museum of Natural History in New York City, took his wife 40 miles north of the city to Bear Mountain State Park to look at woolly bear caterpillars. The woolly bears' variable bands, made up of 13 distinct segments of black and reddish-brown — and their reputed ability to forecast the severity of the coming winter — had long fascinated the entomologist.

Dr. Curran proposed a scientific study. He collected as many caterpillars as he could in a day, determined the average number of reddish-brown segments, and forecast the coming winter weather through a reporter friend at *The New York Herald Tribune*. His experiment, which he continued over the next eight years, attempted to prove scientifically a weather rule of thumb that was as old as the hills around Bear Mountain. The resulting publicity made the woolly bear the most famous and most recognizable caterpillar in North America.

The caterpillar Curran studied, the true woolly bear, is the larval form of *Pyrrharctia isabella*, the Isabella tiger moth. This medium-size moth, with yellowish-orange and cream-colored wings spotted with black, is common from northern Mexico throughout the United States and across the southern third of Canada.

As moths go, the Isabella isn't much to look at compared with some of the other 11,000 species of North American moths, but its immature larva, called the *black-ended bear* or the *woolly bear* (and, throughout the South, *woolly worm*) is one of the few caterpillars most people can identify by name.

Woolly bears do not actually feel much like wool — they are covered with short, stiff bristles of hair. In field guides, they're found among the "bristled" species, which include the all-yellow salt marsh caterpillar and several species in the tiger moth family. Doug Ferguson, an entomologist at the National Museum of Natural History in Washington, D.C., says, "I've heard people call different caterpillars

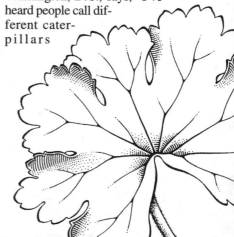

'woolly bears,' even ones that are all black, all brown, yellow, or gray. It's the hairiness they're referring to. I guess you'd better be careful about which caterpillar ter will be. Conversely, a narrow brown band is said to predict a harsh winter.

Between 1948 and 1956, Dr. Curran's average brown-segment counts ranged

Does Mother Nature use the bands on the woolly bear caterpillar to signal a hard winter? Here are a few scientific and not-so-scientific opinions. by Jim Collins

you're looking at before you make your prediction."

Woolly bears, like other caterpillars, hatch during warm weather from eggs laid by a female moth. After feeding on dandelions, asters, birches, clovers, maples, weeds, and other vegetation, mature woolly bears disperse and search for overwintering sites under bark or inside cavities of rocks or logs. (That's why you see so many of them crossing roads and sidewalks in the fall.) When spring arrives, woolly bears spin fuzzy cocoons and transform inside them into full-grown moths.

Typically, the bands at the ends of the caterpillar are black, and the one in the middle is brown or orange, giving the woolly bear its distinctive striped appearance. According to legend, the wider that middle brown section is (i.e., the more brown segments there are), the milder the coming win-

from 5.3 to 5.6 out of the 13-segment total, meaning that the brown band took up more than a third of the woolly bear's

The scientific experiments of Dr. C. H. Curran popularized the folklore of the woolly bear's ability to forecast winter weather.

body. As those relatively high numbers suggested, the corresponding winters were milder than average. But Curran was under no scientific illusion: He knew that his data samples were small. Although the experiments popularized and, to some people, legitimized folklore, they were

simply an excuse for having fun. Curran, his wife, and their group of friends, who called themselves The Original Society of the Friends of the Woolly Bear, escaped New York each fall for the glorious foliage and the meals at the posh Bear Mountain Inn. The naturalist Richard Pough was a member, as was Kim Hunter, the actress who starred in the movie *Planet of the Apes*.

Preparing for the "Woolly Worm Festival" and caterpillar race, Banner Elk, North Carolina.

Thirty years after the last meeting of Curran's society, the woolly bear brown-segment counts and winter forecasts were resurrected by the nature museum at Bear Mountain State Park. The annual counts have continued, more or less tongue in cheek, since then. This fall, museum director Jack Focht will gather a dozen or so caterpillars, as he has done since 1988, and spread them out on the kitchen table of his "folklore consultant," Clarence Conkling. The two men will count the brown segments, average them, and declare another forecast from Woolly Bear Mountain. "We're about 80 percent accurate," he says.

Their forecasts have rekindled interest in the woolly bear. Elementary school classes, like the third grade in Pine Plains, New York, have made woolly bear forecasting into annual science projects. Outdoor columnists, like Dennis Kipp of the *Poughkeepsie Journal,* regularly compare woolly bear forecasts against other predictions, both scientific and not.

For the past ten years, Banner Elk, North Carolina, has held an annual "Woolly Worm Festival" each October, highlighted by a caterpillar race. Retired mayor Charles Von Canon inspects the champion woolly bear and announces his winter forecast. His method differs from the more common number-of-brown-segments method. Counting each of the 13 segments as a week of winter, Von Canon correlates the black segments at the front and rear of the caterpillar with the beginning and end of winter. The more black segments, the worse the winter, and vice versa, with the harshest weather occurring during the black-segment weeks. His predictions, locally famous, are said to be 70 percent accurate.

But most scientists discount the folklore of woolly bear predictions as just that, folklore. Says Ferguson from his office in Washington, "I've never taken the notion very seriously. You'd have to look at an awful lot of caterpillars in one place over a great many years in order to say there's something to it." Randy Morgan, from the insectarium at the Cincinnati Zoo, declares, "In my opinion, woolly bears and other so-called weather indicators — how thick the corn husks are, how high above the ground wasps build their nests — are simply myths."

Mike Peters, an entomologist at the University of Massachusetts, doesn't disagree, but he says there could, in fact, be a link between winter severity and the brown band of a woolly bear caterpillar. "There's evidence," he says, "that the number of brown hairs has to do with the age of the caterpillar — in other words, how late it got going in the spring. The [band] *does* say something about a heavy winter or an early spring. The only thing is . . . it's telling you about the previous year." ☐☐

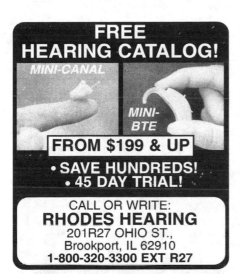

Gather All Ye PEA GROWERS AND LISTEN UP

Here's everything you need to know — and then some — from a gardener who definitely knows her peas (and q's, too).

My family harbors a deep, dark secret. Although we might appear quite typical as we go about planting, supporting, weeding, and watering our garden peas, the truth is that we never, ever cook them. We always eat them raw.

Our dementia began decades ago — the first year my father planted two long rows of peas. On clear June mornings, we started to find ourselves in the garden, just as the dew was drying, nibbling the peas "to see if they were ready." A few years later, as the pea crop expanded from two rows to four rows, we dropped this pretense and openly started grazing. That same year, my mother stopped fretting that there wouldn't be any peas left for dinner.

Now we forage at will, kids and adults side by side. We eat our fill of peas right in the garden whenever the craving hits us, dropping the pods between the rows for mulch. And in the evening, when my father finally sits down to watch the news, he brings along an enormous bowl of peas, which he shells and devours in his easy chair.

It's our conviction that we've done all the work of growing them and we'll enjoy our peas the way they taste best, right from the shell. About one quarter of a pea's weight is sugar, which turns to starch several hours after it's picked. We think peas are better than candy. This justifies our right-from-the-vine obsession — and also tells you why peas you buy even at a farmstand are so sadly lacking in flavor.

BY GEORGIA ORCUTT

– illustrated by Beth Krommes

PEA-GROWING BASICS

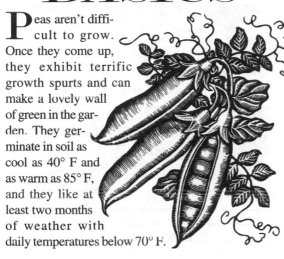

Peas aren't diffi-cult to grow. Once they come up, they exhibit terrific growth spurts and can make a lovely wall of green in the gar-den. They ger-minate in soil as cool as 40° F and as warm as 85° F, and they like at least two months of weather with daily temperatures below 70° F.

In the North, spring plantings have a better chance than fall plantings of making it; vines resist frost better than pods do, and spring rains usually provide the moisture peas need. The most critical time for rain-fall or hand-watering is when peas blossom and when pods form. If peas dry out, they will stop producing.

Though adding compost won't hurt, peas don't need heavy doses of fertilizer. They like phos-phorus and potassium and appreciate a good sprin-kling of wood ashes before planting.

As with other legumes, pea roots support nitro-gen-fixing bacteria, which enrich your soil. If you are planting peas for the first time, you can get everything off to a good start by shaking the seeds in a powdered inoculant that contains billions of teem-ing nitrogen-fixing bacteria. After the first pea year, the bacteria become established in your soil and the inoculant is unnecessary.

TRICKS FOR EARLY PEAS

■

Plant peas in the North as soon as the ground can be worked in the spring. St. Patrick's Day is traditional in many areas, although you might have to drill holes in the soil to put them in this early. To get the best head start, turn over your pea-planting beds in the fall, add manure or compost, and mulch well. When you're ready in the early spring, pull back the mulch and plant your seeds (make

holes with a dibble, if neces-sary). The planting won't be perfect, but you can always add more seeds later if you discover spaces where some don't germinate. A blanket of snow won't hurt emerging pea plants, but several days with

(continued on next page)

temperatures in the teens could. Be prepared to plant again.

■

Southern gardeners follow a different schedule. "The trick here in the hot country is to plant on New Year's Day and pray mightily it doesn't freeze," explains Texas gardening columnist Doreen Howard. "If it freezes before the peas are up, that's OK. But if they get nipped, it's replant! We can harvest peas usually until Tax Day — then it's too hot and the plants do nothing."

■

To get them jump-started, keep pea seeds moist between two pieces of damp paper towels for three or four days until they germinate, and then plant them carefully. Or, before planting, soak pea seeds overnight in warm water or a weak seaweed solution to encourage germination.

TO STAGGER
OR NOT TO STAGGER

■ Some gardeners prefer to stagger their plantings, putting peas in the ground at ten-day or two-week intervals for a steady harvest. But late crops of peas often catch up with early crops and are ready at the same time anyway. Mother Nature will ultimately make the call.

Depending on the variety, peas ripen in response to a measurable "temperature sum" (based on average daily temperature) once the plants begin to grow. Below 40° F, peas virtually do not grow, so these days don't count. And if temperatures get well above 70° F for several consecutive days, mature plants may all begin to flower simultaneously.

Rather than staggering a planting of one variety, plant several different varieties and observe how they respond to your weather. Note the "days to maturity" and try an early variety (such as 'Alaska' or 'Daybreak'), a midseason variety (such as 'Little Marvel' or 'Cascadia'), or a late variety (such as 'Green Arrow' or 'Super Sugar Snap').

PEA PLANTING

The late Jim Crockett was fond of saying, "If you are stingy with your peas, they'll be stingy with you." Plant peas thickly in wide rows so they can climb up both sides of a fence. Use a hoe to make a two-inch trench and sprinkle in the seeds, leaving about an inch between them. Cover with soil and tamp down with a hoe or (gently) with your foot. If you are planting a new garden, make the trench three inches deep, add a one-inch layer of well-rotted manure, cover with soil, and then plant the peas. Water well if the weather is dry. Poke in any seeds that wash out. (A chopstick is an ideal tool for this.)

SUPPORT YOUR
LOCAL PEAS

■ **Keep your peas well picked to encourage more pods to develop. English, or garden, peas are ready to pick when**

Don't pay attention to all the hoopla about bush peas that don't need support. They will form a low tangle no pea picker will enjoy. Plant the peas first and wait for them to come up before putting up your fence. Don't construct a permanent wall or structure; it's best to rotate your pea crop every year or two. We've heard of all sorts of creative ideas for pea fencing, among them old metal bedsprings. Here are three of the most common.

Pea Stakes ■ It's easy to imagine pre-hardware-store gardeners using twiggy brush to support their pea crops. That's just about all they had. In fact, this can be a charming way to hold up your vines, especially if you're growing a two-foot "bush" variety such as 'Knight'. From trees or shrubs on your property, cut thin branches at least a foot taller than you expect your peas to grow. Leave all the little twigs on to give pea tendrils a lot of places to grab. Push the branches about six inches into the ground, forming an overlapping row alongside your pea seedlings.

you can feel the peas in the pods with gentle pressure; if they're wrinkled, faded, or bulging, they are past their prime. Snow peas are ready five to seven days after the plants flower; they should be flat with only tiny seeds. And snap peas are ready to pick when the round pods are filled with peas.

Twine ■ Vermont seedsman Shepherd Ogden swears by growing peas on a twine trellis, a method he learned as a market gardener. Set two posts eight feet apart, with a crossbar along the top. Tie a taut string between the two posts at ground level, and weave a grid of untreated, biodegradable twine between the two posts and between the crossbar and the ground-level string. Let your peas ramble at will on the web. When the season is over, cut down plants and twine and toss them in the compost pile. (Ogden's company, The Cook's Garden, sells a 420-foot roll of untreated twine for $4; three rolls for $10.95. Call 800-457-9703.)

Always use two hands when you pick peas. Secure the vine with one hand and pull the pea off with your other hand. It's never too early to teach kids how to do this properly. Since both your hands are busy, collect the peas in a container with a wide top and a flat bottom.

Chicken Wire ■ This is our favorite. Buy two-inch mesh in 48- or 60-inch width, and support it by nailing it to wooden posts driven into the ground about six feet apart. (We use metal posts and weave them through the mesh.) When the pea harvest is over, peel down the vines and roll up the wire for another year.

(continued)

WHICH VARIETY IS BEST?

Peas fall into two main categories:

EDIBLE PODDED PEAS: This group includes snow peas and snap peas. Snow peas are crisp and very thin, with tiny peas inside the pods. They are eaten whole — raw in salads or barely cooked in stir-fried dishes. By crossing English peas and snow peas, breeders have come up with the revolutionary snap pea, which yields a crunchy three- to four-inch pod with small, round, very sweet peas. It's meant to be eaten whole, not shelled. Some varieties develop a thick string down the back, which you may want to remove before eating. Snap peas often put out vigorous growth, reaching six feet or more. Be sure to supply them with a good high fence.

SHELLING PEAS: Also called English, garden, or green peas, these are sweet enough to eat raw but are meant for shelling. The plants grow up to seven feet tall, depending on the variety, and the pods are usually tough and not very tasty.

We asked experienced pea growers throughout the country to recommend their favorite varieties — those that have great flavor and perform well in the face of spring weather that can swing from 40° to 80° F and back again. Here are their suggestions, along with the average range of days to maturity after planting.

Edible Podded (EP)   Shelling (S)

NORTHEAST
Lee Reich, garden writer and researcher
S-'Green Arrow' (62-70 days)
S-'Lincoln' (65-70 days)
S-'Maestro' (55-60 days)

SOUTHEAST
Jeff McCormack, Southern Exposure Seed Exchange
EP-'Sugar Snap' (53-72 days)
S-'Maestro' (55-60 days)
S-'Wando' (64-72 days)

NORTH CENTRAL
Jim Schmidt, extension specialist, University of Illinois
EP-'Oregon Sugar Pod II' (60-68 days)
EP-'Super Sugar Snap' (70 days)
S-'Alaska' (50-60 days)
S-'Green Arrow' (62-70 days)
S-'Little Marvel' (58-64 days)

SOUTH CENTRAL
Doreen Howard, gardening columnist
EP-'Super Sugar Snap' (70 days)
S-'Little Marvel' (58-64 days)

NORTHWEST
Rose Marie Nichols, Nichols Garden Nursery
EP-'Cascadia' (58-70 days)
EP-'Oregon Sugar Pod II' (60-68 days)
S-'Oregon Pioneer' (61-70 days)

MOUNTAINS
Bill McDorman, High Altitude Gardens
EP-'Cascadia' (58-70 days)
EP-'Oregon Sugar Pod II' (60-68 days)
EP-'Super Sugar Snap' (70 days)
S-'Maestro' (55-60 days)
S-'Montana Marvel' (64 days)

SOUTHWEST
Wendy Krupnick, field trial manager
EP-'Super Sugar Mel' (70-80 days)
EP-'Super Sugar Snap' (70 days)
S-'Knight' (56-62 days)

AUTHOR'S CHOICE
Western New York State
S-'Freezonian' (60-63 days)
S-'Wando' (64-72 days)

Nature's Itchy Revenge

Misconceptions about poison ivy and poison oak have led desperate sufferers to adopt some pretty bizarre (and totally useless) cures. Finally, researchers have found a substance that may help — some of the time. But the best way to foil the itch is by minding the old saying, "Leaflets three, let it be."   by Susan Carol Hauser

American Indians knew the hazards of poison ivy and poison oak, and so did Captain John Smith, the leader of the colony at Jamestown, Virginia. In an early 17th-century personal journal, he described a plant that resembled English ivy but that "causeth redness, itchynge, and finally blysters."

Today we know that an oil called *urushiol* (yoo-ROO-she-ol), found in virtually all parts of the plant, causes the poison reaction in humans. According to the American Academy of Dermatology, approximately 85 percent of the population is sensitive to urushiol, making it one of the most potent allergens on Earth. Once urushiol has bonded chemically with the skin in the first hours after exposure, nothing can stop the allergic process, which can last up to three weeks or longer. Victims are left with tormenting symptoms — weeping blisters, swelling, and an infuriating itch.

It has been a long and scratchy journey to any reliable treatment of the dermatitis caused by contact with *Rhus radicans* (poison ivy) and *Rhus toxicodendron* (poison oak). The road is littered with herbal and home remedies, many of which *do* reduce swelling and itching, such as the teas and poultices that American Indians and pioneers prepared from jewelweed, chamomile, gumweed, goldenseal, and Solomon's seal. But home remedies also included futile treatments concocted by desperate souls: bathing in horse urine, scrubbing with kerosene or gunpowder, and soaking in strychnine, bleach, or ammonia.

Contemporary sufferers have been known to apply hair spray, deodorant, and fingernail polish to poison ivy and poison oak rashes in hopes of suffocating the itch. And a recent conversant on the Internet recommended scrubbing with a mixture of cleanser and rubbing alcohol until the skin turns nicely pink!

All these efforts to confound the natural metabolic process are more likely to cause trouble than to cure it. When the already irritated skin is subjected to abuse from

Poison ivy (Rhus radicans) *grows as a low shrub or as a vine and contains urushiol, which causes blisters and itching, in nearly all its parts.*

"healing" potions, it is vulnerable to secondary infections that can long outlast the original problem.

One of the myths about poison ivy and poison oak is the notion that weeping blisters can spread the rash on the body days after the original outbreak. Actually, the timing of a urushiol reaction is driven by the quantity of the exposure. Areas with the most urushiol will show the reaction first; areas with less exposure will take longer to develop. The clear fluid at blister sites is blood serum and is harmless.

Block That Itch!

■ Preventive barrier creams seem to be the hope of the moment. IvyBlock, a new over-the-counter lotion, has now been approved by the FDA. Spread over exposed parts of the body before venturing outside, it prevents urushiol reactions about 68 percent of the time and lessens the severity of reactions that do occur. In spite of the best efforts of science, woods-goers should still march to the traditional chant, "Leaflets three, let it be."

What to Do if You've Touched Poison Ivy

■ **If it's within the first three to four hours after exposure:** Swab the skin as soon as possible with rubbing alcohol, and wash with copious amounts of water. The key word is *copious.* The more water, the more the urushiol is diluted. Water also works for affected clothing, and water or alcohol can be used on objects such as garden tools and bicycle tires. Harsh yellow laundry soap is no more effective than other kinds of soap, but soap alone won't do it — water is the key.

■ **If the rash has broken out:** The urushiol has bonded to your skin and all you can do is treat the symptoms. Use over-the-counter cortisone creams to relieve minor itching. The traditional calamine lotion or a compress made with Burrow's Solution may also bring temporary relief, as will long, hot showers. Prescription cortisone gels are needed in many cases, especially when the sores are in the weepy stage. In severe cases, systemic prescription cortisone treatment is warranted.

Do not scour the skin, even if self-flagellation seems momentarily appealing. Check your house, car, and garage for objects and clothing that may still carry active urushiol, and wash everything in abundant amounts of water.

Like poison ivy, poison oak (Rhus toxicodendron) *is widely distributed in the United States and is permeated with urushiol.*

How to Get Rid of Poison Ivy and Poison Oak Plants

■ Because urushiol molecules are carried in smoke, it is never safe to burn poison ivy or poison oak in an effort to eradicate it. The plants can be pulled, but broken-off rootlets may sprout again the next year. Some of the worst cases of poison ivy and poison oak dermatitis come from grubbing out the plants and roots. Even the environmentally conscientious usually resort to chemicals; plant and garden stores carry a number of commercial products that destroy *R. radicans* and *R. toxicodendron.* □□

Susan Carol Hauser is the author of *Nature's Revenge: The Secrets of Poison Ivy, Poison Oak, Poison Sumac, and Their Remedies* (Lyons & Burford Publishers, 1996).

OUTDOOR PLANTING TABLE
1998

The best time to plant flowers and vegetables that bear crops above ground is during the *light* of the Moon; that is, between the day the Moon is new to the day it is full. Flowering bulbs and vegetables that bear crops below ground should be planted during the *dark* of the Moon; that is, from the day after

the Moon is full to the day before it is new again. The dates given here are based on the safe periods for planting in areas that receive frost, and the Moon's phases for 1998. Consult page 164 for dates of frosts and length of growing season. See calendar pages 60-86 for the exact days of the new and full Moons.

☞ **Above-Ground Crops Marked (*)** ☞ **E means Early** ☞ **L means Late**

	Planting Dates	Moon Favorable	Planting Dates	Moon Favorable	Planting Dates	Moon Favorable
*Barley	5/15-6/21	5/25-6/10	3/15-4/7	3/27-4/7	2/15-3/7	2/26-3/7
*Beans (E)	5/7-6/21	5/7-11, 5/25-6/10	4/15-30	4/26-30	3/15-4/7	3/27-4/7
(L)	6/15-7/15	6/23-7/9	7/1-21	7/1-9	8/7-31	8/7, 8/21-31
Beets (E)	5/1-15	5/12-15	3/15-4/3	3/15-26	2/7-28	2/12-25
(L)	7/15-8/15	7/15-22, 8/8-15	8/15-31	8/15-20	9/1-30	9/7-19
*Broccoli (E)	5/15-31	5/25-31	3/7-31	3/7-12, 3/27-31	2/15-3/15	2/26-3/12
Plants (L)	6/15-7/7	6/23-7/7	8/1-20	8/1-7	9/7-30	9/20-30
*Brussels Sprouts	5/15-31	5/25-31	3/7-4/15	3/7-12, 3/27-4/11	2/11-3/20	2/11, 2/26-3/12
*Cabbage Plants	5/15-31	5/25-31	3/7-4/15	3/7-12, 3/27-4/11	2/11-3/20	2/11, 2/26-3/12
Carrots (E)	5/15-31	5/15-24	3/7-31	3/13-26	2/15-3/7	2/15-25
(L)	6/15-7/21	6/15-22, 7/10-21	7/7-31	7/10-22	8/1-9/7	8/8-20, 9/7
*Cauliflower (E)	5/15-31	5/25-31	3/15-4/7	3/27-4/7	2/15-3/7	2/26-3/7
Plants (L)	6/15-7/21	6/23-7/9	7/1-8/7	7/1-9, 7/23-8/7	8/7-31	8/7, 8/21-31
*Celery Plants (E)	5/15-6/30	5/25-6/10, 6/23-30	3/7-31	3/7-12, 3/27-31	2/15-28	2/26-28
(L)	7/15-8/15	7/23-8/7	8/15-9/7	8/21-9/6	9/15-30	9/20-30
*Collards (E)	5/15-31	5/25-31	3/7-4/7	3/7-12, 3/27-4/7	2/11-3/20	2/11, 2/26-3/12
(L)	7/1-8/7	7/1-9, 7/23-8/7	8/15-31	8/21-31	9/7-30	9/20-30
*Corn, Sweet (E)	5/10-6/15	5/10-11, 5/25-6/10	4/1-15	4/1-11	3/15-31	3/27-31
(L)	6/15-30	6/23-30	7/7-21	7/7-9	8/7-31	8/7, 8/21-31
*Cucumber	5/7-6/20	5/7-11, 5/25-6/10	4/7-5/15	4/7-11, 4/26-5/11	3/7-4/15	3/7-12, 3/27-4/11
*Eggplant Plants	6/1-30	6/1-10, 6/23-30	4/7-5/15	4/7-11, 4/26-5/11	3/7-4/15	3/7-12, 3/27-4/11
*Endive (E)	5/15-31	5/25-31	4/7-5/15	4/7-11, 4/26-5/11	2/15-3/20	2/26-3/12
(L)	6/7-30	6/7-10, 6/23-30	7/15-8/15	7/23-8/7	8/15-9/7	8/21-9/6
*Flowers (All)	5/7-6/21	5/7-11, 5/25-6/10	4/15-30	4/26-30	3/15-4/7	3/27-4/7
*Kale (E)	5/15-31	5/25-31	3/7-4/7	3/7-12, 3/27-4/7	2/11-3/20	2/11, 2/26-3/12

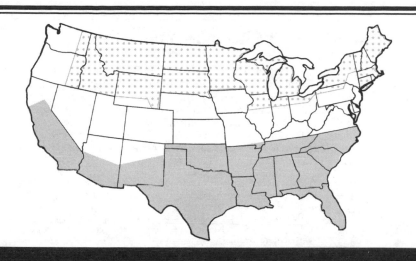

	Planting Dates	Moon Favorable	Planting Dates	Moon Favorable	Planting Dates	Moon Favorable
*Kale (L)	7/1-8/7	7/1-9, 7/23-8/7	8/15-31	8/21-31	9/7-30	9/20-30
Leek Plants	5/15-31	5/15-24	3/7-4/7	3/13-26	2/15-4/15	2/15-25, 3/13-26, 4/12-15
*Lettuce	5/15-6/30	5/25-6/10, 6/23-30	3/1-31	3/1-12, 3/27-31	2/15-3/7	2/26-3/7
*Muskmelon	5/15-6/30	5/25-6/10, 6/23-30	4/15-5/7	4/26-5/7	3/15-4/7	3/27-4/7
Onion Sets	5/15-6/7	5/15-24	3/1-31	3/13-26	2/1-28	2/12-25
*Parsley	5/15-31	5/25-31	3/1-31	3/1-12, 3/27-31	2/20-3/15	2/26-3/12
Parsnips	4/1-30	4/12-25	3/7-31	3/13-26	1/15-2/4	1/15-27
*Peas (E)	4/15-5/7	4/26-5/7	3/7-31	3/7-12, 3/27-31	1/15-2/7	1/28-2/7
(L)	7/15-31	7/23-31	8/7-31	8/7, 8/21-31	9/15-30	9/20-30
*Pepper Plants	5/15-6/30	5/25-6/10, 6/23-30	4/1-30	4/1-11, 4/26-30	3/1-20	3/1-12
Potato	5/1-31	5/12-24	4/1-30	4/12-25	2/10-28	2/12-25
*Pumpkin	5/15-31	5/25-31	4/23-5/15	4/26-5/11	3/7-20	3/7-12
Radish (E)	4/15-30	4/15-25	3/7-31	3/13-26	1/21-3/1	1/21-27, 2/12-25
(L)	8/15-31	8/15-20	9/7-30	9/7-19	10/1-21	10/6-19
*Spinach (E)	5/15-31	5/25-31	3/15-4/20	3/27-4/11	2/7-3/15	2/7-11, 2/26-3/12
(L)	7/15-9/7	7/23-8/7, 8/21-9/6	8/1-9/15	8/1-7, 8/21-9/6	10/1-21	10/1-5, 10/20-21
*Squash	5/15-6/15	5/25-6/10	4/15-30	4/26-30	3/15-4/15	3/27-4/11
Sweet Potatoes	5/15-6/15	5/15-24, 6/11-15	4/21-30	4/21-25	3/23-4/6	3/23-26
*Swiss Chard	5/1-31	5/1-11, 5/25-31	3/15-4/15	3/27-4/11	2/7-3/15	2/7-11, 2/26-3/12
*Tomato Plants	5/15-31	5/25-31	4/7-30	4/7-11, 4/26-30	3/7-20	3/7-12
Turnips (E)	4/7-30	4/12-25	3/15-31	3/15-26	1/20-2/15	1/20-27, 2/12-15
(L)	7/1-8/15	7/10-22, 8/8-15	8/1-20	8/8-20	9/1-10/15	9/7-19, 10/6-15
*Watermelon	5/15-6/30	5/25-6/10, 6/23-30	4/15-5/7	4/26-5/7	3/15-4/7	3/27-4/7
*Wheat, Winter	8/11-9/15	8/21-9/6	9/15-10/20	9/20-10/5, 10/20	10/15-12/7	10/20-11/4, 11/18-12/3
Spring	4/7-30	4/7-11, 4/26-30	3/1-20	3/1-12	2/15-28	2/26-28

FROSTS AND GROWING SEASONS

Courtesy of National Climatic Center

Dates given are normal averages for a light freeze (32° F); local weather and topography may cause considerable variations. The possibility of frost occurring after the spring dates and before the fall dates is 50 percent. The classification of freeze temperatures is usually based on their effect on plants, with the following commonly accepted categories: **Light freeze:** 29° F to 32° F — tender plants killed; little destructive effect on other vegetation. **Moderate freeze:** 25° F to 28° F — widely destructive effect on most vegetation; heavy damage to fruit blossoms and tender and semihardy plants. **Severe freeze:** 24° F and colder — heavy damage to most plants.

CITY	Growing Season (Days)	Last Frost Spring	First Frost Fall	CITY	Growing Season (Days)	Last Frost Spring	First Frost Fall
Mobile, AL	272	Feb. 27	Nov. 26	North Platte, NE	136	May 11	Sept. 24
Juneau, AK	133	May 16	Sept. 26	Las Vegas, NV	259	Mar. 7	Nov. 21
Phoenix, AZ	308	Feb. 5	Dec. 15	Concord, NH	121	May 23	Sept. 22
Tucson, AZ	273	Feb. 28	Nov. 29	Newark, NJ	219	Apr. 4	Nov. 10
Pine Bluff, AR	234	Mar. 19	Nov. 8	Carlsbad, NM	223	Mar. 29	Nov. 7
Eureka, CA	324	Jan. 30	Dec. 15	Los Alamos, NM	157	May 8	Oct. 13
Sacramento, CA	289	Feb. 14	Dec. 1	Albany, NY	144	May 7	Sept. 29
San Francisco, CA	*	*	*	Syracuse, NY	170	Apr. 28	Oct. 16
Denver, CO	157	May 3	Oct. 8	Fayetteville, NC	212	Apr. 2	Oct. 31
Hartford, CT	167	Apr. 25	Oct. 10	Bismarck, ND	129	May 14	Sept. 20
Wilmington, DE	198	Apr. 13	Oct. 29	Akron, OH	168	May 3	Oct. 18
Miami, FL	*	*	*	Cincinnati, OH	195	Apr. 14	Oct. 27
Tampa, FL	338	Jan. 28	Jan. 3	Lawton, OK	217	Apr. 1	Nov. 5
Athens, GA	224	Mar. 28	Nov. 8	Tulsa, OK	218	Mar. 30	Nov. 4
Savannah, GA	250	Mar. 10	Nov. 15	Pendleton, OR	188	Apr. 15	Oct. 21
Boise, ID	153	May 8	Oct. 9	Portland, OR	217	Apr. 3	Nov. 7
Chicago, IL	187	Apr. 22	Oct. 26	Carlisle, PA	182	Apr. 20	Oct. 20
Springfield, IL	185	Apr. 17	Oct. 19	Williamsport, PA	168	Apr. 29	Oct. 15
Indianapolis, IN	180	Apr. 22	Oct. 20	Kingston, RI	144	May 8	Sept. 30
South Bend, IN	169	May 1	Oct. 18	Charleston, SC	253	Mar. 11	Nov. 20
Atlantic, IA	141	May 9	Sept. 28	Columbia, SC	211	Apr. 4	Nov. 2
Cedar Rapids, IA	161	Apr. 29	Oct. 7	Rapid City, SD	145	May 7	Sept. 29
Topeka, KS	175	Apr. 21	Oct. 14	Memphis, TN	228	Mar. 23	Nov. 7
Lexington, KY	190	Apr. 17	Oct. 25	Nashville, TN	207	Apr. 5	Oct. 29
Monroe, LA	242	Mar. 9	Nov. 7	Amarillo, TX	197	Apr. 14	Oct. 29
New Orleans, LA	288	Feb. 20	Dec. 5	Denton, TX	231	Mar. 25	Nov. 12
Portland, ME	143	May 10	Sept. 30	San Antonio, TX	265	Mar. 3	Nov. 24
Baltimore, MD	231	Mar. 26	Nov. 13	Cedar City, UT	134	May 20	Oct. 2
Worcester, MA	172	Apr. 27	Oct. 17	Spanish Fork, UT	156	May 8	Oct. 12
Lansing, MI	140	May 13	Sept. 30	Burlington, VT	142	May 11	Oct. 1
Marquette, MI	159	May 12	Oct. 19	Norfolk, VA	239	Mar. 23	Nov. 17
Duluth, MN	122	May 21	Sept. 21	Richmond, VA	198	Apr. 10	Oct. 26
Willmar, MN	152	May 4	Oct. 4	Seattle, WA	232	Mar. 24	Nov. 11
Columbus, MS	215	Mar. 27	Oct. 29	Spokane, WA	153	May 4	Oct. 5
Vicksburg, MS	250	Mar. 13	Nov. 18	Parkersburg, WV	175	Apr. 25	Oct. 18
Jefferson City, MO	173	Apr. 26	Oct. 16	Green Bay, WI	143	May 12	Oct. 2
Fort Peck, MT	146	May 5	Sept. 28	Janesville, WI	164	Apr. 28	Oct. 10
Helena, MT	122	May 18	Sept. 18	Casper, WY	123	May 22	Sept. 22
Blair, NE	165	Apr. 27	Oct. 10	*Frosts do not occur every year.			

A MONTH-BY-MONTH ASTROLOGICAL TIMETABLE FOR 1998

Herewith we provide the following yearlong chart, based on the Moon signs, showing the most favorable times each month for certain activities. BY CELESTE LONGACRE

	JAN.	FEB.	MAR.	APR.	MAY	JUNE	JULY	AUG.	SEPT.	OCT.	NOV.	DEC.
Give up smoking	13, 18	20, 24	14, 19	10, 20	17, 21	14, 18	11, 15	11, 20	8, 17	13, 18	10, 15	7, 17
Begin diet to lose weight	13, 18	20, 24	14, 19	10, 20	17, 21	14, 18	11, 15	11, 20	8, 17	13, 18	10, 15	7, 17
Begin diet to gain weight	1, 5	1, 5	9	5	2, 7, 30	4, 26	1, 28	7, 25	3, 21	1, 28	2, 29	22, 26
Cut hair to encourage growth	7, 8	3, 4	2, 3	26, 27	7, 8	4, 5	1, 2, 28, 29	25, 26	21, 22	30, 31	3, 27, 28	1, 2, 29, 30
Cut hair to discourage growth	18, 19	15, 16	14, 15	22, 23	24	20, 21	17, 18	13, 14	10, 11	18, 19	14, 15	12, 13
Have dental care	16, 17	12, 13	11, 12	8, 9	5, 6	5, 6	26, 27	22, 23	18, 19	16, 17	12, 13	9, 10
End old projects	26, 27	24, 25	26, 27	24, 25	23, 24	22, 23	21, 22	21, 22	18, 19	18, 19	17, 18	16, 17
Start a new project	29, 30	27, 28	29, 30	27, 28	26, 27	25, 26	24, 25	24, 25	21, 22	21, 22	20, 21	19, 20
Entertain	13, 14	10, 11	9, 10	5, 6	2, 3	26, 27	24, 25	20, 21	16, 17	13, 14	10, 11	7, 8
Go fishing	23, 24	20, 21	19, 20	15, 16	12, 13	9, 10	6, 7	2, 3, 30, 31	26, 27	23, 24	19, 20	17, 18
Breed	21, 22	17, 18	16, 17	13, 14	10, 11	6, 7	3, 4, 31	1, 27, 28	23, 24	21, 22	17, 18	14, 15
Plant above-ground crops	2, 3, 4, 11, 12, 30, 31	7, 8, 26, 27	6, 7, 8	3, 4, 30	1, 10, 11, 27, 28, 29	6, 7, 24, 25	3, 4, 5, 31	1, 27, 28	5, 6, 23, 24, 25	3, 4, 21, 22, 30, 31	18, 27, 28	24, 25
Plant below-ground crops	21, 22	17, 18	16, 17, 18, 25, 26	12, 13, 14, 22, 23	19, 20	15, 16, 17	13, 14, 21, 22	9, 10, 17, 18, 19	14, 15	11, 12	7, 8, 17	5, 6, 14, 15, 16
Destroy pests/weeds	5, 6	1, 2, 28	27, 28	24, 25	21, 22	18, 19	15, 16	11, 12	7, 8	5, 6	1, 2, 29, 30	26, 27
Graft or pollinate	11, 12	7, 8	6, 7, 8, 25, 26	3, 4, 30	19, 20	16, 17, 24, 25	13, 14, 21, 22	9, 10, 18, 19	14, 15	11, 12	7, 8	5, 6
Prune to encourage growth	5, 6	1, 2, 9, 10, 11, 28	1, 9, 10, 27, 28	5, 6	2, 3, 4, 30, 31	8, 9, 10, 26, 27	6, 7, 23, 24, 25	2, 3, 4, 21, 29, 30, 31	26, 27	5, 23, 24, 25	1, 2, 19, 20, 21, 29, 30	18, 26, 27
Prune to discourage growth	13, 14, 23, 24	19, 20, 21	19, 20	15, 16, 24, 25	12, 13, 14, 21, 22	18, 19	15, 16	11, 12, 20	7, 8, 16, 17	6, 13, 14, 15	9, 10, 11	7, 8, 17
Harvest above-ground crops	7, 8	3, 4	2, 3, 26, 27	8, 9	5, 6	1, 2, 28, 29	26, 27	5, 6	28, 29	26, 27	3, 4	28, 29
Harvest root crops	26, 27	12, 13	21, 22	27, 30	15, 16	20, 21	17, 18	13, 14	18, 19	16, 17	12, 13	9, 10
Cut hay	5, 6	1, 2	19, 20	24, 25	12, 13	18, 19	15, 16	11, 12	7, 8	5, 6	1, 29, 30	26, 27
Begin logging	26, 27	22, 23	21, 22	18, 19	15, 16	11, 12	8, 9	5, 6	28, 29	26, 27	22, 23	19, 20
Set posts or pour concrete	26, 27	22, 23	21, 22	18, 19	15, 16	11, 12	8, 9	5, 6	28, 29	26, 27	22, 23	19, 20
Slaughter	21, 22	17, 18	16, 17	13, 14	10, 11	6, 7	3, 4, 31	1, 27, 28	23, 24	21, 22	17, 18	14, 15
Wean	13, 18	20, 24	14, 19	10, 20	17, 21	14, 18	11, 15	11, 20	8, 17	13, 18	10, 15	7, 17
Castrate animals	28, 29	24, 25	23, 24	20, 21	17, 18	13, 14	11, 12	7, 8	3, 4	1, 2, 28, 29	24, 25	22, 23

GARDENING BY THE MOON'S SIGN

It is important to note that *the placement of the planets through the signs of the zodiac is not the same in astronomy and astrology*. The *astrological* placement of the Moon, by sign, is given in the chart below. (The *astronomical*, or actual, placement is given in the Left-Hand Calendar Pages 60-86.)

For planting, the most fertile signs are the three water signs: Cancer, Scorpio, and Pisces. Taurus, Virgo, and Capricorn are good second choices for sowing.

Weeding and plowing are best done when the Moon occupies the signs of Aries, Gemini, Leo, Sagittarius, or Aquarius. In-

sect pests can also be handled at these times. Transplanting and grafting are best done under a Cancer, Scorpio, or Pisces Moon. Pruning is best done under an Aries, Leo, or Sagittarius Moon, with growth encouraged during the waxing stage (between new and full Moon) and discouraged during waning (the day after full to the day before new Moon). (The dates of the Moon's phases can be found on pages 60-86.) Clean out the garden shed when the Moon occupies Virgo so that the work will flow smoothly. Fences or permanent beds can be built or mended when Capricorn predominates. Avoid indecision when under the Libra Moon.

Moon's Place in the Astrological Zodiac

	NOV. 97	DEC. 97	JAN. 98	FEB. 98	MAR. 98	APR. 98	MAY 98	JUNE 98	JULY 98	AUG. 98	SEPT. 98	OCT. 98	NOV. 98	DEC. 98
1	SCO	CAP	AQU	ARI	ARI	GEM	CAN	VIR	LIB	SCO	CAP	AQU	ARI	TAU
2	SAG	CAP	PSC	ARI	TAU	GEM	LEO	VIR	LIB	SAG	CAP	AQU	ARI	TAU
3	SAG	CAP	PSC	TAU	TAU	CAN	LEO	LIB	SCO	SAG	AQU	PSC	TAU	GEM
4	CAP	AQU	PSC	TAU	GEM	CAN	LEO	LIB	SCO	SAG	AQU	PSC	TAU	GEM
5	CAP	AQU	ARI	GEM	GEM	LEO	VIR	LIB	SCO	CAP	PSC	ARI	GEM	CAN
6	CAP	PSC	ARI	GEM	CAN	LEO	VIR	SCO	SAG	CAP	PSC	ARI	GEM	CAN
7	AQU	PSC	TAU	CAN	CAN	VIR	LIB	SCO	SAG	AQU	ARI	TAU	CAN	LEO
8	AQU	ARI	TAU	CAN	CAN	VIR	LIB	SAG	CAP	AQU	ARI	TAU	CAN	LEO
9	PSC	ARI	GEM	LEO	LEO	VIR	LIB	SAG	CAP	PSC	TAU	GEM	LEO	VIR
10	PSC	TAU	GEM	LEO	LEO	LIB	SCO	SAG	AQU	PSC	TAU	GEM	LEO	VIR
11	ARI	TAU	CAN	LEO	VIR	LIB	SCO	CAP	AQU	ARI	TAU	CAN	LEO	VIR
12	ARI	GEM	CAN	VIR	VIR	SCO	SAG	CAP	AQU	ARI	GEM	CAN	VIR	LIB
13	TAU	GEM	LEO	VIR	VIR	SCO	SAG	AQU	PSC	TAU	GEM	LEO	VIR	LIB
14	TAU	GEM	LEO	LIB	LIB	SCO	SAG	AQU	PSC	TAU	CAN	LEO	LIB	SCO
15	GEM	CAN	VIR	LIB	LIB	SAG	CAP	PSC	ARI	GEM	CAN	LEO	LIB	SCO
16	GEM	CAN	VIR	LIB	SCO	SAG	CAP	PSC	ARI	GEM	LEO	VIR	LIB	SCO
17	CAN	LEO	VIR	SCO	SCO	CAP	AQU	PSC	TAU	CAN	LEO	VIR	SCO	SAG
18	CAN	LEO	LIB	SCO	SCO	CAP	AQU	ARI	TAU	CAN	VIR	LIB	SCO	SAG
19	LEO	VIR	LIB	SAG	SAG	CAP	PSC	ARI	GEM	CAN	VIR	LIB	SAG	CAP
20	LEO	VIR	LIB	SAG	SAG	AQU	PSC	TAU	GEM	LEO	VIR	LIB	SAG	CAP
21	LEO	VIR	SCO	SAG	CAP	AQU	ARI	TAU	CAN	LEO	LIB	SCO	SAG	AQU
22	VIR	LIB	SCO	CAP	CAP	PSC	ARI	GEM	CAN	VIR	LIB	SCO	CAP	AQU
23	VIR	LIB	SAG	CAP	AQU	PSC	TAU	GEM	LEO	VIR	SCO	SAG	CAP	AQU
24	LIB	SCO	SAG	AQU	AQU	ARI	TAU	CAN	LEO	LIB	SCO	SAG	AQU	PSC
25	LIB	SCO	CAP	AQU	PSC	ARI	GEM	CAN	LEO	LIB	SCO	SAG	AQU	PSC
26	LIB	SCO	CAP	PSC	PSC	TAU	GEM	LEO	VIR	LIB	SAG	CAP	AQU	ARI
27	SCO	SAG	AQU	PSC	ARI	TAU	CAN	LEO	VIR	SCO	SAG	CAP	PSC	ARI
28	SCO	SAG	AQU	ARI	ARI	GEM	CAN	VIR	LIB	SCO	CAP	AQU	PSC	TAU
29	SAG	CAP	AQU	—	TAU	GEM	CAN	VIR	LIB	SAG	CAP	AQU	ARI	TAU
30	SAG	CAP	PSC	—	TAU	CAN	LEO	VIR	LIB	SAG	CAP	PSC	ARI	TAU
31	—	AQU	PSC	—	GEM	—	LEO	—	SCO	SAG	—	PSC	—	GEM

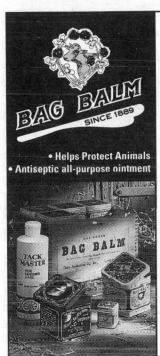

SECRETS OF THE ZODIAC

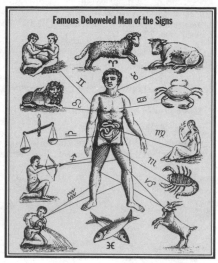
Famous Deboweled Man of the Signs

Ancient astrologers associated each of the signs with a part of the body over which they felt the sign held some influence. The first sign of the zodiac — Aries — was attributed to the head, with the rest of the signs moving down the body, ending with Pisces at the feet.

♈	Aries, head. ARI	Mar. 21-Apr. 20
♉	Taurus, neck. TAU	Apr. 21-May 20
♊	Gemini, arms. GEM	May 21-June 20
♋	Cancer, breast. CAN	June 21-July 22
♌	Leo, heart. LEO	July 23-Aug. 22
♍	Virgo, belly. VIR	Aug. 23-Sept. 22
♎	Libra, reins. LIB	Sept. 23-Oct. 22
♏	Scorpio, secrets. SCO	Oct. 23-Nov. 22
♐	Sagittarius, thighs. SAG	Nov. 23-Dec. 21
♑	Capricorn, knees. CAP	Dec. 22-Jan. 19
♒	Aquarius, legs. AQU	Jan. 20-Feb. 19
♓	Pisces, feet. PSC	Feb. 20-Mar. 20

ASTROLOGY AND ASTRONOMY

Astrology is a tool we use to time events according to the *astrological* placement of the two luminaries (the Sun and the Moon) and eight planets in the 12 signs of the zodiac. Astronomy, on the other hand, is the charting of the *actual* placement of the known planets and constellations, taking into account precession of the equinoxes. As a result, *the placement of the planets in the signs of the zodiac are not the same astrologically and astronomically.* (The Moon's *astronomical* place is given in the Left-Hand Calendar Pages [60-86] and its *astrological* place is given in Gardening by the Moon's Sign, page 168.)

Modern astrology is a study of synchronicities. The planetary movements do not *cause* events. Rather, they *explain* the "flow" or trajectory that events will tend to follow. Because of free will, you can choose to plan a schedule in harmony with the flow, or you can choose to swim against the current.

The dates given in A Month-by-Month Astrological Timetable (page 166) have been chosen with particular care to the astrological passage of the Moon. However, since other planets also influence us, it's best to take a look at *all* indicators before seeking advice on major life decisions. A qualified astrologer can study the current relationship of the planets and your own personal birth chart in order to assist you in the best possible timing for carrying out your plans.

PLANET MERCURY DOES WHAT?

Sometimes when we look out from our perspective here on Earth, the other planets appear to be traveling backward through the zodiac. (They're not actually moving backward, it just looks that way to us.) We call this *retrograde.*

Mercury's retrograde periods, which occur three or four times a year, can cause travel delays and misconstrued communications. Plans have a way of unraveling, too. However, this is an excellent time to be researching or looking into the past. Intuition is high during these periods, and coincidences can be extraordinary.

When Mercury is retrograde, astrologers advise us to keep plans flexible, allow extra time for travel, and avoid signing contracts. It's OK and even useful to look over projects and plans, because we may see them with different eyes at these times. However, our normal system of checks and balances might not be active, so it's best to wait until Mercury is direct again to make any final decisions. In 1998, Mercury will be retrograde from March 27 to April 20, August 2 to 22, and November 21 to December 11. 	*– Celeste Longacre*

RAINY DAY AMUSEMENTS

Answers on page 188.

Word Play

Can you think of English words that meet the following requirements?

1. One that has three *y*'s in it.
2. One that contains four consecutive vowels.
3. One with three double letters in a row.
4. Four one-syllable words of eight letters each. Do not use plurals, or verbs in the past tense that just add *ed*.
5. One that has all five vowels plus *y* in the same order as their alphabetic position (that is, in the order a, e, i, o, u, y).
6. One containing the letter *i* five times.

– Norman E. Duggan

Horse Sense

Two fathers and two sons own 21 horses. Each person is moving to a different part of the country, and they want to divide their horses evenly among them, without resorting to surgery. Is it possible? How?

Number Fun 1

A. Find a number that, when multiplied by 19, gives a product whose digits add up to 19.

B. Find a number whose digit sum equals the difference between its forward and reverse reading.

– David A. Edgar

Earthy Anagrams

Anagrams are words whose letters, when rearranged, form different words. Using the clues, rearrange each four-letter noun into a land area. *Example:* Rearrange *a speed competition* into *43,560 square feet of land.* RACE, ACRE.

– John A. Johnston

Rearrange:

1. *A rate of speed* into *a promontory.*
2. *A metal* into *a small valley.*
3. *A cart* into *house grounds.*
4. *Enthusiasm* into *a narrow road.*
5. *A building division* into *a heath.*
6. *A commercial transaction* into *meadows.*
7. *A garment edge* into *a plateau.*
8. *A groove* into *ground areas.*
9. *A class of things* into *rocky hills.*
10. *An unclothed body* into *a seashore hill.*

Spelling Lessens

This puzzle is called "Spelling Lessens" because the number of letters in the answer words *lessens* with each consecutive step. The top word in the inverted pyramid contains seven letters. Drop one letter, rearrange what remains, and you will form the word that fits the next clue. Continue on to the bottom of the pyramid. We've numbered the clues according to how many letters are in the answer. (Hint: If you can't figure out the first word, try one of the shorter ones and work up instead of down, adding a letter with each step.)

– Teresa M. Hackett

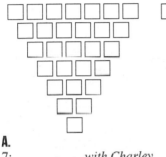
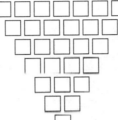
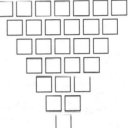

A.
7: _____ *with Charley*
6: Gent's gents
5: Blackboard material
4: Endure
3: College entrance exam
2: Word of comparison
1: Crooked letter

B.
7: Monarchs' chairs
6: Wasp
5: Caruso, e.g.
4: Actor Rip
3: Balderdash
2: 26th president
1: 1/2 *d*

C.
7: Book division
6: Floor covering
5: Slender candle
4: Bosc
3: Primate
2: Ma's mate
1: Softly, in music

Number Fun 2

A. An old music group reunites to put out a new recording. The compact disc they make sells 379,836 copies. If each CD costs $14, what's the name of the group?

B. Using Roman numerals, what is the highest number you can construct that forms an English word? (It must be a proper Roman numeral and form a common word.) *– Rand Higbee*

Changing Moon

Can you change the word *MOON* into the second word in each set in the number of steps indicated? Change only one letter at a time, making a word each time, and do not rearrange the letters. Proper names, slang, and obsolete words are not allowed.

– Monty Gilmer

1. MOON to BUCK (4 steps)
2. MOON to WOLF (4 steps)
3. MOON to SNOW (5 steps)
4. MOON to PINK (6 steps)

From Berries to Bivalves . . .

Culinary Favorites

FROM THE
Northwest

The Pacific Northwest has more topographical and geological variety than any other area of the country: smoking volcanoes, snowcapped mountains, sparkling rivers and alpine lakes, plateaus, deserts, and endless evergreen forests. This spectacular land is so rich in natural resources — timber, minerals, fish, and game — that pioneers and miners risked their lives for a piece of it. But long before explorers made the dangerous trip to this frontier, Native Americans — Makah, Quinault, Skagit, Chehalis, Puyallup — fished the fertile estuaries for clams and oysters, hunted deer and antelope, and harvested berries and salmon galore. Pacific Northwesterners still put indigenous ingredients to use in local specialties. In fact, they say the only thing that rivals their scenery is their food. Here's just a sampling.

BY POLLY BANNISTER

– illustrated by Renée Quintal Daily

Berries and Hazelnuts

The Northwest is Eden for berry lovers. In the temperate climate of Oregon's prized Willamette Valley, you'll find blueberries, strawberries, lingonberries, raspberries, gooseberries, huckleberries, cranberries, and all sorts of caneberries — blackberries, boysenberries, and loganberries. Nearly all the hazelnuts used in the United States are grown in this area, too.

BLUEBERRY PIE WITH GRAHAM HAZELNUT CRUST

Piecrust:
2 cups flour
1/2 cup sugar
2 teaspoons ground cinnamon
1/2 cup crushed graham-cracker crumbs
1/2 cup hazelnuts, finely ground
2/3 cup butter, chilled and cut into small pieces
2 egg yolks
1 teaspoon vanilla
2 tablespoons water
sugar

Filling:
4 cups fresh blueberries
2/3 cup sugar

3 tablespoons flour
1/8 teaspoon salt

For crust: Mix together flour, sugar, and cinnamon. Add graham-cracker crumbs and hazelnuts. Cut in butter until mixture resembles small peas In a separate bowl, beat egg yolks with vanilla, then add to flour mixture. Add water and stir until dough holds together. Form into a ball (dough will be stiff; do not overwork it). Cut dough into 2 equal parts and refrigerate. After dough is chilled, place each ball between 2 sheets of waxed paper and roll out to form top and bottom crusts for a 10-inch pie pan. Put bottom layer in pie pan. Combine filling ingredients in a separate bowl and pour into pie pan. Place top layer on pie, and crimp top and bottom crusts together. Make several knife cuts in crust. Sprinkle top crust with a little sugar. Cover edge of crust with foil and bake in a preheated 350° F oven for 30 minutes. Remove foil and bake 20 minutes longer, or until golden brown and bubbly.
Makes 8 servings.
(Recipe courtesy of Berry Works, Corvallis, Oregon)

(continued on next page)

Lemon-Blueberry Sour Cream Coffee Cake

Topping:
1-1/2 cups fresh blueberries
3/4 cup sugar
1 teaspoon cinnamon
1 cup pecans or walnuts, chopped

Cake:
1 cup butter, softened
1 tablespoon grated lemon peel
1-1/2 cups sugar
2 teaspoons vanilla

2 eggs
2 cups sour cream
1/4 cup lemon juice
2 cups flour
1/2 teaspoon salt
1 tablespoon baking powder

Preheat oven to 375° F. Gently mix topping ingredients in a bowl and divide in half. Cream butter with lemon peel, sugar, and vanilla until fluffy. Add eggs, sour cream, and lemon juice. Sift in flour, salt, and baking powder; fold in batter lightly. Pour a third of the batter into a buttered 10½-inch springform pan. Sprinkle with half of the topping. Fill with remaining batter, and sprinkle with remaining topping, pressing into the batter a bit. Bake for 55 to 60 minutes, or until toothpick comes out clean. **Makes 16 servings.** *(Recipe courtesy of Paisley's Restaurant, Portland, Oregon)*

Hazelnut-Stuffed French Bread

Filling:
2 cloves garlic, minced
1 tablespoon Dijon mustard
3/4 cup hazelnuts, finely chopped
1/3 cup olive oil
1/2 cup chopped sun-dried tomatoes
1/4 cup butter, softened
1 cup grated Swiss cheese

Bread:
2 packages or 2 scant tablespoons dry yeast
2-1/2 cups warm water
7 cups bread flour
1 tablespoon salt

1 tablespoon butter, melted cornmeal
1 egg white with 1 tablespoon water

Thoroughly mix all filling ingredients and set aside.

To make bread, dissolve yeast in warm water. Add flour, salt, and butter, and mix well. Knead until dough is elastic and smooth, about 10 minutes. Place dough in a greased bowl, cover, and let rise until doubled, about an hour. Divide dough into 2 parts and roll into oblong pieces, about 15x12 inches each. Spread each with half the filling, allowing 1-inch margins on long sides, 2 inches on ends, and roll up, sealing as you go. Place seam side down on greased baking sheets that have been dusted with cornmeal. Cover with a towel and let rise for an hour, or until doubled. Make 3 diagonal cuts on each loaf. Bake in preheated 450° F oven for 25 minutes. Remove, brush with egg-white wash, and bake for another 5 minutes. For best results, keep oven very hot and place a pan with 1 inch of water on the bottom oven rack. **Makes 2 loaves.**
(Recipe courtesy of Hazelnut Marketing Board, Tigard, Oregon)

Pears

Ninety-five percent of the nation's commercially grown pears come from five regions in Washington, Oregon, and California. 'Bartlett' production is centered in Washington's Yakima and Wenatchee valleys; winter pears ('Comice', 'Anjou', and 'Bosc') are grown in Oregon's Hood and Medford river valleys.

Pear-Mince-Oatmeal Bars

3/4 cup butter or margarine, softened
3/4 cup brown sugar, packed
1-1/2 cups flour
1-1/4 cups quick rolled oats

1/2 cup chopped walnuts
1/2 teaspoon salt
1/2 teaspoon baking soda
2 winter pears, peeled, cored and chopped

1 cup prepared mincemeat
1 teaspoon lemon juice
1/2 teaspoon grated lemon peel

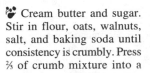

Cream butter and sugar. Stir in flour, oats, walnuts, salt, and baking soda until consistency is crumbly. Press ⅔ of crumb mixture into a 9x13x2-inch pan. Combine pears, mincemeat, lemon juice, and peel; spread over crumb crust. Top with remaining crumb mixture and pat lightly. Bake at 375° F for 25 to 30 minutes, or until crust is golden.

Makes 20 to 25 bars.

CURRIED PEARS AND LAMB

1 medium onion, chopped
1 clove garlic, minced
3 tablespoons vegetable or olive oil
1 pound boneless lamb, cut in 1-inch cubes
2 tablespoons flour
2 tablespoons tomato paste
1 tablespoon curry powder
1 teaspoon paprika
1/2 teaspoon ground ginger
1/4 teaspoon chili powder
1 teaspoon sugar
1/2 teaspoon salt
2 cups chicken broth
2 fresh pears
scallions and chutney for garnish

Sauté onion and garlic in oil until soft. Add lamb, and brown on all sides. Blend in flour, tomato paste, spices, sugar, and salt. Gradually add chicken broth. Cover and simmer for 30 minutes. Core and slice pears (do not peel); add to lamb and cook, uncovered, 15 minutes longer. Serve over hot rice, and garnish with chopped scallions and chutney.

Makes 4 servings.

(Pear recipes courtesy of Oregon-Washington-California Pear Bureau, Portland, Oregon)

Apples

Washington grows over five billion apples a year, producing the largest supply of this country's 'Red Delicious' and 'Golden Delicious' apples. The state's four newest apple varieties are 'Jonagold' (a blend of 'Jonathan' and 'Golden Delicious'), 'Braeburn', 'Fuji', and 'Gala'. Washington also leads the country in sweet cherry production; here the two fruits team up for a winning combination.

WASHINGTON APPLE-CHERRY FRUIT SPREAD

3 'Jonagold' or other sweet variety apples, peeled, cored, and coarsely chopped
1/2 cup dried sweet cherries
1/2 cup apple juice or water
1 cinnamon stick
1/2 teaspoon grated lemon peel

In a medium saucepan, combine apples, cherries, juice, and cinnamon. Cover and bring to a simmer over medium heat. Cook 15 minutes, stirring frequently. Uncover, reduce heat, and cook 15 to 20 minutes longer, or until apples are soft but retain some shape.

Remove cinnamon stick and add lemon peel. Puree in a blender or food processor until mixture becomes a chunky spread. Chill before serving. **Makes about 1 cup.**

(Recipe courtesy of Washington Apple Commission, Wenatchee, Washington)

(c o n t i n u e d   o n   n e x t   p a g e)

Apple-Cherry Crisp

2 cups pitted fresh sweet
   cherries (or 2 cups
   canned, drained and
   rinsed)
2 cups peeled, cored, and
   sliced apples
1 tablespoon lemon juice
1 teaspoon cinnamon
1/2 cup sugar

1/2 cup flour
1/2 cup rolled oats
1/4 cup almonds, chopped
1/2 cup brown sugar, packed
6 tablespoons butter

🍃 Preheat oven to 375° F. Toss cherries and apples with lemon juice, cinnamon,

and sugar. Place in a buttered 2-quart baking dish. Mix flour, rolled oats, almonds, and brown sugar. Cut in butter until mixture is a coarse meal. Spread topping over fruit and bake for 30 to 35 minutes. Serve warm with whipped cream. **Makes 6 to 8 servings.**

Those Briny Bivalves

Washington's chilly Pacific waters and calm bays make for excellent clams, mussels, and oysters. There are dozens of varieties of these bivalves, some of which were brought from Japan and "seeded" in the 1920s. This recipe calls for Pacific oysters and Dungeness crab, named after the town on the Olympic Peninsula where this hard-shell crab was first harvested.

Baked Oysters Stuffed with Dungeness Crab

Crabmeat sauce:
2 tablespoons butter
2 tablespoons flour
1 cup milk
2 tablespoons minced chives
1 tablespoon dry sherry
1 pound cooked crabmeat,
   flaked
salt and pepper, to taste
Oysters:
24 oysters, shucked, and
   placed on half shell
1 cup bread crumbs

2 tablespoons grated
   Parmesan cheese
1/4 cup butter, melted

🍃 Preheat oven to 450° F. In a small saucepan, melt butter over low heat. Add flour and blend well, cooking for 1 to 2 minutes. Slowly stir in milk, whisking until sauce is smooth and thickened. Stir in chives, sherry, and crabmeat. Add salt and

pepper to taste.
   Place oysters in their half shells on a baking sheet or shallow roasting pan, and fill each oyster with crabmeat sauce. Mix bread crumbs with Parmesan and moisten with melted butter. Top each oyster with a teaspoon of bread crumbs. Place in oven and bake for 10 minutes; then brown tops under the broiler. **Makes 6 to 8 servings.**

Salmon

This fish is considered by most to be the ultimate Northwest food. Of the four varieties — King (or Chinook), Sockeye (or Red), Coho (Silver), and Chum — most Washingtonians prefer King for its intense flavor.

Savory Salmon Steaks

3 tablespoons olive oil
1/3 cup finely chopped onion
1/3 cup grated carrot
1/3 cup finely chopped celery
4 salmon steaks
1/2 cup dry white wine

1 eight-ounce can tomatoes,
   chopped
chopped fresh dill for garnish

🍃 Heat oil in a large skillet and sauté the onion, carrot, and celery until soft. Add salmon steaks and brown

lightly on both sides. Pour in wine and tomatoes and cover pan. Simmer salmon over low heat for 10 minutes, or until fish flakes easily. Garnish with dill and serve with buttered new potatoes. **Makes 4 servings.**

☐☐

For Nearly A Century, Americans Have Turned With Confidence To Physicians Mutual

When Physicians Mutual was founded in 1902, the company specialized in health insurance for doctors only.

Today, Physicians Mutual protects Americans from all walks of life. Together with our sister company, Physicians Life, we provide a wide range of coverage, including:

- life insurance and annuities
- supplemental health policies
- Medicare Supplements
- long term care coverage

The Physicians family of companies has earned the trust and confidence of more than <u>1.3 million</u> policyowners from all 50 states and the District of Columbia.

It's a tradition of service we're proud of. And it's one <u>you</u> can depend on.

We're here when you need us®

For more information, Call Toll-Free

1-800-218-3388

Physicians Mutual Insurance Company®
Physicians Life Insurance Company®
2600 Dodge Street • Omaha, NE 68131

SQR

WINNING RECIPES

Appetizers

FIRST PRIZE
Salmon Wontons

Filling:
1 can salmon (6 to 7-1/2 ounces), or
   equivalent fresh salmon, poached
1/4 cup shredded carrot
4 scallions, chopped
1/2 cup alfalfa sprouts
1-1/2 tablespoons soy sauce
1 to 2 teaspoons grated fresh gingerroot,
   or 1/2 teaspoon powdered ginger
2 cloves garlic, crushed

about 30 wonton wrappers
oil for deep-frying

Dipping sauce:
   sweet-and-sour sauce, plum sauce, or a
   combination of 1 cup duck sauce, 1 to 2
   tablespoons soy sauce, 1 teaspoon hoisin
   sauce, and a dash of chili oil

Clean bones and skin from salmon, if necessary. In a medium bowl, combine salmon, carrot, scallions, sprouts, soy sauce, ginger, and garlic, and toss together until crumbly. Heat oil for deep-frying. Moisten the edges of a wonton wrapper with a few drops of water, and drop about 1 teaspoon of the salmon filling on the center. Fold the wonton wrapper diagonally to make a triangle, and press down on the edges to seal. (Fill about 15 wontons at a time, keeping the unused wrappers covered to prevent them from drying out.) Deep-fry in hot oil on one side; then flip over and fry on the other side until golden brown. Drain on brown paper bags or paper towels, and serve hot with dipping sauce. ***Makes about 30.***
    Anne Dirksen, Hastings, Minnesota

SECOND PRIZE
Tuscany Cheese Tortas

3 tablespoons olive oil
1/2 cup diced red onion
1 clove garlic, minced
1/4 cup chopped sun-dried tomatoes
   (not in oil), softened in warm water for
   10 minutes and drained
2-1/2 cups grated zucchini
5 large eggs, lightly beaten
1/3 cup dry, Italian-bread crumbs
1 teaspoon dried oregano
1/4 cup chopped fresh basil
1-1/2 cups grated Cheddar cheese
1-1/2 cups grated Jack cheese
1/2 cup freshly grated Parmesan cheese
1/2 teaspoon salt
pepper, to taste
1/4 cup toasted sesame seeds

Heat oil in a large frying pan over medium-high heat. Add onion, garlic, and tomatoes; cook, stirring, for about 3 minutes. Add zucchini and cook until crisp-tender, about 3 minutes, and remove from heat. In a large bowl, blend eggs, bread crumbs, oregano, basil, cheeses, salt, pepper, and the zucchini mixture. Spread in a greased 9x13-inch baking pan. Sprinkle with sesame seeds. Bake in a preheated 325° F oven for 30 minutes, or until set when lightly touched in the center. Cool on a rack for 15 minutes. Cut into 1-inch squares and serve warm or at room temperature. Can also be refrigerated and served cold. ***Makes 9 to 10 dozen.***
    Kathy Lee, Valley Center, California

Clam-Stuffed Mushrooms

1/4 pound bacon
2 teaspoons reserved bacon drippings
1/2 cup finely chopped onion
1/2 cup finely chopped green pepper
1 clove garlic, minced
1 tablespoon minced fresh parsley
1 teaspoon dried oregano
salt and pepper
one 6-1/2-ounce can chopped clams, drained
1/3 cup grated Parmesan cheese
12 ounces fresh mushrooms, stems removed

Fry bacon until crisp. Drain and crumble into mixing bowl, reserving 2 teaspoons of drippings. Sauté onion and green pepper in bacon drippings until onion is opaque. Remove from heat and stir in garlic, parsley, oregano, salt, and pepper. Mix well and add to crumbled bacon in bowl. Stir in clams and cheese. Spoon into mushroom caps, rounding the filling. Place on baking sheet and bake at 350° F for about 20 minutes, until mushrooms are tender. (Or microwave at 50-percent power for 8 to 10 minutes.) Serve hot. *Makes about 24.*

Susan Straney, Saline, Michigan

Special thanks to Sylvia Wright and Rich Roth for help with recipe judging and testing. – *Ed.*

Announcing

The 1998 RECIPE CONTEST

Chicken

For 1998, cash prizes (first prize, $50; second prize, $25; third prize, $15) will be awarded for the best original recipes using chicken as a main ingredient. All entries become the property of Yankee Publishing Incorporated, which reserves all rights to the materials submitted. Winners will be announced in the 1999 edition of *The Old Farmer's Almanac.* **Deadline is March 1, 1998. Please type all recipes. Address: Recipe Contest,** *The Old Farmer's Almanac,* **P.O. Box 520, Dublin, NH 03444; or send e-mail (subject: Chicken Contest) to almanac@yankeepub.com.**

Winning Essays

in the 1997 ESSAY CONTEST

Best Cures for Picky Eaters

When I was a child, my mother used her own bit of child psychology to introduce new foods to me and my two siblings. After fixing us our spaghetti, or hot dog, or peanut-butter sandwich, she would serve herself and my father something completely different and casually sit down to eat. Our curiosity piqued, we'd ask, "Ooh, what's that?" "Liver," she'd say, for example, "but it's only for grown-ups." Naturally, we had to have some! We may not have actually *liked* what we were trying, but we never refused new foods outright when presented in this manner.

Laurel Parker, Ithaca, New York

The best cures for picky eaters? I consider the question with narrowed, gleaming eyes. I *know* picky eaters. As a waitress, I meet a million people. Many are cheerful and easy to please, but some are . . . *not.* (continued)

I've tried everything: smiling more widely, frowning more fiercely, murmuring soothingly, and speaking firmly, as if to a spoiled child. I've raised the price and lowered the price; once, I even began to cry (quietly). I've watched balding adults all but hurl themselves to the floor, kicking and screaming, because smoked trout was not on the menu. Life is *so* hard and unfair.

The best cure I've found is to threaten perpetrators with something infinitely worse. They become more amenable almost immediately. Losing their options seems to clear their head.

You don't like whole wheat? What a shame. I'll have to bring pumpernickel. You can't live with vanilla malt? I sympathize — you're going to *love* Blue Moon whirled up with milk. Turn turkey into pickled loaf, substitute smoked jalapeño Swiss cheese for cheddar, or switch cream of asparagus with whole-beet borscht, and you've got a sure cure.

Ellen Airgood, Grand Marais, Michigan

THIRD PRIZE

No picky eaters would be tolerated at our house, we decided when the first of our five children began to grace our table. Our rule was, "Take three bites and then decide."

"I hate green food," said David.

"Mother, you *know* I don't like mixed-up food!" cried Anne, as the beef cubes touched the vegetables in the Hungarian goulash.

"Ugh! Rice again. It looks like crawly white bugs," complained Marti.

"I can't eat tuna fish; it smells like cat food," declared Katie.

How did all these little people form such definite opinions about food?

Then Frankie asked, "How come you never make spinach, Mom?"

Before I could stop him, Dad said, "Your mom doesn't like spinach; it reminds her of seaweed."

We no longer have picky eaters at our house — we changed our entire way of looking at individual food preferences. Everyone is now allowed to hate three food items, with no tasting required. Discriminating palates are easier to educate than picky eaters are to eliminate.

Marianna Csizmadia, Cincinnati, Ohio

ANNOUNCING
The 1998 ESSAY CONTEST
The Most Useful Invention of the 20th Century

For 1998, cash prizes (first prize, $50; second prize, $25; third prize, $15) will be awarded for the best 200-word essay on this subject: "The Most Useful Invention of the 20th Century." All entries become the property of Yankee Publishing Incorporated, which reserves all rights to the materials submitted. Winners will be announced in the 1999 edition of *The Old Farmer's Almanac*. Deadline is March 1, 1998. Please type all essays. Address: Essay Contest, *The Old Farmer's Almanac*, P.O. Box 520, Dublin, NH 03444; or send e-mail (subject: Invention Contest) to almanac@yankeepub.com.

Contest Winners Announced
Can You Predict Presidential Elections by the Moon?

We received many wonderful entries for our Presidential Lunations Contest from the 1997 edition of *The Old Farmer's Almanac*. We marveled at the amount of time our readers devoted to tabulating and analyzing the data! We were so impressed by the work of Mary Donovan's fourth grade class at the Crocker Farm Elementary School in Amherst, Massachusetts, that we are pleased to award them First Place and the prize of $100. Congratulations to Stew, Dominga, Jill, Caitlin, Anjali, B. J., Meagan, Kelly, Alex, Daniel, Teddy, Deb,

Nicholas, Adrian, Ryan, Hanna, Orienthia, and Sungha. Ms. Donovan's students were divided into five groups to determine the Moon phase when each president was elected (new, waxing, full, or waning). They tallied, graphed, and charted their findings and concluded: "When the Moon was waxing, the Republicans and the Democrats seem to have had an equal chance of winning (10 and 7); when the Moon was waning, the Republicans and the Democrats seem to have had an equal chance of winning (9 and 8). *We do not think that the Moon influences the outcome of presidential elections.*"

In fact, almost half of you came to the same conclusion, although Janet Hughes, of Forks, Washington, said it best: "According to the Chart of Outcomes of Presidential Elections Through All the Lunations of Voting Days, there is proof the Moon is for lovers and should be totally eliminated in politics; however, it is said both lovers and politicians are fools."

Our hats are off to all the statisticians (and there were several) who analyzed the data. The detailed submissions (complete with mathematical formulas and footnotes) we received from Michael Slattery of Denver, Colorado, and Paul Catalano of Reading, Massachusetts, earned each of them an Honorable Mention. Also receiving an Honorable Mention for his creative and unique "Hypothesis on Presidential Lunacy" is James O. Brown of Flemington, New Jersey. We are posting these and a sampling of other entries on our Web site at www.almanac.com.

We can't resist sharing a few excerpts from our readers' entries:

■ "Entertaining a more complicated model such as

$$\log \frac{\Pr(D)}{1 - \Pr(D)} = \alpha + \beta_1 \text{ Moon's age} + \beta_2 \text{ Moon's age}^2$$

yields estimates of β_1 and β_2 of 0.136 ($p = 0.31$) and –0.00492 ($p = 0.29$), respectively, a result that, again, does not provide any statistical evidence of a significant relationship between the Moon's age and the election outcome." *(Paul Catalano, Reading, Mass.)*

■ "There is the 'Lincoln Principle,' during which the country is experiencing great strife and needs strong leadership, versus the 'Coolidge-Hoover Counterhypothesis' during mediocre times and/or leadership. To be within the Lincoln times, one has to be elected between the first-quarter Moon (9th lunar day) and the last-quarter Moon (23rd). To be within the Coolidge-Hoover phase, one has to be elected between the last-quarter Moon (24th) and the first-quarter Moon (7th). As luck would have it, no one ever gets elected on the 8th lunar day." *(James O. Brown, Flemington, N.J.)*

■ "The Whigs waxed well, but only twice." *(A. Attura, Arlington, Va.)*

■ "The president entering or elected to office on the first day after a new or full Moon would not be in office the next term." *(David Mougakos, Vineland, N.J.)*

■ "Sixty-three percent of the time that the election takes place when the Moon is waning, the new candidate wins. And 78 percent of the time that the Moon is waxing, the incumbent wins." *(Kirk Mona, St. Paul, Minn.)*

■ "Republican incumbents lose if the election is close to the first- or last-quarter Moon. They win if it's closer to the new or full Moon." *(Gary Di Giuseppe, Fort Dodge, Iowa)*

■ "When election day is on an even-numbered day of the Moon's age, the major parties should nominate a candidate with a long last name and an even number of letters in the last name." *(Doug Ward, Battle Ground, Wash.)*

■ "More Republicans were elected to, or took oaths of, office during the waning Moon. More Democrats were elected to, or took oaths of, office during the waxing Moon." *(Charlotte Robinson, New Concord, Ky.)*

■ "I determined from what I observed that rather than the Moon having an effect on an electoral outcome, maybe the answer lies somewhere in the stars." *(John Dallal, Howard Beach, N.Y.)*

SOUTHERN-FRIED CHICKEN?

(The *Real* Southern-Fried Chicken, That Is)

Some might mention barbecued chicken as a rival. But to Southerners — in fact, to people all over the country these days — nothing else even comes close. So here's how to make it correctly . . .

by Jim Auchmutey

■ Mention fried chicken to a Southerner and you're likely to be met with dreamy-eyed remembrance. The preacher coming over for Sunday dinner. A wicker basket of cold chicken on a hot Fourth of July. A heavy, black skillet passed down from grandmother to granddaughter. A slippery tussle over the pully bone, the juicy-meated piece of the chicken that most Americans call the wishbone.

It isn't just Southerners who harbor memories, of course.

Fried chicken is served all over America, particularly in the Midwest, and in many parts of the world, thanks to the efforts of Colonel Sanders and his fast-food brethren. But Southerners created the dish in all its finger-licking forms, whether it be Kentucky-fried, Maryland-fried, Creole-fried, or any of the multitude of styles and cooking techniques.

The first published fried-chicken recipe appeared, fittingly, in the first southern cookbook.

"To know about fried chicken, you have to have been weaned

Mary Randolph, a relative of Thomas Jefferson, wrote *The Virginia Housewife* in 1824 but didn't include her fried-chicken recipe until the third edition four years later. Her technique of dredging chicken parts in flour and frying them in fat remains the standard 170 years later.

Not that every southern cook is in agreement about the method. Only barbecuing rivals frying as a source of debate among the region's cooks.

First, there's the matter of the bird. Some say that only a tender young fryer under three pounds will do. Others hold that the size of the bird matters less than buying it fresh and whole and cutting it up yourself. "Frozen chicken tastes bloody and turns dark at the bone when fried," North Carolina restaurateur Bill Neal wrote in his *Southern Cooking*. "If you find yourself in the possession of one, stew it or bury it."

Then there's the batter and seasonings. People have been known to soak the bird in everything from bourbon to buttermilk, then dip it in flour, cornmeal, potato flour, or some other batter seasoned with salt, pepper, paprika, or anything else that seems to make sense. Atlanta chef Scott Peacock perfected one of the more involved preparations, a three-day process that starts with day-long baptisms in salt water and then buttermilk.

Next comes the frying. Most recipes call for cooking the chicken in an inch or less of oil, using a heavy cast-iron skillet to distribute the heat evenly. Much restaurant chicken, however, is actually deep-fried, like potatoes, in vats of hot oil — a method most traditionalists dislike. Not John Martin Taylor of Charleston, South Carolina. "Deep-frying in really hot fat actually makes the chicken less greasy. It makes a crispier crust, too," says the au-

thor of *Fearless Frying Cookbook,* a volume about Southern-fried foods that he originally wanted to call *The Fryble.*

As for what to fry it in, people use everything from lard and vegetable shortening to sesame and canola oils. Taylor prefers peanut oil or some other neutral-tasting agent. Purists are unwavering in their support of lard.

Finally, there's the question of how to serve the chicken. Cooks usually make a cream gravy with the pan drippings, milk, and flour. In some places — notably Maryland — this gravy is poured over the chicken. Across most of the South, the gravy is instead served on the side with rice, grits, or mashed potatoes. Indeed, many Southerners find the pouring of gravy over chicken a vaguely alien and

and reared on it in the South. Period."

— James Villas, the food editor of *Town and Country* magazine and native of North Carolina

threatening practice. Henrietta Stanley Dull, an Atlanta food editor whose 1928 book *Southern Cooking* taught generations of home economists how to cook, was quite firm on the matter: "Never pour gravy over chicken if you wish Georgia-fried chicken."

And if you're wondering whether it's correct to use your fingers — well, remember what Louis Armstrong said about jazz: "If you have to ask . . ."

So, you see, Southern-fried chicken is more complicated than the old white-meat or dark-meat quandary. The whole

"The women of the North cannot fry a chicken." – Mark Twain

The Recipes

Here are two different approaches to Southern-fried chicken — the first pan-fried, the second deep-fried. The former recipe combines classic techniques set forth by food writers Craig Claiborne and James Villas. The latter is adapted from the recipe of Charleston cookbook author John Martin Taylor.

Basic Southern-Fried Chicken

1 fryer (2-1/2 to 3 pounds), cut into serving pieces
buttermilk to cover
1 cup all-purpose flour
salt and black pepper, to taste
vegetable shortening
1 tablespoon bacon grease

■ Rinse chicken pieces under running water. Pat dry and place in a casserole dish. Cover with buttermilk and soak at least 2 hours in the refrigerator. Remove from refrigerator, and let chicken come to room temperature before cooking.

"If you're that worried about fat, why are you thinking of fried

subject can seem bewildering in its complexity. Perhaps it's best, then, to end with an existential thought.

Reynolds Price, the North Carolina novelist, tells a story about a tourist who stopped at a roadside café that brashly advertised having the best fried chicken, guaranteed. He tried it, and sure enough, it was good. So he called the owner out and asked him his secret.

"How do you prepare your chickens?"

"Nothing special," the man replied. "We just tell 'em they're gonna die."

Too bad he didn't tell them they were going to be immortalized.

In a heavy, brown paper bag, combine flour, salt, and pepper, and shake until blended. Place a 12-inch or larger skillet (cast iron or enameled cast iron is best) over medium-high heat. Melt vegetable shortening to a depth of ½ to 1 inch, add bacon grease, and heat to the point that a drop of water flicked into the oil sputters. Remove chicken from dish, letting excess buttermilk drip off, and place each piece in the bag, shaking until coated evenly. Arrange pieces in skillet, skin side down, being careful not to overcrowd. Fry 15 to 20 minutes on one side, until the skin is crispy and golden; then turn each piece with tongs. Fry 15 minutes on other side. Drain on brown paper bags.

(CONTINUED
ON NEXT PAGE)

chicken in the first place?"
– Damon Lee Fowler, defender of lard and author of *Classical Southern Cooking.*

THE
MAN WHO MADE IT
FINGER-LICKIN' GOOD

···········

■ Colonel Harland Sanders was neither a true colonel nor a native Kentuckian, but it didn't seem to matter to the people who tried the chicken at his café and tourist court in

– courtesy KFC

Corbin, Kentucky. When his business was bypassed by interstate highway construction in the 1950s, he took to the road with his white linen suit, string tie, and neat goatee and sold chicken franchises with the pitch that folks ought to be able to have Sunday dinner seven days a week.

Today, there are more than 5,100 Kentucky Fried Chicken outlets around the nation, and hundreds more like it run by Church's, Popeyes, and other competitors. The strangest bird in the barnyard may be the Kentucky Fried Chicken restaurant in Marietta, Georgia, which is marked by a 56-foot chicken with rolling eyes and a moving beak.

But a funny thing happened. As Americans became more health-conscious, fried foods fell into disfavor and the chicken chains frantically experimented with roasted and grilled poultry to cut the grease. To promote its variety of cooked chicken, Kentucky Fried Chicken renamed itself KFC but maintains it is "selling more fried chicken than ever before."

To raise a cream gravy:

■ Discard all but 2 tablespoons of fat from the skillet, being careful to leave the brown flour drippings in pan. Over high heat, add 2 tablespoons of flour to the fat, whisking until the roux browns. Gradually pour in 2 cups of milk, stirring until gravy comes to a boil. Reduce heat and simmer for 2 minutes, until it reaches a creamy texture, adding salt and pepper to taste. Serve on the side — or over the chicken, if you want to do it Maryland-style.

Stovetop Deep-Fried Chicken

1 fryer (2½ to 3 pounds), cut into serving
    pieces
peanut oil
1 teaspoon salt
1 teaspoon freshly ground black pepper
pinch of paprika and cayenne
1 cup all-purpose flour

■ Rinse chicken well in cold water, drain, and pat dry. In a cast-iron Dutch oven, pour peanut oil 3 inches deep and heat at medium-high. Place the salt, pepper, seasonings, and flour in a paper bag and shake until mixed. Add the chicken pieces one at a time, shaking to coat.

When the oil has reached 365° F, place the chicken in the Dutch oven, skin side down, and cook with the lid on for 5 to 7 minutes. Turn the chicken, replace the lid, and fry for another 5 to 7 minutes. Remove the cover and continue cooking for another 15 minutes, until chicken is crisp. Drain on wire rack.

□□

ANSWERS TO

RAINY DAY AMUSEMENTS
On pages 172-173.

Word Play
1. syzygy
2. queue
3. bookkeeper
4. straight, strength, scrounge, brougham
5. facetiously
6. individualistic

Horse Sense
Yes, if there are three generations: grandfather, father, and son. Each person will take seven horses.

Number Fun 1
A. 46.
46 x 19 = 874; 8 + 7 + 4 = 19. With occasional exceptions, adding 1 to a multiple of 9 gives sequential solutions.

B. 54.
5 + 4 = 9 = 54 - 45

Earthy Anagrams
1. PACE, CAPE
2. LEAD, DALE
3. DRAY, YARD
4. ELAN, LANE
5. ROOM, MOOR
6. SALE, LEAS
7. SEAM, MESA
8. SLOT, LOTS
9. SORT, TORS
10. NUDE, DUNE

Spelling Lessens
A: Travels, valets, slate, last, S.A.T, as, *s*.
B: Thrones, hornet, tenor, Torn, rot, T. R., *r*.
C: Chapter, carpet, taper, pear, ape, pa, *p*.

Number Fun 2
A. The Hollies. (Multiply 379,836 by 14 on a calculator, and turn the calculator upside down to read the answer.)
B. MIX = 1,009

Changing Moon
1. Moon, boon, book, bock, buck.
2. Moon, mood, wood, woof, wolf.
3. Moon, soon, soot, shot, show, snow.
4. Moon, loon, look, lock, lick, link, pink.
(Other answers with the same number of steps may be possible for each set.)

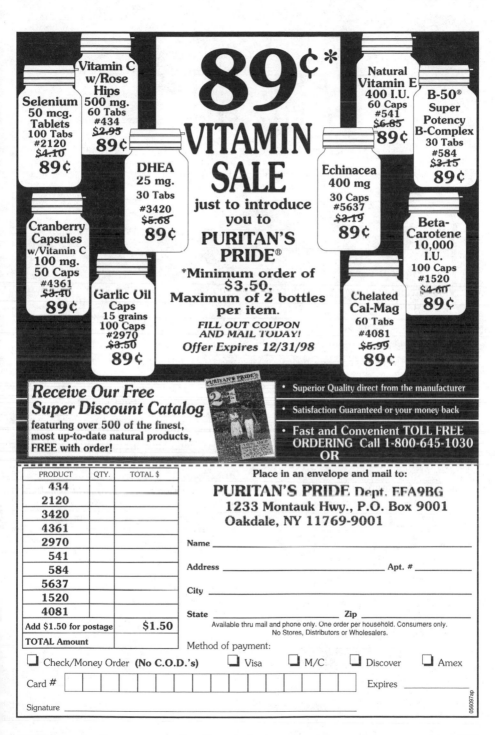

The Last Days of
BABE RUTH

It is 50 years since Babe Ruth died, but he remains America's most magnetic sports personality of the century.

Long before his final days in a small private room on the ninth floor of Memorial Hospital in New York in the summer of 1948, Babe Ruth died slowly and painfully in front of the people who adored him. No man in our time had a more heart-wrenching public death than did Babe Ruth. After two decades of enthralling a nation with almost superhuman feats, it was as though he finally was asked to show how truly mortal we all are.

Although he emerged on the American scene with other sports legends — Jack Dempsey, Bobby Jones, Red Grange, Man o' War — Babe Ruth stood apart. No American athlete towered over his peers the way Ruth did from 1914 into the 1930s.

As a Boston Red Sox pitcher, he once pitched 29⅔ consecutive scoreless innings in the World Series, a record that stood for nearly half a century. He faced the great pitcher Walter Johnson eight times and defeated him six times, three times by 1-0 scores. In 1919, his last season with the Red Sox, he hit 29 home runs, breaking the existing 43-year-old major league record. At the end of the season, when he was sold to the New York Yankees, he predicted he would hit 50 homers the next season. He hit 54. In New York, he grew from baseball star to national icon. In 1927, he hit 60 home runs, 14 percent of the American League's total. (To achieve that percentage today, a player would need to hit about 380 home runs!)

His legend grew off the field as well. One *New York Times* sportswriter summed him up: "He was the most uninhibited human being I have ever known." It was said that Ruth slept only after he had satiated all other appetites. When Ping Bodie, a former roommate was asked how it felt to room with the great Ruth, he replied, "I don't know. I only room with his suitcase."

He was a man who talked a lot, whose voice bellowed and rolled across a room. But in the spring of 1946, 12 years after he left the New York Yankees, Ruth complained that his throat was sore. He grew hoarse, "like gargling with ashes,"

by Mel R. Allen

T*hat fall, he asked the Yankees for a job, any job, no matter the salary. He just wanted to be a part of baseball.*

he said. He had long been plagued with sinus problems, and he started getting frequent headaches and stabbing pains over his left eye. By August, he needed to take aspirin all day long to get through his frequent public appearances.

"Whatever this thing is," he told his wife, Claire, "it's not going to lick me. Maybe I can just work it off."

That fall, he asked the Yankees for a job, any job, no matter the salary. He just wanted to be a part of baseball. Instead, the Yankees urged him to get involved promoting sandlot baseball in the city. His wife never forgot the image of Babe Ruth opening the rejection letter from the Yankees and weeping at the kitchen table in their Manhattan apartment.

By Thanksgiving, no amount of aspirin, or bourbon, could stop the pain. His doctor checked him into French Hospital. He was taken in a wheelchair, his left eye now swollen shut. His throat was too sore to swallow food. He had three teeth removed and was given penicillin for his sinuses. But the pain worsened. Day after day, newspapers reported on the mysterious illness of Babe Ruth. He spent Christmas in the hospital. Then one day in early January, something showed up on an X-ray. His doctors decided to operate.

They never revealed to Ruth what they found: a malignant tumor starting in the nasal passages behind the throat and straddling the major artery on the left side of his neck. The tumor pressing on nerves was the cause of the pain; it also affected his speech. A portion of the cancer was beyond the reach of the surgeon's knife, so the best he could do was to sever the nerves thought to cause most of the pain.

In the weeks after the operation, Ruth's only nourishment was given intravenously. His great bulk withered. His hair fell out from radiation treatment. When Baseball Commissioner Happy Chandler visited the hospital, Ruth simply pointed to his now frail arms and wept. On February 6, his 52nd birthday, he issued a statement for the press: "I'm fighting hard and I'll soon be on top."

Over 30,000 letters and telegrams filled the hospital room. An unknown admirer sent holy water from Lourdes, and he sprinkled it over himself. One woman wrote him that she suspected he had cancer.

"Well, you don't," his wife told him.

When he left the hospital on February 15, he had lost 50 pounds. A sportswriter came to his apartment a few days later. "I can't understand it!" Ruth said. "Why should it happen to me?" He added, "If only I could manage a ball club for a year — for a *week* even! They could fire me at the end of a week!"

Every newswriter in New York knew that Babe Ruth suffered from throat cancer. Yet, in this most competitive of trades, not once did a reporter break the code of silence. They knew that Ruth did not suspect cancer and that just hearing that word might cripple his spirit.

Chandler declared April 27, 1947, "Babe Ruth Day" in all big-league ballparks. The broadcast of the pregame ceremony was piped into all the stadiums. Baseball had never before witnessed such a widespread tribute.

Yankees broadcaster Mel Allen introduced Babe Ruth to the huge Yankee Stadium crowd. Ruth walked out, a camel's hair coat covering him against the chill. "I whispered in his ear," Allen recalled, "but then I had to shout so he could hear above the din. 'Babe, do you want to say something?' I knew cancer had affected his voice. He put his lips to my ear and said, 'I must.'"

In a painful whisper, Ruth's voice carried across the field. "You know how bad my voice sounds," he said. "Well, it feels just as bad." He spoke to the children, telling them baseball was a game they needed to start while young and to play often. "The only real game in the world, I think, is baseball."

It seemed everyone wanted one last piece of Babe Ruth. A publisher hired reporter Bob Considine to work with Ruth on his autobiography, to be ready for the Christmas season. Ford Motor Company named Ruth ambassador to the company-sponsored American Legion youth baseball league and sent him on a cross-country tour until he grew too exhausted to continue. A movie deal was announced with William Bendix, an actor who did not know how to swing a bat, signed on to play the title role.

In February 1948, Ruth and his wife left New York for the Florida sunshine and spring training. "I'd just like to get rid of this pain," he told reporters. "I'd be all right if I could get this nerve straightened out. I don't feel good. I'm weak and I've got no strength." A reporter asked him about his 53rd birthday coming up in a few days.

"It doesn't make any difference how old I am," Ruth said. "I feel 90."

On June 13, 1948, the New York Yankees marked the 25th anniversary of Yankee Stadium, "The House That Ruth Built," by holding a special ceremony and old-timers game featuring the players from the 1923 team. For years, Ruth had pleaded with the Yankees for a job. Now cynics noted that with Ruth rapidly fading, the Yankees had one final chance to fill their park using the power of his name.

The day was cold and rainy, yet nearly 50,000 fans came to the park. Babe Ruth came into the locker room, weak and gaunt, needing friends to help him with the old pregame ritual. W. C. Heinz, one of the

great sportswriters of his time, captured the scene of Ruth's last homecoming:

"He paused for a moment; then he recognized someone and smiled and stuck out his hand. It was quiet around him. The Babe started to undress. His friends helped him. They hung up his clothes and helped him into his uniform. He sat down again to put on his spiked shoes, and when he did this, the photographers who had followed him moved in. They took pictures of him in uniform putting on his shoes, for this would be the last time."

Babe Ruth walked slowly out of the clubhouse into the third-base dugout. Once again, Mel Allen called his name, the last member of the 1923 Yankees team to be introduced. Waite Hoyt, a pitcher on that

Ruth wore his uniform (3) and spikes for the last time on June 13, 1948, in Yankee Stadium.

"The House That Ruth Built" resounded with cheers for its hero as he walked on to the field, leaning on his bat, June 13, 1948.

R uth told the crowd how proud he was to have hit the first home run in the stadium, and then he walked slowly off the field, tears streaming down his face.

team, recalled the moment: "All of us standing along the foul lines heard the deep thunder of the ovation — realizing all this man had done for us, realizing that Babe Ruth was a baseball player apart — a man apart."

Ruth told the crowd how proud he was to have hit the first home run in the stadium, and then he slowly walked off the field, tears streaming down his face.

Thirteen days later, his doctor admitted him to Memorial Hospital. Ruth paused on the steps of the hospital. "This is a cancer hospital," he said to his doctor. "Why are you bringing me here?" The doctor replied that not everyone there had cancer. Not long after, Ruth admitted to a visitor, "They think they're kidding me. But they aren't. I know what I got."

Warren Eberhart, now retired and living in New Hampshire, was a young doctor then, just beginning his surgical residency at Memorial. He had grown up outside New York City, a Yankees fan who often paid one dollar to sit in right field just to be close to his hero, Babe Ruth. When Eberhart first walked into the room, he caught his breath to see Ruth so close, so frail. Ruth's voice then was so weak, the doctor needed to lean close to understand what he was saying. It was his job to start the daily IVs on the dying star. "He liked to have it in the foot," Eberhart recalls. "And he wanted Novocain first. He'd been stuck so many times, I wanted to do whatever I could to make things easier."

On July 26, the world premiere of *The Babe Ruth Story* opened in Manhattan. The promotors of the movie asked that Ruth appear, no matter how briefly. Dr. Eberhart was horrified to see Ruth, dressed in his camel's hair coat and cap, wheeled out of the hospital into a waiting car. "He was exploited to the end," he says. At the theater, throngs waited to see him. As if in slow motion, he walked into

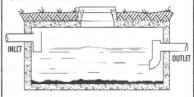

the theater, where he sat staring numbly at the screen. After 20 minutes, he needed to return to his hospital room.

Joe Dugan, one of his best friends from the glory days, came to see him. Sitting in a wheelchair, Ruth grasped Dugan's hand. "I'm gone, Joe, I'm gone," he said.

By August, heavily sedated, he slept much of the time. Both his mother and father had died, previously, in the month of August. On August 9, he signed an updated will. On August 11, the hospital reported that Ruth's condition was now critical. President Truman called to offer his wishes for a recovery.

On August 15, he sat up for 20 minutes. That night, he kissed his wife and told her not to come the next day. "I won't be here," he said.

At 2:20 P.M. on August 16, the hospital issued a bulletin that "pulmonary complications" had reappeared. At 5:10 P.M., a second bulletin said, ". . . condition considered critical." An hour later, ". . . sinking rapidly." Eberhart remembers, "When word got out that he was really dying, 68th Street was jammed with traffic between York Avenue and First Avenue. The streets just filled up with people."

There are at least three conflicting reports of his last hours. In one, Ruth reportedly started walking across the room shortly after 7:00 P.M. A doctor and nurse led him back to bed. "I'm going over the valley," he said. Then he fell into a coma.

A second version came from the Reverend Thomas H. Kaufman, who gave Ruth last rites at 7:30 in the evening. "He said his prayers from 6:30 to 7:30. Then he lapsed into sleep. He died a beautiful death in his sleep."

And in yet a third account, a nurse asked Ruth to autograph his photo; it is said that Ruth signed over a million autographs in his lifetime. Perhaps it befits the man and the legend that his last-known gesture was to scrawl "Babe Ruth."

At 8:01 P.M., Babe Ruth died.

For days, dressed in a blue double-breasted suit, with black rosary beads in his left hand, his body lay in an open casket in the lobby of Yankee Stadium. More than 80,000 people filed past. Those waiting to gain entrance nearly encircled the stadium.

Chandler told his son, "Always remember that you looked upon the face of the one and only Babe Ruth. There will never be another like him."

Rain poured down on Manhattan the day of Babe Ruth's funeral. There were 5,000 people inside St. Patrick's Cathedral, over 75,000 outside, and thousands more lining the 25-mile cortege route to the Gate of Heaven Cemetery in Westchester County.

Two former teammates sat side by side in the pallbearers section of the cathedral. In the stifling heat, Joe Dugan whispered to Waite Hoyt, "Lord. I'd give a hundred dollars for a cold beer."

"So would the Babe," said Hoyt. □ □

Thousands paid their last respects to Babe Ruth: " . . . a baseball player apart — a man apart."

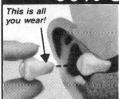

THE MAN Who Used HIS OWN HEART FOR FISH BAIT

...and other **unbelievable** (but true) "no-fail" **bait secrets** from the Deep South

by Gita M. Smith

Find them a stack of Bibles and some Alabama fishermen will swear that Toad Smith once used a piece of his own heart to catch a blue catfish. "Ol' Toad was a devoted catfish angler," recalls John Phillips of Fairfield, Alabama. "When he had heart bypass surgery, he asked the doctor to save the piece of heart that had been removed. Well, Toad put it into a jar with some Berkley's Strike, a real strong-smellin' catfish lure," says Phillips, author of *Masters' Secrets of Catfishing*. "Soon as he was well enough to go fishin' again, he baited up a couple of hooks with pieces of his heart, and before you know it, snap, a blue cat takes the bait. Toad bragged for years he was the only man in America to catch a fish with his own heart."

For eons, we humans have raided our gardens, pantries, and tackle boxes in quest of the perfect, foolproof fish bait. We sling rancid meats at catfish, known for their keen sense of smell. We hurl and dance shiny objects in the direction of toothsome bass, and we nearly blind ourselves sewing microscopic, feathery concoctions onto hooks in hopes of wooing the wily trout.

However, should supplies of the favorite bait run out, the bait du jour becomes whatever's on hand. Take the case of Danny Fields of Oak Grove, Alabama, who ran out of his usual fare while the fish were still biting. Dejected but not defeated, he scooped up a **dead 'possum** from the side of the road near his cabin, cut the freshly killed marsupial into bite-size chunks, and baited his lines. "Don't you just know the 'possum meat caught more and bigger catfish than any of his regular baits?" Phillips says.

Or listen to Lomax Dunham, a highly rated fishing guide for crappie and catfish on Alabama's Lake Martin, who's been known to catch a boatload of catfish on unusual baits. "One time, we ran out of minnows and crickets, but I had a bag of **marshmallows** in the boat," Dunham recalls. "We baited our lines with marshmallows and caught lots of fish. The same happened when we used **Ivory Soap,** cut up in small cubes and left in the water on our weighted lines overnight."

But Mike Bolton, outdoors editor of *The Birmingham News,* says Ivory Soap pales in comparison to **Palmolive Gold** when it comes to catching fish. Bolton went fishing with Jimmy Bedwell, a barber from Livingston, Alabama, who melts down whole cases of the fragrant golden soap in black cast-iron pots in his backyard. "You have to get the soap soft enough to sink your hooks into it. Put out your lines, and when you come back the next day, they'll be full of catfish," promises Bolton.

The overall best bait for catfish? Both Dunham and Phillips vote for **Canadian night crawlers,** the large, reddish-black worms that should be kept cool until you bait your hook.

The best bait for crappies, a favorite with southern cooks in spring and fall? "**Spot-tail minnows and small shad,** if you're using live bait. **White-** or **chartreuse-colored jigs** — that's a hook with a molded-lead head and a tail of fur or feathers — for artificial," says Dunham.

> Should supplies of the favorite bait run out, the bait du jour becomes whatever's on hand.

How to Catch a Finicky Bass

Throughout the South, anglers seek the excitement of hooking into striped or largemouth bass. Unlike catfish, members of the bass family can be picky eaters. The rule of thumb seems to be, if you can make the fish think your bait or lure is a shad, you've got yourself a wall hanger.

For example, consider the striped bass, or "striper," plentiful from the deep lakes of Georgia and the Carolinas to the Tennessee River to the tailraces below almost any dam. "The best year-round bait for stripers is **live shad,** so you may as well learn how to catch them," says Jack Wade of Knoxville, a guide on the Tennessee River.

Shad, which feed on plankton, travel in huge schools. Cast a round, weighted net over the top of a school, let the net sink, pull it up, and immediately release the shad into a bucket or cooler filled with water from the fish's natural environment, Wade says. "Shad are a delicate fish and you'll need to keep the water properly aerated," he adds.

Can't fill up your bucket with shad? "There's one artificial lure I know that will catch more stripers than any other," confides Doug Patterson, a Dadeville, Alabama, guide. "It's called a **Redfin.** It's seven inches long, and you fish it on the surface, reeling it slow to make a V-shaped wake."

Although encyclopedias have been written on the topic of catching bass, Bolton says there's one bait you won't find in your average tackle box, but it's one he'll never forget. "In southern Florida, on Lake Okeechobee, where there are lots of grassy weed beds, I saw bass fishermen use **live white mice** to catch largemouth bass," Bolton says. "They cost about one dollar apiece in pet stores, and you hook them through the skin at the base of the tail. You can imagine the little things scurrying and swimming around in the grass, and how likely a big bass is to strike at them."

Using a live mouse might make some a bit squeamish, but fishermen's zeal knows no end, and the search for the perfect bait goes on. The hitch is, while any angler will claim he or she has a secret no-fail bait, no two can agree about what that bait is. "The quickest way to start an argument in a room full of fishermen is to declare that you know best how to catch a fish," says Phillips. ☐ ☐

Joined at the Chest

Chang and Eng Bunker of North Carolina were successful farmers and businessmen, and between them they fathered 21 children. So why have people found their story to be nothing less than, well, mind-boggling?

by Page Chichester

Below: A Mathew Brady portrait of the Bunker family, c. 1865: Eng (left) with his wife, Sallie, and son Albert; Chang (right) with his wife, Addie, and son Patrick Henry.

– Meserve-Kunhardt Collection

A cry split the night, but for whatever reason, it raised no alarm in the large house outside Mount Airy, North Carolina. A few hours later, the winter stillness was broken yet again, this time by a different voice. Upon awakening and seeing his twin brother dead beside him, Eng Bunker instantly recognized his fate. "Then I am going," he cried in anguish. The bed they had shared through the years, from which neither could escape nor rise alone, became their deathbed.

Chang and Eng Bunker — the world's most famous connected twins, the ones who gave us the term *Siamese twin* — died on a cold January night in 1874. They left the world in virtually the same way they had entered it 63 years before: simultaneously and not without scandal. Their lives raised not only eyebrows, but numerous medical and philosophical questions as well.

Their birth on May 11, 1811, in the isolated kingdom of Siam (which became Thailand in 1939) created a sensation. In fact, they might easily have lost their lives soon after. At the time, Siam was a feudal society, steeped in superstition. Fifty years after the twins were born, when *Anna and the King of Siam* (the autobiography of an English governess at the Siamese court) was written, the country still had not changed. The king's rule was absolute.

When the twins were born, joined at the chest by a three-inch-wide band, no midwife would touch them for fear of becoming cursed. The king heard of the unusual birth and, regarding it as a bad omen, condemned the newborns to death. Luckily, Chang and Eng's mother refused to abandon them, and the king never acted on his impulsive death sentence. Another threat — from medical doctors who wanted to separate the twins with everything from saws to red-hot wires — also was averted.

The boys adapted to their dual life, learning to run, jump, and swim with perfect coordination; their activity helped stretch the connecting ligament to 5½ inches and allowed them to stand side by side instead of face to face. At age 14, their father having died six years before, the two sold duck eggs to provide for the family. About this time, Chang and Eng were discovered by Robert Hunter, a British merchant, who convinced their mother that her sons' future and prosperity lay beyond Siam. It took several years to secure the king's permission for the boys to leave the country. In 1829, whether she realized it or not, Chang and Eng's mother had all but sold her sons to Hunter for $3,000, but unhappily, she received only $500 of the promised sum. The terms of bondage were to expire in 2½ years, upon the twins' 21st birthday.

Hunter and an American partner, Captain Abel Coffin, managed the Siamese twins for the next few years, showing them in theaters and concert halls in America and England. Admission was 50 cents per person.

(continued)

> With only a handful of exceptions, the two seemed to act as one.
> They shared common tastes and opinions to an uncanny degree.

The managers drove the boys at an exhausting pace, exhibiting them for four hours a day, every day, and touring almost constantly with little rest. The twins were treated respectfully by audiences for the most part, and when they turned 21 in 1832, they were able to declare independence and take charge of their own lives.

The twins' intertwined personalities were the subject of much comment in newpaper articles. Chang, who was on the twins' own left, was an inch shorter than his brother, but he made up for it in temper. Chang was usually described as the dominant brother, quicker mentally but also quicker to anger. Eng was quieter and more retiring, with wider intellectual interests.

Despite minor personality differences, the twins never ceased to astound audiences and acquaintances with the apparent harmony and synchronicity of their relationship. With only a handful of exceptions, the two seemed to act as one. They shared common tastes, habits, and opinions to an uncanny degree. Some observers even speculated that they must be telepathic, because the two rarely were heard to talk with one another.

Not surprisingly, the twins' medical history was well documented. Their touring routine included an inspection by the local medical authorities in every new city they visited. This helped counter accusations of fakery, and the newspaper articles that arose from these examinations provided good publicity as well.

The evaluations sought to answer one of the questions that had dogged the twins since birth: Could they be successfully separated? Opinions varied — and evolved through the years

An 1839 drawing of the twins at age 28. Eng is holding an autobiographical booklet sold at their exhibitions.

with increased medical knowledge — but most of the doctors agreed that the operation would be too risky. Certainly before the Civil War, surgeons were not up to the task. Even those who believed that a surgical separation was possible tended to oppose the idea, because the twins seemed perfectly content with their hyphenated existence.

As to the results of the examinations, doctors found the connecting tissue to be tough, like cartilage, and to contain a common navel. Together the two weighed 180 pounds in 1830 (this increased within ten years to 220), and each had a weak eye — Chang's left and Eng's right.

After declaring their independence in 1832, the twins continued touring for about seven years. During this time, they met Dr. James Calloway of Wilkesboro, North Carolina, who talked them into a much-needed vacation in his town. They liked the rural area and the people so much that they decided to retire from the grind of endless touring and settle down.

Financially comfortable, but unable to retire from work entirely, the two soon took up farming and established a large plantation, eventually accumulating about 1,000 acres. They also applied for and received U.S. citizenship (adopting the last name Bunker) and pursued a courtship with two Wilkesboro sisters, Adelaide (Addie) and Sara (Sallie) Yates.

Chang was the first to fall in love, and he chose Addie, who was a year younger than her 18 year-old sister. Eng readily took to Sallie, but she appeared to be uninterested, so the twins and Addie conspired together to pursue the reluctant sister. Certainly, it would have been difficult for either Chang or Eng alone to marry — after all, three's a crowd. And given the fact that privacy would necessarily be in short supply in any dual marriage, having wives who were intimately familiar with one another would be an ideal solution. In any case, Sallie was the last of the foursome to commit to the arrangement.

The girls' parents were adamantly opposed to the union. At this point,

the difficulties of their prospective four-way marriage convinced Chang and Eng to risk a surgical separation, so they secretly traveled to Philadelphia, where surgeons agreed to attempt the risky operation. But before the knife could be employed, Addie and Sallie intervened and brought their future husbands home intact. Still, the girls' parents forbade the marriage but eventually relented after learning that the lovebirds planned to elope.

After the wedding, which was held at the Yates's home in 1843, the newlyweds retired to the house that Chang and Eng had built at Trap Hill, about 20 miles northeast of Wilkesboro. Soon, however, the house with its double-double bed proved to be too cramped.

Not quite a year after their marriage, Sallie delivered a baby girl, and six days later, Addie also gave birth to a girl. The following year saw two more arrivals, this time eight days apart. The two families bought and moved into a new house near Mount Airy, and in short order, more children arrived. Eng ultimately fathered 11 children, and Chang had 10.

Eventually, Addie moved to a separate house, which Chang and Eng built in 1857. This was not only because of the hordes of children, but because the wives were beginning to bicker. This unpleasantness no doubt exacerbated the growing contentiousness between the twins. Heated arguments became more common and for only the second or third time in their lives, the two came to blows. Although the exact cause of this violent dispute is not known, part of the problem was Eng's fondness for all-night poker games and Chang's fondness for the bottle.

So the wives lived apart, and Chang and Eng followed a strict regimen of

An autopsy suggested that Chang died of a blood clot in his brain. One medical camp held that Eng died simply of shock.

---

alternating three days at one house with three at the other, with the "guest" brother submitting to his "host" brother's every whim.

This partial separation helped relieve some pressures, but it created an unforeseen disparity that permanently altered the two families' fortunes. When they divvied up their property, Chang received the lion's share of the land. In return, Eng kept more slaves. The Civil War, during which the slaves were freed, devastated the twins' finances. Eng, who owned 21 slaves in 1864 (almost twice as many as his brother), was hit the hardest. To this day, his descendants consider themselves "the poor side" of the family.

Between 1868 and 1870, the twins twice left North Carolina to tour. They also resolved to try once again for a surgical separation. Although medical exams during each tour left them little hope for separation, the performances were a great success. One daughter of each twin accompanied them on the first tour, of the British Isles; on their next tour, which took them through Europe, they each took along a son. But war between France and Prussia in 1870 forced the twins to return home, and it was on the ship bound for America that Chang suffered a stroke, partially paralyzing his right side.

The stroke marked a decline in Chang's health, which culminated in his death four years later. An autopsy suggested that he died of a blood clot in his brain, but it never explained the cause of Eng's demise. At the time of

their death, one medical camp held that Eng died simply of shock. For security reasons, Chang and Eng were interred first in the cellar of Eng's house and later in the front yard of Chang's house one mile distant. Finally, when Addie died in 1917, the grave was moved to the nearby White Plains Baptist Church, which Chang and Eng had helped build on land they had donated. Although Sallie is included on the common gravestone, she was buried separately on Eng's farm. She, at least, finally found some privacy.

The autopsy settled several questions: Separation as children might have been wise; because the twins' livers were connected through the band, no such operation would have been worth the risk later in life. However, it should have been performed immediately upon Chang's death to try to save Eng. In 1897, the American Medical Association weighed in with a final judgment: Given advances in the use of antiseptics, had the twins lived at that time, they could have been successfully separated.

Today, a historical marker and a gravestone stand on either side of the White Plains Baptist Church. Chang's Mount Airy home is occupied by his late granddaughter Adelaide's husband (since remarried). Eng's house burned in 1956, but another house was built on the site. It is still in the family. □□

This story was excerpted from an article about the Bunker twins that appeared in the November/December 1995 issue of *Blue Ridge Country Magazine*.

Only 0.1 Percent of the

I t won't be long now. The year 2000 is just two years away and closing fast. In other words, an even 99.9 percent of the current millennium is now behind us — perhaps making this a good time to pause, take a deep breath or two, and contemplate the 0.1 percent that still lies ahead.

It's clear that the date of the millennium celebration will be decided — or, rather, has already been decided — not by scholars or scientists but by ordinary people. Although experts at the Royal Greenwich Observatory and elsewhere have announced that the new millennium will definitely not begin until January 1, 2001, the public simply refuses to buy it. The big party is going to begin on New Year's Eve in 1999, and the experts will just have to get used to it. Depending on your point of view, this can be seen as a heartening example of popular sovereignty in action or conclusive proof that civilization as we know it is now in the final stages of collapse.

At least one truly newsworthy story will play itself out in the coming months: the final resolution of a widespread software glitch — the so-called "year 2000 problem" — that leaves many mainframe computers unable to recognize years ending in the digits *00*.

Emergency repair jobs are expensive, of course, and this one will be no exception. It's expected to cost the U.S. government alone somewhere around $30 billion. The Social Security Administration, however, has had its eye on the problem since 1989, and officials there expect to have all necessary changes in place in plenty of time. (It's reassuring to know that if Social Security eventually does go belly-up, its computer system will continue to function flawlessly to the bitter end.)

In general, though, there seems to be a

by Jon Vara

– illustrated by Eldon Doty

Millennium to Go!

dearth of real news to report about this once-in-a-thousand-years story. There's a growing sense that the media opened up with its heavy guns much too soon and is now desperately short of ammunition. The painful truth is that nearly all the stories about the coming millennium that have so far found their way into print are simply minor variations on one of three basic themes:

1. The well-worn 00 vs. 01 debate (see above) — a question that has already received such a thorough going-over that dentists may soon begin using it as a substitute for laughing gas.

2. The impending computer crisis (ditto).

3. The inevitable listing of the New Year's Eve festivities being planned for Times Square, the Great Pyramid, the Taj Mahal, onboard the *Concorde*, and venues like Pitt Island, New Zealand, billed as

Should auld acquaintance be f

"the first terrestrial, accessible, and populated place to usher in the next 1,000 years."

The rest of us, though, can be forgiven for finding this something short of riveting. In fact, we predict that the coming year will see the emergence of a millennial backlash of sorts, as weary citizens begin tuning out on the whole idea. We may soon begin hearing about people whose millennial plans call for staying home, reading a good book, and going to bed early.

TWIST SLOWLY, and Remember to Duck

It's more than likely that the night of December 31, 1999, will be the single biggest evening of champagne drinking in the history of the world. Because true champagne comes only from the Champagne region of France, where it is bottled in quantities limited by French law, there's no way to increase production to meet demand — all of which means that prices will go through the roof. And it's good news for makers of humbler sparkling wines as well, who can — and no doubt will — gear up to produce all the bubbly such an occasion demands.

But to the American Academy of Ophthalmology, the prospect of all that festive cork-popping is worrisome. "Corks are just small enough and hard enough to pass by the facial bones that protect your eyes," says academy spokesperson Monica L. Monica, a practicing ophthalmologist in New Orleans. It's safe (if that's the word) to predict that a record number of American ophthalmologists will usher in the new millennium in hospital emergency rooms, having left the party early to care for other celebrants who should have ducked but didn't.

The Academy recommends the following four-step approach for opening champagne bottles safely: (continued)

1. Keep the bottle cold. A warm bottle is more likely to pop unexpectedly. Champagne tastes best at 45° F.

2. Peel off the foil, and then carefully remove the wire hood while holding the cork down with the palm of your hand.

3. Point the bottle away from yourself and others. Place a towel over the entire top and tilt the bottle at a 45-degree angle. Grasp the cork, slowly and firmly twisting it to break the seal. For a stubborn cork, place the bottle under cool running tap water for about 20 seconds, and repeat the slow twisting under the towel.

4. Keeping the bottle at a 45-degree angle, hold it firmly with one hand, using the other to slowly turn the cork with a slight upward pull. Do this until the cork is almost out of the neck. Counter the force of the cork by using slight downward pressure just as the cork breaks free of the bottle.

REMEMBER TO DUCK
Part II

In Los Angeles, meanwhile, revelers will have more to worry about than champagne corks. That's because a large number of Angelenos make a practice of welcoming the new year by stepping outside and firing their guns in the air.

And at 12:01 A.M. or so — one minute being about the time that it takes a typical bullet to complete its upward flight, turn around, and return to Earth — other Angelenos are struck by the falling projectiles, often with tragic results.

Since 1988, the city's Gunfire Reduction Committee has been urging citizens to hold their fire. A city ordinance now bans ammunition sales in the week before New Year's Eve. All this seems to be having some effect, but the temptation to light up the night with gunfire may be particularly strong next year. If you'll be spending New Year's Eve in the City of the Angels, you may want to stay indoors and keep away from windows — or risk becoming an angel yourself.

THE MORE, the Merrier

For the past 25 years, University of California sociologist David Phillips has been studying a phenomenon known as the death dip: a temporary decline in the death rate that can be linked to an impending event. He has demonstrated, for example, that the death rate tends to drop just before a presidential election and rise immediately afterward, apparently because some on the verge of death hang on a bit longer to find out who won. (Is it the sore losers who then expire?) The same mechanism seems to operate in many other instances as well. Among some religious and ethnic groups, Phillips has discovered, the death rate declines by up to 35 percent in the week leading up to a significant holiday.

Will that translate into a significant death-rate dip just before the turn of the millennium? "It will take a year or two for the numbers to become available," Phillips says. "But if they don't show a pronounced effect, I'll be very surprised." In other words, the population available to welcome January 1, 2000, is going to be a bit larger than expected. Pass the champagne.

A Special Millennium Countdown Activity

(Something to do while waiting for the century — and the millennium — to turn.)

Test yourself against Almanac readers of 100 years ago by trying your hand at these puzzles, taken from the 1898 edition of *The Old Farmer's Almanac*. Answers will be given in the 1999 edition. Anyone who just can't wait that long may request printed answers after March 1, 1998. Send a self-addressed stamped envelope to 1898 Puzzles, *The Old Farmer's Almanac*, P.O. Box 520, Dublin, NH 03444.

CHARADES

1. I built my house upon my last.
So sudden was its fall,
And so surprisingly my first,
It must have been my all.

2. My first is all-embracing, right and left, and front and back,
And my second may be many or a unit, but alack!
My first and third without my second moan and sigh; but once it's there,
My whole incites to mirth, to wit, to banishment of care;
A constant guide, a cheerful friend throughout the changing year;
Seed-time and harvest shall not fail with this companion dear.

CONUNDRUMS

1. Why is a hen immortal?

2. Who was the strongest man mentioned in the Bible?

PUZZLES

1. What two letters express that which all should try to do but which not many in these ages attain, although it is not much beyond middle age?

2. Arrange the numbers from 2 to 10 in three columns so that they will add up to 18 down, across, and diagonally, without repeating any number.

3. Two children were discussing their pocket money. "If you were to give me a cent," said Johnny, "I should have twice as much as you." — "That would not be a fair division," said Tommy. "You had better give *me* a cent, and then we shall be just alike." How much money had each?

ANAGRAMS

1. No more stars.
2. Got as a clue.
3. Sly ware.

☐☐

TIDE CORRECTIONS

Many factors affect the time and height of the tides: the coastal configuration, the time of the Moon's southing (crossing the meridian) at a location, and the phase of the Moon. This table of tidal corrections is a sufficiently accurate guide to the times and heights of the high water at the places shown. (Low tides occur approximately 6.25 hours before and after high tides.) No figures are shown for the West Coast or the Gulf of Mexico, since the method used in compiling this table does not apply there. National Ocean Service tide tables for the East, West, and Caribbean regions are available from Reed's Nautical Almanacs, Thos. Reed Publications, Inc., 13A Lewis St., Boston, MA 02113; telephone 800-995-4995.

The figures for Full Sea on the Left-Hand Calendar Pages 60-86 are the times of high tide at Commonwealth Pier in Boston Harbor. (Where a dash is shown under Full Sea, it indicates that time of high water occurs after midnight and so is recorded on the next date.) The heights of some of these tides are given on the Right-Hand Calendar Pages 61-87. The heights are reckoned from Mean Lower Low Water, and are listed as a set of figures — upper for the morning, lower for the evening. To obtain the times and heights of high water at any of the following places, apply the time difference to the daily times of high water at Boston (pages 60-86) and the height difference to the heights at Boston (pages 61-87).

	Time Difference: Hr. Min.	Height Feet
MAINE		
Bar Harbor	−0 34	+0.9
Belfast	−0 20	+0.4
Boothbay Harbor	−0 18	−0.8
Chebeague Island	−0 16	−0.6
Eastport	−0 28	+8.4
Kennebunkport	+0 04	−1.0
Machias	−0 28	+2.8
Monhegan Island	−0 25	−0.8
Old Orchard	0 00	−0.8
Portland	−0 12	−0.6
Rockland	−0 28	+0.1
Stonington	−0 30	+0.1
York	−0 09	−1.0
NEW HAMPSHIRE		
Hampton	+0 02	−1.3
Portsmouth	+0 11	−1.5
Rye Beach	−0 09	−0.9

	Time Difference: Hr. Min.	Height Feet
MASSACHUSETTS		
Annisquam	−0 02	−1.1
Beverly Farms	0 00	−0.5
Boston	0 00	0.0
Cape Cod Canal		
East Entrance	−0 01	−0.8
West Entrance	−2 16	−5.9
Chatham Outer Coast	+0 30	−2.8
Inside	+1 54	*0.4
Cohasset	+0 02	−0.07
Cotuit Highlands	+1 15	*0.3
Dennis Port	+1 01	*0.4
Duxbury – Gurnet Pt.	+0 02	−0.3
Fall River	−3 03	−5.0
Gloucester	−0 03	−0.8
Hingham	+0 07	0.0
Hull	+0 03	−0.2
Hyannis Port	+1 01	*0.3
Magnolia – Manchester	−0 02	−0.7
Marblehead	−0 02	−0.4
Marion	−3 22	−5.4
Monument Beach	−3 08	−5.4
Nahant	−0 01	−0.5
Nantasket	+0 04	−0.1
Nantucket	+0 56	*0.3
Nauset Beach	+0 30	*0.6
New Bedford	−3 24	−5.7
Newburyport	+0 19	−1.8
Oak Bluffs	+0 30	*0.2
Onset – R.R. Bridge	−2 16	−5.9
Plymouth	+0 05	0.0
Provincetown	+0 14	−0.4
Revere Beach	−0 01	−0.3
Rockport	−0 08	−1.0
Salem	0 00	−0.5
Scituate	−0 05	−0.7
Wareham	−3 09	−5.3
Wellfleet	+0 12	+0.5
West Falmouth	−3 10	−5.4
Westport Harbor	−3 22	−6.4
Woods Hole		
Little Harbor	−2 50	*0.2
Oceanographic Inst.	−3 07	*0.2
RHODE ISLAND		
Bristol	−3 24	−5.3
Sakonnet	−3 44	−5.6
Narragansett Pier	−3 42	−6.2
Newport	−3 34	−5.9
Pt. Judith	−3 41	−6.3
Providence	−3 20	−4.8
Watch Hill	−2 50	−6.8
CONNECTICUT		
Bridgeport	+0 01	−2.6

	Time Difference: Hr. Min.	Height Feet		Time Difference: Hr. Min.	Height Feet
Madison	−0 22	−2.3	Hatteras		
New Haven	−0 11	−3.2	Ocean	−4 26	−6.0
New London	−1 54	−6.7	Inlet	−4 03	−7.4
Norwalk	+0 01	−2.2	Kitty Hawk	−4 14	6.2
Old Lyme			**SOUTH CAROLINA**		
Highway Bridge	−0 30	−6.2	Charleston	−3 22	−4.3
Stamford	+0 01	−2.2	Georgetown	−1 48	*0.36
Stonington	−2 27	−6.6	Hilton Head	−3 22	−2.9
NEW YORK			Myrtle Beach	−3 49	4.4
Coney Island	−3 33	4.9	St. Helena		
Fire Island Lt	−2 43	*0.1	Harbor Entrance	−3 15	−3.4
Long Beach	−3 11	−5.7	**GEORGIA**		
Montauk Harbor	−2 19	−7.4	Jekyll Island	−3 46	−2.9
New York City – Battery	−2 43	−5.0	Saint Simon's Island	−2 50	−2.9
Oyster Bay	+0 04	−1.8	Savannah Beach		
Port Chester	−0 09	−2.2	River Entrance	−3 14	5.5
Port Washington	−0 01	−2.1	Tybee Light	−3 22	−2.7
Sag Harbor	−0 55	−6.8	**FLORIDA**		
Southampton			Cape Canaveral	3 59	6.0
Shinnecock Inlet	−4 20	*0.2	Daytona Beach	−3 28	−5.3
Willets Point	0 00	−2.3	Fort Lauderdale	−2 50	−7.2
NEW JERSEY			Fort Pierce Inlet	−3 32	−6.9
Asbury Park	−4 04	−5.3	Jacksonville		
Atlantic City	−3 56	−5.5	Railroad Bridge	−6 55	*0.10
Bay Head – Sea Girt	−4 04	−5.3	Miami Harbor Entrance	−3 18	−7.0
Beach Haven	−1 43	*0.24	St. Augustine	−2 55	−4.9
Cape May	−3 28	−5.3	**CANADA**		
Ocean City	−3 06	−5.9	Alberton, P.E.I.	−5 45**	−7.5
Sandy Hook	3 30	−5.0	Charlottetown, P.E.I.	−0 45**	−3.5
Seaside Park	−4 03	−5.4	Halifax, N.S.	−3 23	−4.5
PENNSYLVANIA			North Sydney, N.S.	−3 15	−6.5
Philadelphia	+2 40	−3.5	Saint John, N.B.	+0 30	+15.0
DELAWARE			St. John's, Nfld.	4 00	6.5
Cape Henlopen	−2 48	−5.3	Yarmouth, N.S.	−0 40	+3.0
Rehoboth Beach	−3 37	−5.7			
Wilmington	+1 56	−3.8			
MARYLAND					
Annapolis	+6 23	−8.5			
Baltimore	+7 59	−8.3			
Cambridge	+5 05	−7.8			
Havre de Grace	+11 21	−7.7			
Point No Point	+2 28	−8.1			
Prince Frederick					
Plum Point	+4 25	−8.5			
VIRGINIA					
Cape Charles	−2 20	−7.0			
Hampton Roads	−2 02	−6.9			
Norfolk	−2 06	−6.6			
Virginia Beach	−4 00	−6.0			
Yorktown	−2 13	−7.0			
NORTH CAROLINA					
Cape Fear	−3 55	−5.0			
Cape Lookout	−4 28	−5.7			
Currituck	−4 10	−5.8			

* Where the difference in the "Height/Feet" column is so marked, height at Boston should be multiplied by this ratio.

** Varies widely; accurate only within 1½ hours. Consult local tide tables for precise times and heights.

Example: The conversion of the times and heights of the tides at Boston to those of Norfolk, Virginia, is given below:

Sample tide calculation July 1, 1998:

High tide Boston (p. 76)	5:15 A.M., EDT
Correction for Norfolk	−2:06 hrs.
High tide Norfolk	3:09 A.M., EDT
Tide height Boston (p. 77)	9.3 ft.
Correction for Norfolk	−6.6 ft.
Tide height Norfolk	2.7 ft.

THE TWILIGHT ZONE

How to Determine the Length of Twilight and the Times of Dawn and Dark

A stronomical twilight begins (or ends) when the Sun is 18 degrees below the horizon; the latitude of a place, and the time of year determine the length of twilight. To find the latitude of your city or the city nearest you, consult the **Time Correction Tables,** page 214. Check that figure against the chart at the right for the appropriate date, and you will have the length of twilight in your area.

It is also possible to determine when dawn will break and when darkness will descend by applying the length of twilight to the times of sunrise and sunset at any specific place. (Follow the instructions given in "How to Use This Almanac," page 34, to determine sunrise/sunset times for a given locality.) **Subtract** the length of twilight from the time of sunrise for dawn. **Add** the length of twilight to the time of sunset for dark.

Latitude	25° N to 30° N	31° N to 36° N	37° N to 42° N	43° N to 47° N	48° N to 49° N
	H M	H M	H M	H M	H M
Jan. 1 to Apr. 10	1 20	1 26	1 33	1 42	1 50
Apr. 11 to May 2	1 23	1 28	1 39	1 51	2 04
May 3 to May 14	1 26	1 34	1 47	2 02	2 22
May 15 to May 25	1 29	1 38	1 52	2 13	2 42
May 26 to July 22	1 32	1 43	1 59	2 27	—
July 23 to Aug. 3	1 29	1 38	1 52	2 13	2 42
Aug. 4 to Aug. 14	1 26	1 34	1 47	2 02	2 22
Aug. 15 to Sept. 5	1 23	1 28	1 39	1 51	2 04
Sept. 6 to Dec. 31	1 20	1 26	1 33	1 42	1 50

	Boston, Mass. (latitude 42° 22')	Columbia, S.C. (latitude 34° 0')
Sunrise, August 1	5:37 A.M.	6:42 A.M.
Length of twilight	−1:52	−1:38
Dawn breaks	3:45 A.M., EDT	5:04 A.M., EDT
Sunset, August 1	8:04 P.M.	8:31 P.M.
Length of twilight	+1:52	+1:38
Dark descends	9:56 P.M., EDT	10:09 P.M., EDT

Tidal Glossary

Apogean Tide: A monthly tide of decreased range that occurs when the Moon is farthest from Earth (at apogee).

Diurnal: Applies to a location that normally experiences one high water and one low water during a tidal day of approximately 24 hours.

Mean Lower Low Water: The arithmetic mean of the lesser of a daily pair of low waters, observed over a specific 19-year cycle called the National Tidal Datum Epoch.

Neap Tide: A tide of decreased range occurring twice a month, when the Moon is in quadrature (during the first and last quarter Moons, when the Sun and the Moon are at right angles to each other relative to Earth).

Perigean Tide: A monthly tide of increased range that occurs when the Moon is closest to Earth (at perigee).

Semidiurnal: Having a period of half a tidal day. East Coast tides, for example, are semidiur-

nal, with two highs and two lows in approximately 24 hours.

Spring Tide: Named not for the season of spring, but from the German *springen* (to leap up). This tide of increased range occurs at times of syzygy (q.v.) each month. A spring tide also brings a lower low water.

Syzygy: Occurs twice a month, when the Sun and the Moon are in conjunction (lined up on the same side of Earth at the new Moon) and when they are in opposition (on opposite sides of Earth at the full Moon, though usually not so directly in line as to produce an eclipse). In either case, the gravitational effects of the Sun and the Moon reinforce each other, and tidal range is increased.

Vanishing Tide: A mixed tide of considerable inequality in the two highs or two lows, so that the "high low" may become indistinguishable from the "low high." The result is a vanishing tide, where no significant difference is apparent.

TIME CORRECTION TABLES

The times of sunrise/sunset and moonrise/moonset, selected times for observing the visible planets, and the transit times of the bright stars are given for **Boston only** on pages 60-86, 46-47, and 50. Use the **Key Letter** shown to the right of each time on those pages with these tables to find the number of minutes that should be added to or subtracted from Boston time to give the correct time for your city. (Because of the complexities of calculation for different locations, times may not be precise to the minute.) If your city is not listed, find the city closest to you in both latitude and longitude and use those figures. **Boston's latitude is 42° 22' and longitude is 71° 03'.** Canadian cities appear at the end of the list. For a more complete explanation of the use of Key Letters and these tables, see "How to Use This Almanac," page 34.

Time Zone Code: Codes represent *standard time.* Atlantic is -1, Eastern is 0, Central is 1, Mountain is 2, Pacific is 3, Alaska is 4, and Hawaii-Aleutian is 5.

City	North Latitude °	North Latitude '	West Longitude °	West Longitude '	Time Zone Code	A min.	B min.	C min.	D min.	E min.
Aberdeen, SD	45	28	98	29	1	+37	+44	+49	+54	+59
Akron, OH	41	5	81	31	0	+46	+43	+41	+39	+37
Albany, NY	42	39	73	45	0	+ 9	+10	+10	+11	+11
Albert Lea, MN	43	39	93	22	1	+24	+26	+28	+31	+33
Albuquerque, NM	35	5	106	39	2	+45	+32	+22	+11	+ 2
Alexandria, LA	31	18	92	27	1	+58	+40	+26	+ 9	– 3
Allentown-Bethlehem, PA	40	36	75	28	0	+23	+20	+17	+14	+12
Amarillo, TX	35	12	101	50	1	+85	+73	+63	+52	+43
Anchorage, AK	61	10	149	59	4	–46	+27	+71	+122	+171
Asheville, NC	35	36	82	33	0	+67	+55	+46	+35	+27
Atlanta, GA	33	45	84	24	0	+79	+65	+53	+40	+30
Atlantic City, NJ	39	22	74	26	0	+23	+17	+13	+ 8	+ 4
Augusta, GA	33	28	81	58	0	+70	+55	+44	+30	+19
Augusta, ME	44	19	69	46	0	–12	– 8	– 5	– 1	0
Austin, TX	30	16	97	45	1	+82	+62	+47	+29	+15
Bakersfield, CA	35	23	119	1	3	+33	+21	+12	+ 1	– 7
Baltimore, MD	39	17	76	37	0	+32	+26	+22	+17	+13
Bangor, ME	44	48	68	46	0	–18	–13	– 9	– 5	– 1
Barstow, CA	34	54	117	1	3	+27	+14	+ 4	– 7	–16
Baton Rouge, LA	30	27	91	11	1	+55	+36	+21	+ 3	–10
Beaumont, TX	30	5	94	6	1	+67	+48	+32	+14	0
Bellingham, WA	48	45	122	29	3	0	+13	+24	+37	+47
Bemidji, MN	47	28	94	53	1	+14	+26	+34	+44	+52
Berlin, NH	44	28	71	11	0	– 7	– 3	0	+ 3	+ 7
Billings, MT	45	47	108	30	2	+16	+23	+29	+35	+40
Biloxi, MS	30	24	88	53	1	+46	+27	+11	– 5	–19
Binghamton, NY	42	6	75	55	0	+20	+19	+19	+18	+18
Birmingham, AL	33	31	86	49	1	+30	+15	+ 3	–10	–20
Bismarck, ND	46	48	100	47	1	+41	+50	+58	+66	+73
Boise, ID	43	37	116	12	2	+55	+58	+60	+62	+64
Brattleboro, VT	42	51	72	34	0	+ 4	+ 5	+ 5	+ 6	+ 7
Bridgeport, CT	41	11	73	11	0	+12	+10	+ 8	+ 6	+ 4
Brockton, MA	42	5	71	1	0	0	0	0	0	– 1
Brownsville, TX	25	54	97	30	1	+91	+66	+46	+23	+ 5
Buffalo, NY	42	53	78	52	0	+29	+30	+30	+31	+32
Burlington, VT	44	29	73	13	0	0	+ 4	+ 8	+12	+15
Butte, MT	46	1	112	32	2	+31	+39	+45	+52	+57
Cairo, IL	37	0	89	11	1	+29	+20	+12	+ 4	– 2
Camden, NJ	39	57	75	7	0	+24	+19	+16	+12	+ 9
Canton, OH	40	48	81	23	0	+46	+43	+41	+38	+36
Cape May, NJ	38	56	74	56	0	+26	+20	+15	+ 9	+ 5
Carson City–Reno, NV	39	10	119	46	3	+25	+19	+14	+ 9	+ 5

City	North Latitude ° '		West Longitude ° '		Time Zone Code	Key Letters A min.	B min.	C min.	D min.	E min.
Casper, WY........................	42	51	106	19	2	+19	+19	+20	+21	+22
Charleston, SC	32	47	79	56	0	+64	+48	+36	+21	+10
Charleston, WV	38	21	81	38	0	+55	+48	+42	+35	+30
Charlotte, NC...................	35	14	80	51	0	+61	+49	+39	+28	+19
Charlottesville, VA	38	2	78	30	0	+43	+35	+29	+22	+17
Chattanooga, TN..............	35	3	85	19	0	+79	+67	+57	+45	+36
Cheboygan, MI	45	39	84	29	0	+40	+47	+53	+59	+64
Cheyenne, WY..................	41	8	104	49	2	+19	+16	+14	+12	+11
Chicago-Oak Park, IL.......	41	52	87	38	1	+ 7	+ 6	+ 6	+ 5	+ 4
Cincinnati-Hamilton, OH ...	39	6	84	31	0	+64	+58	+53	+48	+44
Cleveland-Lakewood, OH ...	41	30	81	42	0	+45	+43	+42	+40	+39
Columbia, SC...................	34	0	81	2	0	+65	+51	+40	+27	+17
Columbus, OH..................	39	57	83	1	0	+55	+51	+47	+43	+40
Cordova, AK.....................	60	33	145	45	4	−55	+13	+55	+103	+149
Corpus Christi, TX............	27	48	97	24	1	+86	+64	+46	+25	+ 9
Craig, CO	40	31	107	33	2	+32	+28	+25	+22	+20
Dallas-Fort Worth, TX......	32	47	96	48	1	+71	+55	+43	+28	+17
Danville, IL......................	40	8	87	37	1	+13	+ 9	+ 6	+ 2	0
Danville, VA.....................	36	36	79	23	0	+51	+41	+33	+24	+17
Davenport, IA	41	32	90	35	1	+20	+19	+17	+16	+15
Dayton, OH.......................	39	45	84	10	0	+61	+56	+52	+48	+44
Decatur, AL......................	34	36	86	59	1	+27	+14	+ 4	− 7	−17
Decatur, IL........................	39	51	88	57	1	+19	+15	+11	+ 7	+ 4
Denver-Boulder, CO.........	39	44	104	59	2	+24	+19	+15	+11	+ 7
Des Moines, IA	41	35	93	37	1	+32	+31	+30	+28	+27
Detroit-Dearborn, MI.......	42	20	83	3	0	+47	+47	+47	+47	+47
Dubuque, IA	42	30	90	41	1	+17	+18	+18	+18	+18
Duluth, MN.......................	46	47	92	6	1	+ 6	+16	+23	+31	+38
Durham, NC......................	36	0	78	55	0	+51	+40	+31	+21	+13
Eastport, ME.....................	44	54	67	0	0	−26	−20	−16	−11	− 8
Eau Claire, WI	44	49	91	30	1	+12	+17	+21	+25	+29
El Paso, TX	31	45	106	29	2	+53	+35	+22	+ 6	− 6
Elko, NV	40	50	115	46	3	+ 3	0	− 1	− 3	− 5
Ellsworth, ME...................	44	33	68	25	0	−18	−14	−10	− 6	− 3
Erie, PA............................	42	7	80	5	0	+36	+36	+35	+35	+35
Eugene, OR.......................	44	3	123	6	3	+21	+24	+27	+30	+33
Fairbanks, AK	64	48	147	51	4	127	+ 2	+61	+131	+205
Fall River–New Bedford, MA	41	42	71	9	0	+ 2	+ 1	0	0	− 1
Fargo, ND	46	53	96	47	1	+24	+34	+42	+50	+57
Flagstaff, AZ....................	35	12	111	39	2	+64	+52	+42	+31	+22
Flint, MI	43	1	83	41	0	+47	+49	+50	+51	+52
Fort Myers, FL.................	26	38	81	52	0	+87	+63	+44	+21	+ 4
Fort Scott, KS	37	50	94	42	1	+49	+41	+34	+27	+21
Fort Smith, AR.................	35	23	94	25	1	+55	+43	+33	+22	+14
Fort Wayne, IN	41	4	85	9	0	+60	+58	+56	+54	+52
Fresno, CA	36	44	119	47	3	+32	+22	+15	+ 6	0
Gallup, NM	35	32	108	45	2	+52	+40	+31	+20	+11
Galveston, TX	29	18	94	48	1	+72	+52	+35	+16	+ 1
Gary, IN	41	36	87	20	1	+ 7	+ 6	+ 4	+ 3	+ 2
Glasgow, MT	48	12	106	38	2	− 1	+11	+21	+32	+42
Grand Forks, ND	47	55	97	3	1	+21	+33	+43	+53	+62
Grand Island, NE	40	55	98	21	1	+53	+51	+49	+46	+44
Grand Junction, CO	39	4	108	33	2	+40	+34	+29	+24	+20
Great Falls, MT................	47	30	111	17	2	+20	+31	+39	+49	+58
Green Bay, WI.................	44	31	88	0	1	0	+ 3	+ 7	+11	+14
Greensboro, NC	36	4	79	47	0	+54	+43	+35	+25	+17

City	North Latitude ° '	West Longitude ° '	Time Zone Code	Key Letters A min.	B min.	C min.	D min.	E min.
Hagerstown, MD	39 39	77 43	0	+35	+30	+26	+22	+18
Harrisburg, PA..................	40 16	76 53	0	+30	+26	+23	+19	+16
Hartford-New Britain, CT...	41 46	72 41	0	+ 8	+ 7	+ 6	+ 5	+ 4
Helena, MT.......................	46 36	112 2	2	+27	+36	+43	+51	+57
Hilo, HI............................	19 44	155 5	5	+94	+62	+37	+ 7	−15
Honolulu, HI.....................	21 18	157 52	5	+102	+72	+48	+19	− 1
Houston, TX	29 45	95 22	1	+73	+53	+37	+19	+ 5
Indianapolis, IN	39 46	86 10	0	+69	+64	+60	+56	+52
Ironwood, MI....................	46 27	90 9	1	0	+ 9	+15	+23	+29
Jackson, MI......................	42 15	84 24	0	+53	+53	+53	+52	+52
Jackson, MS.....................	32 18	90 11	1	+46	+30	+17	+ 1	−10
Jacksonville, FL..............	30 20	81 40	0	+77	+58	+43	+25	+11
Jefferson City, MO	38 34	92 10	1	+36	+29	+24	+18	+13
Joplin, MO	37 6	94 30	1	+50	+41	+33	+25	+18
Juneau, AK	58 18	134 25	4	−76	−23	+10	+49	+86
Kalamazoo, MI	42 17	85 35	0	+58	+57	+57	+57	+57
Kanab, UT........................	37 3	112 32	2	+62	+53	+46	+37	+30
Kansas City, MO	39 1	94 20	1	+44	+37	+33	+27	+23
Keene, NH	42 56	72 17	0	+ 2	+ 3	+ 4	+ 5	+ 6
Ketchikan, AK	55 21	131 39	4	−62	−25	0	+29	+56
Knoxville, TN...................	35 58	83 55	0	+71	+60	+51	+41	+33
Kodiak, AK.......................	57 47	152 24	4	0	+49	+82	+120	+154
LaCrosse, WI....................	43 48	91 15	1	+15	+18	+20	+22	+25
Lake Charles, LA..............	30 14	93 13	1	+64	+44	+29	+11	− 2
Lanai City, HI	20 50	156 55	5	+99	+69	+44	+15	− 6
Lancaster, PA....................	40 2	76 18	0	+28	+24	+20	+17	+13
Lansing, MI......................	42 44	84 33	0	+52	+53	+53	+54	+54
Las Cruces, NM	32 19	106 47	2	+53	+36	+23	+ 8	− 3
Las Vegas, NV	36 10	115 9	3	+16	+ 4	− 3	−13	−20
Lawrence-Lowell, MA	42 42	71 10	0	0	0	0	0	+ 1
Lewiston, ID	46 25	117 1	3	−12	− 3	+ 2	+10	+17
Lexington-Frankfort, KY..	38 3	84 30	0	+67	+59	+53	+46	+41
Liberal, KS.......................	37 3	100 55	1	+76	+66	+59	+51	+44
Lihue, HI..........................	21 59	159 23	5	+107	+77	+54	+26	+ 5
Lincoln, NE......................	40 49	96 41	1	+47	+44	+42	+39	+37
Little Rock, AR.................	34 45	92 17	1	+48	+35	+25	+13	+ 4
Los Angeles incl. Pasadena and Santa Monica, CA ...	34 3	118 14	3	+34	+20	+ 9	− 3	−13
Louisville, KY	38 15	85 46	0	+72	+64	+58	+52	+46
Macon, GA	32 50	83 38	0	+79	+63	+50	+36	+24
Madison, WI.....................	43 4	89 23	1	+10	+11	+12	+14	+15
Manchester-Concord, NH...	42 59	71 28	0	0	0	+ 1	+ 2	+ 3
McAllen, TX.....................	26 12	98 14	1	+93	+69	+49	+26	+9
Memphis, TN....................	35 9	90 3	1	+38	+26	+16	+ 5	− 3
Meridian, MS....................	32 22	88 42	1	+40	+24	+11	− 4	−15
Miami, FL........................	25 47	80 12	0	+88	+57	+37	+14	− 3
Miles City, MT	46 25	105 51	2	+ 3	+11	+18	+26	+32
Milwaukee, WI.................	43 2	87 54	1	+ 4	+ 6	+ 7	+ 8	+ 9
Minneapolis-St. Paul, MN	44 59	93 16	1	+18	+24	+28	+33	+37
Minot, ND........................	48 14	101 18	1	+36	+50	+59	+71	+81
Moab, UT.........................	38 35	109 33	2	+46	+39	+33	+27	+22
Mobile, AL	30 42	88 3	1	+42	+23	+ 8	− 8	−22
Monroe, LA	32 30	92 7	1	+53	+37	+24	+ 9	− 1
Montgomery, AL...............	32 23	86 19	1	+31	+14	+ 1	−13	−25
Muncie, IN.......................	40 12	85 23	0	+64	+60	+57	+53	+50
Nashville, TN...................	36 10	86 47	1	+22	+11	+ 3	− 6	−14
New Haven, CT	41 18	72 56	0	+11	+ 8	+ 7	+ 5	+ 4

City	North Latitude °	North Latitude '	West Longitude °	West Longitude '	Time Zone Code	A min.	B min.	C min.	D min.	E min.
New London, CT	41	22	72	6	0	+ 7	+ 5	+ 4	+ 2	+ 1
New Orleans, LA	29	57	90	4	1	+52	+32	+16	− 1	−15
New York, NY	40	45	74	0	0	+17	+14	+11	+ 9	+ 6
Newark–Irvington– East Orange, NJ	40	44	74	10	0	+17	+14	+12	+ 9	+ 7
Norfolk, VA	36	51	76	17	0	+38	+28	+21	+12	+ 5
North Platte, NE..............	41	8	100	46	1	+62	+60	+58	+56	+54
Norwalk-Stamford, CT.....	41	7	73	22	0	+13	+10	+ 9	+ 7	+ 5
Oakley, KS	39	8	100	51	1	+69	+63	+59	+53	+49
Ogden, UT	41	13	111	58	2	+47	+45	+43	+41	+40
Ogdensburg, NY	44	42	75	30	0	+ 8	+13	+17	+21	+25
Oklahoma City, OK	35	28	97	31	1	+67	+55	+46	+35	+26
Omaha, NE	41	16	95	56	1	+43	+40	+39	+37	+36
Orlando, FL.....................	28	32	81	22	0	+80	+59	+42	+22	+ 6
Ortonville, MN	45	19	96	27	1	+30	+36	+40	+46	+51
Oshkosh, WI	44	1	88	33	1	+ 3	+ 6	+ 9	+12	+15
Palm Springs, CA	33	49	116	32	3	+28	+13	+ 1	−12	−22
Parkersburg, WV	39	16	81	34	0	+52	+46	+42	+36	+32
Paterson, NJ	40	55	74	10	0	+17	+14	+12	+ 9	+ 7
Pendleton, OR..................	45	40	118	47	3	− 1	+ 4	+10	+16	+21
Pensacola, FL...................	30	25	87	13	1	+39	+20	+ 5	−12	−26
Peoria, IL	40	42	89	36	1	+19	+16	+14	+11	+ 9
Philadelphia-Chester, PA..	39	57	75	9	0	+24	+19	+16	+12	+ 9
Phoenix, AZ.....................	33	27	112	4	2	+71	+56	+44	+30	+20
Pierre, SD........................	44	22	100	21	1	+49	+53	+56	+60	+63
Pittsburgh-McKeesport, PA ..	40	26	80	0	0	+42	+38	+35	+32	+29
Pittsfield, MA	42	27	73	15	0	+ 8	+ 8	+ 8	+ 8	+ 8
Pocatello, ID	42	52	112	27	2	+43	+44	+45	+46	+46
Poplar Bluff, MO	36	46	90	24	1	+35	+25	+17	+ 8	+ 1
Portland, ME....................	43	40	70	15	0	− 8	− 5	− 3	− 1	0
Portland, OR....................	45	31	122	41	3	+14	+20	+25	+31	+36
Portsmouth, NH...............	43	5	70	45	0	− 4	− 2	− 1	0	0
Presque Isle, ME..............	46	41	68	1	0	−29	−19	−12	− 4	+ 2
Providence, RI	41	50	71	25	0	+ 3	+ 2	+ 1	0	0
Pueblo, CO......................	38	16	104	37	2	+27	+20	+14	+ 7	+ 2
Raleigh, NC	35	47	78	38	0	+51	+39	+30	+20	+12
Rapid City, SD.................	44	5	103	14	2	+ 2	+ 5	+ 8	+11	+13
Reading, PA.....................	40	20	75	56	0	+26	+22	+19	+16	+13
Redding, CA	40	35	122	24	3	+31	+27	+25	+22	+19
Richmond, VA..................	37	32	77	26	0	+41	+32	+25	+17	+11
Roanoke, VA....................	37	16	79	57	0	+51	+42	+35	+27	+21
Roswell, NM....................	33	24	104	32	2	+41	+26	+14	0	−10
Rutland, VT	43	37	72	58	0	+ 2	+ 5	+ 7	+ 9	+11
Sacramento, CA...............	38	35	121	30	3	+34	+27	+21	+15	+10
Salem, OR.......................	44	57	123	1	3	+17	+23	+27	+31	+35
Salina, KS	38	50	97	37	1	+57	+51	+46	+40	+35
Salisbury, MD..................	38	22	75	36	0	+31	+23	+18	+11	+ 6
Salt Lake City, UT	40	45	111	53	2	+48	+45	+43	+40	+38
San Antonio, TX..............	29	25	98	30	1	+87	+66	+50	+31	+16
San Diego, CA.................	32	43	117	9	3	+33	+17	+ 4	− 9	−21
San Francisco incl. Oak- land and San Jose, CA ...	37	47	122	25	3	+40	+31	+25	+18	+12
Santa Fe, NM	35	41	105	56	2	+40	+28	+19	+ 9	0
Savannah, GA	32	5	81	6	0	+70	+54	+40	+25	+13
Scranton–Wilkes Barre, PA	41	25	75	40	0	+21	+19	+18	+16	+15
Seattle-Tacoma- Olympia, WA	47	37	122	20	3	+ 3	+15	+24	+34	+42

City	North Latitude °	'	West Longitude °	'	Time Zone Code	Key Letters A min.	B min.	C min.	D min.	E min.
Sheridan, WY	44	48	106	58	2	+14	+19	+23	+27	+31
Shreveport, LA	32	31	93	45	1	+60	+44	+31	+16	+ 4
Sioux Falls, SD	43	33	96	44	1	+38	+40	+42	+44	+46
South Bend, IN	41	41	86	15	0	+62	+61	+60	+59	+58
Spartanburg, SC	34	56	81	57	0	+66	+53	+43	+32	+23
Spokane, WA	47	40	117	24	3	−16	− 4	+ 4	+14	+23
Springfield, IL	39	48	89	39	1	+22	+18	+14	+10	+ 6
Springfield-Holyoke, MA	42	6	72	36	0	+ 6	+ 6	+ 6	+ 5	+ 5
Springfield, MO	37	13	93	18	1	+45	+36	+29	+20	+14
St. Johnsbury, VT	44	25	72	1	0	− 4	0	+ 3	+ 7	+10
St. Joseph, MI	42	5	86	26	0	+61	+61	+60	+60	+59
St. Joseph, MO	39	46	94	50	1	+43	+38	+35	+30	+27
St. Louis, MO	38	37	90	12	1	+28	+21	+16	+10	+ 5
St. Petersburg, FL	27	46	82	39	0	+87	+65	+47	+26	+10
Syracuse, NY	43	3	76	9	0	+17	+19	+20	+21	+22
Tallahassee, FL	30	27	84	17	0	+87	+68	+53	+35	+22
Tampa, FL	27	57	82	27	0	+86	+64	+46	+25	+ 9
Terre Haute, IN	39	28	87	24	0	+74	+69	+65	+60	+56
Texarkana, AR	33	26	94	3	1	+59	+44	+32	+18	+ 8
Toledo, OH	41	39	83	33	0	+52	+50	+49	+48	+47
Topeka, KS	39	3	95	40	1	+49	+43	+38	+32	+28
Traverse City, MI	44	46	85	38	0	+49	+54	+57	+62	+65
Trenton, NJ	40	13	74	46	0	+21	+17	+14	+11	+ 8
Trinidad, CO	37	10	104	31	2	+30	+21	+13	+ 5	0
Tucson, AZ	32	13	110	58	2	+70	+53	+40	+24	+12
Tulsa, OK	36	9	95	60	1	+59	+48	+40	+30	+22
Tupelo, MS	34	16	88	34	1	+35	+21	+10	− 2	−11
Vernal, UT	40	27	109	32	2	+40	+36	+33	+30	+28
Walla Walla, WA	46	4	118	20	3	− 5	+ 2	+ 8	+15	+21
Washington, DC	38	54	77	1	0	+35	+28	+23	+18	+13
Waterbury-Meriden, CT	41	33	73	3	0	+10	+ 9	+ 7	+ 6	+ 5
Waterloo, IA	42	30	92	20	1	+24	+24	+24	+25	+25
Wausau, WI	44	58	89	38	1	+ 4	+ 9	+13	+18	+22
West Palm Beach, FL	26	43	80	3	0	+79	+55	+36	+14	− 2
Wichita, KS	37	42	97	20	1	+60	+51	+45	+37	+31
Williston, ND	48	9	103	37	1	+46	+59	+69	+80	+90
Wilmington, DE	39	45	75	33	0	+26	+21	+18	+13	+10
Wilmington, NC	34	14	77	55	0	+52	+38	+27	+15	+ 5
Winchester, VA	39	11	78	10	0	+38	+33	+28	+23	+19
Worcester, MA	42	16	71	48	0	+ 3	+ 2	+ 2	+ 2	+ 2
York, PA	39	58	76	43	0	+30	+26	+22	+18	+15
Youngstown, OH	41	6	80	39	0	+42	40	+38	+36	+34
Yuma, AZ	32	43	114	37	2	+83	+67	+54	+40	+28
CANADA										
Calgary, AB	51	5	114	5	2	+13	+35	+50	+68	+84
Edmonton, AB	53	34	113	25	2	− 3	+26	+47	+72	+93
Halifax, NS	44	38	63	35	− 1	+21	+26	+29	+33	+37
Montreal, PQ	45	28	73	39	0	− 1	+ 4	+ 9	+15	+20
Ottawa, ON	45	25	75	43	0	+ 6	+13	+18	+23	+28
Peterborough, ON	44	18	78	19	0	+21	+25	+28	+32	+35
Saint John, NB	45	16	66	3	− 1	+28	+34	+39	+44	+49
Saskatoon, SK	52	10	106	40	1	+37	+63	+80	+101	+119
Sydney, NS	46	10	60	10	− 1	+ 1	+ 9	+15	+23	+28
Thunder Bay, ON	48	27	89	12	0	+47	+61	+71	+83	+93
Toronto, ON	43	39	79	23	0	+28	+30	+32	+35	+37
Vancouver, BC	49	13	123	6	3	0	+15	+26	+40	+52
Winnipeg, MB	49	53	97	10	1	+12	+30	+43	+58	+71

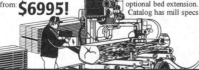

The OLD FARMER'S
GENERAL STORE

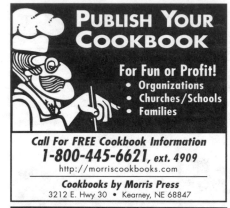

The OLD FARMER'S GENERAL STORE

NAUTICAL ANTIQUES, books, lighthouse, coast guard. Catalog $2. Claflin Antiques, 30 Hudson St., Northborough MA 01532.

$AVE! Kitchen dealer's tips on how to buy a new kitchen without being taken! Send $12.95 to Tenibac, PO Box 116, Peckville PA 18452.

FREE NEW-AGE BOOK LIST. Hundreds of titles! Book List, Box 5588(OF-2), Santa Fe NM 87502-5588. www.sunbooks.com.

CASINO GAMBLERS: FREE copyrighted "Beat Slots" report and catalog. Send $1 s/h to Barens Books, 422F Elmwood, Lansing MI 48917.

MAGIC/SPIRITUALITY: 400+ TITLES. Candle-burning, oils, incense, herbs, dreams, spells, spirituality. Send $2. Original Publications, PO Box 236F, Old Bethpage NY 11804-0236.

HAWAIIAN LUAU of taste treats. Original Macadamia Nut Korn Krunch, 100% Kona Coffee, scrumptious chocolates, Hamakua Macnuts, factory direct prices. Free catalog. Kona Confections, PO Box 2579, Kailua-Kona HI 96745. 800-437-7477. Check out our Web site www.konaconfections.com.

ORISON SWETT MARDEN, James Allen, Ralph Waldo Trine, etc! Inspirational Book List, Box 5588(OF-3), Santa Fe NM 87502-5588. Web site www.sunbooks.com.

GRACE LIVINGSTON HILL BOOKS! Free list. Arnold Publications-A, 2440 Bethel Rd., Nicholasville KY 40356. 800-854-8571.

SAVE $400 a year on your grocery bill. All home delivery. Call 800-354-0386.

BUSINESS OPPORTUNITIES

MAKE $25 PER POUND from free aluminum scrap? Yes! Free report! Ameriscrap-FA98, Alexandria Bay NY 13607-0127.

COMPANY DOWNSIZING? Worried? Stressed out? Self-determined entrepreneurial type? PT/FT 800-927-2527 ext. 7262 (CT096171).

EARN $1,000 WEEKLY stuffing envelopes at own premises. Rush SASE: Lightning Quik Mail Distributors, PO Box 18027, Philadelphia PA 19147.

LET THE GOVERNMENT FINANCE your small business. Grants/loans to $800,000. Free recorded message: 707-448-0270. (KE1).

NATIONAL DIRECTORY lists over 100 companies seeking home workers. Good pay. Easy work. Free information. Gulf Books, Box 263484, Tampa FL 33685-3484. Web site www.concentric.net/~gulf40/index.htm.

$1,800 WEEKLY RECORDING VIDEOTAPES at home. No copyright violation. Free start-up information. CMS Video, 210 Lorna Sq. #163-FA8, Birmingham AL 35216.

$27,000 IN BACKYARD growing new specialty plants. Start with $60. Free booklet. Growers, Box 2010-FA, Port Townsend WA 98368.

LEARN SMALL-BUSINESS MANAGEMENT at home. Free information. Call 800-326-9221 or write Lifetime Career Schools, Dept. 0B0997, 101 Harrison St., Archbald PA 18403.

JOIN HOME-WORKER'S ASSOCIATION. Get "guaranteed legitimate" home-employment offers! Many choices! Write: Association-FA98, Alexandria Bay NY 13607-0250.

MAKE $575 WEEKLY! Guaranteed! Mail list advertisements from home. Free supplies! Send stamped envelope: Superior(#FA-98), Box 7, Bedford Park IL 60499.

EXCELLENT PROFITS possible growing trees and flowers! Professional newsletter $2! Moonflower Farm, Moon VA 23119.

GET PAID $268.20/roll taking easy snapshots at home! Film supplied. Phototek, Box 3706-FO, Idyllwild CA 92549-3706. 909-659-9757 ext. 207.

CASINO MANIA! Win consistently. Slot machines, blackjack, craps, roulette, and bingo. "Free info packet." Write: JSA, Box 7038, North Arlington NJ 07031.

FREE GOVERNMENT GRANTS, loans, auctions. Bonus: We incorporate you free. 800-619-9681. 24-hour free recorded message.

HOME-BUSINESS REVOLUTION SWEEPS ACROSS AMERICA! Free catalog. Choose from hundreds of legitimate businesses — make one your very own! Janus Marketing, Dept. FA, Box 770631, Coral Springs FL 33077.

RECEIVE $9,840 A MONTH! I made a fortune and I'll show you how. Write for free information. PO Box 27345, Fort Worth TX 76127.

LEARN BOOKKEEPING at home. Free information. Call 800-326-9221 or write Lifetime Career Schools, Dept. 0B0997, 101 Harrison St., Archbald PA 18403.

$80,000 FROM ONE ACRE! Grow ginseng, other herbs. Information, long SASE. Lee's, Box 68276-FA, New Augusta IN 46268.

WATKINS PRODUCTS since 1868. Has sincere ways to have a successful home-based business. 800-828-1868.

SPECTACULAR MAIL-ORDER HOME BUSINESS. We drop-ship 3,500 best-selling products. Lowest, below-wholesale prices. Immediate delivery. Free book, tape. SMC, 9401 De Soto Ave., Dept. 358-105, Chatsworth CA 91311-4991.

BUY IT WHOLESALE

39,457 PRODUCTS, FACTORY DIRECT. Taiwan, Hong Kong, Mexico! Save 500%-900%. Echomark, Box 739-FA67, Shalimar FL 32579-0739.

FREE BULK CANDY CATALOG! Old-fashioned specialty candies — home, work, travel, resale. Peter's Candies, 138-F West Court St., Cincinnati OH 45202.

CARNIVOROUS PLANTS

CARNIVOROUS (insect-eating) plants, seeds, supplies, and books. Peter Paul's Nurseries, Canandaigua NY 14424-8713. www.peterpauls.com.

CHEESEMAKING SUPPLIES

MAKE DELICIOUS CHEESES AT HOME. Complete kit $16.95. Free catalog: New England Cheesemaking, Box 85FA, Ashfield MA 01330. www.cheesemaking.com.

COLLECTIBLES/NOSTALGIA

VINTAGE POCKET-WATCH RESTORATION. Twenty years experience, guarantee, free estimates. The Escapement, Box 606, Chenango Bridge NY 13745. 607-648-3777.

ATTENTION BABY BOOMERS. Stand up! Be counted! Own the official Baby Boomers T-shirt. Great gift idea, too! Free brochure 800-346-2382 or www.phunphit.com.

ALADDIN LAMPS and parts. Kerosene lamps, repair service, beautiful, collectible. Catalog $1. MGS Co., Box 11-FA, Mitchellville TN 37119.

CRAFTS

WOODEN HOME ACCESSORIES. Quality pine. Brochure $1 (refundable with order). PO Box 504-OFA, Hillsboro NH 03244-0504. 603-464-4026 or fax 603-464-5548.

PICTURE CLOCK PLAN. Make big bucks! Send $6.95 to J. Meyer, E. 1995 Hill Rd., Luxemburg WI 54217.

INDIAN CRAFTS. Free brochure showing materials used. Recommended to Indian guides, Scout troops, etc. Cleveland Leather, 2629 Lorain Ave., Cleveland OH 44113.

DEER CONTROL

DEER PROBLEMS? We can help! Free catalog. Call Deerbusters, 800-248-DEER (3337). www.deerbusters.com.

DO IT YOURSELF

BUILD A CLIMBING-VINE POLE that attracts birds, butterflies, people! $3 for instructions, material lists, seeds. Myers, PO Box 105, Vicksburg MI 49097.

EDUCATION/INSTRUCTION

EARN YOUR HIGH SCHOOL DIPLOMA. Home study. P.C.D.I., Atlanta, Georgia. Free literature. 800-362-7070 Dept. JMK554.

BECOME A MEDICAL TRANSCRIPTIONIST. Home study. Free career literature. P.C.D.I., Atlanta, Georgia. 800-362-7070 Dept. YYK554.

DEATH BEGINS IN THE COLON. Headaches, indigestion, constipation, diarrhea, heartburn, fatigue, irritable bowel, gas, and big stomach all have been directly attributed to a toxic colon. Raw dietary fiber and enzymes are the answer. Call 800-610-1958 to reclaim your health.

MAGNETIC PRODUCTS. Free information reports and catalog. Dealer inquiries welcome. American Health Service Magnetics 800-544-7521.

TRAVELER'S REMEDIES — natural, safe relief from jet lag, motion sickness, diarrhea, nerves, and backaches. 800-HOMEOPATHY (466-3672).

CHOCOLATE LOVERS, COFFEE ADDICTS, stop bingeing! Hair restorers, aphrodisiacs, natural remedies, and recipes $3.99. Nehalem Farm, Box 272-F, Vernonia OR 97064.

DENTAL IMPRESSION KIT. Make impressions and a model of your own mouth. Examine your teeth and dental work. Good positive identification. Send $59.95 to A. Joyner, PO Box 1963, St. Cloud MN 56302.

FREE CATALOG! Edgar Cayce natural remedies, dental products, homeopathy, oils, shampoos, vitamins, herbs, etc. The Heritage Store, PO Box 444-FA, Virginia Beach VA 23458. 800-862-2923.

KILLER BEES SURVIVAL advice experts say could save lives. Everyone's allergic! $5, stamp. 311 North Robertson #825. Beverly Hills CA 90211

HELP WANTED

GREAT EXTRA INCOME! Assemble simple craft products at home! Guaranteed! Call now! 800-377-6000 ext. 8440.

HOME TYPISTS, PC users needed. $45,000 income potential. Call 800-513-4343 ext. B-2838.

EASY WORK! EXCELLENT PAY! Assemble products at home. Call toll-free 800-467-5566 ext. 12627.

LIST OF OVER 100 JOB classifications open to continuous application with the state of Minnesota. Send $12.50 to A. Joyner, PO Box 1963, St. Cloud MN 56302.

HERBS

FREE GRANDMA'S HOME REMEDIES BOOKLET. Collection of recipes, herbs, and folklore. Send long stamped envelope. Champion's RX-Herb Store, 2369 Elvis Presley, Memphis TN 38106.

HYDROPONICS

Latest hydroponics and lighting equipment and supplies. Guaranteed lowest prices. Free catalog. Higher Yield, Dept. F, 29211 NE Wylie Rd., Camas WA 98607.

INVENTIONS/PATENTS

PATENT IT ECONOMICALLY! Free details. Licensed since 1958. Near Washington, D.C.; Ph.D. Associates, 800-546-2649.

LEARN HOW to offer your invention for sale or license. Free booklet outlines procedures, royalty rates, requirements. Kessler Sales Corp., C-42-8, Fremont OH 43420. 800-537-1133.

INVENTIONS, IDEAS, NEW PRODUCTS! Presentation to industry/exhibition at national innovation exposition. Patent services. 800-288-IDEA (4332).

LIVESTOCK

ALL ABOUT DAIRY GOATS. $17/year. United Caprine News, PO Box 365A, Granbury TX 76048.

LOTTERY/LOTTERY PRODUCTS

HOW-TO-WIN books will change your life to a winner in lotteries/sweepstakes. Bingo, video poker, dice, blackjack, refund, coupon, and more. Free details. JAPA, Box 807, Leominster MA 01453-0807.

MUSIC/RECORDS/TAPES

ACCORDIONS, CONCERTINAS, button boxes. New, used, buy, sell, trade, repair. Hohners, Martin guitars. Catalog $5. Castiglione, Box 40-A, Warren MI 48090. 810-755-6050.

CASH FOR OLD RECORDS! Illustrated 72-page catalog, including thousands of specific prices we pay for 78s on common labels (Columbia, Decca, Victor, etc.), information about scarce labels, shipping instruction, etc. Send $2 (refundable). Discollector, Box 691035(FA), San Antonio TX 78269.

WATERBUG: Renegade singer-songwriters, folk musicians, etc. Free catalog, free sampler with order. 800-466-0234. www.waterbug.com.

FIDDLING AND FOLK MUSIC instruction, catalog. Captain Fiddle, 4 Elm Ct., Newmarket NH 03857. 603-659-2658. www.tiac.net/users/cfiddle.

NURSERY STOCK

WILDFLOWERS. Nursery-propagated woodland and prairie plants, for sun, shade, and bogs. Catalog $1. Contact Cattail Meadows, Ltd., PO Box 39391, Dept. OL, Solon OH 44139.

EVERGREEN TREE SEEDLINGS. Direct from growers. Free catalog. Carino Nurseries, Box 538, Dept. AL, Indiana PA 15701.

RARE FRUITS, ETHNOBOTANICALS, Chinese, Himalayan, Andean; also hundreds of new figs, persimmons, jujubes, pawpaws, passion fruits, subzero citrus, more. "A godsend!" says American Horticulturist. "Fascinating!" says Macmillan Books. "A treasure trove of exotic edibles!" says The Portland Oregonian. 100-page catalog, $3. Oregon Exotics Nursery, 1065 Messinger, Grants Pass OR 97527.

BEAUTIFUL DAYLILIES! Tremendous range of colors and hybrids. Sparrow's Nursery, 405 Sparrow Ln., Colfax LA 71417. 318-627-5294.

OF INTEREST TO ALL

PHOTOS COPIED, restored, enlarged. Request price list: Big Foto, PO Box 521, Cataula GA 31804.

FOUNDATION GRANTS for individuals, to $180,000 for widely varied uses. Free recorded message: 707-448-2668. (2KE1).

TINY TEA. Perfect anytime friendship gift. Adorable teatime keepsake your friend(s) will love! 3" book, whimsical artwork, nostalgic verse, tea, magnet. $3.95 plus $1.05 s/h. Send check: TT, Box 6874, Arlington VA 22206.

RELIEF! From problems, stress, loneliness, heartache, anxiety. Order today. Powerful booklet. Conquer Anxiety and Frustration. $2. Dr. Frank Cassidy, M.D., PO Box 2230-QV, Pine AZ 85544. www.anewlife.org.

TWELVE-MONTH BIORHYTHM CHARTS — $7. Send birth date and year. John Morgan, 1208 Harris, Bartlesville OK 74006.

GIFTS BY MAIL. For all occasions. Send $1 for colorful catalog. V.P. Enterprise, PO Box 1196, Hightstown NJ 08520.

CAN'T SLEEP? Drift off into natural sleep and wake up refreshed. By listening to safe, hypnotic suggestions on tape, restful sleep can be yours. $22 includes guaranteed delivery. U-Neeq Networks, PO Box 5667, Tacoma WA 98415.

OUTDOOR SPORTS/ACTIVITIES

FISHING SECRETS REVEALED. Six practical booklets provide new tips for rigging line and artificial fresh/saltwater baits. Gulf Books, Box 263484, Tampa FL 33685-3484. Web site www.concentric.net/~gulf40/index.htm.

FREE CATFISH CATALOG! Bait, tackle, books, videos, T-shirts. Ford's Outdoor World, Dept. FA, 18405 Garden Blvd., Cleveland OH 44128-2628.

PERSONALS

THAI ASIAN worldwide ladies desire lifemates, free color photo-brochure! TAWL, Box 937(FA), Kailua-Kona HI 96745-0937. 808-329-5559. Web site http://tawl.com.

BEAUTIFUL ASIAN LADIES overseas seek love, marriage. Lowest rates! Free brochure: PR, Box 1245FA, Benicia CA 94510. 707-747-6906.

ASIAN WOMEN desire marriage! Overseas. $2 for details, photos! Sunshine International, Box 5500-YH, Kailua-Kona HI 96745-5500. Web site http://sunshine-girls.com.

NEW AGE contacts, occultists, circles, wicca, companionship, love, etc. America/worldwide. Dollar bill: Dion, Golden Wheel, Liverpool L15 3HT England.

RUSSIAN LADIES, truly beautiful, educated, seek companionship. 3,000 selected from 80,000+ ladies. Exciting Moscow tours, videos. Free color photocatalog. Euro182, PO Box 888851, Atlanta GA 30356. 770-458-0909.

JAPANESE, ASIAN, European pen pals seek correspondence! All ages! Inter Pacific, Box 304-K, Birmingham MI 48012.

MRS. NANCY, INDIAN HEALER. Are you facing difficult problems? Are you sick, suffering, in pain and misery? Has your loved one left you? Are you unhappy? Mrs. Nancy reunites lovers fast. Will give you options you never considered. Call now at 803-981-7679 for total answers. 3045 N. Cherry Rd., Rock Hill SC 29730.

DOMINIQUE REVEALS FUTURE, love, finance, career. Helps all problems. Reunites lovers, calls enemies names. 423-472-3035.

ATTENTION: SISTER LIGHT, Spartanburg, South Carolina. One free reading when you call. I will help in all problems. 864-576-9397.

WATKINS! MY HUSBAND LAUGHED when I started selling Watkins Products like grandma used. Now he borrows from me! Information/catalog. Angela International, Marketing Director, Dept. A, 888-203-4321, fax 913-758-0470. Your Watkins source!

ASIAN DREAM GIRLS abroad desire love, marriage. Lowest price! Tours! Free brochure. ADG, Box 1821FA, Sanford FL 32772. 407-321-8558.

MEET LATIN LADIES! Mexico/South America. Photo-magazines, videos, tours. Free photo-brochures! TLC, Box 924904AL, Houston TX 77292-4994. 713-896-9224.

LATIN, ORIENTAL LADIES seek friendship, marriage. Free photo-brochure. "Latins," Box 1716-OF, Chula Vista CA 91912.

NICE SINGLES with Christian values meet others. Nationwide since 1981. Free magazine. Send age/interests. Singles, Box 310-OFA, Allardt TN 38504.

FREE INFORMATION! Unmarried Catholics. Large membership. Unlimited choice. Established 1980. Sparks, Box 872-F, Troy NY 12181.

ASIAN BEAUTIES! WORLDWIDE! Romance, pen pals, marriage! Color photos $5. P.I.C., Box 461873-FA, Los Angeles CA 90046. Web site www.paclsl.com.

LONELY? UNLUCKY? UNHAPPY? Lost nature? Lost love? Linda solves all problems quickly. Free readings. 912-995-3611.

MOTHER DORA can influence others. Bring luck. Help with all problems. Correct wrongs. Results! 912-888-5999.

SISTER RUBY helps in all problems. One free reading by phone. Removes bad luck. 912-776-3069.

SISTER SONYA SPIRITUAL HEALER. Specializes in reuniting loved ones. Removes evil influences. Powerful, immediate results. 804-792-6935.

BEAUTIFUL EAST EUROPEAN WOMEN overseas seek romance and marriage! Free 500-photo color magazine. Clubprima, 1101-D Thorpe, #110DP, San Marcos TX 78666. 512-396-5522; 24 hours. http://clubprima.com.

ALOHA! MEET WOMEN WORLD-WIDE! Thousands of happy marriages since 1974. Complimentary photo-magazine: Cherry Blossoms, Box 190-FA, Kapaau HI 96755. 619-262-6025 ext. 71.

MOTHER DOROTHY, reader and adviser. Advice on all problems — love, marriage, health, business, and nature. Gifted healer, she will remove your sickness, sorrow, pain, bad luck. ESP. Results in three days. Write or call about your problems. 1214 Gordon St., Atlanta GA 30310. 404-755-1301.

SISTER JOSIE can solve all problems in life such as love, business, health, marriage, financial. 706-353-9259.

WONDERING ABOUT TOMORROW? Find out today! Let Sister Hope help you with love, marriage, business, good luck. Whatever your problem may be, call today, for tomorrow may be too late. 706-548-8598.

POULTRY

GOSLINGS, DUCKLINGS, CHICKS, guineas, turkeys, bantams, pheasants, quail, swans. Books, medications. Hoffman Hatchery, Gratz PA 17030.

FREE CATALOG. Baby chicks, ducks, geese, turkeys, game birds, Canadian honkers, wood ducks. Eggs to incubators. Books and supplies. Call 800-720-1134. Stromberg's, Pine River 45, MN 56474-0400.

PULLETS, BROILERS, STANDARD BREEDS, plus rare and exotics, bantams, turkeys, ducks, guineas, jungle fowl — hatched weekly. Write for free color catalog. Grain Belt Hatchery, Box 125-FA, Windsor MO 65360. Phone 816-647-2711.

GOSLINGS, DUCKLINGS, CHICKS, turkeys, guineas, books. Picture catalog $1, deductible. Pilgrim Goose Hatchery, OF-98, Williamsford OH 44093.

AMERICAN POULTRY ASSOCIATION, promoting all breeds of domestic poultry and waterfowl. $10/year, $25/3 years. Free brochure. American Poultry Association, 133 Millville St., Mendon MA 01756.

REAL ESTATE

LET THE GOVERNMENT PAY for your new or existing home. Over 100 different programs available. Free recorded message: 707-448-3210. (8KE1).

GOVERNMENT LAND now available for claim. Up to 160 acres/person. Free recorded message: 707-448-1887. (4KE1).

OZARK MOUNTAIN OR LAKE ACREAGES. From $30/month, nothing down, environmental protection codes, huge selection. Free catalog. WOODS & WATERS, Box 1-FA, Willow Springs MO 65793. 417-469-3187 or www.ozarkland.com.

ARKANSAS — FREE CATALOG. Natural beauty. Low taxes. The good life for families and retirement. Century 21 Fitzgerald-Olsen Realtors, PO Box 237-A, Booneville AR 72927. Call toll-free 800-432-4595 ext. 641A.

MAINE. PENOBSCOT. 273 REMOTE, WOODED ACRES. High elevations. Private, seasonal road. Near salt water. $125,000. Cochrane, 207-942-4941.

BARGAIN HOMES — foreclosed, HUD, VA, S&L bailout properties. Low down. Fantastic savings. Call 800-513-4343 ext. H-2838 for list.

ESCAPE TO THE HILLS OF SOUTH-CENTRAL KENTUCKY. Secluded country properties. Inexpensive homes. Call Century 21, Vibbert Realty, 800-267-2600 for free brochure.

ARKANSAS LAND. Free lists! Recreational, investment, retirement homes, acreages. Gatlin Farm Agency, Box 790, Waldron AR 72958. Toll-free 800-562-9078 ext. OFA.

RECIPES/COOKBOOKS

BLUE CHEESE from scratch. Simple, old recipe. Send $5. Hawkshaven Farms, PO Box 111, Trenton OH 45067.

THE CAT'S MEOW — Victorian Inn offers family-favorite recipes — including the Inn's feline favorites! Send $21 to The Albert Stevens Inn, 127 Myrtle Ave., Cape May NJ 08204.

RELIGION

A MIRACLE IN CLEARWATER. TV broadcast–quality, documented video apparition . . . "The Virgin Mary." On the windows of an office building in Clearwater, Florida, Christmas 1996. Includes apparition of Baby Jesus on same windows. $19.95 video, $6.99 poster, plus $4.99 s/h, or send check/mo: B. Shears, 321 5th Ave., Pelham NY 10803. Fax/phone 914-738-4162. Visa/MC.

FREE: Four booklets of Bible verses: Vernon-O8F, 11613 N. 31st Dr., Phoenix AZ 85029-3201.

FREE ADULT OR CHILD Bible study courses. Project Philip, Box 35A, Muskegon MI 49443.

INSPIRATIONAL, SELF-HELP, positive-thinking books. Many titles! Inspirational Book List, Box 5588(OF-4), Santa Fe NM 87502-5588. Web site www.sunbooks.com.

CHRISTIAN PROGRAM debt freedom — monthly gifts. Free information. LSASE. 25 Pleasant St. (1005), Lynn MA 01902-4429.

WHAT IS THIS WORLD COMING TO? An end or new beginning? What Bible prophecies predict for the future. Free booklet. Clearwater Bible Students, PO Box 8216, Clearwater FL 33758.

THE BOOK OF REVELATION by Clarence Larken. $18 plus $3.50 shipping: Sunbooks, Box 5588(OF-5), Santa Fe NM 87502-5588. Web site www.sunbooks.com.

SAWMILLS

CALL SAWMILL EXCHANGE to buy/sell used portable sawmills (Wood-Mizer, TimberKing, etc.). Also *Portable Sawmill Encyclopedia,* only $14.95! 205-969-3963. Web site www.sawmill-exchange.com.

SEEDS

ENDANGERED/HEIRLOOM flower, herb, vegetable seeds. Catalog $1. greenseeds™, 4N381-FA Maple Ave., Bensenville IL 60106.

TOBACCO, HOT PEPPERS, medicinal plants, supplies, and more. Free catalog. Eons Inc., PO Box 4604, Hallandale FL 33008. 954-455-0229.

FREE CATALOG. Quality flower, herb, and vegetable seeds. Burrell, Box 150-FA, Rocky Ford CO 81067.

RARE HILARIOUS peter, female, and squash pepper seeds. $3/pkg. Any two $5. All three $7.50. Over 100 rare peppers. Seeds, 2119 Hauss Nursery Rd., Atmore AL 36502.

GOURDS. More than 15 different shapes and sizes! The Gourd Garden and Curiosity Shop, 4808 E. C-30A, Santa Rosa Beach FL 32459. 850-231-2007.

OPIUM POPPY SEEDS. Guaranteed fertile. 10,000 seeds for $10. Not intended for illegal use. Jones Seed Co., PO Box 1989, Douglas GA 31534.

VACATION RENTALS

POCONO RETREAT IN HONESDALE, PENNSYLVANIA. Furnished, sleeps 8, secluded, cozy, private ponds. $85/night. Kevin 717-282-7545.

WANTED

WE BUY ROYALTIES and minerals in producing oil and gas wells. Please write Marienfeld Royalty Corp., PO Box 25914, Houston TX 77265, or call 800-647-2580, or visit www.marienfeld.com.

WANTED: AUTOGRAPHS, signed photos, letters, documents of famous people. Gray, Box 5084, Cochituate MA 01778, or 617-426-4912.

BOY SCOUT patches, jamboree items, OA patches, uniforms, etc. wanted. Doug Bearce, Box 4742, Salem OR 97302. 503-399-9872.

WEATHER VANES

WEATHER VANES AND CUPOLAS — Special sale! America's largest selection. Antique and custom designs. Free catalog 800-724-2548, 410-757-5637.

WORK CLOTHES

WORK CLOTHES. Save 80%. Shirts, pants, coveralls. Free folder. Write: Galco, 4004 East 71st St., Dept. OF-5, Cleveland OH 44105.

MISCELLANEOUS

LET THE GOVERNMENT FINANCE your career in writing or the arts. Free recorded message 707-448-0200. (5KE1).

FREE DEGREES! Counseling, metaphysics, hypnotherapy, parapsychology! Ministerial license! P.U.L.C., Box 276265-FR, Sacramento CA 95827.

JEHOVAH'S WITNESSES, friends, family, find out facts the society doesn't want you to know. Free and confidential. JW FACTS, 454 Metaline Falls WA 99153.

STOP SMOKING NOW. Free information request from Hal Miller, PO Box 811, Mancos CO 81328.

STAINLESS STEEL high-pressure steam cleaners, to 4,000 PSI, 210° F. Factory Direct Cost. Financing. 800-324-2822.

BURIED TREASURE, water, mineral deposits. Sensitive equipment allows locating from a distance. Brochure free. Simmon Scientific, Box 10057PA, Wilmington NC 28405.

The Old Farmer's Almanac accepts classified ads for products and services we feel will be of interest to our readers. However, we cannot verify the quality or reliability of the products or services offered.

ATTENTION, CLASSIFIED ADVERTISERS!

Reach millions of readers with your classified ad in the five publications from *The Old Farmer's Almanac* listed below. For rates on the individual publications or special group rates, call Donna Stone at 800-729-9265, ext. 314, or write to *The Old Farmer's Almanac*, Attn.: Donna Stone, P.O. Box 520, Dublin, NH 03444.

CLOSING DATES:

The Old Farmer's Almanac
Gardener's Companion
For people who love to grow things.
$6 per word — October 27, 1997

The Old Farmer's Almanac
Good Cook's Companion
A publication dedicated to good food and the joys of cooking.
$6 per word — January 9, 1998

The Old Farmer's Almanac
HomeOwner's Companion
The magazine for people who care about their home.
$6 per word — April 1, 1998

The Old Farmer's Almanac
The original Robert B. Thomas Farmer's Almanac published every year since 1792.
$12 per word — May 8, 1998

The Old Farmer's Almanac
Holiday Recipes Companion
Great traditional recipes for the season.
$6 per word — August 3, 1998

ANECDOTES and PLEASANTRIES

A motley collection of useful (and useless) facts, stories, advice, and observations compiled mostly from reader correspondence received over the past 12 months.

"My Friends Think I'm Nuts, but My Wife Is Impressed"

Forecasting the Weather with Body Parts

For the past year or so, we've been running down reports from dozens of readers who claim to be able to accurately predict the local weather by recognizing certain sensations in their anatomies. Here's a sampling of what we have so far . . .

Gwynne Wolin, Florida: "When I was living up North, I could tell within 12 to 24 hours when it was going to snow. I did it with my 'snow bone,' some sort of bone tucked at the right side of my skull. When my snow bone began to throb, my family always ran for the tire chains and shovels."

Deborah Anderson, Arizona: "When I was a registered nurse in Englewood, Ohio, working long hours on my feet, I noticed that I became wobbly in the knees with approaching wind storms. Sure, anyone could be blown around on a breezy day, but I would begin to sway 24 hours *before* the wind came."

Dr. Jack Stone, New Jersey: "I know there's going to be a big change in the weather when I start to itch all over. The more I need to scratch, the bigger the change, whether it's in anticipation of rain, snow, heat, cold, or even humidity. I've found the best treatment for this itching is my own concoction of a pepper ointment I mix in the kitchen. It burns so much that I forget about the itching."

David Hill, California: "I've never been quite the same since I fell from a telephone pole while working in San Diego a few years ago. Now, my back becomes sore if it's going to rain. I can spot the biggest, blackest clouds heading my way, but if my back isn't sore, that storm will glide right over me without a drop. I've never missed. My friends think I'm nuts, but my wife is impressed."

Kate Cunningham, Indiana: "The sky can be clear and blue and the sun shining bright, but if I begin to feel a pain in my stomach, it's going to rain — never fails."

Iola Davies, Washington: "I always go into one of my famous sneezing fits the minute the seasons change. Never at any other time. Just four times a year. My family re-

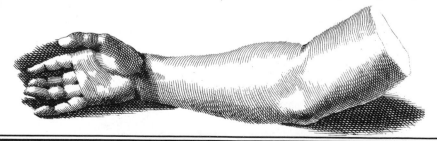

lies on it to know when — exactly — it's winter, spring, summer, and fall."

Richard Bennett, Connecticut: "Whenever it's going to rain, we notice that our daugh-

ter Megan's ordinarily straight hair turns into what we call 'banana curls.' The more severe the coming storm, the tighter her curls." *— compiled by Jeff Brein, Bainbridge Island, Washington*

Editor's Note: If you can forecast the weather with different body parts from those listed above, or by any odd anatomical method, please write and maybe we'll include you next year. Just send to: Body Parts, *The Old Farmer's Almanac*, Box 520, Dublin, NH 03444.

About the Man Who Drank Himself into Bolivia

The following was sent to us by Dr. Stephen Davis and psychotherapist Tina Kenyon (former colleagues at the Department of Family Medicine, Memorial Hospital, Brown University, Providence, R.I.). Our thanks to Yankee Magazine cartoonist Don Bousquet, who put them up to it.

SEA ROACH

We have fun collecting malapropisms. As you and many of your readers would know, a malapropism is the misuse of a word that sounds similar to the correct word the person had in mind. It's a mistake we all make from time to time. Our collection, to which we hope your readers will contribute, began when a colleague said she preferred to drink **"decapitated coffee."** Since then, some of the malaprop maladies we've encountered here at the hospital include **"old timer's disease," "prostrate cancer," "chickenpops," "smiling mighty Jesus"** (for spinal meningitis), and **"65 roses"** (for cystic fibrosis).

Another colleague once reported that one of his patients said her father, a longtime Navy man, had died from **"sea roaches of the liver."**

Describing a beautiful sunset, a patient of ours, presumably mixing up *rainbow* and *spectrum*, said, **"It had all the colors of the rectum."**

Last month, we had a pregnant woman who, after nine months, said she was ready to be **"reduced."**

Another woman told us that she was going through **"mental pause."** She also said her husband had quit smoking **"cold duck."** (Did she mean he quit drinking Cold Duck?)

Finally, a woman reported to a counselor here that she was certain she did not have a sexually transmitted disease because she and her husband, despite a recent **"falling down,"** were unfailingly **"monotonous."**

Only 100 Years Ago

Did you know that there were about twice as many opiate addicts in the United States (per capita) in 1898 as there are today?

In 1898, a particularly effective cough medicine was introduced to this country by the Bayer Company of Germany. It was called heroin, a drug produced from morphine (an opium derivative). Two years later, there were 4.59 drug addicts (including heroin users) in the United States for every 1,000 citizens, about twice the rate of official estimates today. (continued on next page)

By 1902, the American Medical Association had issued a warning regarding the addictive nature of this new cough medicine, but doctors nonetheless continued to prescribe it, and people went on buying over-the-counter patent medicines containing heroin well into the 1950s, when federal legislation finally put a stop to it.

P.S. Know what else happened in 1898? Well, a Hungarian fellow by the name of Dêzso Bánky invented a gizmo that sprays an explosive mixture of gasoline and air into an internal combustion engine. It was called a carburetor.   – *courtesy of Randy Miller, Alstead, New Hampshire*

A Secret Way of Removing a Ring from a Swollen Finger

Hint: All you need is a little string . . .

Perhaps you and your readers would be interested in knowing how to remove a ring from a finger that's become swollen by obesity, old age, or injury (such as a sprain). In the latter case, it is imperative that you act quickly because more swelling happens in mere minutes.

So here's what you do:

Push a piece of string (two or three feet long) under the ring and hold it firmly while winding the long end tightly around the finger and knuckle over which the ring must slide. Then unwrap the string by pulling the short end toward the tip of the ring finger, and presto, the ring is off.   – *courtesy of Margo Burkhardt, Antioch, California*

How You, Too, Can Watch an Apple Fall from Sir Isaac Newton's Tree

Maybe, if you're lucky, one will even fall on your head.

Back around 1666, Isaac Newton supposedly watched an apple fall from a tree in the garden of his family home at Woolsthorpe, near Grantham, England. Whether the apple actually clunked him on the head or not, Newton eventually credited that apple for his discovery of the gravitational force that holds the planets and our Moon in their respective orbits *and* causes objects to fall to Earth.

So whatever happened to that apple tree? It lives on in grafts that have found their way to many parts of the world. Here are a few places you can find Newton apple trees, scions of the original, in the United States:

■ The National Institute of Standards and Technology (NIST) complex near Gaithersburg, Maryland. Telephone 301-975-3058 for directions.

■ Pennsbury Manor, William Penn's home, in Morrisville, Pennsylvania. Call 215-946-0400 for directions and hours of tours.

■ The American Society for Metals, headquartered in Russell, Ohio. For an appointment and directions, call Gloria Terpay at 800-336-5152.

■ The University of Nebraska in Lincoln, Nebraska. Call 402-472-2023 for tours, directions, and maps.

■ The Massachusetts Institute of Technology in Cambridge, Massachusetts. Call 617-253-4795 for a map and tour information.

– *courtesy of Richard A. Dengrove, Alexandria, Virginia*

The Luckiest Person of the 1990s

In 1994, 44-year-old Mary Clamser of Oklahoma City, Oklahoma, who suffered from multiple sclerosis, was struck by lightning (or at least lightning struck her house) while she happened to be grasping metal objects in each hand and wearing her metal leg brace. Within minutes, she found she could walk easily and without pain. Her doctors told her the "cure" was probably temporary, but she continues to walk easily to this day.

In April of 1995, she was invited to appear on a television show in California to be interviewed about this miraculous occurrence. She was happy to accept the invitation, but to do so, she had to cancel a local appointment for 9:00 A.M. on April 19 at the Oklahoma City federal building (which, as we all know, was blown up that morning).

– *courtesy of Kenneth R. Rotch, Decatur, Georgia*
from *The Sunday Oklahoman*

A Dozen Facts to Contemplate

Some are interesting. (The others are appropriate for preceding the question, "So?")

1 If you toss a penny 10,000 times, it will not come up heads 5,000 times. More likely 4,950 times. The reason is that the "heads" side weighs slightly more, so it tends to end up on the bottom.

2 If NASA sent birds into space, they would soon die. They need gravity to swallow.

3 One hundred and twenty drops of water are needed to fill a teaspoon.

4 All birds have either three or four toes, except the ostrich, which has only two.

5 Armored knights raised their visors to identify themselves when they rode past their king. This custom has become the modern military salute.

6 Dr. Samuel A. Mudd was the physician who set the broken leg of Lincoln's assassin, John Wilkes Booth . . . and whose shame created the expression for ignominy, "His name is Mudd."

7 The longest recorded flight of a chicken is just over 210 yards.

8 The first bomb dropped by the allies on Berlin during World War II killed the only elephant in the Berlin Zoo.

9 Studies show that if a cat falls off the 7th floor of a building, it has about a 30 percent less chance of surviving than if it falls off the 20th floor. It supposedly takes about eight floors for a cat to realize what is occurring, relax, and correct its position. (If anyone else tries this with a cat, he or she will cook in hell for all of eternity. Guaranteed. – *Ed.*)

10 Your stomach produces a new layer of mucus every two weeks; if it didn't, it would digest itself.

11 The housefly hums in the middle octave, key of F.

12 The saying, "It's so cold out there it could freeze the balls off a brass monkey," comes from the Civil War. In those days, cannonballs were stacked beside cannons in a pyramid formation called a *brass monkey*. When it became extremely cold outside, these stacked cannonballs would crack and break off.

– *courtesy of Diane Chen, Boston, Massachusetts*

How to Lovingly Care for Your Poinsettia Plant

Here are a few tips about poinsettias from a Canadian reader who writes, "I have kept some of my Christmas poinsettias going for years by following these rules."

1 Select healthy plants with green foliage all the way down to the soil line. This is a good indication that the plants have active, healthy roots.

2 Look for plants that have small, green buttons (cyathia) in the center of the colored bracts. These buttons will eventually develop into little flowers.

3 Place poinsettias in a room with at least six hours of bright, indirect natural light each day. Water thoroughly, but don't overwater.

4 Fertilize the plants within several days of acquiring them. They are without nutrients during the whole marketing process and will need feeding.

5 Keep plants away from drafts, radiators, and hot-air registers. To prolong the bright color of the bracts, temperatures should not exceed 72° F during the day.

6 In January, when the bracts fade, cut back the plants and repot them. In March and April, start fertilizing them every two weeks. The plants may be moved outside in the summer, into filtered light, as long as there is no danger of frost. Repot if needed before bringing them back inside. From the third week of September through the end of October, they need at least 14 hours each day of uninterrupted darkness: Use a spare bedroom for this, or move them into a closet each evening. Your poinsettias should be blooming again before Christmas.

P.S. It is not true that poinsettias are highly toxic. According to POISONDEX, a 50-pound child would have to eat more than 1-1/4 pounds of poinsettia bracts (or 500 to 600 leaves) to exceed the experimental doses that found no toxicity. (A slight tummy ache, maybe?)

– courtesy of Martin P. Waterman, Petitcodiac, New Brunswick

Six Who Rest in Pieces

We include the following, sent to us from reader Melissa Bienvenu, of Franklinton, Louisiana, with some misgivings. It's a list of people buried in multiple graves. Maybe it's an item we could have skipped.

● *The Return of the Native* author **Thomas Hardy** left his heart in his first wife's grave, but the ashes of the rest of him are next to those of Charles Dickens in Westminster Abbey.

● Confederate General **Stonewall Jackson** retired his left arm (amputated in 1863 because of a bullet wound) in the private family plot of Major James Horace Lacy in Spotsylvania County, Virginia. Eight days later, Jackson died of pneumonia; his one-armed body was laid to rest in Presbyterian Cemetery in Lexington, Virginia. A Virginia highway marker commemorates the site of the gruesome severing.

(continued)

SUPER YOHIMBE

Yohimbe comes from the bark of an African tree. It was first introduced centuries ago by sailors returning from Africa, where tribesmen swore it was an aphrodisiac. Reports of its efficacy were scoffed at by scientists until recently, when Its mechanism of action was discovered.

When a man is sexually aroused, there is an increased flow of blood that causes an erection. To facilitate this process, norepinephrine is released by the body's sympathetic nervous system.

Yohimbe belongs to a class of drugs that enhance stimulation of the sympathetic nervous system, causing more rapid, more frequent and stronger erections. With an erection, the increased stimulation of the sympathetic nervous system by Yohimbe increases both desire and sexual pleasure.

Dr. Christiaan Barnard, the world renowned heart transplant surgeon, reported that 3 out of 4 heart transplant patients had immediate return of sexual potency after taking Yohimbe.

Yohimbe is 100% Natural. Physicians and researchers agree that using Yohimbe is the natural way to increase and enjoy sexual strength, stamina and endurance. Super Yohimbe (500mg) is guaranteed to have maximum potency. Available without a prescription. Daily dosage: 3 tablets per day.
☐ **90 Tablets $39.95** plus $4. post & handl
☐ SAVE $7.95! **180 Tabs $79.95** (incls P&H)
WILLOWS NUTRITION, Dept. SY-106
179 Post Road West, Westport CT 06880

100% Natural, Herbal
BLADDER CONTROL

"My wife has benefited from taking your HB Healthy Bladder 100% natural tablets" Dr. Dominic A. Vavala
Cranston, R.I. 02920

Millions of men and women of all ages and every social and economic level suffer from this embarrassing condition. Adult diapers are ill fitting, uncomfortable and very expensice.

URINARY INCONTINENCE
CAN BE CURED WITH HERBS

Healthy Bladder with Cranberry Extract
All orders shipped by FIRST CLASS MAIL.
Satisfaction guaranteed or return for full refund of purchase price (less P&H)
☐ 60 Tabs only $19.95 plus $3. P&H
☐ 120 Tabs $35.95 plus $4. P&H
☐ 240 Tabs $64.95 plus $5. P&H
☐ 360 Tabs $100.00 (includes P&H)
WILLOWS NUTRITION, Dept HBC-197
179 Post Rd West, Westport CT 06880
CREDIT CARD ORDERS 1-800-770-1155

● **King John**, brother of Richard the Lion-Hearted, was laid to rest under the high altar at Worcester Cathedral — all except for his bowels, which were autopsied for signs of poisoning and buried separately at Croxton Abbey.

● A friend snatched the heart of **Percy Bysshe Shelley** from the flames during the English poet's seaside cremation in Italy in 1822. The organ was given to Shelley's lover and then, after a quarrel, to his wife, *Frankenstein* author Mary Shelley. Finally the restless heart was buried beside Percy's son in England. The poet's ashes are in Rome.

● **St. Lawrence**, roasted over hot coals in A.D. 258 for giving church treasures to the poor, was buried in Rome — or what was left of him. A dozen churches claimed pieces of the martyr, including his shoulder blade, arm, jaw, backbone joint, finger, foot, two ribs, and some melted fat.

● After **Sir Walter Raleigh**'s beheading in 1618, his body was buried in a London church. However, Raleigh's wife kept his embalmed noggin in a red leather bag until she died 29 years later, giving new meaning to the term "head of the household."

Editor's Postscript: Reader Melissa Bienvenu also tells us that the American woman who is commemorated by the most statues — at least 19 of them — in the United States is . . . can you guess? Well, it's Sacagawea (1787-1812). She was the young Shoshoni Indian guide who helped Lewis and Clark explore the West. Now we know.

The Proper Position for an Outhouse

Courtesy of Sherman Hines of Poplar Grove, Nova Scotia — who found this item in Yankee Home Hints *by* Yankee *Magazine columnist Earl Proulx (Rodale Press).*

I've built a lot of outhouses. Back before the invention of 'Portapotties,' I'd have to build an outhouse every time the con-tracting firm I worked for took on a big road-building project for the state.

"Only the crudest camps use outhouses today. The factors in positioning an outhouse, however, are the same as they have been for centuries. You want it near the house, downwind, out of sight, in a place that's easy to dig. One other factor: Make sure the path to it goes by your woodpile. When you're returning from the outhouse, you can bring in an armload of wood. Better yet, guests who are embarrassed about heading in that direction can pretend they just went out to get more wood. If you put your woodpile along the path to the outhouse, you'll never have an empty woodbox."

A Health Tip for Those Who Hate Health Tips

According to a recent study by Deakin University in Melbourne, Australia, nine weekly workouts of just ten minutes each has exactly the same cardiovascular benefits as three weekly half-hour sessions. So, for three days each week, those who really can't face a long exercise workout or who don't have time for one can do ten minutes of brisk walking before work, another ten minutes of running or maybe stair climbing at noon, and a final ten minutes on a bicycle in the evening before supper. Or maybe spread it out. Do just one of those ten-minute workouts every day and two on two days. Seems do-able.

– courtesy of R. Arnold, Naples, Florida
from *UC Berkeley Wellness Letter*, January 1997

1997

JANUARY
S	M	T	W	T	F	S
–	–	–	1	2	3	4
5	6	7	8	9	10	11
12	13	14	15	16	17	18
19	20	21	22	23	24	25
26	27	28	29	30	31	–

FEBRUARY
S	M	T	W	T	F	S
–	–	–	–	–	–	1
2	3	4	5	6	7	8
9	10	11	12	13	14	15
16	17	18	19	20	21	22
23	24	25	26	27	28	–

MARCH
S	M	T	W	T	F	S
–	–	–	–	–	–	1
2	3	4	5	6	7	8
9	10	11	12	13	14	15
16	17	18	19	20	21	22
23	24	25	26	27	28	29
30	31					

APRIL
S	M	T	W	T	F	S
–	–	1	2	3	4	5
6	7	8	9	10	11	12
13	14	15	16	17	18	19
20	21	22	23	24	25	26
27	28	29	30	–	–	–

MAY
S	M	T	W	T	F	S
–	–	–	–	1	2	3
4	5	6	7	8	9	10
11	12	13	14	15	16	17
18	19	20	21	22	23	24
25	26	27	28	29	30	31

JUNE
S	M	T	W	T	F	S
1	2	3	4	5	6	7
8	9	10	11	12	13	14
15	16	17	18	19	20	21
22	23	24	25	26	27	28
29	30					

JULY
S	M	T	W	T	F	S
–	–	1	2	3	4	5
6	7	8	9	10	11	12
13	14	15	16	17	18	19
20	21	22	23	24	25	26
27	28	29	30	31	–	–

AUGUST
S	M	T	W	T	F	S
–	–	–	–	–	1	2
3	4	5	6	7	8	9
10	11	12	13	14	15	16
17	18	19	20	21	22	23
24	25	26	27	28	29	30
31						

SEPTEMBER
S	M	T	W	T	F	S
–	1	2	3	4	5	6
7	8	9	10	11	12	13
14	15	16	17	18	19	20
21	22	23	24	25	26	27
28	29	30				

OCTOBER
S	M	T	W	T	F	S
–	–	–	1	2	3	4
5	6	7	8	9	10	11
12	13	14	15	16	17	18
19	20	21	22	23	24	25
26	27	28	29	30	31	–

NOVEMBER
S	M	T	W	T	F	S
–	–	–	–	–	–	1
2	3	4	5	6	7	8
9	10	11	12	13	14	15
16	17	18	19	20	21	22
23	24	25	26	27	28	29
30						

DECEMBER
S	M	T	W	T	F	S
–	1	2	3	4	5	6
7	8	9	10	11	12	13
14	15	16	17	18	19	20
21	22	23	24	25	26	27
28	29	30	31	–	–	–

1998

JANUARY
S	M	T	W	T	F	S
–	–	–	–	1	2	3
4	5	6	7	8	9	10
11	12	13	14	15	16	17
18	19	20	21	22	23	24
25	26	27	28	29	30	31

FEBRUARY
S	M	T	W	T	F	S
1	2	3	4	5	6	7
8	9	10	11	12	13	14
15	16	17	18	19	20	21
22	23	24	25	26	27	28

MARCH
S	M	T	W	T	F	S
1	2	3	4	5	6	7
8	9	10	11	12	13	14
15	16	17	18	19	20	21
22	23	24	25	26	27	28
29	30	31				

APRIL
S	M	T	W	T	F	S
–	–	–	1	2	3	4
5	6	7	8	9	10	11
12	13	14	15	16	17	18
19	20	21	22	23	24	25
26	27	28	29	30	–	–

MAY
S	M	T	W	T	F	S
–	–	–	–	–	1	2
3	4	5	6	7	8	9
10	11	12	13	14	15	16
17	18	19	20	21	22	23
24	25	26	27	28	29	30
31						

JUNE
S	M	T	W	T	F	S
–	1	2	3	4	5	6
7	8	9	10	11	12	13
14	15	16	17	18	19	20
21	22	23	24	25	26	27
28	29	30				

JULY
S	M	T	W	T	F	S
–	–	–	1	2	3	4
5	6	7	8	9	10	11
12	13	14	15	16	17	18
19	20	21	22	23	24	25
26	27	28	29	30	31	–

AUGUST
S	M	T	W	T	F	S
–	–	–	–	–	–	1
2	3	4	5	6	7	8
9	10	11	12	13	14	15
16	17	18	19	20	21	22
23	24	25	26	27	28	29
30	31					

SEPTEMBER
S	M	T	W	T	F	S
–	–	1	2	3	4	5
6	7	8	9	10	11	12
13	14	15	16	17	18	19
20	21	22	23	24	25	26
27	28	29	30	–	–	–

OCTOBER
S	M	T	W	T	F	S
–	–	–	–	1	2	3
4	5	6	7	8	9	10
11	12	13	14	15	16	17
18	19	20	21	22	23	24
25	26	27	28	29	30	31

NOVEMBER
S	M	T	W	T	F	S
1	2	3	4	5	6	7
8	9	10	11	12	13	14
15	16	17	18	19	20	21
22	23	24	25	26	27	28
29	30					

DECEMBER
S	M	T	W	T	F	S
–	–	1	2	3	4	5
6	7	8	9	10	11	12
13	14	15	16	17	18	19
20	21	22	23	24	25	26
27	28	29	30	31	–	–

1999

JANUARY
S	M	T	W	T	F	S
–	–	–	–	–	1	2
3	4	5	6	7	8	9
10	11	12	13	14	15	16
17	18	19	20	21	22	23
24	25	26	27	28	29	30
31						

FEBRUARY
S	M	T	W	T	F	S
–	1	2	3	4	5	6
7	8	9	10	11	12	13
14	15	16	17	18	19	20
21	22	23	24	25	26	27
28						

MARCH
S	M	T	W	T	F	S
–	1	2	3	4	5	6
7	8	9	10	11	12	13
14	15	16	17	18	19	20
21	22	23	24	25	26	27
28	29	30	31			

APRIL
S	M	T	W	T	F	S
–	–	–	–	1	2	3
4	5	6	7	8	9	10
11	12	13	14	15	16	17
18	19	20	21	22	23	24
25	26	27	28	29	30	–

MAY
S	M	T	W	T	F	S
–	–	–	–	–	–	1
2	3	4	5	6	7	8
9	10	11	12	13	14	15
16	17	18	19	20	21	22
23	24	25	26	27	28	29
30	31					

JUNE
S	M	T	W	T	F	S
–	–	1	2	3	4	5
6	7	8	9	10	11	12
13	14	15	16	17	18	19
20	21	22	23	24	25	26
27	28	29	30			

JULY
S	M	T	W	T	F	S
–	–	–	–	1	2	3
4	5	6	7	8	9	10
11	12	13	14	15	16	17
18	19	20	21	22	23	24
25	26	27	28	29	30	31

AUGUST
S	M	T	W	T	F	S
1	2	3	4	5	6	7
8	9	10	11	12	13	14
15	16	17	18	19	20	21
22	23	24	25	26	27	28
29	30	31				

SEPTEMBER
S	M	T	W	T	F	S
–	–	–	1	2	3	4
5	6	7	8	9	10	11
12	13	14	15	16	17	18
19	20	21	22	23	24	25
26	27	28	29	30		

OCTOBER
S	M	T	W	T	F	S
–	–	–	–	–	1	2
3	4	5	6	7	8	9
10	11	12	13	14	15	16
17	18	19	20	21	22	23
24	25	26	27	28	29	30
31						

NOVEMBER
S	M	T	W	T	F	S
–	1	2	3	4	5	6
7	8	9	10	11	12	13
14	15	16	17	18	19	20
21	22	23	24	25	26	27
28	29	30				

DECEMBER
S	M	T	W	T	F	S
–	–	–	1	2	3	4
5	6	7	8	9	10	11
12	13	14	15	16	17	18
19	20	21	22	23	24	25
26	27	28	29	30	31	–

A Reference Compendium
compiled by Mare-Anne Jarvela and Sarah Hale

Is It Raining, Drizzling, or Misting?

	Drops (per sq. ft. per sec.)	Diameter of Drops (mm)	Intensity (in. per hr.)
Cloudburst	113	2.85	4.00
Excessive rain	76	2.40	1.60
Heavy rain	46	2.05	.60
Moderate rain	46	1.60	.15
Light rain	26	1.24	.04
Drizzle	14	.96	.01
Mist	2,510	.10	.002
Fog	6,264,000	.01	.005

A Table Foretelling the Weather Through All the Lunations of Each Year (Forever)

This table is the result of many years of actual observation and shows what sort of weather will probably follow the Moon's entrance into any of its quarters. For example, the table shows that the week following May 11, 1998, will have frequent showers because the Moon becomes full that day at 10:29 A.M., EDT. (See Left-Hand Calendar Pages 60-86 for 1998 Moon phases.)

Editor's note: While the data in this table is taken into consideration in the yearlong process of compiling the annual long-range weather forecasts for _The Old Farmer's Almanac,_ we rely far more on our projections of solar activity.

Time of Change	Summer	Winter
Midnight to 2 A.M.	Fair	Hard frost, unless wind is south or west
2 A.M. to 4 A.M.	Cold, with frequent showers	Snow and stormy
4 A.M. to 6 A.M.	Rain	Rain
6 A.M. to 8 A.M.	Wind and rain	Stormy
8 A.M. to 10 A.M.	Changeable	Cold rain if wind is west; snow if east
10 A.M. to noon	Frequent showers	Cold with high winds
Noon to 2 P.M.	Very rainy	Snow or rain
2 P.M. to 4 P.M.	Changeable	Fair and mild
4 P.M. to 6 P.M.	Fair	Fair
6 P.M. to 10 P.M.	Fair if wind is northwest; rain if south or southwest	Fair and frosty if wind is north or northeast; rain or snow if wind is south or southwest
10 P.M. to midnight	Fair	Fair and frosty

This table was created more than 160 years ago by Dr. Herschell for the Boston Courier; _it first appeared in_ The Old Farmer's Almanac _in 1834._

Windchill Table

A s wind speed increases, the air temperature against your body falls. The combination of cold temperatures and high winds creates a cooling effect so severe that exposed flesh can freeze. (Inanimate objects, such as cars, do not experience windchill.)

To gauge wind speed: At 10 miles per hour, you can feel wind on your face; at 20, small branches move and dust or snow is raised; at 30, large branches move and wires whistle; at 40, whole trees bend. — *courtesy Mount Washington Observatory*

Wind Velocity (mph)	Temperature (° F)											
	50	41	32	23	14	5	−4	−13	−22	−31	−40	−49	−58
	Equivalent Temperature (° F) (Equivalent in cooling power on exposed flesh under calm conditions)											
5	48	39	28	19	10	1	−9	−18	−27	−36	−51	56	−65
10	41	30	18	7	−4	−15	−26	−36	−49	−60	−71	−81	−92
20	32	19	7	−6	−18	−31	−44	−58	−71	−83	−96	−108	−121
30	28	14	1	−13	−27	−40	−54	−69	−81	−96	−108	−123	137
40	27	12	−2	−17	−31	−45	−60	−74	−89	−103	−116	−130	−144
50	25	10	−4	−18	−33	−47	−62	−76	−90	−105	−119	−134	−148

Little Danger	Increasing Danger	Great Danger

Danger from freezing of exposed flesh (for properly clothed person)

Heat Index

A s humidity increases, the air temperature feels hotter to your skin. The combination of hot temperature and high humidity reduces your body's ability to cool itself. For example, the heat you feel when the actual temperature is 90 degrees Fahrenheit with a relative humidity of 70 percent is 106 degrees.

Humidity (%)	Temperature (° F)										
	70	75	80	85	90	95	100	105	110	115	120
	Equivalent Temperature (° F)										
0	64	69	73	78	83	87	91	95	99	103	107
10	65	70	75	80	85	90	95	100	105	111	116
20	66	72	77	82	87	93	99	105	112	120	130
30	67	73	78	84	90	96	104	113	123	120	148
40	68	74	79	86	93	101	110	123	137	135	
50	69	75	81	88	96	107	120	135	150		
60	70	76	82	90	100	114	132	149			
70	70	77	85	93	106	124	144				
80	71	78	86	97	113	136					
90	71	79	88	102	122						
100	72	80	91	108							

Average Monthly Temperatures for Selected U.S. Cities

Daily maximum (**bold numbers**) and minimum averages in degrees Fahrenheit

	JAN.	FEB.	MAR.	APR.	MAY	JUNE	JULY	AUG.	SEPT.	OCT.	NOV.	DEC.
Mobile,	**59.7**	**63.6**	**70.9**	**78.5**	**84.6**	**90.0**	**91.3**	**90.5**	**86.9**	**79.5**	**70.3**	**62.9**
Alabama	40.0	42.7	50.1	57.1	64.4	70.7	73.2	72.9	68.7	57.3	49.1	43.1
Anchorage,	**21.4**	**25.8**	**33.1**	**42.8**	**54.4**	**61.6**	**65.2**	**63.0**	**55.2**	**40.5**	**27.2**	**22.5**
Alaska	8.4	11.5	18.1	28.6	38.8	47.2	51.7	49.5	41.6	28.7	15.1	10.0
Phoenix,	**65.9**	**70.7**	**75.5**	**84.5**	**93.6**	**103.5**	**105.9**	**103.7**	**98.3**	**88.1**	**74.9**	**66.2**
Arizona	41.2	44.7	48.8	55.3	63.9	72.9	81.0	79.2	72.8	60.8	48.9	41.8
Little Rock,	**49.0**	**53.9**	**64.0**	**73.4**	**81.3**	**89.3**	**92.4**	**91.4**	**84.6**	**75.1**	**62.7**	**52.5**
Arkansas	29.1	33.2	42.2	50.7	59.0	67.4	71.5	69.8	63.5	50.9	41.5	33.1
San Francisco,	**55.6**	**59.4**	**60.8**	**63.9**	**66.5**	**70.3**	**71.6**	**72.3**	**73.6**	**70.1**	**62.4**	**56.1**
California	41.8	45.0	45.8	47.2	49.7	52.6	53.9	55.0	55.2	51.8	47.1	42.7
Denver,	**43.2**	**46.6**	**52.2**	**61.8**	**70.8**	**81.4**	**88.2**	**85.8**	**76.9**	**66.3**	**52.5**	**44.5**
Colorado	16.1	20.2	25.8	34.5	43.6	52.4	58.6	56.9	47.6	36.4	25.4	17.4
Hartford,	**33.2**	**36.4**	**46.8**	**59.9**	**71.6**	**80.0**	**85.0**	**82.7**	**74.8**	**63.7**	**51.0**	**37.5**
Connecticut	15.8	18.6	28.1	37.5	47.6	56.9	62.2	60.4	51.8	40.7	32.8	21.3
Washington,	**42.3**	**45.9**	**56.5**	**66.7**	**76.2**	**84.7**	**88.5**	**86.9**	**80.1**	**69.1**	**58.3**	**47.0**
D.C.	26.8	29.1	37.7	46.4	56.6	66.5	71.4	70.0	62.5	50.3	41.1	31.7
Miami,	**75.2**	**76.5**	**79.1**	**82.4**	**85.3**	**87.6**	**89.0**	**89.0**	**87.8**	**84.5**	**80.4**	**76.7**
Florida	59.2	60.4	64.2	67.8	72.1	75.1	76.2	76.7	75.9	72.1	66.7	61.5
Atlanta,	**50.4**	**55.0**	**64.3**	**72.7**	**79.6**	**85.8**	**88.0**	**87.1**	**81.8**	**72.7**	**63.4**	**54.0**
Georgia	31.5	34.5	42.5	50.2	58.7	66.2	69.5	69.0	63.5	51.9	42.8	35.0
Honolulu,	**80.1**	**80.5**	**81.6**	**82.8**	**84.7**	**86.5**	**87.5**	**88.7**	**88.5**	**86.9**	**84.1**	**81.2**
Hawaii	65.6	65.4	67.2	68.7	70.3	72.2	73.5	74.2	73.5	72.3	70.3	67.0
Boise,	**36.4**	**44.2**	**52.9**	**61.4**	**71.0**	**80.9**	**90.2**	**88.1**	**77.0**	**64.6**	**48.7**	**37.7**
Idaho	21.6	27.5	31.9	36.7	43.9	52.1	57.7	56.7	48.2	39.0	31.1	22.5
Chicago,	**29.0**	**33.5**	**45.8**	**58.6**	**70.1**	**79.6**	**83.7**	**81.8**	**74.8**	**63.3**	**48.4**	**34.0**
Illinois	12.9	17.2	28.5	38.6	47.7	57.5	62.6	61.6	53.9	42.2	31.6	19.1
Indianapolis,	**33.9**	**38.2**	**50.0**	**62.4**	**73.2**	**82.3**	**85.6**	**83.8**	**78.0**	**65.8**	**52.2**	**39.2**
Indiana	17.2	20.3	30.9	41.2	51.6	61.1	65.4	62.9	55.8	43.4	34.4	23.1
Des Moines,	**28.1**	**33.7**	**46.9**	**61.8**	**73.0**	**82.2**	**86.7**	**84.2**	**75.6**	**64.3**	**48.0**	**32.6**
Iowa	10.7	15.6	27.6	40.0	51.5	61.2	66.5	63.6	54.5	42.7	29.9	16.1
Wichita,	**39.8**	**45.9**	**57.2**	**68.3**	**76.9**	**86.8**	**92.8**	**90.7**	**81.4**	**70.6**	**55.3**	**43.0**
Kansas	19.2	23.7	33.6	44.5	54.3	64.6	69.9	67.9	81.4	46.6	33.9	23.0
Louisville,	**40.3**	**44.8**	**56.3**	**67.3**	**76.0**	**83.5**	**87.0**	**85.7**	**80.3**	**69.2**	**56.8**	**45.1**
Kentucky	23.2	26.5	36.2	45.4	54.7	62.9	67.3	65.8	58.7	45.8	37.3	28.6
New Orleans,	**61.3**	**64.5**	**71.8**	**78.7**	**84.5**	**89.4**	**90.8**	**90.5**	**87.1**	**80.0**	**71.5**	**64.8**
Louisiana	44.1	47.1	54.2	60.9	67.5	73.0	74.9	74.8	71.7	61.8	54.1	47.6
Portland,	**30.3**	**33.1**	**41.4**	**52.3**	**63.2**	**72.7**	**78.8**	**77.4**	**69.3**	**58.7**	**47.0**	**35.1**
Maine	11.4	13.5	24.5	34.1	43.4	52.1	58.3	57.1	48.9	38.3	30.4	17.8
Boston,	**35.7**	**37.5**	**45.8**	**55.9**	**66.6**	**76.3**	**81.8**	**79.8**	**72.8**	**62.7**	**52.2**	**40.4**
Massachusetts	21.6	23.0	31.3	40.2	49.8	59.1	65.1	64.0	56.8	46.9	38.3	26.7
Detroit,	**30.3**	**33.3**	**44.4**	**57.7**	**69.6**	**78.9**	**83.3**	**81.3**	**73.9**	**61.5**	**48.1**	**35.2**
Michigan	15.6	17.6	27.0	36.8	47.1	56.3	61.3	59.6	52.5	40.9	32.2	21.4
Minneapolis-	**20.7**	**26.6**	**39.2**	**56.5**	**69.4**	**78.8**	**84.0**	**80.7**	**70.7**	**58.8**	**41.0**	**25.5**
St. Paul, Minnesota	2.8	9.2	22.7	36.2	47.6	57.6	63.1	60.3	50.3	38.8	25.2	10.2

	JAN.	FEB.	MAR.	APR.	MAY	JUNE	JULY	AUG.	SEPT.	OCT.	NOV.	DEC.
Jackson,	55.6	60.1	69.3	77.4	84.0	90.6	92.4	92.0	88.0	79.1	69.2	59.5
Mississippi	32.7	35.7	44.1	51.9	60.0	67.1	70.5	69.7	63.7	50.3	42.3	36.1
St. Louis,	37.7	42.6	54.6	66.9	76.1	85.2	89.3	87.3	79.9	68.5	54.7	41.7
Missouri	20.8	25.1	35.5	46.4	56.0	65.7	70.4	69.7	60.5	48.3	37.7	26.0
Butte,	28.5	33.9	39.9	50.4	60.3	70.2	80.1	78.4	66.4	55.5	39.3	29.4
Montana	5.0	10.0	16.7	25.9	34.0	41.7	45.7	44.0	35.1	26.4	16.0	5.5
Omaha,	29.7	35.0	47.6	62.4	72.8	82.4	86.5	84.0	74.9	64.0	47.7	32.9
Nebraska	11.2	16.6	27.8	40.3	51.8	61.4	66.5	63.8	54.7	43.0	29.7	15.9
Reno,	45.1	51.7	56.3	63.7	72.9	83.1	91.9	89.6	79.5	68.6	53.8	45.5
Nevada	20.7	24.2	29.2	33.3	40.1	46.9	51.3	49.6	41.3	32.9	26.7	19.9
Albuquerque,	46.8	53.5	61.4	70.8	79.7	90.0	92.5	89.0	81.9	71.0	57.3	47.5
New Mexico	21.7	26.4	32.2	39.6	48.6	58.3	64.4	62.6	55.2	43.0	31.2	23.1
Buffalo,	30.2	31.6	41.7	54.2	66.1	75.3	80.2	77.9	70.8	59.4	47.1	35.3
New York	17.0	17.4	25.9	36.2	47.0	56.5	61.9	60.1	53.0	42.7	33.9	22.9
Charlotte,	49.0	53.0	62.3	71.2	78.3	85.8	88.9	87.7	81.9	72.0	62.6	52.3
North Carolina	29.6	31.9	39.4	47.5	56.4	65.6	69.6	68.9	62.9	50.6	41.5	32.8
Bismarck,	20.2	26.4	38.5	54.9	67.8	77.1	84.4	82.7	70.8	58.7	39.3	24.5
North Dakota	-1.7	5.1	17.8	31.0	42.2	51.6	56.4	53.9	43.1	32.5	17.8	3.3
Columbus,	34.1	38.0	50.5	62.0	72.3	80.4	83.7	82.1	76.2	64.5	51.4	39.2
Ohio	18.5	21.2	31.2	40.0	50.1	58.0	62.7	60.8	54.8	42.9	34.3	24.6
Tulsa,	45.4	51.0	62.1	73.0	79.7	87.7	93.7	92.5	83.8	73.8	60.3	48.8
Oklahoma	24.9	29.5	39.1	49.9	58.8	67.7	72.8	70.6	63.0	50.7	39.5	28.9
Portland,	45.4	51.0	56.0	60.6	67.1	74.0	79.9	80.3	74.6	64.0	52.6	45.6
Oregon	33.7	36.1	38.6	41.3	47.0	52.9	56.5	56.9	52.0	44.9	39.5	34.8
Philadelphia,	37.9	41.0	51.6	62.6	73.1	81.7	86.1	84.6	77.6	66.3	55.1	43.4
Pennsylvania	22.8	24.8	33.2	42.1	52.7	61.8	67.2	66.3	58.7	46.4	37.6	28.1
Charleston,	57.8	61.0	68.6	75.8	82.7	87.6	90.2	89.0	84.9	77.2	69.5	61.6
South Carolina	37.7	40.0	47.5	53.9	62.9	69.1	72.7	72.2	67.9	56.3	47.2	40.7
Huron,	24.1	29.7	42.1	58.6	70.4	80.3	87.1	84.8	74.2	61.5	43.0	28.3
South Dakota	2.3	9.1	21.7	34.0	44.8	55.5	61.7	58.8	47.3	35.4	21.8	7.8
Nashville,	45.9	50.8	61.2	70.8	78.8	86.5	89.5	88.4	82.5	72.6	60.4	50.2
Tennessee	26.5	29.9	39.1	47.5	56.6	64.7	68.9	67.7	61.1	48.3	39.6	30.9
Houston,	61.0	65.3	71.1	78.4	84.6	90.1	92.7	92.5	88.4	81.6	72.4	64.7
Texas	39.7	42.6	50.0	58.1	64.4	70.6	72.4	72.0	67.9	57.6	49.6	42.2
Salt Lake City,	36.4	43.6	52.2	61.3	71.9	82.8	92.2	89.4	79.2	66.1	50.8	37.8
Utah	19.3	24.6	31.4	37.9	45.6	55.4	63.7	61.8	51.0	40.2	30.9	21.6
Burlington,	25.1	27.5	39.3	53.6	67.2	75.8	81.2	77.9	69.0	57.0	44.0	30.4
Vermont	7.5	8.9	22.0	34.2	45.4	54.6	59.7	57.9	48.8	38.6	29.6	15.5
Richmond,	45.7	49.2	59.5	70.0	77.8	85.1	88.4	87.1	80.9	70.7	61.3	50.2
Virginia	25.7	28.1	36.3	44.6	54.2	62.7	67.5	66.4	59.0	46.5	37.9	29.9
Seattle-Tacoma,	45.0	49.5	52.7	57.2	63.9	69.9	75.2	75.2	69.3	59.7	50.5	45.1
Washington	35.2	37.4	38.5	41.2	46.3	51.9	55.2	55.7	51.9	45.8	40.1	35.8
Charleston,	41.2	45.3	56.7	66.8	75.5	83.1	85.7	84.4	78.8	68.2	57.3	46.0
West Virginia	23.0	25.7	35.0	42.8	51.5	59.8	64.4	63.4	56.5	44.2	36.3	28.0
Madison,	24.8	30.1	41.5	56.7	68.9	78.2	82.4	79.6	71.5	59.9	44.0	29.8
Wisconsin	7.2	11.1	23.0	34.1	44.2	54.2	59.5	56.9	48.2	37.7	26.7	13.5
Cheyenne,	37.7	40.5	44.9	54.7	64.6	74.4	82.2	80.0	71.1	60.0	46.8	38.8
Wyoming	15.2	18.1	22.1	30.1	39.4	48.3	54.6	52.8	43.7	33.9	23.7	16.7

(courtesy Dr. Richard Head and National Climatic Data Center)

Beaufort's Scale of Wind Speeds

"Used Mostly at Sea but of Help to all who are interested in the Weather"

A scale of wind velocity was devised by Admiral Sir Francis Beaufort of the British Navy in 1806. The numbers 0 to 12 were arranged by Beaufort to indicate the strength of the wind from a calm, force 0, to a hurricane, force 12. Here's a scale adapted to land.

Beaufort Force	Description	When You See This	mph	km/h
0	Calm	Smoke goes straight up. No wind.	less than 1	0-1.6
1	Light air	Direction of wind is shown by smoke drift but not by wind vane.	1-3	1.7-5
2	Light breeze	Wind felt on face. Leaves rustle. Wind vane moves.	4-7	6-11
3	Gentle breeze	Leaves and small twigs move steadily. Wind extends small flag straight out.	8-12	12-19
4	Moderate wind	Wind raises dust and loose paper. Small branches move.	13-18	21-29
5	Fresh breeze	Small trees sway. Waves form on lakes.	19-24	30-38
6	Strong wind	Large branches move. Wires whistle. Umbrellas are hard to use.	25-31	40-50
7	High wind	Whole trees are in motion. Hard to walk against the wind.	32-38	52-60
8	Gale	Twigs break from trees. Very hard to walk against wind.	39-46	62-72
9	Strong gale	Small damage to buildings. Roof shingles are removed.	47-54	74-87
10	Whole gale	Trees are uprooted.	55-63	88-101
11	Violent storm	Widespread damage from wind.	64-72	102-116
12	Hurricane	Widespread destruction from wind.	73+	117+

Winter Weather Terms

Winter Storm Watch

■ Possibility of a winter storm. Be alert to changing weather conditions. Avoid unnecessary travel.

Winter Storm Warning

■ A severe winter storm has started or is about to begin in the forecast area. You should stay indoors during the storm. If you must go outdoors, wear several layers of lightweight clothing, which will keep you warmer than a single heavy coat. In addition, wear gloves or mittens and a hat to prevent loss of body heat. Cover your mouth to protect your lungs.

Heavy Snow Warning

■ Snow accumulations are expected to approach or exceed six inches in 12 hours but will not be accompanied by significant wind. This warning could also be issued if eight inches or more of snow accumulation is expected in a 24-hour period. During a heavy snow warning, freezing rain and sleet are not expected.

Blizzard Warning

■ Sustained winds or frequent gusts of 35 miles per hour or greater will occur in combination with considerable falling and/or blowing snow for a period of at least three hours. Visibility will often be reduced to less than ¼ mile in a blizzard.

Ice Storm Warning

■ A significant coating of ice, ½ inch thick or more, is expected.

Windchill Warning

■ Windchills reach life-threatening levels of minus 50 degrees Fahrenheit or lower.

Windchill Advisory

■ Windchill factors fall between minus 35 and minus 50 degrees Fahrenheit.

Sleet

■ Frozen or partially frozen rain in the form of ice pellets hit the ground so fast they bounce off with a sharp click.

Freezing Rain

■ Rain falls as a liquid but turns to ice on contact with a frozen surface to form a smooth ice coating called glaze.

Hurricane Names for 1998

Alex	Earl	Jeanne	Nicole	Tomas
Bonnie	Frances	Karl	Otto	Virginie
Charley	Georges	Lisa	Paula	Walter
Danielle	Hermine	Mitch	Richard	
	Ivan		Shary	

Retired Hurricane Names

These are some of the most destructive and costly storms whose names have been retired from the six-year rotating hurricane list.

Year Retired	Name	Year Retired	Name
1970	Celia	1985	Elena
1972	Agnes	1985	Gloria
1974	Carmen	1988	Gilbert
1975	Eloise	1988	Joan
1977	Anita	1989	Hugo
1979	David	1990	Diana
1979	Frederic	1990	Klaus
1980	Allen	1991	Bob
1983	Alicia	1992	Andrew

Temperature Conversion Formulas

Fahrenheit to Celsius

To convert temperatures in degrees Fahrenheit to Celsius, subtract 32 and multiply by .5556 (or 5/9).
Example: (50° F - 32) x .5556 = 10° C

Celsius to Fahrenheit

To convert temperatures in degrees Celsius to Fahrenheit, multiply by 1.8 (or 9/5) and add 32.
Example: 30° C x 1.8 + 32 = 86° F

Cricket Chirps to Temperature

To convert cricket chirps to degrees Fahrenheit, count number of chirps in 14 seconds and add 40 to get temperature.
Example: 30 chirps + 40 = 70° F

To convert cricket chirps to degrees Celsius, count number of chirps in 25 seconds, divide by 3, and add 4 to get temperature.
Example: 48 chirps ÷ 3 + 4 = 20° C

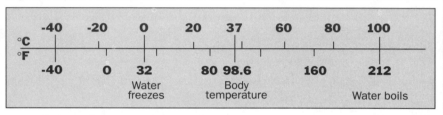

°C	-40	-20	0	20	37	60	80	100
°F	-40	0	32	80	98.6	160		212

Water freezes / Body temperature / Water boils

1" Water = How Much Snow?

	Water	Average Snow	Heavy, Wet Snow	Dry, Powdery Snow
Inches	1	10	4-5	15
Centimeters	2.5	25	10-13	38

Fujita Scale (or F Scale) for Tornadoes

This is a system developed by Dr. Theodore Fujita to classify tornadoes based on wind damage. All tornadoes, and most other severe local windstorms, are assigned a single number from this scale according to the most intense damage caused by the storm.

F0 (weak) . . . . 40- 72 mph, light damage
F1 (weak) . . . . 73-112 mph, moderate damage
F2 (strong) . . . . 113-157 mph, considerable damage
F3 (strong) . . . . 158-206 mph, severe damage
F4 (violent). . . . . 207-260 mph, devastating damage
F5 (violent). . . . . 261-318 mph, (rare) incredible damage

Month Names

JANUARY	Named for the Roman god Janus, protector of gates and doorways. Janus is depicted with two faces, one looking into the past, the other into the future.
FEBRUARY	From the Latin word *februare*, "to cleanse." The Roman Februalia was a month of purification and atonement.
MARCH	Named for the Roman god of war, Mars. This was the time of year to resume military campaigns that had been interrupted by winter.
APRIL	From the Latin word *aperire*, "to open (bud)," because plants begin to grow in this month.
MAY	Named for the Roman goddess Maia, who oversaw the growth of plants. Also from the Latin word *maiores*, meaning "elders," who were celebrated during this month.
JUNE	Named for the Roman goddess Juno, patroness of marriage and the well-being of women. Also from the Latin word *juvenis*, "young people."
JULY	Named to honor Roman dictator Julius Caesar (100 B.C.- 44 B.C.). In 46 B.C., Julius Caesar made one of his greatest contributions to history: With the help of Sosigenes, he developed the Julian calendar, the precursor to the Gregorian calendar we use today.
AUGUST	Named to honor the first Roman emperor (and grand-nephew of Julius Caesar), Augustus Caesar (63 B.C.-14 A.D.)
SEPTEMBER	From the Latin word *septem*, "seven," because this had been the seventh month of the early Roman calendar.
OCTOBER	From the Latin word *octo*, "eight," because this had been the eighth month of the early Roman calendar.
NOVEMBER	From the Latin word *novem*, "nine," because this had been the ninth month of the early Roman calendar.
DECEMBER	From the Latin word *decem*, "ten," because this had been the tenth month of the early Roman calendar.

Phases of the Moon

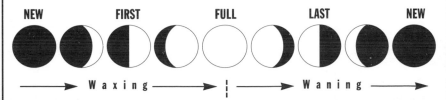

NEW   FIRST   FULL   LAST   NEW

W a x i n g | W a n i n g

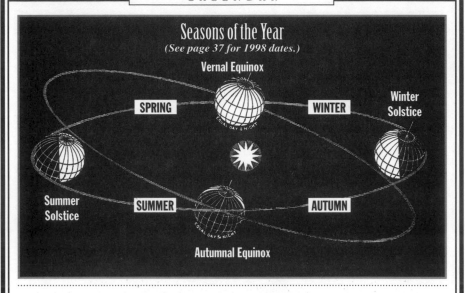

Seasons of the Year
(See page 37 for 1998 dates.)

Vernal Equinox

SPRING

WINTER

Winter Solstice

Summer Solstice

SUMMER

AUTUMN

Autumnal Equinox

☞ Glossary of Almanac Oddities

Many readers have expressed puzzlement over the rather obscure notations that appear on our Right-Hand Calendar Pages (pages 61-87). These "oddities" have long been fixtures in the Almanac, and we are pleased to provide some definitions. (Once explained, it would seem that they are not so odd after all!)

■ Ember Days (Movable)

The four periods set apart by the Roman Catholic and Anglican churches for special prayer and fasting and the ordination of clergy. The Ember Weeks are the complete weeks following 1) the First Sunday in Lent; 2) Pentecost (Whitsunday); 3) the Feast of the Holy Cross (September 14); and 4) the Feast of St. Lucy (December 13). The Wednesdays, Fridays, and Saturdays of these weeks are the Ember Days — days marked for fasting. (The word *ember* is thought to derive from an Old English term that refers to the revolution of time.)

Folklore has it that the weather on each of the three days foretells weather for three successive months — that is, in September Ember Days, Wednesday forecasts weather for October, Friday for November, and Saturday for December.

■ Plough Monday (January)

The first Monday after the Epiphany; so called because it was the end of the Christmas holidays, when men returned to their plough — or daily work. It was customary for farm laborers to draw a plough through the village, soliciting money for a "plough-light," which was kept burning in the parish church all year. In some areas, the custom of blessing the plough is maintained.

■ Three Chilly Saints (May)

Mammertius, Pancratius, and Gervatius, three early Christian saints, whose feast days occur on May 11, 12, and 13, respectively. Because these days are traditionally cold (an old French saying goes: "St. Mammertius, St. Pancras, and St. Gervais do not pass without a frost"), they have come to be known as the Three Chilly Saints.

■ Midsummer Day (June 24)

Although it occurs near the summer solstice, to the farmer it is the midpoint of the growing season, halfway between planting and harvest and an occasion for festivity. The English church considered it a "Quarter Day," one of the four major divisions of the liturgical year. It also marks the feast day of St. John the Baptist.

■ Cornscateous Air (July)

A term first used by the old almanac makers to signify warm, damp air. While it signals ideal climatic conditions for growing corn, it also poses a danger to those affected by asthma, pneumonia, and other respiratory problems.

■ Dog Days (July-August)

The hottest and most unhealthy days of the year. Also known as "Canicular Days," the name derives from the Dog Star, Sirius. The Almanac lists the traditional timing of Dog Days: The 40 days beginning July 3 and ending August 11, coinciding with the heliacal (at sunrise) rising of Sirius.

■ Cat Nights Begin (August)

The term harks back to the days when people believed in witches. An old Irish legend has it that a witch could turn herself into a cat eight  times and then regain herself, but on the ninth time — August 17 — she couldn't change back. Hence the saying, "A cat has nine lives." Since August is a "yowly" time for cats, this may have prompted the speculation about witches on the prowl in the first place.

■ Harvest Home (September)

In both Europe and Britain, the conclusion of the harvest each autumn was once marked by great festivals of fun, feasting, and thanksgiving known as "Harvest Home." It was also a time to hold elections, pay workers, and collect rents. These festivals usually took place around the time of the autumnal equinox. Certain ethnic groups in this country, particularly the Pennsylvania Dutch, have kept the tradition alive.

■ St. Luke's Little Summer (October)

A spell of warm weather occurring about the time of the saint's feast day, October 18. This period is sometimes referred to as "Indian Summer."

■ Indian Summer (November)

A period of warm weather following a cold spell or a hard frost. While there are differing dates for the time of occurrence, for 206 years the Almanac has adhered to the saying, "If All Saints brings out winter, St. Martin's brings out Indian Summer." Accordingly, Indian Summer can occur between St. Martin's Day (November 11) and November 20. As for the origin of the term, some say it comes from the early Indians, who believed the condition was caused by a warm wind sent from the court of their southwestern God, Cautantowwit.

■ Halcyon Days (December)

A period (about 14 days) of calm weather, following the blustery winds of autumn's end. The ancient Greeks and Romans believed them to occur around the time of the winter solstice when the halcyon, or kingfisher, was brooding. In a nest floating on the sea, the bird was said to have charmed the wind and waves so the waters were especially calm during this period.

■ Beware the Pogonip (December)

The word *pogonip* is a meteorological term used to describe an uncommon occurrence — frozen fog. The word was coined by American Indians to describe the frozen fogs of fine ice needles that occur in the mountain valleys of the western United States. According to Indian tradition, breathing the fog is injurious to the lungs.

Full Moon Names

H istorically, the Indians of what are now the northern and eastern United States kept track of the seasons by giving a distinctive name to each recurring full Moon, this name being applied to the entire month in which it occurred. With some variations, the same Moon names were used throughout the Algonquin tribes from New England to Lake Superior.

Name	Month	Other Names Used
Full Wolf Moon	January	Full Old Moon
Full Snow Moon	February	Full Hunger Moon
Full Worm Moon	March	Full Crow Moon, Full Crust Moon, Full Sugar Moon, Full Sap Moon
Full Pink Moon	April	Full Sprouting Grass Moon, Full Egg Moon, Full Fish Moon
Full Flower Moon	May	Full Corn Planting Moon, Full Milk Moon
Full Strawberry Moon	June	Full Rose Moon, Full Hot Moon
Full Buck Moon	July	Full Thunder Moon, Full Hay Moon
Full Sturgeon Moon	August	Full Red Moon, Full Green Corn Moon
Full Harvest Moon*	September	Full Corn Moon, Full Barley Moon
Full Hunter's Moon	October	Full Travel Moon, Full Dying Grass Moon
Full Beaver Moon	November	Full Frost Moon
Full Cold Moon	December	Full Long Nights Moon

* The Harvest Moon is always the full Moon closest to the autumnal equinox. If the Harvest Moon occurs in October, the September full Moon is usually called the Corn Moon.

How to Find the Day of the Week for Any Given Date

To compute the day of the week for any given date as far back as the mid-18th century, proceed as follows:

A dd the last two digits of the year to one-quarter of the last two digits (discard any remainder if it doesn't come out even), the given date, and the month key from the key box below. Divide the sum by 7; the number left over is the day of the week (1 is Sunday, 2 is Monday, and so on). If it comes out even, the day is Saturday. If you go back before 1900, add 2 to the sum before dividing; before 1800, add 4. Don't go back before 1753. From 2000 to 2099, subtract 1 from the sum before dividing.

Example: **The Dayton Flood was on Tuesday, March 25, 1913.**

Last two digits of year:	13
One-quarter of these two digits:	3
Given day of month:	25
Key number for March:	4
Sum:	45

45/7=6, with a remainder of 3. The flood took place on Tuesday, the third day of the week.

KEY	
January	1
leap year	0
February	4
leap year	3
March	4
April	0
May	2
June	5
July	0
August	3
September	6
October	1
November	4
December	6

Day Names

The Romans named the days of the week after the Sun, the Moon, and the five known planets. These names have survived in European languages, but English names also reflect an Anglo-Saxon influence.

Latin	French	Italian	Spanish	Saxon	English
Solis (Sun)	dimanche	domenica	domingo	Sun	Sunday
Lunae (Moon)	lundi	lunedì	lunes	Moon	Monday
Martis (Mars)	mardi	martedì	martes	Tiw (the Anglo-Saxon god of war, equivalent to the Norse Tyr or the Roman Mars)	Tuesday
Mercurii (Mercury)	mercredi	mercoledì	miércoles	Woden (the Anglo-Saxon equivalent to the Norse Odin, or the Roman Mercury)	Wednesday
Jovis (Jupiter)	jeudi	giovedì	jueves	Thor (the Norse god of thunder, equivalent to the Roman Jupiter)	Thursday
Veneris (Venus)	vendredi	venerdì	viernes	Frigg (the Norse god of love and fertility, the equivalent of the Roman Venus)	Friday
Saturni (Saturn)	samedi	sabato	sábado	Saterne (Saturn, the Roman god of agriculture)	Saturday

Easter Sunday (1998-2002)

Christian churches that follow the Gregorian calendar (Eastern Orthodox churches follow the Julian calendar) celebrate Easter on the first Sunday after the full Moon that occurs on or just after the vernal equinox.

In . . .	Easter will fall on . . .
1998	April 12
1999	April 4
2000	April 23
2001	April 15
2002	March 31

Triskaidekaphobia

Here are a few conclusions on Friday the 13th

Of the 14 possible configurations for the annual calendar (see any perpetual calendar), the occurrence of Friday the 13th is this:

- 6 of 14 years have one Friday the 13th.
  6 of 14 years have two Fridays the 13th.
  2 of 14 years have three Fridays the 13th.
  There is no year without one Friday the 13th, and no year with more than three.

- 1998 has three Fridays the 13th; the next year to have three Fridays the 13th is 2009.

- The reason we say "Fridays the 13th" is that no one can pronounce "Friday the 13ths."

Dining by the Calendar: Traditional Foods for Feasts and Fasts

JANUARY

Feast of the Circumcision: Black-eyed peas and pork (United States); oat-husk gruel or oatmeal porridge (Scotland).

Epiphany: Cake with a lucky bean baked in it; the one who finds the bean is the king or queen of the feast, in memory of the three wise men (France).

Robert Burns Day: Haggis — sheep's stomach stuffed with suet, chopped organ meat (heart, lungs, liver), onions, oatmeal, and seasonings (Scotland). Haggis is a traditional Scottish delicacy served on all holidays of national importance.

FEBRUARY

Candlemas Day: Pancakes eaten today will prevent hemorrhoids for a full year (French American).

St. Agatha: Round loaves of bread blessed by a priest (southern Europe).

Shrove Tuesday: Pancakes (England); oatcakes (Scotland); rabbit (Ireland). Rich foods are eaten to usher in the Lenten fast; pancakes use up the last of the eggs and butter.

Lent: Simnel, a large fruitcake baked so hard it has sometimes been mistaken by recipients for a hassock or footstool (Great Britain).

MARCH

St. David: Leeks, to be worn (Wales) or eaten raw (England). Recalls a Welsh victory over the Saxons in A.D. 640; the Welsh wore leeks in their hats to distinguish them from the enemy.

St. Benedict: Nettle soup (ancient monastic practice). Picking nettles, which irritate the skin, was a penance in keeping with the spirit of the monastic rule of St. Benedict.

Purim: Strong drink and three-cornered cookies flavored with poppy seed (Jewish). These cookies, called hamantaschen, are said to represent the three-cornered hat of Haman, the enemy of the Jewish people, whose downfall is celebrated on this holiday.

Maundy Thursday: Green foods or foods colored green (southern Europe). The medieval liturgical observance called for green vestments; in some parts of Europe, it is still called Green Thursday.

Good Friday: Hot cross buns. If made properly on this day, they will never get moldy (England).

APRIL

Easter: Lamb as symbol of sacrifice; ham.

Beltane, May Day Eve: Strong ale (England); oatcakes with nine knobs to be broken off one by one and offered to each of nine supernatural protectors of domestic animals (Scotland).

MAY

Ascension Day: Fowl, or pastries molded in the shape of birds, to commemorate the taking of Jesus into the skies (medieval Europe).

Whitsunday (Pentecost): Dove or pigeon in honor of the Holy Spirit (southern Europe); strong ale (England).

St. Dunstan: Beer. Cider pressed today will go bad (England).

Corpus Christi: Orange peel dipped in chocolate, chicken stuffed with sauerkraut (Basque Provinces).

JUNE

St. Anthony of Padua: Liver, possibly based on the pre-Christian custom of eating liver on the summer solstice.

Feast of St. John the Baptist: First fruits of spring harvest eaten.

JULY

St. Swithin: Eggs, because the saint miraculously restored intact a basket of eggs that had been broken by a poor woman taking them to market; he also looks after apples (medieval England).

St. James: Oysters, because James was a fisherman (England).

AUGUST

Lammas Day: Oatcakes (Scotland); loaves made from new grain of the season (England); toffee; seaweed pudding. Blueberries in baskets as an offering to a sweetheart are the last vestige of this holiday as a pagan fertility festival (Ireland).

St. Lawrence of Rome: Because the saint was roasted to death on a gridiron, it is courteous to serve only cold meat today (southern Europe).

Feast of the Assumption: Onions, possibly because they have always been considered wholesome and potent against evil (Polish American).

SEPTEMBER

St. Giles: Tea loaf with raisins (Scotland).

Nativity of Mary: Blackberries, possibly because the color is reminiscent of the depiction of the Virgin's blue cloak (Brittany).

Michaelmas Day: New wine (Europe); goose, originally a sacrifice to the saint (Great Britain); cake of oats, barley, and rye (Scotland); carrots (Ireland).

OCTOBER

Rosh Hashanah: Sweet foods; honey; foods colored orange or yellow to represent a bright, joyous, and sweet new year (Jewish).

Yom Kippur: Fast day; the day before, eat kreplach (filled noodles), considered by generations of mothers to be good and filling (Jewish).

St. Luke: Oatcakes flavored with anise and cinnamon (Scotland).

Sts. Simon and Jude: Dirge cakes, simple fried buns made for distribution to the poor. Also apples or potatoes, for divination (Scotland and England). Divination with apples is accomplished by peeling the fruit in one long strip and tossing the peel over one's shoulder. The letter formed by the peel is then interpreted.

All Hallows Eve: Apples and nuts for divination

(England); buttered oat-husk gruel (Scotland); bosty, a mixture of potatoes, cabbage, and onions (Ireland).

NOVEMBER

All Saints Day: Chestnuts (Italy); gingerbread and oatcakes (Scotland); milk (central Europe); doughnuts, whose round shape indicates eternity (Tyrol).

All Souls Day: Skull-shaped candy (Mexico); beans, peas, and lentils, considered food of the poor, as penance for souls in purgatory (southern Europe).

St. Martin: Last religious feast day before the beginning of the Advent fast. Goose, last of fresh-killed meat before winter; blood pudding (Great Britain).

St. Andrew: Haggis — stuffed sheep's stomach (Scotland).

DECEMBER

St. Nicholas: Fruit, nuts, candy for children (Germany). Commemorates, in part, the miracle by which the saint restored to life three young boys who had been murdered by a greedy innkeeper.

St. Lucy: Headcheese; cakes flavored with saffron or cardamom, raisins, and almonds (Sweden). The saffron imparts a yellow color to the cakes, representing sunlight, whose return is celebrated at the solstice.

Christmas: Boar's head or goose, plum pudding, nuts, oranges (England); turkey (United States); spiced beef (Ireland).

St. John the Evangelist: Small loaves of bread made with blessed wine (medieval Europe). This is a feast on which wine is ritually blessed in memory of the saint, who drank poisoned wine and miraculously survived.

Chanukah: Latkes — potato pancakes (Jewish).

Holy Innocents Day: Baby food, pablum, Cream of Wheat, in honor of the children killed by King Herod of Judea (monastic observance).

St. Sylvester: Strong drink (United States); haggis, oatcakes and cheese, oat-husk gruel or porridge (Scotland).   *— E. Brady*

Chinese Zodiac

The animal designations of the Chinese zodiac follow a 12-year cycle and are always used in the same sequence. The Chinese year of 354 days begins three to seven weeks into the western 365-day year, so the animal designation changes at that time, rather than on January 1.

RAT

Ambitious and sincere, you can be generous with your financial resources. Compatible with the dragon and the monkey. Your opposite is the horse.

1900	1960
1912	1972
1924	1984
1936	1996
1948	2008

RABBIT (HARE)

Talented and affectionate, you are a seeker of tranquility. Compatible with the sheep and the pig. Your opposite is the rooster.

1903	1963
1915	1975
1927	1987
1939	1999
1951	2011

HORSE

Physically attractive and popular, you like the company of others. Compatible with the tiger and the dog. Your opposite is the rat.

1906	1966
1918	1978
1930	1990
1942	2002
1954	2014

ROOSTER (COCK)

Seeking wisdom and truth, you have a pioneering spirit. Compatible with the snake and the ox. Your opposite is the rabbit.

1909	1969
1921	1981
1933	1993
1945	2005
1957	2017

OX (BUFFALO)

A leader, you are bright and cheerful. Compatible with the snake and the rooster. Your opposite is the sheep.

1901	1961
1913	1973
1925	1985
1937	1997
1949	2009

DRAGON

Robust and passionate, your life is filled with complexity. Compatible with the monkey and the rat. Your opposite is the dog.

1904	1964
1916	1976
1928	1988
1940	2000
1952	2012

SHEEP (GOAT)

Aesthetic and stylish, you enjoy being a private person. Compatible with the pig and the rabbit. Your opposite is the ox.

1907	1967
1919	1979
1931	1991
1943	2003
1955	2015

DOG

Generous and loyal, you have the ability to work well with others. Compatible with the horse and the tiger. Your opposite is the dragon.

1910	1970
1922	1982
1934	1994
1946	2006
1958	2018

TIGER

Forthright and sensitive, you possess great courage. Compatible with the horse and the dog. Your opposite is the monkey.

1902	1962
1914	1974
1926	1986
1938	1998
1950	2010

SNAKE

Strong-willed and intense, you display great wisdom. Compatible with the rooster and the ox. Your opposite is the pig.

1905	1965
1917	1977
1929	1989
1941	2001
1953	2013

MONKEY

Persuasive and intelligent, you strive to excel. Compatible with the dragon and the rat. Your opposite is the tiger.

1908	1968
1920	1980
1932	1992
1944	2004
1956	2016

PIG (BOAR)

Gallant and noble, your friends will remain at your side. Compatible with the rabbit and the sheep. Your opposite is the snake.

1911	1971
1923	1983
1935	1995
1947	2007
1959	2019

Planning Your Garden

Sow or plant in cool weather	Beets/chard, cabbage, broccoli, brussels sprouts, lettuce, onions, parsley, peas, radishes, spinach, turnips
Sow or plant in warm weather	Beans, carrots, corn, cucumbers, eggplant, peppers, squash tomatoes, melons, okra
One crop per season	Corn, eggplant, melons, leeks, peppers, tomatoes, summer squash, winter squash, New Zealand spinach, potatoes
Resow for additional crops	Beans, beets, carrots, cabbage family, kohlrabi, lettuce, radishes, rutabagas, spinach, turnips

Vegetable Seeds Best Sown in the Ground

Beans, bush and pole	Endive	Radishes
Beets	Kale	Spinach
Carrots	Kohlrabi	Squash, summer and
Collards	Mustard greens	winter
Corn	Parsnips	Swiss chard
Cucumbers	Peas	Turnips
	Potatoes	

Vegetables and Herbs Best Started Indoors

Seeds	Weeks before last frost in spring
Basil	6
Broccoli	6-8
Brussels sprouts	4-8
Cabbage	6-8
Cauliflower	6-8
Celeriac	6-8
Celery	6-8
Chives	8-12
Eggplant	8-10
Leeks	8-12
Lettuce	4-6
Onions	10-12
Parsley	8
Peppers	8-10
Sweet marjoram	8
Tomatoes	6-8

Herb Companions in the Garden and Kitchen

Herbs are great companions to food in your culinary masterpieces, and they are great companions in the garden, too.

Anise

In the garden: Plant with coriander, which promotes its germination and growth.

In the kitchen: Use in cookies, cakes, fruit fillings, and breads, or with cottage cheese, shellfish, and spaghetti dishes.

Basil

In the garden: Plant with tomatoes. Repels flies and mosquitoes.

In the kitchen: Use in tomato dishes, pesto, sauces, and salad dressings.

Borage

In the garden: Plant with tomatoes, squash, and strawberries. Deters tomato worm.

In the kitchen: Use leaves in salads; flowers in soups and stews.

Caraway

In the garden: Plant here and there. Loosens soil.

In the kitchen: Use in rye breads, cheese dips and rarebits, soups, applesauce, salads, coleslaw, and over pork or sauerkraut.

Chervil

In the garden: Plant with radishes.

In the kitchen: Use with soups, salads, sauces, eggs, fish, veal, lamb, and pork.

Chives

In the garden: Plant with carrots.

In the kitchen: Related to the onion, chives enliven vegetable dishes, dressings, casseroles, rice, eggs, cheese dishes, sauces, gravies, and dips.

Dill

In the garden: Plant with cabbages. Keep away from carrots.

In the kitchen: Use seed for pickles and also to add aroma and taste to strong vegetables like cauliflower, cabbage, and turnips. Use fresh with green beans, potato dishes, cheese, soups, salads, seafood, and sauces.

Fennel

In the garden: Plant away from other herbs and vegetables.

In the kitchen: Use to flavor pastries, confectionery, sweet pickles, sausages, tomato dishes, soups, and to flavor vinegars and oils. Gives warmth and sweetness to curries.

Garlic

In the garden: Plant near roses and raspberries. Deters Japanese beetle.

In the kitchen: Use in tomato dishes, garlic bread, soups, dips, sauces, marinades, or with meats, poultry, fish, and vegetables.

Lovage

In the garden: Plant here and there to improve the health and flavor of other plants.

In the kitchen: It's a great flavoring for soups, stews, and salad dressings. Goes well with potatoes. The seeds can be used on breads and biscuits.

Marjoram

In the garden: Good companion to all vegetables.

In the kitchen: Excellent in almost any meat, fish, dairy, or vegetable dish that isn't sweet. Add near the end of cooking.

Mint

In the garden: Plant near cabbage and tomatoes. Deters white cabbage moth.

In the kitchen: It is common in Middle Eastern dishes. Use with roast lamb or fish and in salads, jellies, or teas.

Oregano

In the garden: Good companion to all vegetables.

In the kitchen: Of Italian origin, its taste is zesty and strong, good in any tomato dish. Try oregano with summer squash and potatoes, mushroom dishes, beans, or in a marinade for lamb or game.

Parsley

In the garden: Plant near asparagus, corn, and tomatoes.

In the kitchen: Use fresh parsley in soups, sauces, and salads. It lessens the need for salt in soups. You can fry parsley and use it as a side dish with meat or fish. It is, of course, the perfect garnish.

Rosemary

In the garden: Plant near cabbage, beans, carrots, and sage. Deters cabbage moth, bean beetles, and carrot fly.

In the kitchen: Use for poultry, lamb, and tomato dishes, stews, soups, and vegetables. Try it finely chopped in breads and custards.

Sage

In the garden: Plant near rosemary, cabbage, and carrots; away from cucumbers. Deters cabbage moth and carrot fly.

In the kitchen: Use in cheese dishes, stuffings, soups, pickles, with beans and peas, and in salads. Excellent for salt-free cooking.

Summer Savory

In the garden: Plant with beans and onions to improve growth and flavor.

In the kitchen: Popular in soups, stews, stuffings, and with fish, chicken, green beans, and eggs.

Tarragon

In the garden: Good companion to most vegetables.

In the kitchen: Great with meat, eggs, poultry, seafood, and in salad dressings, marinades, and sauces.

Thyme

In the garden: Plant near cabbage. Deters cabbage worm.

In the kitchen: Use in casseroles, stews, soups, ragouts, and with eggs, potatoes, fish, and green vegetables.

Herbs to Plant in Lawns

Choose plants that suit your soil and your climate. All these can withstand mowing and considerable foot traffic.

- Ajuga or bugleweed (*Ajuga reptans*)
- Roman chamomile (*Chamaemelum nobile*)
- Dwarf cinquefoil (*Potentilla tabernaemontani*)
- Corsican mint (*Mentha requienii*)
- English pennyroyal (*Mentha pulegium*)
- Thyme (*Thymus serpyllum*)
- Pearly everlasting (*Anaphalis margaritacea*)
- Rupturewort (*Herniaria glabra*)
- Speedwell (*Veronica officinalis*)
- White clover (*Trifolium repens*)
- Wild strawberries (*Fragaria virginiana*)
- Sweet violets (*Viola odorata* or *tricolor*)
- Wintergreen or partridgeberry (*Mitchella repens*)
- Green Irish moss (*Sagiona subulata*)
- Stonecrop (*Sedum ternatum*)

Heat-Loving Wildflowers

Asclepias tuberosa (butterfly weed)

Baptisia (wild indigo)

Echinacea purpurea (purple coneflower)

Liatris (blazing star)

Mirabilis (four-o'clock)

Monarda (bee balm)

Ratibida pinnata (prairie coneflower)

Rudbeckia (black-eyed Susan)

Herbs That Attract Butterflies

Dill . . . . *Anethum graveolens*

Catmint . . . . *Nepeta*

Sweet marjoram . . *Origanum majorana*

Mint . . . . *Mentha*

Oregano . . . . *Origanum vulgare*

Parsley . . . . *Petroselinum crispum*

Mealy-cup sage . . . . . . *Salvia farinacea*

Creeping thyme . . . . *Thymus serpyllum*

Flowers That Attract Butterflies

Allium . . . . *Allium*	Helen's flower *Helenium*	Purple coneflower
Aster . . . . *Aster*	Hollyhock . . . . *Alcea*	. . . . *Echinacea*
Bee balm . . . . . . *Monarda*	Honeysuckle . . . . *Lonicera*	Purple loosestrife . *Lythrum*
Butterfly bush . . *Buddleia*	Lavender . . . . . *Lavendula*	Rock cress . . . . *Arabis*
Clove pink . . . . . *Dianthus*	Lilac . . . . *Syringa*	Sea holly . . . . *Eryngium*
Cornflower . . . . *Centaurea*	Lupine . . . . *Lupinus*	Shasta daisy *Chrysanthemum*
Daylily . . . . *Hemerocallis*	Lychnis . . . . *Lychnis*	Snapdragon . . *Antirrhinum*
False indigo . . . . . *Baptisia*	Mallow . . . . *Malva*	Stonecrop . . . . *Sedum*
Fleabane . . . . *Erigeron*	Milkweed . . . . . . *Asclepias*	Sweet alyssum . . *Lobularia*
Floss flower . . *Ageratum*	Pansy . . . . *Viola*	Sweet rocket . . . . . *Hesperis*
Globe thistle . . . . *Echinops*	Phlox . . . . *Phlox*	Tickseed . . . . *Coreopsis*
Goldenrod . . . . . *Solidago*	Privet . . . . *Ligustrum*	Zinnia . . . . *Zinnia*

Flowers That Attract Hummingbirds

	Flag . . . . *Iris*
	Flowering tobacco . . . . . . *Nicotiana alata*
	Foxglove . . . . *Digitalis*
	Larkspur . . . . *Delphinium*
	Lily . . . . *Lilium*
	Lupine . . . . *Lupinus*
	Petunia . . . . *Petunia*
	Pincushion flower . . . . *Scabiosa*
	Red-hot poker . . . . *Kniphofia*
Beard tongue . . . . *Penstemon*	Scarlet sage . . . . *Salvia splendens*
Bee balm . . . . *Monarda*	Scarlet trumpet
Butterfly bush . . . . *Buddleia*	honeysuckle . . . . *Lonicera sempervirens*
Catmint . . . . *Nepeta*	Soapwort . . . . *Saponaria*
Clove pink . . . . *Dianthus*	Summer phlox . . . . *Phlox paniculata*
Columbine . . . . *Aquilegia*	Verbena . . . . *Verbena*
Coral bells . . . . *Heuchera*	Weigela . . . . *Weigela*
Daylily . . . . *Hemerocallis*	
Desert candle . . . . *Yucca*	**Note: Choose varieties in red and orange shades.**

Forcing Bulbs Indoors

The technique is simple. Plant bulbs in pots of rich soil so tips are just even with pot rims. Store in cold frame, cellar, or refrigerator at a cold temperature for two to several months. Water bulbs just enough to keep them from drying out. When roots can be seen poking out through bottoms of pots, bring them into a lighted room to flower.

The table below shows estimated times for rooting and ideal temperatures for flowering for some of the most common spring bulbs.

Name of Bulb	Time for Rooting	Temperature for Flowering
Chionodoxa (glory-of-the-snow)	10-14 weeks	55-60° F
Convallaria (lily-of-the-valley)	10-12 weeks	60-65° F
Crocus (crocus)	8-12 weeks	55-60° F
Freesia (freesia)	8-12 weeks	50-55° F
Galanthus (snowdrop)	9-12 weeks	55-60° F
Hyacinthus (hyacinth)	8-10 weeks	55-60° F
Iris reticulata (netted iris)	10-14 weeks	55-60° F
Muscari (grape hyacinth)	10-12 weeks	55-60° F
Narcissus (daffodil)	10-12 weeks	50-60° F
Puschkinia (striped squill)	8-12 weeks	50-55° F
Scilla (squill)	12-16 weeks	55-60° F
Tulipa (tulip)	12-16 weeks	55-60° F

Spring-Flowering Bulbs

These bulbs, planted in the fall, will be welcome heralds of spring.

	Planting Depth (inches)	Flower Height (inches)		Planting Depth (inches)	Flower Height (inches)
Early Spring Blooms			**Mid-Spring Blooms**		
Galanthus (snowdrop)	5	6	Daffodil	8	20
Crocus	5	6	Darwin hybrid tulip	8	28
Anemone blanda (Grecian windflower)	5	6	Fritillaria imperialis (crown imperial)	8	40
Muscari (grape hyacinth)	5	10	**Late Spring Blooms**		
Greigii tulip	8	14	Spanish bluebell	5	10
Hyacinth	8	14	Dutch iris	8	24
			Late tulip	8	32
			Allium giganteum (ornamental onion)	8	50

Forcing Indoor Blooms

Here is a list of shrubs and some trees that can be forced to flower indoors. (The trees tend to be stubborn, and their blossoms may not be as rewarding as those of the shrubs.) The numbers indicate the approximate number of weeks they will take to flower.

Buckeye	5	Lilac	4
Cherry	4	Magnolia	3
Cornelian dogwood	2	Pussy willow	2
Crab apple	4	Red maple	2
Deutzia	3	Redbud	2
Flowering almond	3	Red-twig dogwood	5
Flowering dogwood	5	Spicebush	2
Flowering quince	4	Spirea	4
Forsythia	1	Wisteria	3
Honeysuckle	3		
Horse chestnut	5		

Source: Purdue University Cooperative Extension Service

Houseplant Harmonies

Experiments conducted in a controlled environment during the 1960s and 1970s suggest that you may want to consider the health and well-being of your houseplants when making musical selections.

Type of Music / Effect on Plant Growth

Type of Music	Effect on Plant Growth
Classical	Lush and abundant growth; good root development
Indian Devotional	Lush and abundant growth; good root development
Country	No abnormal growth reaction
Silence	No abnormal growth reaction
Jazz	Abundant growth
Rock 'n' Roll	Poor growth; roots scrawny and sparse
White Noise	Plants died quickly

Perennials for Cutting Gardens

Aster (*Aster*)

Baby's-breath (*Gypsophila*)

Bellflower (*Campanula*)

Black-eyed Susan (*Rudbeckia*)

Blanket flower (*Gaillardia*)

Chrysanthemum (*Chrysanthemum*)

Delphinium (*Delphinium*)

False sunflower (*Heliopsis*)

Flowering onion (*Allium*)

Foxglove (*Digitalis*)

Gay-feather (*Liatris*)

Globe thistle (*Echinops*)

Goldenrod (*Solidago*)

Iris (*Iris*)

Lavender (*Lavandula*)

Meadow rue (*Thalictrum*)

Peony (*Paeonia*)

Phlox (*Phlox*)

Purple coneflower (*Echinacea*)

Sea holly (*Eryngium*)

Speedwell (*Veronica*)

Tickseed (*Coreopsis*)

Yarrow (*Achillea*)

THE GARDEN

When Is a Good Time to Fertilize Your Vegetables?

Crop	Time of Application
Asparagus	Before growth starts in spring
Beans	After heavy blossom and set of pods
Broccoli	Three weeks after transplanting
Cabbage	Three weeks after transplanting
Cauliflower	Three weeks after transplanting
Corn	When eight to ten inches tall and again when silk first appears
Cucumber	One week after blossoming and again three weeks later
Eggplant	After first fruit-set
Kale	When plants are one-third grown
Lettuce, Head	Two to three weeks after transplanting
Muskmelon	One week after blossoming and again three weeks later
Onions	When bulbs begin to swell and again when plants are one foot tall
Peas	After heavy bloom and set of pods
Peppers	After first fruit-set
Potatoes	At blossom time or time of second hilling
Spinach	When plants are one-third grown
Squash	Just before vines start to run, when plants are about one foot tall
Tomatoes	One to two weeks before first picking and again two weeks after first picking
Watermelon	Just before vines start to run, when plants are about one foot tall

Manure Guide

Type of Manure	Water Content	Primary Nutrients (pounds per ton)		
		Nitrogen	Phosphate	Potash
Cow, horse	60%-80%	12-14	5-9	9-12
Sheep, pig, goat	65%-75%	10-21	7	13-19
Chicken: Wet, sticky, and caked	75%	30	20	10
Moist, crumbly to sticky	50%	40	40	20
Crumbly	30%	60	55	30
Dry	15%	90	70	40
Ashed	none	none	135	100

Type of Garden	Best Type of Manure	Best Time to Apply
Flower	Cow, horse	Early spring
Vegetable	Chicken, cow, horse	Fall, spring
Potato or root crop	Cow, horse	Fall
Acid-loving plants (blueberries, azaleas, mountain laurel, rhododendrons)	Cow, horse	Early fall or not at all

General Rules for Pruning

What	When	How
Apple	Early spring	Prune moderately. Keep tree open with main branches well spaced. Avoid sharp V-shaped crotches.
Cherry	Early spring	Prune the most vigorous shoots moderately.
Clematis	Spring	Cut weak growth. Save as much old wood as possible.
Flowering dogwood	After flowering	Remove dead wood only.
Forsythia	After flowering	Remove old branches at ground. Trim new growth.
Lilac	After flowering	Remove diseased, scaly growth, flower heads, and suckers.
Peach	Early spring	Remove half of last year's growth. Keep tree headed low.
Plum	Early spring	Cut dead, diseased branches; trim rank growth moderately.
Rhododendron	After flowering	Prune judiciously. Snip branches from weak, leggy plants to induce growth from roots.
Roses (except climbers)	Spring, after frosts	Cut dead and weak growth; cut branches or canes to four or five eyes.
Roses, climbers	After flowering	Cut half of old growth; retain new shoots for next year.
Rose of Sharon	When buds begin	Cut all winter-killed wood to swell growth back to live wood.
Trumpet vine	Early spring	Prune side branches severely to main stem.
Virginia creeper	Spring	Clip young plants freely. Thin old plants and remove dead growth.
Wisteria	Spring, summer	Cut new growth to spurs at axils of leaves.

Symbolic Meanings of Herbs and Plants

Aloe . . . . Healing, protection, affection
Angelica . . . . Inspiration
Arbor vitae . . . . Unchanging friendship
Bachelor's button . . . . Single blessedness
Basil . . . . Good wishes, love
Bay . . . . Glory
Black-eyed Susan . . . . Justice
Carnation . . . . Alas for my poor heart
Chamomile . . . . Patience
Chives . . . . Usefulness
Clover, white . . . . Think of me
Coriander . . . . Hidden worth
Cumin . . . . Fidelity
Fennel . . . . Flattery
Fern . . . . Sincerity
Geranium, oak-leaved . . . . True friendship
Goldenrod . . . . Encouragement
Heliotrope . . . . Eternal love
Holly . . . . Hope

Hollyhock . . . . Ambition
Honeysuckle . . . . Bonds of love
Horehound . . . . Health
Hyssop . . . . Sacrifice, cleanliness
Ivy . . . . Friendship, continuity
Lady's mantle . . . . Comforting
Lavender . . . . Devotion, virtue
Lemon balm . . . . Sympathy
Marjoram . . . . Joy, happiness
Mint . . . . Eternal refreshment
Morning glory . . . . Affection
Nasturtium . . . . Patriotism
Oak . . . . Strength
Oregano . . . . Substance
Pansy . . . . Thoughts
Parsley . . . . Festivity
Pine . . . . Humility
Poppy, red . . . . Consolation
Rose . . . . Love

Rosemary	Remembrance	Tansy	Hostile thoughts
Rue	Grace, clear vision	Tarragon	Lasting interest
Sage	Wisdom, immortality	Thyme	Courage, strength
Salvia, blue	I think of you	Valerian	Readiness
Salvia, red	Forever mine	Violet	Loyalty, devotion
Savory	Spice, interest	Violet, blue	Faithfulness
Sorrel	Affection	Violet, yellow	Rural happiness
Southernwood	Constancy, jest	Willow	Sadness
Sweet pea	Pleasures	Zinnia	Thoughts of absent friends
Sweet woodruff	Humility		

Fall Palette

TREE	COLOR
Sugar maple and sumac	Flame red and orange
Red maple, dogwood, sassafras, and scarlet oak	Dark red
Poplar, birch, tulip tree, willow	Yellow
Ash	Plum purple
Oak, beech, larch, elm, hickory, and sycamore	Tan or brown
Locust	Stays green (until leaves drop)
Black walnut and butternut	Drops leaves before turning color

Vegetable Gardening in Containers

Lack of yard space is no excuse for not gardening, since many vegetables can be readily grown in containers. In addition to providing five hours or more of full sun, attention must be given to choosing the proper container, using a good soil mix, planting and spacing requirements, fertilizing, watering, and variety selection.

VEGETABLE	TYPE OF CONTAINER	RECOMMENDED VARIETIES
Beans, snap	5-gallon window box	Bush 'Romano', Bush 'Blue Lake', 'Tender Crop'
Broccoli	1 plant/5-gallon pot 3 plants/15-gallon tub	'Green Comet', 'DeCicco'
Carrot	5-gallon window box at least 12 inches deep	'Short 'n Sweet', 'Danvers Half Long', 'Tiny Sweet'
Cucumber	1 plant/1-gallon pot	'Patio Pik', 'Spacemaster', 'Pot Luck'
Eggplant	5-gallon pot	'Slim Jim', 'Ichiban', 'Black Beauty'
Lettuce	5-gallon window box	'Salad Bowl', 'Ruby'
Onion	5-gallon window box	'White Sweet Spanish', 'Yellow Sweet Spanish'
Pepper	1 plant/2-gallon pot 5 plants/15-gallon tub	'Sweet Banana', 'Yolo', 'Wonder', 'Long Red', 'Cayenne'
Radish	5-gallon window box	'Cherry Belle', 'Icicle'
Tomatoes	Bushel basket	'Tiny Tim', 'Small Fry', 'Early Girl', 'Sweet 100', 'Patio'

Courtesy North Carolina Cooperative Extension Service

How to Speak Plant Latin

by Mary Cornog

You don't have to delve very deeply into gardening to realize that those mysterious Latin (and latinized Greek) names that appear in italics in catalogs and on plant labels are as important in identifying specific plants as your own name is in identifying you.

The translation of the scientific name of a familiar plant gives clues to the history and original uses of the plant. *Paeonia officinalis,* a member of the large peony family, is an old-fashioned single red peony that has long been in cultivation and once had medicinal (*officinalis*) applications.

Carl Linnaeus, the Swedish naturalist, began the modern system of classification and Latin nomenclature in the 18th century. Linnaeus gave each plant a permanent set of names drawn from early Greek and Latin efforts (some as old as Aristotle) that indicate genus, species, and sometimes variety.

In 1867, scientists began to formulate an International Code of Botanical Nomenclature, an intricate set of rules for identifying and naming all living things. The scientific name of even the most modern genetically engineered variety has this highly structured code and centuries of precedence behind it.

The list that follows is no substitute for a schooling in the classics but will help gardeners decipher catalogs and make good choices about plants. All terms are Latin unless followed by a (G) for Greek.

How to Pronounce Botanical Latin and Wow Your Local Plant Supplier

Pronunciation of Latin plant names follows general English pronunciation, with few exceptions. To give a few examples:

Senecio cineraria =
seh-né-see-oh sï-ne-rá-ri-a (dusty miller)

Salvia officinalis =
sál-vi-a of-fi-shi-ná-lis (common sage)

Cardiocrinum giganteum =
car-di-o-crí-num ji-gán-te-um
(giant Himalayan lily)

Centaurea cyanus =
sen-táur-e-a si-á-nus (cornflower)

-ae = long e
ch = k
c = s before i, e, y; = k before a, o, u
g = hard before a, o, u; = soft (j) before i, e, y

Accent: In two-syllable words, the accent falls on the first syllable. For longer words, it generally falls, as in English, on the second-last (penultimate) syllable of the word if that syllable is long (e.g., for-mó-sus), and on the third-last (antepenultimate) syllable if the second-last is short (e.g., fló-ri-dus).

A Brief Glossary of Terms Commonly Used in Plant Names

acanthus thorn (G)
aestivalis summer
alatus winged
altus tall
amoenus harmless, charming
angustifolius narrow-leaved
arborenscens treelike
asper rough
aureus golden
australis southern
autumnalis of autumn
baccatus berry- or pearl-like
barbatus bearded or barbed
bellus beautiful
borealis northern (G)
brevis short
caeruleus blue
campanulatus bell-shaped
campestris growing in fields
candidus white
canescens grayish
capillaris hairlike
cardinalis bright red
carneus flesh-colored
caudatus tailed
cinnamomeus cinnamon brown
coccineus scarlet
cordatus heart-shaped
coriaceus leathery
corniculatus horned
cuneifolius wedge-shaped leaves
cyaneus blue (G)
dactyloides finger-shaped (G)
didymus in pairs (G)
digitatus finger-shaped
dulcis sweet
echinatus spiny, bristly (G)
edulis edible
elatus tall
erythrocarpus red-fruited (G)
esculentus edible
fasciculatus clustered, bundled
ferrugineus rust-colored

flavens yellowish
fulvus brownish yellow
germinatus twin
gibbosus humped, swollen on one side
glabratus smooth
glaucescens becoming bluish- or greenish-gray (G)
hastatus spear-shaped
heterophyllus with leaves of several shapes (G)
hirsutus hairy or shaggy
humifusus sprawling
humilis dwarf
inodorus without odor
junceus rushlike
kewensis relating to Kew Gardens
labiatus lipped
lacteus milky
laevigatus smooth
lanosus woolly
latiflorus broad-flowered
laxiflorus loose-flowered
leucanthus white-flowered (G)
lignosus like wood
limosus of muddy places
lucidus shiny
luteus muddy yellow
macrophyllus large-leaved (G)
maculatus spotted
microcarpus small-fruited (G)
mirabilis wonderful
nanus dwarf (G)
natans floating
nemoralis growing in woods
niger black
nitens shining
niveus snow-white
noctiflorens night-flowering
nyctagineus night-flowering (G)
occidentalis western
officinalis a formerly recognized medicinal
oleraceus from a vegetable garden

pallens pale
paludosus marshy
parviflorens small-flowering
patens spreading
pauciflorus few-flowered
pratensis growing in meadows
pubens downy
pumilus dwarf, small
puniceus reddish-purple
quadrifolius four-leaved
quinquefolius five-leaved
radicans rooting
regalis royal
repens creeping
reptans crawling
reticulans netlike
riparius growing near a river
roseus rose-colored
rubens red
ruderalis growing among rubbish
rugosus wrinkled
sativus cultivated
scandens climbing
sericeus silky
setosus bristly
speciosus beautiful
spinosus with spines
stellatus starlike
stramineus straw-colored
strigosus stiff-bristled
tenuis slender
tinctorius used for dyeing
tomentosus like felt
tuberosus with tubers
urens stinging
vacillans swaying
velutinus velvety
vernalis spring-flowered
verus true
villosus with soft hairs
violaceus violet
viridis green
vulgaris common
xanthinus yellow (G)

How Much Water Is Enough?

When confronted with a dry garden and the end of a hose, many gardeners admit to a certain insecurity about just how much water those plants really need. Here's a guide to help you estimate when and how much to water, assuming rich, well-balanced soil. Increase frequency during hot, very dry periods.

Vegetable	Critical time(s) to water
● **Beans**	When flowers form and during pod-forming and picking.
■ **Beets**	Before soil gets bone-dry.
■ **Broccoli**	Don't let soil dry out for 4 weeks after transplanting.
■ **Brussels sprouts**	Don't let soil dry out for 4 weeks after transplanting.
▲ **Cabbage**	Water frequently in dry weather for best crop.
■ **Carrots**	Before soil gets bone-dry.
▲ **Cauliflower**	Water frequently for best crop.
▲ **Celery**	Water frequently for best crop.
● **Corn**	When tassels form and when cobs swell.
▲ **Cucumbers**	Water frequently for best crop.
▲ **Lettuce/Spinach**	Water frequently for best crop.
■ **Onions**	In dry weather water in early stage to get plants going.
■ **Parsnips**	Before soil gets bone-dry.
● **Peas**	When flowers form and during pod-forming and picking.
● **Potatoes**	When the size of marbles.
▲ **Squash (all types)**	Water frequently for best crop.
● **Tomatoes**	For 3 to 4 weeks after transplanting and when flowers and fruit form.

▲ Needs a lot of water during dry spells.   ● Needs water at critical

Number of gallons of water needed for a 5-foot row	Comments
2 per week depending on rainfall	Dry soil when pods are forming will adversely affect quantity and quality.
1 at early stage; 2 every 2 weeks	Water sparingly during early stages to prevent foliage from becoming too lush at the expense of the roots; increase water when round roots form.
1 to 1-1/2 per week	Best crop will result with no water shortage.
1 to 1-1/2 per week	Plants can endure dry conditions once they are established. Give 2 gallons the last 2 weeks before harvest for most succulent crop.
2 per week	If crop suffers some dry weather, focus efforts on providing 2 gallons 2 weeks before harvest. (Too much water will cause heads to crack.)
1 at early stage; 2 every 2 weeks as roots mature	Roots may split if crop is watered after soil has become too dry.
2 per week	Give 2 gallons before harvest for best crop.
2 per week	If conditions are very dry, water daily.
2 at important stages (left)	Cob size will be smaller if plants do not receive water when ears are forming.
1 per week	Water diligently when fruits form and throughout growth; give highest watering priority.
2 per week	Best crop will result with no water shortage.
1/2 to 1 per week if soil is very dry	Withhold water from bulb onions at later growth stages to improve storage qualities; water salad onions anytime soil is very dry.
1 per week in early stages	Water when dry to keep plants growing steadily. Too much water will encourage lush foliage and small roots.
2 per week	To reduce excess foliage and stem growth, do not water young seedlings unless wilting.
2 per week	In dry weather give 2 gallons throughout the growing season every 10 days. Swings from very dry to very wet produce oddly shaped and cracked tubers.
1 per week	Water diligently when fruits form and throughout their growth; give highest watering priority.
1 twice a week or more	Frequent watering may increase yield but adversely affect flavor.

stages of development. ■ Does not need frequent watering.

Animal Terminology

Animal	Male	Female	Young
Ant	Male-ant (reproductive)	Queen (reproductive), worker (nonreproductive)	Antling
Antelope	Ram	Ewe	Calf, fawn, kid, yearling
Ass	Jack, jackass	Jenny	Foal
Bear	Boar, he-bear	Sow, she-bear	Cub
Beaver	Boar	Sow	Kit, kitten
Bee	Drone	Queen or queen bee, worker (nonreproductive)	Larva
Buffalo	Bull	Cow	Calf, yearling, spike-bull
Camel	Bull	Cow	Calf, colt
Caribou	Bull, stag, hart	Cow, doe	Calf, fawn
Cat	Tom, tomcat, gib, gibcat, boarcat, ramcat	Tabby, grimalkin, malkin, pussy, queen	Kitten, kit, kitling, kitty, pussy
Cattle	Bull	Cow	Calf, stot, yearling, bullcalf, heifer
Chicken	Rooster, cock, stag, chanticleer	Hen, partlet, biddy	Chick, chicken, poult, cockerel, pullet
Deer	Buck, stag	Doe	Fawn
Dog	Dog	Bitch	Whelp
Duck	Drake, stag	Duck	Duckling, flapper
Elephant	Bull	Cow	Calf
Fox	Dog	Vixen	Kit, pup, cub
Giraffe	Bull	Cow	Calf
Goat	Buck, billy, billie, billie-goat, he-goat	She-goat, nanny, nannie, nannie-goat	Kid
Goose	Gander, stag	Goose, dame	Gosling
Horse	Stallion, stag, horse, stud	Mare, dam	Colt, foal, stot, stag, filly, hog-colt, hogget
Kangaroo	Buck	Doe	Joey
Leopard	Leopard	Leopardess	Cub
Lion	Lion, tom	Lioness, she-lion	Shelp, cub, lionet
Moose	Bull	Cow	Calf
Partridge	Cock	Hen	Cheeper
Quail	Cock	Hen	Cheeper, chick, squealer
Reindeer	Buck	Doe	Fawn
Seal	Bull	Cow	Whelp, pup, cub, bachelor
Sheep	Buck, ram, male-sheep, mutton	Ewe, dam	Lamb, lambkin, shearling, yearling, cosset, hog
Swan	Cob	Pen	Cygnet
Swine	Boar	Sow	Shoat, trotter, pig, piglet, farrow, suckling
Termite	King	Queen	Nymph
Walrus	Bull	Cow	Cub
Whale	Bull	Cow	Calf
Zebra	Stallion	Mare	Colt, foal

Collective

Colony, nest, army, state, swarm

Herd

Pace, drove, herd

Sleuth, sloth

Family, colony

Swarm, grist, cluster, nest, hive, erst

Troop, herd, gang

Flock, train, caravan

Herd

Clowder, clutter (kindle or kendle of kittens)

Drove, herd

Flock, run, brood, clutch, peep

Herd, leash

Pack (cry or mute of hounds, leash of greyhounds)

Brace, team, paddling, raft, bed, flock, flight

Herd

Leash, skulk, cloud, troop

Herd, corps, troop

Tribe, trip, flock, herd

Flock (on land), gaggle, skein (in flight), gaggle or plump (on water)

Haras, stable, remuda, herd, string, field, set, pair, team

Mob, troop, herd

Leap

Pride, troop, flock, sawt, souse

Herd

Covey

Bevy, covey

Herd

Pod, herd, trip, rookery, harem

Flock, drove, hirsel, trip, pack

Herd, team, bank, wege, bevy

Drift, sounder, herd, trip (litter of pigs)

Colony, nest, swarm, brood

Pod, herd

Gam, pod, school, herd

Herd

More Animal Collectives

army of caterpillars, frogs

bale of turtles

band of gorillas

bed of clams, oysters

brood of jellyfish

business of flies

cartload of monkeys

cast of hawks

cete of badgers

charm of goldfinches

chatter of budgerigars

cloud of gnats, flies, grasshoppers, locusts

colony of penguins

congregation of plovers

convocation of eagles

crash of rhinoceri

descent of woodpeckers

dole of turtles

down of hares

dray of squirrels

dule of turtle doves

exaltation of larks

family of sardines

flight of birds

flock of lice

gang of elks

hatch of flies

horde of gnats

host of sparrows

hover of trout

husk of hares

knab of toads

knot of toads, snakes

murder of crows

murmuration of starlings

mustering of storks

nest of vipers

nest or nide of pheasants

pack of weasels

pladge of wasps

plague of locusts

scattering of herons

sedge or siege of cranes

smuck of jellyfish

span of mules

spring of teals

steam of minnows

tittering of magpies

troop of monkeys

troubling of goldfish

volery of birds

watch of nightingales

wing of plovers

yoke of oxen

Gestation and Mating Table

	Proper age for first mating	Period of fertility, in years	No. of females for one male	Period of gestation in days Range	Average
Ewe	90 lbs. or 1 yr.	6		142-154	147 / 151[8]
Ram	12-14 mos., well matured	7	50-75[2] / 35-40[3]		
Mare	3 yrs.	10-12		310-370	336
Stallion	3 yrs.	12-15	40-45[4] / Record 252[5]		
Cow	15-18 mos.[1]	10-14		279-290[6] 262-300[7]	283
Bull	1 yr., well matured	10-12	50[4] / Thousands[5]		
Sow	5-6 mos. or 250 lbs.	6		110-120	115
Boar	250-300 lbs.	6	50[2] / 35-40[3]		
Doe goat	10 mos. or 85-90 lbs.	6		145-155	150
Buck goat	Well matured	5	30		
Bitch	16-18 mos.	8		58-67	63
Male dog	12-16 mos.	8			
She cat	12 mos.	6		60-68	63
Doe rabbit	6 mos.	5-6		30-32	31
Buck rabbit	6 mos.	5-6	30		

[1]Holstein & beef: 750 lbs.; Jersey: 500 lbs. [2]Handmated. [3]Pasture. [4]Natural. [5]Artificial. [6]Beef; 8-10 days shorter for Angus. [7]Dairy. [8]For fine wool breeds.

Bird and Poultry Incubation Periods, in Days

Chicken......21	Goose 30-34	Guinea........26-28
Turkey........28	Swan 42	Canary........14-15
Duck 26-32	Pheasant ..22-24	Parakeet......18-20

Gestation Periods, Wild Animals, in Days

Black bear 210   Seal 330
Hippo...................225-250   Squirrel, gray 44
Moose 240-250   Whale, sperm..........480
Otter.....................270-300   Wolf....................60-63
Reindeer 210-240

Maximum Life Spans of Animals in Capitivity, in Years

Ant (queen) ...... 18+
Badger 26
Beaver .... 15+
Box turtle
  (Eastern) 138
Camel .... 35+
Cat (domestic) 34
Chicken (domestic) 25
Chimpanzee 51
Coyote .... 21+
Dog (domestic) 29
Dolphin 25
Duck (domestic) ... 23

Eagle 55
Elephant 75
Giraffe 36
Goat (domestic) 20
Goldfish 41
Goose (domestic) .. 20
Gorilla .... 50+
Horse 62
Housefly .... .04
  (17 days)
Kangaroo 30
Lion 29
Monarch butterfly .. 1+

Mouse (house) 6
Mussel
  (freshwater) ... 70-80
Octopus 2-3
Quahog 150
Rabbit .... 18+
Squirrel, gray 23
Tiger 26
Toad 40
Tortoise
  (Marion's) .... 152+
Turkey (domestic) .. 16

	Recurs if not bred	Estrual cycle incl. heat period (days)		In heat for		Usual time of ovulation
	Days	Avg.	Range	Avg.	Range	
Mare	21	21	10-37	5-6 days	2-11 days	24-48 hours before end of estrus
Sow	21	21	18-24	2-3 days	1-5 days	30-36 hours after start of estrus
Ewe	16½	16½	14-19	30 hours	24-32 hours	12-24 hours before end of estrus
Goat	21	21	18-24	2-3 days	1-4 days	Near end of estrus
Cow	21	21	18-24	18 hours	10-24 hours	10-12 hours after end of estrus
Bitch	pseudo-pregnancy	24		7 days	5-9 days	1-3 days after first acceptance
Cat	pseudo-pregnancy		15-21	3-4 if mated	9-10 days in absence of male	24-56 hours after coitus

Dogs: Gentle, Fierce, Smart, Popular

GENTLEST BREEDS

Golden retriever
Labrador retriever
Shetland sheepdog
Old English
   sheepdog
Welsh terrier
Yorkshire terrier
Beagle
Dalmatian
Pointer

FIERCEST BREEDS

Pit bull
German shepherd
Husky
Malamute
Doberman pinscher

Rottweiler
Great Dane
Saint Bernard

SMARTEST BREEDS

Border collie
Poodle
German shepherd
   (Alsatian)
Golden retriever
Doberman pinscher
Shetland sheepdog
Labrador retriever
Papillon
Rottweiler
Australian cattle dog

MOST POPULAR BREEDS

Labrador retriever
Rottweiler
Cocker spaniel
German shepherd
Poodle
Golden retriever
Beagle
Dachshund
Shetland sheepdog
Chow chow

How Old Is Your Dog?

Multiplying your dog's age by seven is easy, but it doesn't always hold true. The more carefully graded system below has the human equivalency years piled onto a dog's life more quickly during the dog's rapid growth to maturity, after which each year for a dog becomes the equivalent of four human years, and after age 13 it slows down to 2½ years.

Dog Age		Equivalent Human Age	
6 months. . 10 years		16 . . . . 75½
1 year.	15	17. 78
2 years.	24	18 . . . . 80½
3.	28	19 83
4.	32	20 . . . . 85½
5.	36	21. 88
6.	40	22 . . . . 90½
7.	44	23. 93
8.	48	24 . . . . 95½
9.	52	25. 98
10.	56	26 . . . . 100½
11.	60	27 103
12.	64	28 . . . . 105½
13.	68	29 108
14.	70½	30 110
15.	73	

Don't Poison Your Pussycat!

Certain common houseplants are poisonous to cats. They should not be allowed to eat the following:

- *Caladium* (elephant's ears)
- *Nerium oleander* (oleander)
- *Dieffenbachia* (dumb cane)
- *Philodendron* (philodendron)
- *Euphorbia pulcherrima* (poinsettia)
- *Prunus laurocerasus* (common or
   cherry laurel)
- *Hedera* (true ivy)
- *Rhododendron* (azalea)
- *Solanum capiscastrum* (winter or
   false Jerusalem cherry)
- *Ficus deltoidea* (mistletoe)

Ten Most Intelligent Animals
(Besides Humans)

According to Edward O. Wilson, behavioral biologist, professor of zoology, Harvard University, they are:

1. **Chimpanzee** (two species)
2. **Gorilla**
3. **Orangutan**
4. **Baboon** (seven species, including drill and mandrill)
5. **Gibbon** (seven species)
6. **Monkey** (many species, especially the macaques, the patas, and the Celebes black ape)
7. **Smaller toothed whale** (several species, especially killer whale)
8. **Dolphin** (many of the approximately 80 species)
9. **Elephant** (two species)
10. **Pig**

For the Birds

	Sunflower seeds	Millet (white proso)	Niger (thistle seeds)	Safflower seeds	Corn, cracked	Corn, whole	Peanuts	Peanut butter	Suet	Raisins	Apples	Oranges and grapefruit
Blue jay	■			■	■	■	■			■		
Bunting	■	■	■	■	■							
Cardinal	■	■		■	■					■	■	■
Catbird										■	■	■
Cedar waxwing											■	■
Chickadee	■	■		■	■		■	■	■			
Cowbird		■										
Crossbill	■	■		■				■				
Duck		■			■	■						
Finch	■	■	■	■	■		■	■				■
Flicker							■	■	■			
Goldfinch	■		■									
Goose					■	■						
Grackle	■											
Grosbeak	■	■		■			■			■	■	■
Junco	■	■	■	■	■							
Mockingbird										■	■	
Mourning dove	■	■		■	■	■						
Nuthatch	■	■		■			■	■	■			
Oriole												■
Pheasant					■							
Pine siskin	■	■	■	■			■			■		■
Redpoll	■	■	■	■								
Sparrow	■	■		■	■		■					
Starling					■							
Tanager												■
Thrasher					■		■			■	■	
Thrush										■	■	
Titmouse	■	■		■	■		■	■	■			
Towhee		■										
Warbler							■					■
Woodpecker							■	■	■			

What Counts as a Serving?

Bread Group
1 slice of bread
1 ounce of ready-to-eat cereal
½ cup of cooked cereal, rice, or pasta

Vegetable Group
1 cup of raw leafy vegetable
½ cup of other vegetable, cooked or
    chopped raw
¾ cup of vegetable juice

Fruit Group
1 medium apple, banana, or orange
½ cup of chopped, cooked, or canned fruit
¾ cup of fruit juice

Milk Group
1 cup of milk or yogurt
1½ ounces of natural cheese
2 ounces of processed cheese

Meat Group
2 to 3 ounces of cooked lean meat,
    poultry, or fish
½ cup of cooked dry beans, 1 egg, or 2
    tablespoons of peanut butter count as
    1 ounce of meat (about ⅓ serving)

Fats, Oils,
and Sweets
(use sparingly)

Milk Group — **2 - 3 SERVINGS** | **2 - 3 SERVINGS** — Meat Group

Vegetable Group — **3 - 5 SERVINGS** | **2 - 4 SERVINGS** — Fruit Group

6 - 11 SERVINGS — Bread Group

Suggested Daily Servings

The best Dietary Guidelines for a healthful diet from the USDA (United States Department of Agriculture) and HHS (Department of Health and Human Services) are:

- Eat a variety of foods

- Maintain healthy weight

- Choose a diet low in fat, saturated fat, and cholesterol

- Choose a diet with plenty of vegetables, fruits, and grain products

- Use sugars only in moderation

- Use salt only in moderation

- If you drink alcoholic beverages, do so in moderation

Food for Thought

☞ A piece of pecan pie = 580 calories
☞ Grilled cheese sandwich = 440 calories
☞ A chocolate shake = 364 calories
☞ Bagel with cream cheese = 361 calories
☞ 20 potato chips = 228 calories
☞ 10 french fries = 214 calories
☞ Half a cantaloupe = 94 calories
☞ Corn on the cob = 70 calories (no butter)
☞ One carrot = 30 calories

Don't Freeze These

Bananas
Canned hams
Cream fillings and
    puddings
Cooked eggs
Cooked potatoes
Custards
Fried foods
Gelatin dishes
Mayonnaise

Raw vegetables, such
    as cabbage, celery,
    green onions,
    radishes, and salad
    greens
Soft cheeses, cottage
    cheese
Sour cream
Yogurt

Substitutions for Common Ingredients

ITEM	QUANTITY	SUBSTITUTION
Allspice	1 teaspoon	½ teaspoon cinnamon plus ⅛ teaspoon ground cloves
Arrowroot, as thickener	1½ teaspoons	1 tablespoon flour
Baking powder	1 teaspoon	¼ teaspoon baking soda plus ⅝ teaspoon cream of tartar
Bread crumbs, dry	¼ cup	1 slice bread
Bread crumbs, soft	½ cup	1 slice bread
Buttermilk	1 cup	1 cup plain yogurt
Chocolate, unsweetened	1 ounce	3 tablespoons cocoa plus 1 tablespoon butter or fat
Cracker crumbs	¾ cup	1 cup dry bread crumbs
Cream, heavy	1 cup	¾ cup milk plus ⅓ cup melted butter (this will not whip)
Cream, light	1 cup	⅞ cup milk plus 3 tablespoons melted butter
Cream, sour	1 cup	⅞ cup buttermilk or plain yogurt plus 3 tablespoons melted butter
Cream, whipping	1 cup	⅔ cup well-chilled evaporated milk, whipped; **or** 1 cup nonfat dry milk powder whipped with 1 cup ice water
Egg	1 whole	2 yolks
Flour, all-purpose	1 cup	1⅛ cups cake flour; **or** ⅝ cup potato flour; **or** 1¼ cups rye or coarsely ground whole grain flour; **or** 1 cup cornmeal
Flour, cake	1 cup	1 cup minus 2 tablespoons sifted all-purpose flour
Flour, self-rising	1 cup	1 cup all-purpose flour plus 1¼ teaspoons baking powder plus ¼ teaspoon salt
Garlic	1 small clove	⅛ teaspoon garlic powder; **or** ½ teaspoon instant minced garlic
Herbs, dried	½ to 1 teaspoon	1 tablespoon fresh, minced and packed
Honey	1 cup	1¼ cups sugar plus ½ cup liquid

Measuring Vegetables

Asparagus: 1 pound = 3 cups chopped
Beans (string): 1 pound = 4 cups chopped
Beets: 1 pound (5 medium) = 2-1/2 cups chopped
Broccoli: 1/2 pound = 6 cups chopped
Cabbage: 1 pound = 4-1/2 cups shredded
Carrots: 1 pound = 3-1/2 cups sliced or grated
Celery: 1 pound = 4 cups chopped
Cucumbers: 1 pound (2 medium) = 4 cups sliced
Eggplant: 1 pound = 4 cups chopped (6 cups raw, cubed = 3 cups cooked)

Garlic: 1 clove = 1 teaspoon chopped
Leeks: 1 pound = 4 cups chopped (2 cups cooked)
Mushrooms: 1 pound = 5 to 6 cups sliced = 2 cups cooked
Onions: 1 pound = 4 cups sliced = 2 cups cooked
Parsnips: 1 pound unpeeled = 1-1/2 cups cooked, pureed
Peas: 1 pound whole = 1 to 1-1/2 cups shelled
Potatoes: 1 pound (3 medium) sliced = 2 cups mashed
Pumpkin: 1 pound = 4 cups chopped = 2 cups cooked and drained
Spinach: 1 pound = 3/4 to 1 cup cooked

ITEM	QUANTITY	SUBSTITUTION
Lemon	1	1 to 3 tablespoons juice, 1 to 1½ teaspoons grated rind
Lemon juice	1 teaspoon	½ teaspoon vinegar
Lemon rind, grated	1 teaspoon	½ teaspoon lemon extract
Milk, skim	1 cup	⅓ cup instant nonfat dry milk plus about ¾ cup water
Milk, to sour	1 cup	Add 1 tablespoon vinegar or lemon juice to 1 cup milk minus 1 tablespoon. Stir and let stand 5 minutes.
Milk, whole	1 cup	½ cup evaporated milk plus ½ cup water; or 1 cup skim milk plus 2 teaspoons melted butter
Molasses	1 cup	1 cup honey
Mustard, prepared	1 tablespoon	1 teaspoon dry or powdered mustard
Onion, chopped	1 small	1 tablespoon instant minced onion; or 1 teaspoon onion powder; or ¼ cup frozen chopped onion
Sugar, granulated	1 cup	1 cup firmly packed brown sugar; or 1¾ cups confectioners' sugar (do not substitute in baking); or 2 cups corn syrup; or 1 cup superfine sugar
Tomatoes, canned	1 cup	½ cup tomato sauce plus ½ cup water; or 1⅓ cups chopped fresh tomatoes, simmered
Tomato juice	1 cup	½ cup tomato sauce plus ½ cup water plus dash each salt and sugar; or ¼ cup tomato paste plus ¾ cup water plus salt and sugar
Tomato ketchup	½ cup	½ cup tomato sauce plus 2 tablespoons sugar, 1 tablespoon vinegar, and ⅛ teaspoon ground cloves
Tomato puree	1 cup	½ cup tomato paste plus ½ cup water
Tomato soup	1 can (10¾ oz.)	1 cup tomato sauce plus ¼ cup water
Vanilla	1-inch bean	1 teaspoon vanilla extract
Yeast	1 cake (⅗ oz.)	1 package active dried yeast (1 scant tablespoon)
Yogurt, plain	1 cup	1 cup buttermilk

Squash (summer): 1 pound = 4 cups grated = 2 cups salted and drained

Squash (winter): 2 pounds = 2-1/2 cups cooked, pureed

Sweet Potatoes: 1 pound = 4 cups grated = 1 cup cooked, pureed

Swiss Chard: 1 pound = 5 to 6 cups packed leaves = 1 to 1-1/2 cups cooked

Tomatoes: 1 pound (3 or 4 medium) = 1-1/2 cups seeded pulp

Turnips: 1 pound = 4 cups chopped = 2 cups cooked, mashed

Measuring Fruits

Apples: 1 pound (3 or 4 medium) = 3 cups sliced
Bananas: 1 pound (3 or 4 medium) = 1-3/4 cups mashed
Berries: 1 quart = 3-1/2 cups
Dates: 1 pound = 2-1/2 cups pitted
Lemon: 1 whole = 1 to 3 tablespoons juice; 1 to 1-1/2 teaspoons grated rind
Lime: 1 whole = 1-1/2 to 2 tablespoons juice
Orange: 1 medium = 6 to 8 tablespoons juice; 2 to 3 tablespoons grated rind
Peaches: 1 pound (4 medium) = 3 cups sliced
Pears: 1 pound (4 medium) = 2 cups sliced
Rhubarb: 1 pound = 2 cups cooked
Strawberries: 1 quart = 4 cups sliced

Basic Kitchen Equipment

FOOD PREPARATION
Measuring cups
   Dry measure: set
      of 4 cups
   Wet measure:
      1-cup and 2-cup
Measuring spoons
Ruler
Thermometers
   Meat
   Candy/frying
   Freezer
Timer
Mixing bowls (3 sizes)
Chopping board
Knives
   Chef's knife
   Paring knife
   Bread knife
      (serrated edge)
   Carving knife
Knife sharpener
Kitchen shears
Vegetable parer
Openers

Bottle opener
Corkscrew
Jar opener
Can opener
Pepper grinder
Rotary egg beater
Nutcracker
Funnel
Grater
Colander
Strainer
Juicer

COOKING
Pots, skillets, and pans
   Saucepans: 1- to
      2-cup, 1-quart,
      2-quart, and 8-
      quart
   Skillets/frying
      pans: 7-inch,
      10-inch, and
      12-inch
   Griddle

Flameproof
   casserole or
   Dutch oven
Casseroles and
   baking dishes
Roasting pan
   (with rack)
Double boiler
Steamer

Kettle
Coffeepot
Wooden spoons
Rubber spatula
Metal utensils
   Metal spatula
   Slotted spoon
   Cooking fork
   Ladle
   Potato masher
   Tongs
   Whisk

Skewers
Bulb baster
Brush

BAKING
Pastry blender
Rolling pin
Sifter
Cake pans
   Pair of 8 (and/or 9)
      x1½-inch
      round
   8- or 9-inch
      square
   9x12-inch
      rectangular
   10-inch tube
Loaf pans
Cookie sheets (at least 2)
Jelly-roll pan
Muffin tins
Pie pans
Custard cups
Cooling racks

Appetizing Amounts

Occasion	Number of bites per person
Hors d'oeuvres (with meal following)	4
Cocktail party	10
Grand affair, no dinner following **(e.g., wedding reception)**	10-15

Pass the Pasta

All pastas, when cooked, are not created equal. Four ounces of dried pasta, the usual serving size, yields different amounts depending on the pasta shape.

Type of pasta, 4 ounces uncooked	Cooked yield (in cups)
Spaghetti, vermicelli, capellini, linguine	2
Elbow macaroni, conchiglie (seashells), rotini, ruote (cartwheels), mostaccioli, ziti, penne	2½
Medium egg noodles, tagliatelle	3

Unexpected Uses for Household Items

SALT

■ Rub salt on fruit stains while still wet, then put item in the wash.

■ For mildew spots, rub  in some buttermilk and salt, and let item dry in the sun.

■ If you spill wine or fruit juice on your tablecloth, pour salt on the spot at once to absorb the stain.

■ Apply a paste of salt and olive oil to ugly heat rings on your table. Let sit for about an hour, and then wipe off with a soft cloth.

■ To catch a wild bird easily, first sprinkle some salt on its tail.

■ Sprinkle salt on a piece of paper and run your sticky iron over it a few times while the iron is hot. You should notice a big improvement next time you use the iron.

■ To restore some of the color to faded fabric, soak it in a strong solution of salt and water.

■ You can get rid of an evil spell by throwing a pinch of salt over your left shoulder.

■ Mix a tablespoon of salt into the water of a vase of cut flowers to keep them fresh longer.

VINEGAR

■ Bring a solution of 1 cup vinegar and 4 tablespoons baking soda to a boil in teapots and coffeepots to rid them of mineral deposits.

■ A solution of vinegar and baking soda will easily remove cooking oil from your stovetop.

■ Clean the filter on your humidifier by removing it and soaking it in a pan of white vinegar until all the sediment is off.

■ Vinegar naturally breaks down uric acid and soapy residue, leaving baby clothes and diapers soft and fresh. Add a cup of vinegar to each load during the rinse cycle.

■ Saturate a cloth with vinegar and sprinkle with baking soda, then use it to clean fiberglass tubs and showers. Rinse well and rub dry for a spotless shine.

■ To remove chewing gum, rub it with full-strength vinegar.

■ For a clean oven, combine vinegar and baking soda, then scrub.

■ Soak paint stains in hot vinegar to remove them.

BAKING SODA

■ Add baking soda to your bath water to relieve sunburned or itchy skin.

■ Make a paste of baking soda and water, and apply to a burn or an insect bite for relief.

■ Clean your refrigerator with a solution of 1 teaspoon baking soda to 1 quart of warm water.

■ Pour a cup of baking soda into the opening of your clogged drain and then add a cup of hot vinegar. After a few minutes, flush the drain with a quart of boiling water.

■ To remove perspiration stains, make a thick paste of baking soda and water. Rub paste into the stain, let sit for an hour, and launder as usual.

■ If you crave sweets, rinse your mouth with 1 teaspoon baking soda dissolved in a glass of warm water. Don't swallow the mixture; spit it out. Your craving should disappear at once.

■ Tough meat can be tenderized by rubbing it with baking soda. Let stand for several hours before rinsing and cooking.

How Long Household Items Last

ITEMS	YEARS (Approx. Averages)
Electric shavers	4
Personal computers	6
Lawn mowers	6
Automatic coffee makers	6
VCRs	6
Food processors	7
Electric can openers	7
CD players	7
Camcorders	7
Toasters	8
Stereo receivers	8
Color TV sets	8
Blenders	8
Room air conditioners	9
Vacuum cleaners	10
Microwave ovens	10
Dishwashers	11
Dehumidifiers	12
Washing machines	13
Electric dryers	13
Refrigerators	14
Gas dryers	14
Electric ranges	15
Gas ranges	18

The life span of a product depends not only on its actual durability but also on your desire for some new convenience found only on a new model.

– courtesy Consumer Reports

How Long Does Litter Last?

Glass bottles	1,000,000 years
Aluminum cans/tabs	80-100 years
Rubber boot soles	50-80 years
Leather	up to 50 years
Nylon fabric	30-40 years
Plastic film containers	20-30 years
Plastic bags	10-20 years
Plastic-coated papers	5 years
Cigarette butts	1-5 years
Wool socks	1-5 years
Orange/banana peels	2-5 weeks

– courtesy the NPS

How Much Water Is Used?

The greatest water waste is in your bathroom. The numbers below show a typical distribution of household water use with standard fixtures:

	Percent
Dishwashers	3.1
Toilet leaks	5.5
Baths	8.9
Faucets	11.7
Showers	21.2
Washing machines	21.2
Toilets	28.4

	Gallons
To brush your teeth (water running)	1-2
To flush a toilet	5-7
To run a dishwasher	9-12
To shave (water running)	10-15
To wash dishes by hand	20
To take a shower	15-30
By an average person daily	123
In the average residence during a year	110,000

Heat Values of Fuels
(approximate)

Fuel	BTU	Unit of Measure
Oil	141,000	gallon
Coal	31,000	pound
Natural gas	1,000	cubic foot
Steam	1,000	cubic foot
Electricity	3,413	kilowatt-hour
Gasoline	124,000	gallon

Stovewood — Best Heat Value

You will pay more for these hardwoods, but you will get more heat for your dollar.

Ash, white	Locust, black
Beech	Maple, sugar
Birch, yellow	Oak, red
Hickory, shagbark	Oak, white
Hop hornbeam	

A Few Clues About Cords of Wood

1. A cord of wood is a pile of logs 4 feet wide by 4 feet high by 8 feet long.
2. A cord of wood may contain from 77 to 96 cubic feet of wood.
3. The larger the unsplit logs, the larger the gaps, with fewer cubic feet of wood actually in the cord.

Hand Thermometer for Outdoor Cooking

Hold your palm close to where the food will be cooking: over the coals or in front of a reflector oven. Count "one-and-one, two-and-two," and so on, for as many seconds as you can hold your hand still.

SECONDS COUNTED	HEAT	TEMPERATURE
6-8	Slow	250-350° F
4-5	Moderate	350-400° F
2-3	Hot	400-450° F
1 or less	Very hot	450-500° F

Homeowner's Tool Kit

THE ESSENTIALS

Butt chisel
Putty knife
Adjustable wrench
Slip-joint pliers
Needle-nose pliers
Block plane
Four-in-one rasp
Hacksaw
Crosscut saw
Retractable steel ruler
Drain auger
C-clamp
Nail set
Curved-claw hammer
Push drill and drill point

3 standard screwdrivers
  (3 sizes)
2 Phillips screwdrivers
  (2 sizes)
Combination square
Level
Utility knife
Toilet plunger
Screws and nails

OTHER SUPPLIES

Machine oil
Penetrating lubricant
Pencils
Bolts and nuts, hollow-
  wall fasteners, etc.
Adhesives
Sandpaper and steel
  wool
Sharpening stone

Wire brush
Paintbrushes
Dustpan and brush
Lint-free rags or
  cheesecloth
Clip-on light
Grounded extension cord
Single-edge razor blades
  with holder
Scissors
Toolbox
Stepladder

Cost of a Load of Laundry

Electric Water Heater (8¢/kWh)			Gas Water Heater (60¢/therm)		
Wash/rinse settings	kWh used	Average cost per load (cents)	Wash/rinse settings	Therms used	Average cost per load (cents)
Water-heater thermostat set at 140° F					
Hot/Hot	8.3	66	Hot/Hot	.329	20
Hot/Warm	6.3	50	Hot/Warm	.247	15
Hot/Cold	4.3	34	Hot/Cold	.164	10
Warm/Warm	4.3	34	Warm/Warm	.164	10
Warm/Cold	2.3	18	Warm/Cold	.082	5
Cold/Cold	0.4	3	Cold/Cold	—	3
Water-heater thermostat set at 120° F					
Hot/Hot	6.5	52	Hot/Hot	.248	15
Hot/Warm	4.9	39	Hot/Warm	.186	10
Hot/Cold	4.3	27	Hot/Cold	.124	7
Warm/Warm	3.4	27	Warm/Warm	.124	7
Warm/Cold	1.9	15	Warm/Cold	.062	4
Cold/Cold	0.4	3	Cold/Cold	—	3

Paper Clutter — Save, Stash, or Scrap?

SAVE For a While or Forever

- Canceled checks that substantiate tax deductions (file with tax material) or major purchases (file with product warranties)
- Purchase and sale documents (including tax form 2119) for every home you've owned
- Documents relating to capital home-improvement expenditures (new roofs, remodeled kitchen/bath, land-scaping, etc.)
- Credit-card records (for six years)
- Health records (forever)
- Contracts (for seven years past expiration date)
- Loan papers (for three years after final payment)
- Records of all contributions to non-deductible IRAs, including form 8606
- Current will (copy — leave original with your attorney)
- Tax returns (for six years, in individual folders)

STASH In a Safe Deposit Box

- Valuable, hard-to-replace papers (keep photocopies at home)
- Deeds and other records of ownership (inventory, appraisals, photos, receipts)
- Birth and marriage certificates
- Passports
- Stock and bond certificates
- List of all insurance policies and agents (store original documents at home)
- Adoption papers
- Divorce decrees
- Custody agreements

SCRAP What You Can Safely Throw Away
(When in doubt, consult your CPA or lawyer)

- Expired insurance policies (with no possibility of claim)
- Nontax-related checks more than three years old
- Records for items you no longer own (cars, boats)
- Pay stubs going back more than two years

The Right Wood for the Job

Doors	Birch, oak
Cabinet doors	Maple, oak, birch, cherry
Shelving	Ash, birch, maple, oak, walnut, poplar, Douglas fir, redwood, ponderosa pine, sugar pine, Idaho white pine
Paneling	Oak, redwood, cypress, walnut, cedar, ash, birch, pine
Stairways	Oak, birch, maple, walnut, beech, ash, cherry
Interior trim, natural finish	Oak, birch, maple, cypress, cherry, sycamore, beech, walnut. Knotty surface: cedar, ponderosa pine, spruce, sugar pine, gum, lodgepole pine
Interior trim, painted finish	Northern and Idaho white pine, ponderosa pine, sugar pine, poplar
Exterior trim	Cedar, cypress, redwood, northern and Idaho white pine, ponderosa pine, sugar pine
Frames and sash	Cypress, cedar, redwood, northern and Idaho white pine, ponderosa pine, sugar pine
Siding	Western red cedar, cypress, redwood
Decking and outdoor steps	White oak, locust, walnut
Exposed platforms and porches	Redwood, locust, white oak
Shingles	Cedar, cypress, redwood
Plank roof decking	Southern yellow pine, Douglas fir, other softwood
Fence posts	Black locust, Osage orange, white oak, cedar, cypress, redwood, catalpa, chestnut
Gates and fences	Douglas fir, western larch, southern yellow pine, redwood, white oak
Roof sheathing	Douglas fir, western larch, southern yellow pine
Wall sheathing	Cedar, hemlock, northern and Idaho white pine, redwood, aspen, spruce, balsam, white fir, basswood, lodgepole pine, poplar, sugar pine, ponderosa pine
Subfloors	Douglas fir, western larch, southern yellow pine, ash, oak

Guide to Lumber and Nails

Lumber Width and Thickness in Inches

NOMINAL SIZE	ACTUAL SIZE Dry or Seasoned
1 x 3	¾ x 2½
1 x 4	¾ x 3½
1 x 6	¾ x 5½
1 x 8	¾ x 7¼
1 x 10	¾ x 9¼
1 x 12	¾ x 11¼
2 x 3	1½ x 2½
2 x 4	1½ x 3½
2 x 6	1½ x 5½
2 x 8	1½ x 7¼
2 x 10	1½ x 9¼
2 x 12	1½ x 11¼

Nail Sizes

The nail on the left is a 5d (penny) finish nail; on the right, 20d common. The numerals below the nail sizes indicate the approximate number of common nails per pound.

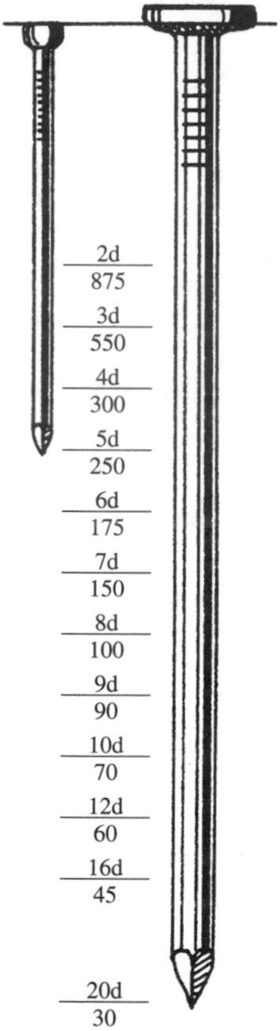

Size	Nails per pound
2d	875
3d	550
4d	300
5d	250
6d	175
7d	150
8d	100
9d	90
10d	70
12d	60
16d	45
20d	30

Lumber Measure in Board Feet

LENGTH Size in Inches	12 ft.	14 ft.	16 ft.	18 ft.	20 ft.
1 x 4	4	4⅔	5⅓	6	6⅔
1 x 6	6	7	8	9	10
1 x 8	8	9⅓	10⅔	12	13⅓
1 x 10	10	11⅔	13⅓	15	16⅔
1 x 12	12	14	16	18	20
2 x 3	6	7	8	9	10
2 x 4	8	9⅓	10⅔	12	13⅓
2 x 6	12	14	16	18	20
2 x 8	16	18⅔	21⅓	24	26⅔
2 x 10	20	23⅓	26⅔	30	33⅓
2 x 12	24	28	32	36	40
4 x 4	16	18⅔	21⅓	24	26⅔
6 x 6	36	42	48	54	60
8 x 8	64	74⅔	85⅓	96	106⅔
10 x 10	100	116⅔	133⅓	150	166⅔
12 x 12	144	168	192	216	240

Daily Caloric Requirements

These hypothetical examples demonstrate changing caloric requirements
at different times of life.

Age range	MALE Weight in pounds	MALE Calories needed	FEMALE Weight in pounds	FEMALE Calories needed
1	24	1,100	24	1,100
2-3	31	1,300	31	1,300
4-6	40	1,800	40	1,800
7-9	55	2,200	55	2,200
10-12	75	2,500	79	2,200
13-15	110	2,800	106	2,200
16-18	136	3,200	117	2,100
19-24	156	3,000	128	2,100
25-49	163	2,700	130	1,900
50-74	161	2,300	139	1,800

PLEASE NOTE: If pregnant or nursing, add 300 to 500 calories.

Prescription-ese

Abbreviation	Latin	Meaning
ac	ante cibum	before meals
ad lib	ad libitum	at pleasure
bid	bis in die	twice a day
cum	cum	with
disp #50		pharmacist should dispense 50 pills
et	et	and
gtt	guttae	drops
hs	hora somni	at bedtime
npo	nihil per os	nothing by mouth
pc	post cibum	after meals
po	per os	by mouth
prn	pro re nata	as needed
qd	quaque die	every day
qh	quaque hora	every hour
qid	quater in die	four times a day
Rx	recipe	take
semis	semis	a half
Sig	signetur	let it be labeled
sine	sine	without
stat	statim	immediately
tid	ter in die	three times a day

Health Hot Lines

Aging
National Council on Aging
800-424-9046

AIDS
CDC National AIDS Hot Line
800-342-AIDS (2437)

Alcohol and Drug Abuse
National Clearinghouse for
Alcohol and Drug Information
800-729-6686

Cancer
Cancer Information Service
800-4-CANCER (422-6237)

Child Abuse
National Child Abuse Hot Line
800-422-4453

Food and Drug Safety
Food and Drug Administration,
Office of Consumer Affairs
301-827-4420

Heart, Lung, and Blood Diseases
National Heart, Lung, and
Blood Institute Education
Programs Center
301-251-1222

Maternal and Child Health
National Maternal and Child
Health Clearinghouse
703-821-8955, ext. 254

Mental Health
National Mental Health
Association
800-969-6642

Occupational Safety and Health
National Institute for
Occupational Safety and Health
800-35-NIOSH (356-4674)

Physical Activity and Fitness
Aerobic and Fitness
Foundation
800-BE FIT 86 (233-4886)

Safety and Injury Prevention
Consumer Product Safety
Commission
800-638-CPSC (2772)

National Highway Traffic
Safety Administration,
Auto Safety Hot Line
800-424-9393

Sexually Transmitted Diseases
CDC National STD Hot Line
800-227-8922

Are You Skinny, Just Right, or Overweight?

Here's an easy formula to figure your Body Mass Index (BMI), now thought to be a more accurate indicator of relative body size than the old insurance charts. **W** is your weight in pounds and **H** is your height in inches.

$$BMI = \frac{(W \times 705) \div H}{H}$$

■ If the result is 25 or less, you are within a healthy weight range.

■ If it's 19 or below, you are too skinny.

■ Between 25 and 27, you are as much as 8 percent over your healthy weight.

■ Between 27 and 30, you are at increased risk for health problems.

■ Above 30, you are more than 20 percent over your healthy weight. It puts you at a dramatically increased risk for serious health problems.

There are a couple of exceptions to the above. Very muscular people with a high BMI generally have nothing to worry about, and extreme skinniness is generally a symptom of some other health problem, not the cause.

Here's another way to see if you are dangerously overweight. Measure your waistline. A waist measurement of 35 inches or more in women and 41 inches or more in men, regardless of height, suggests a serious risk of weight-related health problems.

Life Expectancy by Current Age

If your age now is . . .	You can expect to live to age . . .	
	Men	Women
0	72	79
20	74	80
25	74	80
30	75	80
35	75	81
40	76	81
45	76	81
50	77	82
55	78	82
60	79	83
65	80	84
70	82	86
75	85	87
80	87	89
85	90	92

Source: U.S. Department of Health and Human Services, 1995

Calorie Burning

If you hustle through your chores to get to the fitness center, relax. You're getting a great workout already. The left-hand column lists "chore" exercises, the middle column shows number of calories you burn per minute per pound of your body weight, the right-hand column lists comparable "recreational" exercises. For example, a 150-pound person forking straw bales burns 9.45 calories per minute, the same workout he/she would get playing basketball.

Chopping with an ax, fast	0.135	Skiing, cross country, uphill
Climbing hills, with 44-pound load	0.066	Swimming, crawl, fast
Digging trenches	0.065	Skiing, cross country, steady walk
Forking straw bales	0.063	Basketball
Chopping down trees	0.060	Football
Climbing hills, with 9-pound load	0.058	Swimming, crawl, slow
Sawing by hand	0.055	Skiing, cross country, moderate
Mowing lawns	0.051	Horseback riding, trotting
Scrubbing floors	0.049	Tennis
Shoveling coal	0.049	Aerobic dance, medium
Hoeing	0.041	Weight training, circuit training
Stacking firewood	0.040	Weight lifting, free weights
Shoveling grain	0.038	Golf
Painting houses	0.035	Walking, normal pace, asphalt road
Weeding	0.033	Table tennis
Shopping for food	0.028	Cycling, 5.5 mph
Mopping floors	0.028	Fishing
Washing windows	0.026	Croquet
Raking	0.025	Dancing, ballroom
Driving a tractor	0.016	Drawing, standing position

pho·bi·a (fō-bē-ə) *noun*

1. A persistent, abnormal, or irrational fear of a specific thing or situation that compels one to avoid the feared stimulus.

2. A strong fear, dislike, or aversion.

PHOBIA SUBJECT	PHOBIA TERM
Air, drafts	Aerophobia
Animals	Zoophobia
Beards	Pogonophobia
Books	Bibliophobia
Cats	Ailurophobia
Churches	Ecclesiaphobia
Crowds	Ochlophobia
Dirt, contamination	Mysophobia
Dreams	Oneirophobia
England, the English	Anglophobia
Flowers	Anthophobia
Food	Sitophobia
Foreign persons or things; strangers	Xenophobia
Gay or homosexual people or their lifestyle or culture	Homophobia
Graves	Taphophobia
Great height, being near something of (e.g., skyscraper, mountain)	Batophobia
High places	Acrophobia
Infection	Nosemaphobia
Lakes	Limnophobia
Leaves	Phyllophobia
Lightning and thunder	Astraphobia
Men	Androphobia
Mites, small insects, worms	Acarophobia
Money	Chrometophobia
Music	Musicophobia
Narrow or enclosed places, being in	Claustrophobia
Newness	Cainotophobia
Night, darkness	Nyctophobia
Number 13	Triskaidekaphobia
Open or public places	Agoraphobia
Sex	Genophobia
Shadows	Sciophobia
Sharply pointed objects, especially needles	Belonephobia
Spiders	Arachnophobia
Sun	Heliophobia
Touch	Haptophobia
Trees	Dendrophobia
Walking	Basiphobia
Water	Hydrophobia
Women	Gynophobia
Work	Ergophobia
Writing	Graphophobia

First-Aid Essentials

Cuts and Abrasions
+ Antibacterial soap
+ Adhesive bandages (Band-Aids) of various sizes
+ Roll of adhesive tape
+ Sterile dressings (especially 4" x 4" gauze pads)
+ Roll of 4" gauze (to hold dressings)
+ Pair of blunt-end scissors

Eye Injuries
+ Prepared eyewash and eyecup

Burns (minor)
+ Burn ointment or spray

Skin Problems
+ Hydrocortisone cream or calamine lotion (itches and rashes)
+ Petroleum jelly
+ Antifungal powder or spray for athlete's foot
+ Sunscreen and sunburn spray for relief
+ Insect repellent

Poison (swallowed)
+ Syrup of ipecac (to induce vomiting, after consulting physician or poison-control center)
+ Activated charcoal (to absorb poisons that shouldn't be regurgitated)
+ Epsom salts (to speed excretion of poison)

Heat Exhaustion
+ Sodium bicarbonate (mix a pinch with ¼ teaspoon salt in a quart of water, and drink)

Pain Relief
+ Aspirin or other over-the-counter pain reliever

Miscellaneous
+ Surgical tweezers for removing splinters
+ Cotton balls
+ Elastic bandage for sprains
+ Ice bag to reduce swellings
+ Hot-water bottle and heating pad for aches and pains
+ Aspirin and/or acetaminophen for pain relief and fever reduction
+ Thermometer
+ Sodium bicarbonate for bee, ant, and wasp stings

EMERGENCY CAR KIT

- Battery-powered radio, flashlight, and extra batteries
- Blanket
- Booster cables
- Fire extinguisher (5-lb., A-B-C type)
- First-aid kit and manual
- Bottled water and nonperishable high-energy foods such as granola bars, raisins, and peanut butter
- Maps, shovel, flares
- Tire repair kit and pump

Origins of Sports

Badminton: Probably originated in China. The first badminton club was formed in the United States in 1878.

Baseball: Early 19th century; derived from the English games of cricket and rounders.

Basketball: Originated in 1891 in Springfield, Massachusetts, by Dr. James Naismith of the YMCA.

Billiards: Various games played in England and France in the 15th and 16th centuries.

Bowling: Originated in ancient Germany; introduced in America in the 17th century by the Dutch.

Boxing: One of the oldest forms of competition known. After the fall of Rome, boxing declined but was revived in England in the early 18th century. Modern boxing is based on a code of rules introduced in 1867 by the Marquess of Queensberry. Boxing was illegal in the United States until 1896, when New York became the first state to legalize it.

Checkers: Popular game in Europe since the 16th century; similar to a game played in ancient times.

Chess: Probably originated in India. Popular throughout Europe by the 15th century. First modern international chess tournament was held in London in 1851.

Croquet: Developed in France in the 17th century. The modern form of the game was devised in England in 1857.

Field hockey: Of ancient origin. Played in England for centuries before spreading to other countries.

Football: Developed from English games of soccer and rugby. American football evolved slowly in the 19th century.

Golf: Origin unknown; played in Scotland as early as 1457. The British Open Tournament was established in 1860.

May have been played in the American colonies in the 17th century; first United States club organized in 1888.

Ice Hockey: Originated in Canada in the mid-19th century. It later spread to the United States and other countries. The first formal hockey game was played in Kingston, Ontario, in 1855.

Lacrosse: Of Native American origin. Developed in Canada and introduced into the United States in the 1870s.

Polo: Probably originated in ancient Persia about 600 B.C. Played in India in the 19th century by British officers and thereafter spread to England and the United States.

Rodeo: Based on the riding and roping skills of the Western cowboy. Prescott, Arizona, held the first formal rodeo in 1888.

Rugby: Originated at the Rugby School in England ca. 1840.

Soccer: Earliest recorded game played in England in A.D. 217. By the 12th century, it was a regular Shrove Tuesday event. Refined in the 19th century to emphasize only the kicking aspects. It arrived in the United States in the late 19th century. Today soccer is played in more than 140 countries, making it the most popular international sport.

Softball: Invented in Chicago in 1888. International rules were established in 1933.

Swimming: Swimming contests were organized in Japan as early as the 1st century B.C. It became organized as an amateur sport in the late 19th century.

Table tennis: Originated in England in the late 19th century. The first world championships were held in London in 1926.

Tennis: Englishman Major Walter C. Wingfield borrowed from older forms of the game to found the sport of modern tennis in 1873. The first United States tennis championship was held in 1881.

Volleyball: Originated in Holyoke, Massachusetts, in 1895. It was invented by YMCA physical-fitness director William G. Morgan. The International Volleyball Federation was formed in 1947.

Pitches

CURVEBALL
Veers or breaks to the left when thrown with the right hand and to the right when thrown with the left hand.

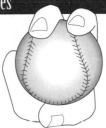

SLIDER
A fast pitch that breaks in the same direction as a curveball at the last moment.

KNUCKLEBALL
A slow, randomly fluttering pitch thrown by gripping the ball with the tips or nails of two or three fingers.

FASTBALL
A pitch thrown at the pitcher's maximum speed.

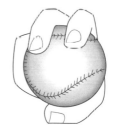

FORKBALL
A pitch with the ball placed between the index and middle fingers so that the ball takes a sharp dip near home plate.

Safe Ice Thickness *

Ice Thickness	Permissible Load
2 inches	one person on foot
3 inches	group in single file
7½ inches	passenger car (2-ton gross)
8 inches	light truck (2½-ton gross)
10 inches	medium truck (3½-ton gross)
12 inches	heavy truck (8-ton gross)
15 inches	10 tons
20 inches	25 tons
30 inches	70 tons
36 inches	110 tons

* Solid clear blue/black pond and lake ice

☞ Slush ice has only half the strength of blue ice.

☞ Strength value of river ice is 15 percent less.

Source: American Pulpwood Association

Sports Halls of Fame

Association of Sports Museums and Halls of Fame
101 W. Sutton Place
Wilmington, DE 19810

Pro Football Hall of Fame
2121 George Halas Dr. N.W.
Canton, OH 44708
330-456-8207

National Football Foundation and Hall of Fame
1865 Palmer Ave.
Larchmont, NY 10538
914-834-0474

National Soccer Hall of Fame
5-11 Ford Ave.
Oneonta, NY 13820
607-432-3351

Pro Rodeo Hall of Fame
101 Pro Rodeo Dr.
Colorado Springs, CO 80919
719-528-4764

International Boxing Hall of Fame
P.O. Box 425
Canastota, NY 13032
315-697-7095

National Baseball Hall of Fame and Museum
P.O. Box 590
Cooperstown, NY 13326
607-547-7200

Naismith Memorial Basketball Hall of Fame
1150 W. Columbus Ave.
Springfield, MA 01101
413-781-6500

National Softball Hall of Fame
2801 N.E. 50th St.
Oklahoma City, OK 73111
405-424-5266

Hockey Hall of Fame and Museum
BCE Place, 30 Yonge St.
Toronto, ON M5E 1X8
Canada
416-360-7765

National Tennis Foundation and Hall of Fame
100 Park Ave.
New York, NY 10017
212-880-4179

International Swimming Hall of Fame
1 Hall of Fame Dr.
Fort Lauderdale, FL 33316
305-462-6536

Bowling Hall of Fame and Museum
111 Stadium Plaza
St. Louis, MO 63102
314-231-6340

International Checker Hall of Fame
220 Lynn Ray Rd.
(P.O. Box 365)
Petal, MS 39465
601-582-7090

National Freshwater Fishing Hall of Fame
1 Hall of Fame Dr.
(P.O. Box 33)
Hayward, WI 54843
715-634-4440

Abbreviations Approved by the U.S. Postal Service to Be Used in Addressing Mail

Alabama .... AL	North Dakota ...... ND	East .... E
Alaska .... AK	North Mariana Islands MP	Estates .... EST
American Samoa ..... AS	Ohio .... OH	Expressway ...... EXPY
Arizona .... AZ	Oklahoma .... OK	Extension .... EXT
Arkansas .... AR	Oregon .... OR	Freeway .... FWY
California .... CA	Pennsylvania .... PA	Gardens .... GDNS
Colorado .... CO	Puerto Rico .... PR	Grove .... GRV
Connecticut .... CT	Rhode Island .... RI	Heights .... HTS
Delaware .... DE	South Carolina ...... SC	Highway .... HWY
District of Columbia .. DC	South Dakota ...... SD	Island .... IS
Florida .... FL	Tennessee .... TN	Junction .... JCT
Georgia .... GA	Texas .... TX	Lake .... LK
Guam .... GU	Trust Territory .... TT	Lane .... LN
Hawaii .... HI	Utah .... UT	Manor .... MNR
Idaho .... ID	Vermont .... VT	Mountain .... MTN
Illinois IL	Virgin Islands, U.S. ... VI	North .... N
Indiana .... IN	Virginia .... VA	Park .... PK
Iowa .... IA	Washington .... WA	Parkway .... PKY
Kansas .... KS	West Virginia ...... WV	Place .... PL
Kentucky .... KY	Wisconsin .... WI	Plaza .... PLZ
Louisiana .... LA	Wyoming .... WY	Point .... PT
Maine .... ME		Road .... RD
Maryland .... MD	Alley .... ALY	Room .... RM
Massachusetts ...... MA	Apartment .... APT	Rural .... R
Michigan .... MI	Arcade .... ARC	South .... S
Minnesota .... MN	Avenue .... AVE	Square .... SQ
Mississippi .... MS	Boulevard .... BLVD	Station .... STA
Missouri .... MO	Branch .... BR	Street .... ST
Montana .... MT	Bypass .... BYP	Suite .... STE
Nebraska .... NE	Causeway .... CSWY	Terrace .... TER
Nevada .... NV	Center .... CTR	Trail .... TRL
New Hampshire ..... NH	Circle .... CIR	Turnpike .... TPKE
New Jersey .... NJ	Court .... CT	Viaduct .... VIA
New Mexico .... NM	Courts .... CTS	Vista .... VIS
New York .... NY	Crescent .... CRES	Valley .... VLY
North Carolina ...... NC	Drive .... DR	West .... W

Canadian Province and Territory Postal Codes

Alberta .... AB	Nova Scotia .... NS
British Columbia .... BC	Ontario .... ON
Manitoba .... MB	Prince Edward Island .... PE
New Brunswick .... NB	Quebec .... QC
Newfoundland .... NF	Saskatchewan .... SK
Northwest Territories .... NT	Yukon Territory .... YT

Presidential Libraries

Office of Presidential Libraries
National Archives and Records Administration
Washington, DC 20408
PHONE: 202-501-5700
FAX: 202-501-5709

Herbert Hoover Library
210 Parkside Dr., P.O. Box 488
West Branch, IA 52358-0488
PHONE: 319-643-5301
FAX: 319-643-5825
E-MAIL: library@hoover.nara.gov

Franklin D. Roosevelt Library
511 Albany Post Rd.
Hyde Park, NY 12538-1999
PHONE: 914-229-8114
FAX: 914-229-0872
E-MAIL: library@roosevelt.nara.gov

Harry S. Truman Library
500 West U.S. Highway 24
Independence, MO 64050-1798
PHONE: 816-833-1400
FAX: 816-833-4368
E-MAIL: library@truman.nara.gov

Dwight D. Eisenhower Library
200 S.E. 4th St., Abilene, KS 67410-2900
PHONE: 785-263-4751
FAX: 785-263-4218
E-MAIL: library@eisenhower.nara.gov

John Fitzgerald Kennedy Library
Columbia Point, Boston, MA 02125-3398
PHONE: 617-929-4500
FAX: 617-929-4538
E-MAIL: library@kennedy.nara.gov

Lyndon Baines Johnson Library
2313 Red River St., Austin, TX 78705-5702
PHONE: 512-916-5137
FAX: 512-478-9104
E-MAIL: library@johnson.nara.gov

Nixon Presidential Materials Staff
National Archives at College Park
8601 Adelphi Rd.
College Park, MD 20740-6001
PHONE: 301-713-6950
FAX: 301-713-6916
E-MAIL: nixon@arch2.nara.gov

Richard Nixon Library and Birthplace (private)
18001 Yorba Linda Blvd.
Yorba Linda, CA 92686
PHONE: 714-993-5075
FAX: 714-528-0544

Gerald R. Ford Library
1000 Beal Ave., Ann Arbor, MI 48109-2114
PHONE: 313-741-2218
FAX: 313-741-2341
E-MAIL: library@fordlib.nara.gov

Gerald R. Ford Museum
303 Pearl St., N.W.
Grand Rapids, MI 49504-5353
PHONE: 616-451-9263
FAX: 616-451-9570
E-MAIL: information.museum@fordmus.nara.gov

Jimmy Carter Library
441 Freedom Parkway, Atlanta, GA 30307-1406
PHONE: 404-331-3942
FAX: 404-730-2215
E-MAIL: library@carter.nara.gov

Ronald Reagan Library
40 Presidential Dr.
Simi Valley, CA 93065-0666
PHONE: 805-522-8444
FAX: 805-522-9621
E-MAIL: library@reagan.nara.gov

George Bush Presidential Materials Project
701 University Dr. E., Suite 300
College Station, TX 77840-1897
PHONE: 409-260-9552
FAX: 409-260-9557
E-MAIL: library@bush.nara.gov

Presidents of the United States......................................Service

1.	George Washington (1732-1799)	1789-1797
2.	John Adams (1735-1826)	1797-1801
3.	Thomas Jefferson (1743-1826)	1801-1809
4.	James Madison (1751-1836)	1809-1817
5.	James Monroe (1758-1831)	1817-1825
6.	John Quincy Adams (1767-1848)	1825-1829
7.	Andrew Jackson (1767-1845)	1829-1837
8.	Martin Van Buren (1782-1862)	1837-1841
9.	William Henry Harrison (1773-1841)	1841
10.	John Tyler (1790-1862)	1841-1845
11.	James K. Polk (1795-1849)	1845-1849
12.	Zachary Taylor (1784-1850)	1849-1850
13.	Millard Fillmore (1800-1874)	1850-1853
14.	Franklin Pierce (1804-1869)	1853-1857
15.	James Buchanan (1791-1868)	1857-1861
16.	Abraham Lincoln (1809-1865)	1861-1865
17.	Andrew Johnson (1808-1875)	1865-1869
18.	Ulysses S. Grant (1822-1885)	1869-1877
19.	Rutherford B. Hayes (1822-1893)	1877-1881
20.	James A. Garfield (1831-1881)	1881
21.	Chester A. Arthur (1830-1886)	1881-1885
22.	Grover Cleveland (1837-1908)	1885-1889
23.	Benjamin Harrison (1833-1901)	1889-1893
24.	Grover Cleveland (1837-1908)	1893-1897
25.	William McKinley (1843-1901)	1897-1901
26.	Theodore Roosevelt (1858-1919)	1901-1909
27.	William H. Taft (1857-1930)	1909-1913
28.	Woodrow Wilson (1856-1924)	1913-1921
29.	Warren G. Harding (1865-1923)	1921-1923
30.	Calvin Coolidge (1872-1933)	1923-1929
31.	Herbert C. Hoover (1874-1964)	1929-1933
32.	Franklin D. Roosevelt (1882-1945)	1933-1945
33.	Harry S. Truman (1884-1972)	1945-1953
34.	Dwight D. Eisenhower (1890-1969)	1953-1961
35.	John F. Kennedy (1917-1963)	1961-1963
36.	Lyndon B. Johnson (1908-1973)	1963-1969
37.	Richard M. Nixon (1913-1994)	1969-1974
38.	Gerald R. Ford (1913-)	1974-1977
39.	James (Jimmy) Carter (1924-)	1977-1981
40.	Ronald Reagan (1911-)	1981-1989
41.	George Bush (1924-)	1989-1993
42.	William (Bill) Clinton (1946-)	1993-

America's Seacoasts

STATE	LENGTHS IN STATUTE MILES	
	1. General Coastline	2. Tidal Shoreline
Atlantic Coast		
Maine	228	3,478
New Hampshire	13	131
Massachusetts	192	1,519
Rhode Island	40	384
Connecticut	–	618
New York	127	1,850
New Jersey	130	1,792
Pennsylvania	–	89
Delaware	28	381
Maryland	31	3,190
Virginia	112	3,315
North Carolina	301	3,375
South Carolina	187	2,876
Georgia	100	2,344
Florida (Atlantic)	580	3,331
Total	**2,069**	**28,673**
Gulf Coast		
Florida (Gulf)	770	5,095
Alabama	53	607
Mississippi	44	359
Louisiana	397	7,721
Texas	367	3,359
Total	**1,631**	**17,141**
Pacific Coast		
California	840	3,427
Oregon	296	1,410
Washington	157	3,026
Hawaii	750	1,052
Alaska (Pacific)	5,580	31,383
Total	**7,623**	**40,298**
Arctic Coast		
Alaska (Arctic)	1,060	2,521
Total	**1,060**	**2,521**
UNITED STATES TOTAL	**12,383**	**88,633**

1. Figures are lengths of general outline of seacoast. Measurements made with unit measure of 30 minutes of latitude on charts as near scale of 1:1,200,000 as possible. Coastline of bays and sounds is included to point where they narrow to width of unit measure, and distance across at such point is included.

2. Figures obtained in 1939-1940 with recording instrument on largest-scale maps and charts then available. Shoreline of outer coast, offshore islands, sounds, bays, rivers, and creeks is included to head of tidewater or to point where tidal waters narrow to width of 100 feet.

Source: Department of Commerce, National Oceanic and Atmospheric Administration, National Ocean Service

The Sequence of Presidential Succession

1. Vice President
2. Speaker of the House
3. President Pro Tempore of the Senate
4. Secretary of State
5. Secretary of the Treasury
6. Secretary of Defense
7. Attorney General
8. Secretary of the Interior
9. Secretary of Agriculture
10. Secretary of Commerce
11. Secretary of Labor
12. Secretary of Health and Human Services
13. Secretary of Housing and Urban Development
14. Secretary of Transportation
15. Secretary of Energy
16. Secretary of Education

Top Ten Ancestries of the U.S. Population
According to the 1990 U.S. Census*

	Ancestry Group	Number
1.	German	57,947,873
2.	Irish	38,735,539
3.	English	32,651,788
4.	African	23,777,098
5.	Italian	14,644,550
6.	American	12,395,999
7.	Mexican	11,586,983
8.	French	10,320,935
9.	Polish	9,366,106
10.	American Indian	8,708,220

*Survey asked people to identify the ancestry group to which they believed themselves to belong.

Dear Congressman...

Address a letter to your senator or representative as follows:

[Senator's name]
United States Senate
Washington, DC 20510

[Representative's name]
United States House of
Representatives
Washington, DC 20515

Selected Federal Agencies

Consumer Product Safety Commission	800-638-2772
Environmental Protection Agency	202-260-2090
Farm Credit Administration	703-883-4000
Federal Communications Commission	202-418-0200
Federal Maritime Commission	202-523-5707
General Services Administration	202-708-5082
National Endowment for the Arts	202-682-5400
National Science Foundation	703-306-1234
Peace Corps	800-424-8580
Small Business Administration	800-827-5722
Smithsonian Institution	202-357-1300
U.S. Information Agency	202-619-4700
U.S. Postal Service	202-268-2000

Federal Information Center

If you have a question about the federal government but don't know whom to call, start with the Federal Information Center. Following is a list of numbers for major metropolitan areas. If you are outside the areas listed, call **301-722-9000**.

800-347-1997

Connecticut: Hartford, New Haven
Florida: Fort Lauderdale, Jacksonville, Miami, Orlando, St. Petersburg, Tampa, West Palm Beach
Georgia: Atlanta
Indiana: Indianapolis
Kentucky: Louisville
Maryland: Baltimore
Massachusetts: Boston
Michigan: Detroit, Grand Rapids
New Jersey: Newark, Trenton
New York: Albany, Buffalo, New York, Rochester, Syracuse
North Carolina: Charlotte
Ohio: Akron, Cinncinnati, Cleveland, Columbus, Dayton, Toledo
Pennsylvania: Philadelphia,

Pittsburgh
Rhode Island: Providence
Tennessee: Chattanooga
Virginia: Norfolk, Richmond, Roanoke

800-366-2998

Alabama: Birmingham, Mobile
Arkansas: Little Rock
Illinois: Chicago
Indiana: Gary
Louisiana: New Orleans
Minnesota: Minneapolis
Missouri: St. Louis
Nebraska: Omaha
Oklahoma: Oklahoma City, Tulsa
Tennessee: Memphis, Nashville
Texas: Austin, Dallas, Fort Worth, Houston, San Antonio
Wisconsin: Milwaukee

800-359-3997

Arizona: Phoenix
Colorado: Colorado Springs, Denver, Pueblo
New Mexico: Albuquerque
Utah: Salt Lake City

800-726-4995

California: Los Angeles, Sacramento, San Diego, San Francisco, Santa Ana
Oregon: Portland
Washington: Seattle, Tacoma

800-733-5996

Hawaii: Honolulu

800-729-8003

Alaska: Anchorage

800-735-8004

Iowa: all locations
Kansas: all locations

United States Paper Currency

Currency	Portrait	Reverse
One Dollar Bill	George Washington	Great Seal of the U.S.
Two Dollar Bill	Thomas Jefferson	Declaration of Independence
Five Dollar Bill	Abraham Lincoln	Lincoln Memorial
Ten Dollar Bill	Alexander Hamilton	U.S. Treasury Building
Twenty Dollar Bill	Andrew Jackson	White House
Fifty Dollar Bill	Ulysses Grant	U.S. Capitol
One Hundred Dollar Bill	Benjamin Franklin	Independence Hall
Five Hundred Dollar Bill *	William McKinley	$500
One Thousand Dollar Bill *	Grover Cleveland	ONE THOUSAND DOLLARS
Five Thousand Dollar Bill *	James Madison	$5,000
Ten Thousand Dollar Bill *	Salmon P. Chase	$10,000

* No longer printed and being withdrawn from circulation

Did you know that until 1929 our currency measured 7.42 x 3.13 inches? Since then, U.S. paper currency has measured 6.14 x 2.61 inches — an easier size to handle and store.

U.S. Department of the Treasury

Greatest Hits

The top ten songs represented by BMI (Broadcast Music Incorporated), based on the most American radio and television broadcasts.

Title	Composer(s)
"Yesterday"	John Lennon & Paul McCartney
"Never My Love"	Donald & Richard Addrisi
"By the Time I Get to Phoenix"	Jim Webb
"Gentle on My Mind"	John Hartford
"You've Lost That Lovin' Feelin'"	Phil Spector, Barry Mann & Cynthia Weil
"More"	Norman Newell, Nino Oliviero, Riz Ortalani & Marcello Ciorcioloni
"Georgia on My Mind"	Hoagy Carmichael & Stuart Gorrell
"Bridge over Troubled Water"	Paul Simon
"Something"	George Harrison
"Mrs. Robinson"	Paul Simon

Car Dollars

Figures are given in cents per mile (average) and are based on suburban driving conditions.

	LARGE (weight more than 3,500 pounds)	INTERMEDIATE (weight less than 3,500 pounds)	COMPACT (weight less than 3,000 pounds)	SUBCOMPACT (weight less than 2,500 pounds)	PASSENGER VAN (weight less than 5,000 pounds)
Depreciation	9.6	8.6	7.3	5.9	10.7
Maintenance	6.0	5.2	4.6	5.1	6.9
Gas and oil	7.0	5.7	4.6	4.4	9.1
Parking and tolls	0.9	0.9	0.9	0.9	0.9
Insurance	4.9	5.6	4.3	5.0	8.9
Taxes	2.2	1.8	1.6	1.4	2.7
Total costs	30.6	27.8	23.3	22.7	39.2

Richter Scale for Measuring Earthquakes

MAGNITUDE	POSSIBLE EFFECTS
1	Detectable only by instruments
2	Barely detectable, even near the epicenter
3	Felt indoors
4	Felt by most people; slight damage
5	Felt by all; damage minor to moderate
6	Moderately destructive
7	Major damage
8	Total and major damage

Devised by American geologist Charles W. Richter in 1935 to measure the magnitude of an earthquake.

Knots

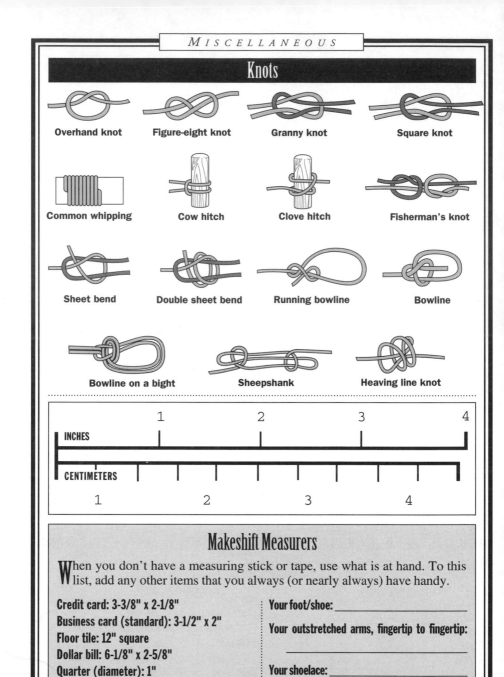

Overhand knot

Figure-eight knot

Granny knot

Square knot

Common whipping

Cow hitch

Clove hitch

Fisherman's knot

Sheet bend

Double sheet bend

Running bowline

Bowline

Bowline on a bight

Sheepshank

Heaving line knot

| INCHES | 1 | 2 | 3 | 4 |

| CENTIMETERS | 1 | 2 | 3 | 4 |

Makeshift Measurers

When you don't have a measuring stick or tape, use what is at hand. To this list, add any other items that you always (or nearly always) have handy.

Credit card: 3-3/8" x 2-1/8"
Business card (standard): 3-1/2" x 2"
Floor tile: 12" square
Dollar bill: 6-1/8" x 2-5/8"
Quarter (diameter): 1"
Penny (diameter): 3/4"
Sheet of paper: 8-1/2" x 11"
   (legal size: 8-1/2" x 14")

Your foot/shoe: _____

Your outstretched arms, fingertip to fingertip:

_____

Your shoelace: _____

Your necktie: _____

Your belt: _____

Decibels

Decibels (dB) are used to measure the loudness or intensity of sounds. One decibel is the smallest difference between sounds detectable by the human ear. Intensity varies exponentially: A 20-dB sound is 10 times louder than a 10-dB sound; a 30-dB sound is 100 times louder than a 10-dB sound; a 40-dB sound is 1,000 times louder than a 10-dB sound; and so on. A 120-dB sound is painful.

DECIBELS	COMPARABLE SOUND
10	light whisper
20	quiet conversation
30	normal conversation
40	light traffic
50	typewriter, loud conversation
60	noisy office
70	normal traffic, quiet train
80	rock music, subway
90	heavy traffic, thunder
100	jet plane at takeoff

Metric Conversion

CONVENTIONAL TO METRIC, MULTIPLY BY		METRIC TO CONVENTIONAL, MULTIPLY BY	
inch	2.54	centimeter	0.39	inch
foot	30.48	centimeter	0.033	foot
yard	0.91	meter	1.09	yard
mile	1.61	kilometer	0.62	mile
square inch	6.45	square centimeter	0.15	square inch
square foot	0.09	square meter	10.76	square foot
square yard	0.8	square meter	1.2	square yard
square mile	0.84	square kilometer	0.39	square mile
acre	0.4	hectare	2.47	acre
ounce	28.0	gram	0.035	ounce
pound	0.45	kilogram	2.2	pound
short ton (2,000 pounds)	0.91	metric ton	1.10	short ton
ounce	30.0	milliliter	0.034	ounce
pint	0.47	liter	2.1	pint
quart	0.95	liter	1.06	quart
gallon	3.8	liter	0.26	gallon

If you know the conventional measurement and want to convert it to metric, multiply it by the numbers in the first column (**example: 1 inch equals 2.54 centimeters**). If you know the metric measurement, multiply it by the numbers in the second column (**example: 2 meters equals 2.18 yards**).

Know Your Angels

I.	**First Group — nearest to God**	Seraphim Cherubim Thrones
II.	**Second Group — receives the reflection of Divine Presence from the first group**	Dominions Virtues Powers
III.	**Angelic Group — ministers directly to human beings**	Principalities Archangels Angels

Animals in the Bible

In addition to the following list of references to specific animals, there are numerous general references: beast (337), cattle (153), fowl (90), fish (56), and bird (41).

Animal	Old Testament	New Testament	Total
Sheep	155	45	200
Lamb	153	35	188
Lion	167	9	176
Ox	156	10	166
Ram	165	0	165
Horse	137	27	164
Bullock	152	0	152
Ass	142	8	150
Goat	131	7	138
Camel	56	6	62

Best-Bet Wedding Gifts

At a loss for an appropriate gift? Emily Post has a few ready suggestions.

For the couple just starting out:

- Set of folding tables on rack
- Mirror for entry or hall
- Crystal vase
- Food processor
- Electric hot tray
- Lamp
- Set of glasses
- Carving set
- Microwave cookware
- Wooden salad bowl
- Large pepper grinder or salt-and-pepper set
- Framed print or photograph
- Wastebasket
- Hors d'oeuvres tray
- Items of the silver or china selected by the bride
- Answering machine

Second-marriage gifts, for couples who have already set up housekeeping:

- A plant, tree, or shrub
- A selection of fine wines or champagnes
- If they are collectors, something to add to their collection
- A picture frame containing a meaningful photo
- Ceramic or copper molds for cooking or decoration
- A subscription to a magazine related to their special interests
- A gift package of gourmet-food selections
- A painting or lithograph (if you know their tastes)
- If either one has small children, sitter service for a specified period (either yourself or hired)

Principal Religions of the World

The figures given for membership in each religious affiliation are estimates based on 1991 statistics.

Christians . . . . 1.8 billion
Muslims . . . . 1 "
Nonreligious . . . . 900 million
Hindus . . . . 750 "
Buddhists . . . . 325 "
Atheists . . . . 250 "
Chinese folk religionists . . 200 "
New-Religionists . . . . 150 "
Tribal religionists . . . . 100 "
Sikhs . . . . 19 "
Jews . . . . 18 "
Shamanists . . . . 10 "
Confucians . . . . 6 "
Baha'is . . . . 5.5 "
Jains . . . . 3.8 "
Shintoists . . . . 3.2 "
Other religionists . . . . 18 "

The Golden Rule
(It's true in all faiths.)

BRAHMANISM:
This is the sum of duty: Do naught unto others which would cause you pain if done to you. *Mahabharata 5:1517*

BUDDHISM:
Hurt not others in ways that you yourself would find hurtful. *Udana-Varga 5:18*

CONFUCIANISM:
Surely it is the maxim of loving-kindness: Do not unto others what you would not have them do unto you. *Analects 15:23*

TAOISM:
Regard your neighbor's gain as your own gain and your neighbor's loss as your own loss. *T'ai Shang Kan Ying P'ien*

ZOROASTRIANISM:
That nature alone is good which refrains from doing unto another whatsoever is not good for itself. *Dadistan-i-dinik 94:5*

JUDAISM:
What is hateful to you, do not to your fellowman. That is the entire Law; all the rest is commentary. *Talmud, Shabbat 31a*

CHRISTIANITY:
All things whatsoever ye would that men should do to you, do ye even so to them; for this is the law and the prophets. *Matthew 7:12*

ISLAM:
No one of you is a believer until he desires for his brother that which he desires for himself. *Sunnah*

– courtesy Elizabeth Pool

Every Minute Counts

The Tax Foundation gives a breakdown of the amount of time you work in an eight-hour day to pay for certain expenses as follows:

Federal and state taxes . . . . 2 hours, 45 minutes		**Transportation** . . . . 39 minutes	
Housing . . . . 1 hour, 25 minutes		**Recreation** . . . . 25 minutes	
Food, tobacco . . . . 57 minutes		**Other** . . . . 1 hour, 3 minutes	
Medical care . . . . 46 minutes			

Rules of Introduction

Countless situations call for introductions. Here are some basic guidelines to help you through. Even if you forget the proper order of introduction, forget names, or make another mistake in your introduction, it is a far greater blunder to neglect this social courtesy altogether. To easily carry out a "proper" introduction, say first the name of the person who is having someone introduced *to* them. For example, you would say: "Mary, this is Tom Smith; Tom, Mary Jones."

a man	**TO**	**a woman**
a young person	**TO**	**an older person**
a less important person	**TO**	**a more important person**
a peer in your own company	**TO**	**a peer in another company**
a nonofficial person	**TO**	**an official person**
a junior executive	**TO**	**a senior executive**
a fellow executive	**TO**	**a customer or client**

Having Tea with the Queen?

On the off chance that you may have the honor of conversing with members of the British Royal Family or members of the nobility, use these forms of address:

Your Majesty (to the queen or king)

Your Royal Highness (to the monarch's spouse, children, and siblings)

Your Highness (to nephews, nieces, and cousins of the monarch)

Duke or Duchess (to a duke or duchess if you are also among the nobility)

Your Grace (to a duke or duchess if you are a commoner; to an archbishop of the Church of England)

My Lord (to a peer below a duke; to a bishop of the Church of England)

Lord (to an earl, marquis, or viscount; an earl and marquis is usually "of" somewhere, but you don't say the "of," just Lord

Derby for the Earl of Derby, for instance)

Lady (to a marchioness, countess, viscountess, or baroness; as in Lord, you don't say the "of")

Sir (to a baronet or knight, using his first name; i.e., Sir Thomas Lipton)

Lady (to the wife of a baronet or knight; in olden days, the title was Dame)

Appropriate Finger Foods

Asparagus, if crisp.

Bananas. Peel completely, then break pieces off with fingers.

Corn on the cob. Eat the corn "typewriter-style."

Grapes. Break off a small bunch. Then pluck and eat one by one.

Lemon. Squeeze wedges with fingers to trickle juice on food.

Lobster. Crack first with tools provided.

Olives. Remove pits from mouth with fingers.

Spare ribs and rack of lamb. Use knife and fork to get easy meat first.

Steamed clams. Lift each out by its neck, dip in butter, eat in one bite.